THE DEVELOPMENT OF PLATO'S
POLITICAL THEORY

The Development of Plato's Political Theory

Second Edition

GEORGE KLOSKO

OXFORD
UNIVERSITY PRESS

OXFORD

UNIVERSITY PRESS

Great Clarendon Street, Oxford ox2 6DP

Oxford University Press is a department of the University of Oxford.
It furthers the University's objective of excellence in research, scholarship,
and education by publishing worldwide in

Oxford New York

Auckland Cape Town Dar es Salaam Hong Kong Karachi
Kuala Lumpur Madrid Melbourne Mexico City Nairobi
New Delhi Shanghai Taipei Toronto

With offices in

Argentina Austria Brazil Chile Czech Republic France Greece
Guatemala Hungary Italy Japan Poland Portugal Singapore
South Korea Switzerland Thailand Turkey Ukraine Vietnam

Oxford is a registered trade mark of Oxford University Press
in the UK and in certain other countries

Published in the United States
by Oxford University Press Inc., New York

© George Klosko 2006

The moral rights of the author have been asserted
Database right Oxford University Press (maker)

First published 2006

British Library Cataloguing in Publication Data
Data available

Library of Congress Cataloging in Publication Data
Data available

Typeset by SPI Publisher Services, Pondicherry, India
Printed in Great Britain
on acid-free paper by
Biddles Ltd., King's Lynn, Norfolk

ISBN 0–19–927995–0   978–0–19–927995–1
ISBN 0–19–927996–9 (Pbk.)   978–0–19–927996–8

1 3 5 7 9 10 8 6 4 2

φασὶ δ' οἱ σοφοί, ὦ Καλλίκλεις, καὶ οὐρανὸν καὶ γῆν καὶ θεοὺς καὶ
ἀνθρώπους τὴν κοινωνίαν συνέχειν καὶ φιλίαν καὶ κοσμιότητα καὶ
σωφροσύνην καὶ δικαιότητα, καὶ τὸ ὅλον τοῦτο διὰ ταῦτα κόσμον
καλοῦσιν ... οὐκ ἀκοσμίαν οὐδὲ ἀκολασίαν.

Gorgias 507e–508a

(Wise men say, Callicles, that heaven and earth and gods and men
are bound together by communion and friendship, by orderliness,
temperance, and justice, and that is the reason why they call the whole
of this world cosmos [order] ... not disorder or dissoluteness.)

*For Meg, Caroline, and Susanna
(and Debby)*

Contents

Contents

Preface

For this edition, I have gone through all chapters, editing and rewriting as needed, and incorporating what I view as significant, new scholarly findings. This has been more necessary in some chapters than others. In particular, because of important recent studies, I have gained a fuller appreciation of the *Statesman* and thoroughly reworked my discussion, though this has not substantially altered my view of its place in the development of Plato's political theory. My account of the *Laws* has been significantly revised in places, in part through the influence of Christopher Bobonich's *Plato's Utopia Recast* (2002). In spite of the evident brilliance of much of Bobonich's account, I disagree with his central claims concerning the movement of Plato's moral and political thought, and have not felt the need significantly to revise my overall interpretation of the *Laws*. Although my basic understanding of the Platonic Socrates and the *Republic* has not changed, I have expanded discussion in various ways, in particular of questions concerning Plato's alleged racism and totalitarianism, and addressed other matters more briefly, for example, the so-called 'Straussian' interpretation of the *Republic*, which has received much attention in the American political theory community. Other subjects I have discussed in more detail include the status of the nocturnal council in the *Laws*. But on the whole, this edition, although improved and expanded in important ways and addressing the last two decades of Plato scholarship, is faithful to the first edition.

In many ways, I view this as a traditional work. In my original preface, I note my desire to be 'reliable rather than new'. That desire has not changed, although with the passage of twenty years, it may be more difficult to realize. As in the first edition, I provide a generally literal reading of Plato's main political texts. Because of the prominence questions of interpretation have assumed in recent years, I have expanded my discussion in Chapter 2 to provide a fuller defence of literal interpretation. However out of fashion this view may be at the present time, I believe Plato is a pre-eminent political theorist, whose ideas should be taken on their own terms. Tracing out the implications of his basic assumptions allows us to recognize the deeply *political* nature of his political theory—Plato's deep concern with the actual politics of the Greek world of his time. As argued in Chapter 1, Plato essentially turned his back on existing political systems, in favour of overall reform and wrote his dialogues with this end in mind. As I say in my initial preface, on these issues, Plato has much of interest to say to modern readers.

In writing this edition, I have drawn on the following previously published articles: 'The "Straussian" Interpretation of Plato's *Republic*', *History of Political Thought*, 7 (1986), 275–93; 'The "Rule" of Reason in Plato's Psychology', *History of Philosophy Quarterly*, 9 (1988), 341–56; 'The Nocturnal Council in Plato's *Laws*', *Political Studies*, 36 (1988), 74–88; '"Racism" in Plato's *Republic*', *History of Political Thought*, 12 (1991), 1–13; 'Popper's Plato: An Assessment', *Philosophy of Social Science*, 26 (1996), 509–27; 'Politics and Method in Plato's Political Theory', *Polis*, 23 (2006), 1–22; 'Knowledge and Law in Plato's *Laws*', *Political Studies* (forthcoming). I am grateful to the publishers of these journals for permission to draw on these pieces and to Robin Waterfield and Oxford University Press, for permission to quote from Waterfield's translation of the *Republic*.

I am grateful to the University of Virginia and the Henry L. and Grace Doherty Charitable Foundation for a semester's leave during the fall of 2005. Friends and colleagues who have read and commented on portions of this work include Ernie Alleva, Lawrie Balfour, Colin Bird, Daniel Devereux, Jon Mikalson, Ryan Pevnick, and Stephen White. I am grateful to Will Umphres, who checked references and made helpful editorial suggestions. I wish to thank the audience for the Covey Lectures in Political Analysis, delivered at Loyola University Chicago, in 2001, for questions and comments and to my students in graduate level Plato classes in 2005 at the University of Virginia and Central European University in Budapest. Dominic Byatt, of Oxford University Press, has been a model editor, while I am grateful to Oxford's reviewers, as well as reviewers and other scholars for their comments on the first edition. As ever, I acknowledge my great debt to my wife Meg, and daughters, Carrie, Sukey, and Debby, for moral support.

PREFACE TO FIRST EDITION

It comes as something of a surprise to realize that the last comprehensive treatment of Plato's political theory written in English appeared almost seventy years ago. Ernest Barker's *Greek Political Theory: Plato and His Predecessors* (London, 1918; rpt. 1947) is still a valuable reading, and to some extent the lack of a comparable work can be attributed to the quality of Barker's scholarship and judgement, and the charm and lucidity of his prose. But much has changed in our understanding of politics since 1918 while there have also been major developments in Classical scholarship. Despite its merits, Barker has become dated, leaving a rather large gap in the literature.

This essay is intended partially to remedy this situation. I attempt to pull together the main themes of Plato's political theory, while providing reasonable commentary and criticism. I trace the course of his political thought from early to middle dialogues and middle to late, and attempt to work out the connections between his political theory and other aspects of his system. Towards this end, I discuss numerous works often considered to be non-political. Because I discuss Plato's political thought in the political and social context of his times, I also draw heavily from the works of other Greek political writers, mainly Thucydides and Aristotle. Finally, I also draw on much modern Plato scholarship, hoping to make this material available to a wide circle of readers. In these respects I have attempted to write an up-to-date, comprehensive account of Plato's political philosophy.

In another sense, however, this study is not intended to be comprehensive. Whereas Barker pursues an approach that might be termed 'encyclopedic', in that he calls attention to and discusses virtually all aspects of Plato's corpus dealing with things 'political', I have concentrated on a somewhat narrower area and, I suppose, on a thesis. I remember reading Barker as an undergraduate and being struck by his remark (slightly altered here) that it is impossible to read the *Republic*—or other political dialogues—'without believing that political reform was the preoccupation of Plato's mind' (pp. 277–8). I believe that this is true, and I have centred my discussion of Plato's political thought on problems of moral and political reform. My account of the development of Plato's political thought is constructed around what I take to be Plato's continuing attempts to grapple with questions of moral reform from rather different angles as his overall philosophical premises changed and evolved.

On the whole, I have not attempted to be highly original. I am aware of the views of current scholars and have tried to avoid controversy as far as possible. Because Plato scholars are a contentious lot, this has not always been possible, especially in regard to such issues as the unity or development of Plato's thought, which will probably never be resolved (see Chapter 2). I depart from the current mainstream—to the extent that there is such a thing—on a few important points, which specialists will recognize. But I have generally preferred to be reliable rather than new. In terms of approach, I am perhaps most original in the degree of attention I devote to questions of moral reform. On this topic, I believe, Plato has much of interest to say to modern readers.

In writing this essay I have incurred numerous debts which I would like to acknowledge. Portions of several chapters can be traced back to a series of articles: 'On the Analysis of *Protagoras* 351B–360E', *Phoenix*, 34 (1980); 'Implementing the Ideal State', *Journal of Politics*, 43 (1981); 'Dêmotikê Aretê in the *Republic*', *History of Political Thought*, 3 (1982); 'The Insufficiency of Reason in Plato's *Gorgias*', *Western Political Quarterly*, 36 (1983); 'Plato's Utopianism: The Political Content of the Early Dialogues,' *Review of Politics*, 45 (1983); 'Provisionality in Plato's Ideal State', *History of Political Thought*, 5

(1984). I am grateful to these publications and to their editors for allowing me to draw on the chapters below. I am also grateful to William Hackett and the Hackett Publishing Company for permission to quote from G. M. A. Grube's translation of the *Republic*.

Much of the argument of this essay originated in my dissertation (Columbia University, 1977), the completion of which was greatly assisted by a Columbia University Graduate School of Arts and Sciences Traveling Fellowship, which allowed me to spend the year 1975–6 in Oxford. I am grateful to Herbert Deane and Julian Franklin, who were the sponsors of my dissertation, and James Coulter, one of the original readers.

I wrote this essay while I was teaching at two institutions, Purdue University and the University of Virginia, and received substantial assistance from both. Summer grants were provided for the 1982 summer by Purdue and the 1984 summer by Virginia. I am grateful to the Department of Political Science at Purdue and the Department of Government and Foreign Affairs at Virginia, and their respective chairmen, David Caputo and Robert Evans, and David O'Brien, graduate adviser at Virginia, for making available valuable research assistance. Daryl Rice, my research assistant at Purdue, read several chapters and made valuable comments. Jeff Hockett, my research assistant at Virginia, checked references and offered editorial suggestions.

Portions of the manuscript were read by Daniel Devereux and Dante Germino, and two earlier versions of the entire manuscript by Peter Nicholson. Their criticisms and suggestions helped me avoid numerous errors and infelicities of style. Valuable comments, criticisms, and suggestions were also provided by anonymous readers of my manuscript and of the articles listed above. I am also grateful to Nancy Marten of Methuen for editorial assistance. All of these people helped me to improve the manuscript a good deal, though I have not always followed their suggestions and am of course responsible for the imperfections that remain. In this technological age, I am also grateful to Bill Bormann, of Academic Computing Services at Purdue, who helped me transfer my files out of the University word processing system and onto floppy disks.

As is true of anyone doing scholarly work on Plato, I have incurred enormous debts to previous scholars—Cornford, Guthrie, Burnet, Adam, Dodds, Friedlander, Murphy, Nettleship, and Barker, to name only a few. I am grateful to Professor Guthrie for granting me access to Cornford's papers while I was working on my dissertation, as Cornford's unpublished lectures on Socrates and Plato, along with his other works, did much to shape my thinking. The value of previous scholarship has been called into question by many in my discipline in recent years. For this, political theory is much the worse.

Special thanks are owed to my wife Meg for editorial assistance and, along with my daughters, Caroline and Susanna, for moral support.

Note on Sources and Substantiation

Because this work is not intended primarily for specialists, I have dispensed with much of the usual scholarly apparatus. I have also been unable to offer detailed defences of various positions I assume. I have argued for many of my positions in the articles noted in the *Bibliography*, while in various general contexts I have drawn heavily from the works of particular scholars and would like to indicate these debts.

In addition to discussion in Chapter 2, I have addressed questions of interpreting Plato in relationship to evidence concerning his life, in my article, 'Politics and Method in Plato's Political Theory', *Polis*, 23 (2006), 1–22.

I have defended portions of the argument in Chapter 4 in: 'On the Analysis of *Protagoras* 351B–360E', *Phoenix*, 34 (1980), 307–22; 'Plato's Utopianism: The Political Content of the Early Dialogues', *Review of Politics*, 45 (1983), 483–509; 'The Insufficiency of Reason in Plato's *Gorgias*', *Western Political Quarterly*, 36 (1983), 579–95; 'Rational Persuasion in Plato's Political Theory', *History of Political Thought*, 7 (1986), 15–31.

My view of the workings of the tripartite soul is argued for in 'The "Rule" of Reason in Plato's Psychology', *History of Philosophy Quarterly*, 9 (1988), 341–56 and 'Dêmotikê Aretê in the *Republic*', *History of Political Thought*, 3 (1982), 363–81. Chapter 10, sections 2 and 3 are argued for respectively in: 'Provisionality in Plato's Ideal State', *History of Political Thought*, 5 (1984), 171–93; and 'Implementing the Ideal State', *Journal of Politics*, 43 (1981), 365–89. Plato is discussed in the context of the political theory of radical reform in *Jacobins and Utopians: The Political Theory of Fundamental Moral Reform* (Notre Dame, 2003).

My overall conception of the development of Plato's thought is similar to those of W. K. C. Guthrie, *A History of Greek Philosophy*, 6 vols. (Cambridge, 1962–81), esp. Vols. IV and V; and F. M. Cornford, in various works (see *Bibliography*). Though I have avoided footnotes as much as possible, specific debts are noted. A few works from which I have drawn heavily for less particular matters are as follows:

J. Burnet, 'The Socratic Doctrine of the Soul', *Proceedings of the British Academy*, 7 (1915–16) (esp. in Ch. 3, sec. 1);

G. Santas, *Socrates: Philosophy in Plato's Early Dialogues* (London, 1979) (esp. in Ch. 4, sec. 1);

F. M. Cornford, 'Plato's Commonwealth', in *The Unwritten Philosophy and Other Essays* (Cambridge, 1950) (in Ch. 4, sec. 2);

Cornford, 'The Doctrine of Eros in Plato's *Symposium*', *The Unwritten Philosophy* (in Ch. 7, sec. 4).

My interpretation of the *Republic* is most heavily indebted to N. R. Murphy, *The Interpretation of Plato's Republic* (Oxford, 1951) and J. Adam, *The Republic of Plato*, 2 vols. (Cambridge, 1902). I have also been influenced by R. C. Cross and A. D. Woozley, *Plato's Republic: A Philosophical Commentary* (London, 1964); R. Robinson, *Plato's Earlier Dialectic*, 2nd edn. (Oxford, 1953); R. L. Nettleship, *Lectures on the Republic of Plato*, 2nd edn. (London, 1901); J. C. Gosling, *Plato* (London, 1973); J. Annas, *An Introduction to Plato's Republic* (Oxford, 1981).

For the *Statesman*, I have benefited especially from M. Lane, *Method and Politics in Plato's Statesman* (Cambridge, 1998) and C. Rowe, ed. and trans., *Plato: Statesman* (Warminster, 1995). On the *Laws*, my most important debt is to the great work of G. Morrow, *Plato's Cretan City* (Princeton, NJ, 1960). I should also acknowledge my general debt to E. Barker, *Greek Political Theory: Plato and His Predecessors* (London, 1918; rpt. 1947).

Texts and Translations

Greek authors are quoted from Oxford Classical Texts. This means that for Plato the edition used is J. Burnet, *Platonis Opera*, 5 vols. (Oxford, 1900–7). Vol. I has been revised by E. A. Duke, W. F. Hicken, W. S. M. Nicoll, D. B. Robinson, and J. C. G. Strachan (*Platonis Opera*, Vol. I [Oxford, 1995]). The *Republic* has been revised by S. Slings, ed., *Platonis Res Publica* (Oxford, 2003). All departures from this edition are noted.

Unless otherwise indicated, all translations of ancient authors used are from Loeb Classical Library editions. I have occasionally modified these slightly, substituted other published translations or translations of my own. I have taken slight liberties with translation and quotations in general. For example, for the sake of uniformity, I have made minor alterations by omitting quotation marks in certain translations of Plato (e.g. in Fowler's rendering of the narrated dialogue in the *Phaedo*).

For various reasons, I have employed a few more recent translations. Unless otherwise indicated, translations of the following works of Plato are as listed: *Republic*, trans. by R. Waterfield (Oxford, 1998); *Statesman*, trans. by C. Rowe (Warminster, 1995); *Laws*, trans. by T. Saunders (Harmondsworth, UK, 1970); *Epistles*, trans. by G. Morrow (Indianapolis, IN, 1962). I occasionally use language from G. M. A. Grube's translation of the *Republic*, revised by C. D. C. Reeve (Indianapolis, IN, 1992), and W. A. Woodhead's translation of the *Gorgias* (reference in *Bibliography*).

In addition, for translations of Aristotle's *Ethics*, I have occasionally substituted W. D. Ross's translation, revised by J. L. Ackrill, in Ackrill, ed., *Aristotle's Ethics* (London, 1973), for Loeb translations. Translations of Xenophon's *Memorabilia* are by A. Benjamin, *Recollections of Socrates* and *Socrates' Defense Before the Jury* (Indianapolis, IN, 1965). I have used Penguin translations of Thucydides (trans. by R. Warner, revised edn., Harmondsworth, UK, 1972); Herodotus (trans. by A. de Selincourt, revised edn., Harmondsworth, UK, 1972); Aristophanes (*The Birds* and *Ecclesiazusae* both trans. by D. Barrett, Harmondsworth, UK, 1978); and Euripides (*Medea*, trans. by P. Vellacott, Harmondsworth, UK, 1963).

Full references for other translations used are found in the *Bibliography*.

List of Abbreviations

For ancient authors in general, standard abbreviations are used. These are listed in a systematic form in Liddell and Scott's *Greek English Lexicon*. A few abbreviations that might be confusing are as follows:

Ath. Pol. *Constitution of Athens* (Aristotle)

EN *Nicomachean Ethics* (Aristotle)

EE *Eudemian Ethics* (Aristotle)

MM *Magna Moralia* (pseudo-Aristotle)

DL Diogenes Laertius, *Lives of Eminent Philosophers*

Frag. H. Diels and W. Kranz, eds., *Die Fragmente der Vorsokratiker*, 6th edn., 3 vols. (Berlin, 1951–2). This work is divided into two sections: A., testimonia and B., fragments; thus the Fragments of the Pre-Socratics referred to can be found in the B section of Diels–Kranz; English translation by K. Freeman, *Ancilla to the Pre-Socratic Philosophers* (Oxford, 1956).

1

Plato and Greek Politics

Plato was born in 428 BC to a distinguished, well-connected Athenian family. His early years were passed in the shadow of the wars between Athens and Sparta, which culminated in the complete victory of Sparta in the year 404. Plato probably saw military service during this conflict, but in the remarkable autobiographical statement preserved in his *Seventh Epistle*,[1] he does not mention this but rather comments on political events during the closing years of the war. The Athenian democracy was overthrown and replaced by an oligarchy, important members of which were Plato's relatives and associates. He watched with horror as this regime, which he had considered joining and in which he had lodged great hopes, degenerated into a tyranny. The democracy returned and completed Plato's disillusionment with politics, by executing Socrates, 'the best and wisest and most righteous man' then living (*Phaedo* 118a). Thus, Plato's early years were filled with political turmoil and strife. He saw Athens pass from a position of political supremacy in the Greek world to defeat and near destruction. But Athens rose again, and Plato witnessed her resumption of her earlier course.

Specific political events will be discussed below. For now we should note that Plato's understanding of politics was shaped by the conditions in which he lived. The aftermath of the Peloponnesian War was a period of hardship throughout the Greek world, and though subsequent years witnessed a commercial upsurge, this exacerbated conditions within many cities, enriching some inhabitants but increasing the poverty of others. City after city was beset by civil strife, *stasis*, pitting rich against poor, oligarch against democrat. In both the *Republic* and *Laws*, Plato describes all cities as actually two cities conjoined—cities of the rich and of the poor, at each other's throats

---

[1] I regard this as genuine. For defence of the authenticity of *Epistle* 7, see G. Morrow, ed., *Plato's Epistles*, revised edn. (Indianapolis, IN, 1962), pp. 3–17; G. G. Field, *Plato and His Contemporaries*, 3rd edn. (London, 1967), pp. 197–201; W. K. C. Guthrie, *A History of Greek Philosophy*, 6 vols. (Cambridge, 1962–81), V, 399–401. For the contrary view, see L. Edelstein, *Plato's Seventh Letter* (Leiden, Germany, 1966). Also note the compromise position of P. A. Brunt, who does not insist on the validity of the epistle, but accepts its evidence in regard to both Plato's early political experiences and voyages to Sicily (*Studies in Greek History and Culture* [Oxford, 1993], pp. 319, 339–41). For brief discussion of the issue and additional references, see G. Klosko, 'Politics and Method in Plato's Political Theory', *Polis*, 23 (2006).

(*Rep.* 422e–23b; *Laws* 715b–d). War between cities as well was the rule throughout Plato's lifetime, as the great powers struggled for supremacy. Unending warfare gradually sapped the vitality of Greece and its ability to resist foreign encroachment—by Persia, Carthage, and Macedon. Plato was about 50 years old when Athens formed a second naval alliance in the hopes of recapturing something of her past power and prestige. He was about 70 when this possibility was dashed by defeat in the Social War of 357–55. Plato died in 347, nine years before the triumph of Phillip of Macedon over the united forces of Athens and Thebes at the battle of Chaeronea, which marked the decline of freedom and influence of the Greek city-state.

Thus, Plato's world was one of decay and decline. The 'inherited conglomerate' of traditional values and institutions was in dissolution.[2] The forces responsible for this—social, political, economic, intellectual—could be traced back to the fifth century, and Plato opposed them throughout his life. Plato was especially concerned with the situation in moral thought. In his autobiographical statement he laments the 'corruption of our written laws and customs', which he saw proceeding at 'amazing speed' (*Ep.* 7 325d). We begin with the situation he encountered in this area.

1.1. NATURE AND CONVENTION

At the time Plato was writing, traditional Greek moral standards had been undermined, and revolutionary doctrines of ethical relativism and immoralism were in the air. According to time-honoured Greek moral and political thought, the laws of the *polis* were divinely sanctioned and were a repository of its values, of the moral ideal to which its citizens were to be raised. These laws were generally both written and unwritten, some explicitly legislated, others resting on tradition, a situation reflected in the Greek word *nomos*, which means both 'law' and 'custom'. The divine sanction of the laws is seen in the first line of Plato's *Laws*, where Plato's spokesman, the Athenian Stranger, asks his companion from Crete if gods or men made the laws of that city (*Laws* 624a).

During the fifth century BC, the divine status of cities' laws was called into question and with this their role as moral arbiters. Greek thought came to be permeated with the distinction between *nomos* and *phusis*, commonly translated as 'convention' and 'nature'. The distinction took on a number of different forms, but basically it distinguished what was enacted by man—primarily laws and customs, the results of agreements between people—and

---

[2] The phrase, 'inherited conglomerate', is Gilbert Murray's, used by E. R. Dodds, *The Greeks and the Irrational* (Berkeley, CA, 1951), chs. 6 and 7.

what was more firmly rooted in divine or natural processes. The distinction came to play an important role in moral thought.

The convention/nature distinction first began to be recognized when the Greeks became aware of significant differences between their own and other cultures. A well-known illustration of this is Herodotus' report of the reactions of certain Greeks and certain inhabitants of India upon discovering the funeral customs of the other society. The Indians reacted with horror at the Greek custom of burning the bodies of the dead, while the Greeks reacted similarly to the Indians' custom of eating the bodies. Thus, Herodotus concludes: 'Everyone without exception believes his own native customs, and the religion he was brought up in, to be the best. ... ' (III, 38). The historian quotes Pindar's dictum that *nomos* is 'king of all'.

The relativism reported by Herodotus was developed into a philosophical position by certain thinkers, especially Protagoras, from the city of Abdera. Protagoras argued that 'Man is the measure of all things' (Frag. 1), that there is no truth beyond people's opinions, and implicitly that truth can vary between societies. Protagoras despaired of ever discovering a deeper reality. He believed that it was impossible to learn about the gods; such knowledge is barred by the obscurity of the subject matter and the shortness of man's life (Frag. 4).

Though Protagoras apparently subscribed to this extreme relativism without drawing radical ethical implications, subsequent thinkers proved less conservative. If the laws and moral standards of cities were founded upon nothing but custom and opinion, it became necessary to account for their existence. Various positions were proffered. A sociological account is presented by Thrasymachus in Book I of the *Republic*. Thrasymachus argues that the laws of each society were created by the rulers for their own benefit, that the laws' reason for existing is to promote the interest of the rulers (*Rep.* 338d–39a). Other thinkers declared that laws were actually created by the weaker and less fortunate members of society to protect themselves from exploitation by the stronger. Critias, who was Plato's cousin and later a leading member of the Thirty Tyrants, presented a similar explanation for the existence of the gods in his play, *Sisyphus*. He said that the gods were invented to frighten potential wrongdoers, to deter them from committing crimes (Frag. 25).

Regardless of what specific account of the origin of laws was presented, the crucial implication was that the human origin of laws made them inferior to other standards that were more securely rooted in 'nature'—however defined. This contrast could be harmful to the morality of the *polis*. If the laws of the state were merely man's creations, they could be disregarded with impunity. The Sophist Antiphon, for one, argues that individuals should practise justice only when there are witnesses. If people can commit injustice unobserved, they should do so, as the only penalties attached to injustice come from being detected (Frag. 44).

Various thinkers developed alternative moral precepts by observing aspects of the 'natural' world. The first discussions of so-called 'laws of nature' date from this period. The first usage of the term in Greek is found in Plato's *Gorgias*, where it is given voice by Callicles, Socrates' main interlocutor. Taking his examples from international affairs and the animal world, Callicles declares that it is the 'law of nature' (*nomon ... ton tês phuseôs*) that the strong rule over the weak and have more (*Gorgias* 483a–e). Additional evidence of the prevalence of this belief is afforded by Thucydides, especially in his report of the conduct of the city of Athens and its representatives during the Peloponnesian War. Among the many memorable speeches presented by Thucydides, perhaps the most memorable is a series of statements put into the mouth of unnamed Athenian envoys, who attempt to persuade the small island of Melos to join their empire. The Athenians refer to the standard of justice that applies in the real world, that the strong take what they will and the weak suffer what they must (V, 89). They go on and describe this principle as divinely rooted:

Our opinion of the gods and our knowledge of men leads us to conclude that it is a general and necessary law of nature to rule wherever one can. This is not a law that we made ourselves, nor were we the first to act upon it when it was made. We found it already in existence, and we shall leave it to exist for ever among those who come after us. (V, 105)

As the examples just quoted indicate, the new morality of 'nature' was frequently a morality of self-aggrandizement. Glaucon in the *Republic* argues that an individual with the power to take advantage of others and reap the benefits, who chooses not to do so, must be mad (*Rep.* 359b). He speaks of the urge to have more than one's share that every creature naturally pursues (*Rep.* 359c). Again, an extreme view is presented by Callicles, who declares that the most desirable kind of life is having strong desires and the ability to satisfy them: 'Luxury and licentiousness and liberty, if they have the support of force, are virtue and happiness, and the rest of these embellishments—the unnatural covenants of mankind—are all mere stuff and nonsense' (*Grg.* 492c).

Thus, at the time Plato was writing, Greek society was torn by an intellectual revolution. The old standards had been undermined with little to take their place. The conclusion reached by Ivan Karamazov in *The Brothers Karamazov* was in the air: 'If God is dead, then everything is permitted'. Plato saw a direct connection between the relativism of Herodotus and Protagoras, and the blunt immoralism of Thucydides' Athenians and Callicles. It is no exaggeration to say that countering these tendencies lay at the heart of his philosophic endeavours. Both Socrates and Plato believed it to be crucial to find a philosophical foundation for the laws of justice, to prove that they were rooted in something more than human enactments and that a life of adherence to these standards was superior to a life of unbridled self-indulgence.

1.2. POLITICAL DEVELOPMENTS

The political world of Plato's day was also beset by instability. A series of geographical features divide Greece into numerous, relatively small, separated regions, which developed self-contained political units: *poleis*. Though commonly translated as both 'city' and 'state', the *polis* is both and neither. 'City-state' is probably more accurate, though cumbersome; throughout this book I will use all three terms. It is difficult to generalize about *poleis*; they were both numerous and diverse. But clearly, during Plato's time, the traditional, ideal-typical *polis* was shaken to its foundations.

For our purposes, three aspects of the *polis* should be discussed briefly: its size, the kind of moral unity this size allowed, and its tradition of political independence or autonomy. Beginning with size, the typical *polis* was quite small. The ideal state discussed in Plato's *Laws* is intended to contain 5,040 citizen families; the ideal state in the *Republic* is to be defended by an army of some 1,000 men (*Rep.* 423a). Along similar lines, in *Politics* VIII Aristotle remarks that the entire citizenry should be able to hear a single herald (1326b5–7).

Actual population figures can be judged only roughly.[3] A reasonable estimate for Athens at its peak would be 40,000 citizens. Including women and children, this figure would be 110,000–150,000, while the entire population, including metics (foreign residents) and slaves was perhaps 300,000. In comparison, Sparta at its height had approximately 4,000–5,000 full citizens (12,000–15,000 including women and children), ruling over a subject population of some 200,000–300,000. In the light of the fact that Athens and Sparta were by far the largest *poleis*, Plato's ideal states may seem a bit small, but not unusually so.

Typically, the *polis* would contain both rural and urban areas, generally a series of agricultural villages ringing a walled central city. These territories were, again, small and can be assessed quite accurately. Athens was relatively large, encompassing some 1,000 square miles. Sparta, including subject areas, encompassed some 3,300 square miles, but other *poleis* were much smaller.

---

[3] The following population and territory figures are taken from V. Ehrenberg, *The Greek State* (Oxford, 1960); I also use some of Ehrenberg's comparison examples and have rounded off some of his estimated figures.

Corinth had 340 square miles, Samos 180, Aegina 33, and Delos less than 2. For comparison, a few modern figures are: Texas 267,000 square miles, Scotland 30,400, Rhode Island 1,200, Luxembourg 1,010, Manhattan 30.

The small size of the typical *polis* fostered intense political involvement in its citizens. The *polis* is not simply a city or state; it implies active participation, a joint undertaking on the part of its citizens. According to Aristotle, the essence of the *polis* does not lie in the physical contiguity of its citizens, or even in their sharing a walled enclosure. What is paramount is the *polis'* moral dimension; the *polis'* reason for being is not to promote life, but good life (*Politics* 1252b29–30). Aristotle says that a human being can achieve his full potential only through participation in a *polis*. Thus man is a *zôon politikon*, literally a 'political animal'—an animal by nature meant to live in a *polis*. The individual capable of achieving his full development without a *polis* must be either more than or less than human, either a beast or a god (*Pol.* 1253a1–29).

The *polis* was able to afford its citizens a degree of political participation that has probably not been equalled since. In a city such as Athens, at any one time a high percentage of the citizens would be drawing state pay—as jurors, for sitting in the Assembly, in military service, as magistrates, etc. But even more than this financial relationship was a spiritual relationship. The *polis* recognized no separation between state and church. Greek religion was state religion; the individual performed religious service by worshipping the gods of his *polis*. Socrates of course was condemned to death for not worshipping them, one of several prosecutions for impiety in Athens during this period. The Greeks recognized little distinction between state and society. Society was political society. Their art was public art, just as their most important athletic competitions, the Olympics, were organized around competition between *poleis* and aroused strong patriotic sentiments. The subordination of economic activity to political life is seen in the fact that economies were largely sustained by non-citizens, by slaves and metics. In many cities, legislation restricted the economic activity of those politically engaged. For instance, at Thebes citizens who had sold goods in the marketplace within the past ten years were not eligible to sit in the Assembly (Aristotle, *Pol.* 1278a25–26). The subordination of economic life achieved its fullest expression in Sparta, where the citizens, the Spartiates, devoted their time to military and political activity, and were forbidden to trade, while their land was farmed by subject peoples.

As the citizen fulfilled himself by becoming part of the state, so it was, ideally, the business of the state to raise him to this height. The *polis* was an educational institution, designed to improve its citizens, to make them virtuous according to its conception of the good. As the poet Simonides says, 'The *polis* educates man' (Frag. 53D). An extreme instance of this was found in Sparta, where the state as a whole was carefully geared towards education. Male children were taken from their families at an early age and publicly raised. Forced to live under harsh conditions and subjected to rigorous military training and discipline, Spartan youths were instilled with the martial virtues. We see below that something very like this is imitated in Plato's *Republic* and *Laws,* though Plato hoped to produce a personality type more rounded than the Spartan warrior.

The intensity that the Greeks brought to political life also depended on the traditional autonomy and political independence of their cities. The value of political autonomy was deeply engrained in the Greek psyche. The wars against Persia were largely fought in its name, and throughout the entire Hellenic period it stood in the way of cooperation between cities, opening the door for a national power from the north, Macedonia, to divide and conquer. For the Greeks, deprivation of political autonomy was regarded as slavery. This is seen in Thucydides' account of the dialogue between representatives of Athens and Melos. Confronted with a powerful Athenian force, facing a strong possibility of complete destruction, the Melians prefer to fight rather than 'give up in a short moment the liberty which our city has enjoyed from its foundation for 700 years' (V, 112).

By the time of the Peloponnesian War, complete autonomy was a thing of the past. Traditionally, the political independence of a Greek city rested upon a foundation of economic independence. The ideal-type city would be self-supporting, feeding its population with the produce of its land, engaging in relatively little trade with other cities or countries. But by the fifth century extensive foreign trade had replaced the old, indigenous economy. Thus, at the outbreak of the Peloponnesian War, Pericles boasts that the fruits of all the world are readily available in Athenian markets (Thucydides II, 38). The degree to which Athens had come to rely on imports is seen in her policy during the war. The Athenians allowed their enemies to devastate their land, as they retreated behind the walls of their city to live exclusively upon what was brought in by sea.

Economic interaction contributed to conflict between cities and exacerbated divisions within cities, between bitterly opposed oligarchic and democratic camps. The classic account of civil war and the horrors it occasioned is Thucydides' description of what overtook Corcyra during the Peloponnesian War. I quote only part of Thucydides' account:

There was death in every shape and form. And, as usually happens in such situations, people went to every extreme and beyond it. There were fathers who killed their sons; men were dragged from the temples or butchered on the very altars; some were actually walled up in the temple of Dionysius and died there.

So savage was the progress of this revolution, and it seemed all the more so because it was one of the first which had broken out. Later, of course, practically the whole of the Hellenic world was convulsed, with rival parties in every state.... In the various cities these revolutions were the cause of many calamities—as happens and always will happen while human nature is what it is. (III, 81–2)

Civil war between democrat and oligarch broke out in Athens too during the closing years of the war. As noted above, Plato's family and associates were engulfed. Such horrors undoubtedly contributed to the weight Plato places on stability and harmony as important political values.

The conflict that convulsed the Greek world points to profound destabilizing conditions. The relevant factors were especially in evidence in Athens, which in many ways represented a new kind of political entity. During the fifth century, a series of related factors had led Athens from being a relatively minor power to the greatest and most powerful city in the Greek world. The basis of Athenian power lay on the seas. During the sixth and fifth centuries, Athens moved from a predominantly agricultural economy to one based on trade. The city grew progressively larger at the expense of the surrounding countryside, eventually outgrowing the ability of her own land to support her. One reason Athenian naval power was necessary was to maintain access to foreign grain.

The growth of Athenian naval power was also connected with the rise of democracy and imperialism. These developments proceeded in conjunction. As Athens began to put more stock in sea power, she naturally came to rely less heavily on the armoured foot soldier, the hoplite. Since Greek citizens were required to furnish their own armour, hoplite forces were made up of relatively prosperous strata of society. Naval service, which required not armour but the ability to row in the fleets, went hand in hand with democracy. In the years after the navy rescued Athens from the Persian invasion, at Salamis, the democracy achieved numerous inroads, eventually developing political institutions that lodged power directly in the hands of the people.

Democracy also developed in conjunction with the growth of Athenian imperialism. This connection was clearly drawn by Plato and other like-minded critics. After the war with Persia, the Delian League was formed between Athens and a number of other cities, many of them on islands in the Aegean Sea, for the purpose of mutual defence from Persia. During succeeding years, as the menace of Persia receded, the alliance was gradually transformed into an Athenian empire. Cities that attempted to leave the alliance were forcibly subjugated, and the Athenians began to use the League's revenues to enrich and beautify their own city. League revenue made possible the construction of such monuments as the Parthenon and also enabled the state to employ numerous citizens in its service. According to Aristotle, in the early years of the empire, at least 20,000 citizens were maintained by imperial revenues (*Ath. Pol.* 24, 3). With the empire under the control of the democratic government, the demand for further expansion was ever in the air. The Athenians are described by Thucydides as unable to enjoy the possessions that they have in their eagerness for more. They are 'by nature incapable of either living a quiet life themselves or of allowing anyone else to do so' (I, 70). Even during the twenty-seven year period of war with Sparta, the Athenians could not resist the prospect of further gains and so invaded Sicily. To Thucydides, the motive for this was apparent: 'The general masses and the average soldier himself saw the prospect of getting pay for the time being and of adding to the empire so as to secure permanent paid employment in the future' (VI, 24).

Needless to say, Plato despised the imperial greatness of Athens and the coterie of political leaders who had made it what it was, Themistocles, Miltiades, Cimon, and Pericles:

People say they have made the city great; but never realizing that it is swollen and festering.... For with no regard to temperance and justice they have stuffed the city with harbors and arsenals and walls and tribute and suchlike trash. (*Grg.* 518e–19a)

Throughout his political writings, Plato opposed the factors responsible for Athens' development into an expansive imperial power. Combatting democracy, commerce, and the urge for aggrandizement that these elements both promoted and fed off, Plato advocated the traditional, economically independent *polis* of times long past.

To some extent Plato's hostility to the democracy can be attributed to his economic and social background. The conservative landholding classes from which he came saw the rise of the commercial economy as a threat to their economic position. Democratic government undermined their traditional claims to political preeminence, while militant, expansionist, imperial foreign policies also threatened their interests. Being the wealthier elements in society, they had the most to lose through war. War taxes fell upon them especially hard, and during the Peloponnesian War, when Athens retreated behind its walls, it was their land that was ravaged by the Spartans. Thus, in the *Ecclesiazusae*, produced in 392, Aristophanes describes what happens when a new military venture is proposed. Someone moves that the fleets be launched; the poor vote 'Yes', and the rich and farmers 'No' (*Ec.* 197). Faced with the need to protect their interests, conservative elements were not above attempting to subvert the democratic system, while, as we have noted, in the closing years of the Peloponnesian War two attempts were made.

Throughout his writings Plato reveals many of his class's attitudes and biases. Many of his criticisms of the Athenian system, and of democracy in general, were common to his class, and it should be realized that much of what he says along these lines is coloured by an almost inbred hatred of these features of his state. Supporters and defenders of the Athenian system have long accused him of unfairness and have amassed considerable evidence to counter his depiction of the democratic regime.

Plato's criticism of the Athenian democracy is carried on in many of his works. The *Republic* and *Gorgias* contain direct political critiques, but in addition to what is said in these works is what is implied. The fact that Plato does not talk about alliances or other forms of cooperation between cities in his political works is significant, as is his low opinion of intercity commerce. It is significant that the ideal states in the *Republic* and *Laws* are to be without commercial relations with other states. According to Plato, not only does foreign trade foster undesirable customs and beliefs, but it also upsets the economic balance of a city, enriching some and impoverishing others. In the *Laws*, Plato says that commerce makes a city unfriendly within itself and to other cities (705a). In his political dialogues Plato retreats from the Greek world of his own time to an earlier, more ideal situation—perhaps one that never fully existed—in which the *polis* was able to do its job of forming and morally educating its inhabitants, free from outside interference.

In another respect as well, the political view expressed in the *Republic* and *Laws* represents a return to earlier times. As the separate Greek cities retreated from economic and political isolation, the ties binding the citizen to his community weakened. The communal spirit idealized by many Greek political philosophers gave way, before ever growing individualism. The religious underpinning of the state's laws was widely questioned, and individuals more frequently put their own welfare before the welfare of their cities. Such individualism is reflected in numerous changes in the political scene, for example, the rise of mercenary soldiers. Whereas in former times cities had been defended by armies of citizen soldiers, during the fourth century they increasingly turned to hired hands. Other forms of public service were also on the wane. In Athens, citizens increasingly demanded payment for performing state functions, while the conduct of political affairs passed into the hands of a class of professional politicians. During the fifth century pay was introduced for serving in the Assembly and on jury duty. During subsequent decades the practice of state pay expanded, as citizens began to receive payment for attending state festivals. In the year 358 a special fund, the theoric fund, was set up to provide poor relief on a regular basis. Management of the theoric fund became a locus of power in Athenian politics, eventually coming to control state finances as a whole.

These changes are indicative of important changes in the nature of the *polis* itself. From a moral community, it was evolving in the direction of an association of individuals interested primarily in their own well-being. Thus, in *Republic* II (358e–59b) Glaucon presents the view that justice was founded by individuals motivated by self-interest, a view that approaches liberal, social contract theory, and is the first recognizable account of the contract in the Western tradition. Along similar lines, the Sophist Lycophron asserted that the *polis* exists merely to protect the rights of its citizens (Aristotle, *Pol.* 1280b10–12). The degree of self-interest in Athens is attested to by the orator Aeschines. 'You leave the Assembly', he said to his fellow citizens, 'not after deliberating but after dividing up the surplus like shareholders' (III, 251). Here too Plato's political writings contain an implicit critique and a return to an earlier state of affairs. In the ideal cities described in the *Republic* and *Laws*, the *polis* reasserts its claims upon the individual. The primary task of the *polis* is to promote the virtue of its citizens, while the sharp divide between economics and politics in both works marks another return to an earlier, more ideal era.

1.3. PLATO AND GREEK POLITICS

By family, Plato seemed destined for a political career. His father, Ariston, claimed descent from Codrus, the legendary last king of Athens. The family of Perictione, his mother, was connected with Solon, one of Athens' greatest statesmen, and contained two of the Thirty Tyrants, Critias, her cousin, and Charmides, her brother. Both of these were killed in the fighting in 403 when the democracy regained power. But despite their bad end, Plato apparently took pride in Critias and Charmides. He included them in the *Charmides*, which, of course, is named after the latter. As one scholar says: 'The opening scene of the *Charmides* is a glorification of the whole connection'.[4] In the *Seventh Epistle*, Plato describes his early desire to pursue a political career. He was especially tempted when the Thirty seized power and asked him to join them. He says he hoped this regime would restore just rule to Athens. But the Thirty established a reign of terror and attempted to implicate Socrates in one of their crimes. When the Thirty were overthrown, Plato was at first surprised at the moderation and restraint exhibited by the returning democracy. But again Socrates fell afoul of the established regime, this time paying with his life. Plato was profoundly shaken by these experiences. He describes his reaction in the *Seventh Epistle*:

The more I reflected upon what was happening, upon what kind of men were active in politics, and upon the state of our laws and customs, and the older I grew, the more I realized how difficult it is to manage a city's affairs rightly. For I saw it was impossible

---

[4] J. Burnet, *Greek Philosophy: Part I, Thales to Plato* (London, 1914), p. 208.

to do anything without friends and loyal followers; and to find such men ready to hand would be a piece of sheer good luck, since our city was no longer guided by the customs and practices of our fathers, while to train up new ones was anything but easy. And the corruption of our written laws and our customs was proceeding at such amazing speed that whereas at first I had been full of zeal for public life, when I noted these changes and saw how unstable everything was, I became in the end quite dizzy; and though I did not cease to reflect how an improvement could be brought about in our laws and in the whole constitution, yet I refrained from action, waiting for the proper time. At last I came to the conclusion that all existing states are badly governed and the condition of their laws practically incurable, without some miraculous remedy and the assistance of fortune. (325c–26a)

Plato goes on to explain the form he believed this miraculous assistance must take:

I was forced to say, in praise of true philosophy, that from her heights alone was it possible to discern what the nature of justice is, either in the state or in the individual, and that the ills of the human race would never end until either those who are sincerely and truly lovers of wisdom come into political power, or the rulers of our cities, by the grace of God, learn true philosophy. (326a–b)

This hope assumed more concrete form in the *Republic*, as the philosopher-king. Clearly, the impetus for the central idea of Plato's greatest work lay in the political conditions he experienced.

Two important motifs in Plato's political thought are indicated in the above passages. First is his deep concern with political reform. As a result of his early experiences, perhaps also because of his background and upbringing, Plato was dissatisfied with the politics and political systems of the cities he encountered. Throughout his life he wished to return them to the path of justice and righteousness. Though his early expectation that his relatives would rule justly was disappointed, he never ceased hoping for a just regime. Second, because Plato thought so little of the regimes he witnessed, he came to believe that political reform would have to be accomplished outside existing political systems. He believed that existing governments were corrupt and would resist improvement. As Socrates says in the *Apology*, 'A man who really fights for the right, if he is to preserve his life for even a little while, must be a private citizen, not a public man' (*Ap.* 31e–32a). Throughout his philosophical career, Plato presents a profound meditation on political reform and its possibilities. In the passage from the *Seventh Epistle* quoted above, Plato says that he refrained from political action, waiting for the proper time. But as F. M. Cornford remarks, for someone of Plato's temperament, dreaming of the perfect society, it is not surprising that the right opportunity never came.[5]

---

[5] F. M. Cornford, *The Republic of Plato* (Oxford, 1941), p. xviii.

As he stood on the sidelines, Plato's political interests found expression in his writings. Though politics and political theory are not the only concern of the dialogues, they are an important concern at all stages of his career, most clearly in such works as the *Gorgias, Republic, Statesman,* and *Laws.* In addition, Plato made three voyages to Sicily in the hope of converting the tyrants of Syracuse, Dionysius I, and later his son, Dionysius II, to philosophy. These attempts failed, but Plato was closely associated with Dion, who in 357 successfully invaded and took control of Syracuse—for a time (see Chapter 11, sec. 1). Finally, Plato opened the Academy, which was intended as a training ground for future statesmen and advisers of rulers. Several of Plato's students did manage to achieve positions as advisers to rulers or teachers of future rulers, the most important of whom was Aristotle, who became tutor to the young Alexander of Macedon (see Chapter 11, sec. 1).

This study concentrates on Plato's writings, especially the development of his political thought throughout the different stages of his career. We trace the interconnections between his political doctrines on the one hand and his other philosophical views, especially moral and psychological, on the other. We see that throughout his career, Plato maintains the two attitudes evidenced in the *Seventh Epistle*: (*a*) desiring political reform but (*b*) profoundly distrustful of contemporary political institutions and so looking for a way to accomplish this outside them. We examine the ways in which Plato's ideas concerning political reform changed and evolved in connection with the more general develop ment of his philosophy as a whole, and we see the central place these themes occupied at all stages of his career. In general, it is seen that Plato's political theory developed in the direction of increasing pessimism. There is a marked drop in his estimation of human nature and human potential, while he came increasingly to lodge his hope for reform in political institutions, described in ever more elaborate detail, which could be used to shape and condition human beings. Though he had little faith in existing political institutions, Plato came to rely on those that could be erected in a properly run state.

2

Plato's Corpus

A set of interrelated problems concerning the interpretation of Plato should be discussed, before we move on to his political thought. These are explored from different points of view in the voluminous scholarly literature. Full discussion could well take a book in itself, and so I will not examine them in detail. But it is advisable briefly to indicate and to justify the positions I assume on some major questions of interpretation. Scholars who discuss Plato necessarily commit themselves to positions on these issues, however aware of this they are. Given the state of the evidence, different positions are defensible. Classical scholars are notorious for the intensity of their disagreements, and many disputes are unlikely ever to be resolved. Because of the variety of issues that are subject to dispute and widely different combinations of positions scholars assume, the result is an often bewildering variety of interpretations in the literature.

Although firm proof is impossible on many issues, some positions are more defensible than others. Needless to say, I believe the positions presented in this work are the most defensible. For the most past, as I note in my Preface, they fall in the traditional mainstream of interpretations, to the extent there is such a thing.[1] However, several of these positions have come under strong attack in recent years. Although I am often impressed by the power and ingenuity of different scholars' arguments, I believe they can be rebutted. Because it is not possible to provide detailed discussions of many issues, I refer the reader to the critical literature cited in the notes to this chapter and the suggestions for Further Reading at the end of this volume. I will discuss four matters: (1) the chronology of the dialogues; (2) problems of interpretation raised by Plato's use of the dialogue form; (3) the 'Socratic problem'; and (4) the unity or development of Plato's thought. To some degree, the questions are interrelated and we must refer forwards and backwards in discussing them.

(1) In studying Plato, questions of chronology are important, because of significant differences between dialogues. These are generally explained

---

[1] I should note that the proleptic approach, discussed below, pp. 27–8, is less widely accepted than the other points I discuss.

according to the hypothesis that Plato held different views at different times. As noted below, other explanations have been advanced, but for the last 200 years or so, most scholars have subscribed to chronological views.[2] The dialogues can be dated in two respects: in regard to the actual dates at which various works were written, and in regard to the chronological relationships between different dialogues. Throughout the dialogues, there are few direct references to contemporaneous events, and so with few exceptions, it is not possible to say exactly when Plato wrote specific works. For the purposes of this study, the order in which the dialogues were written is more significant, and I generally confine attention to that. However, because of the state of the evidence, the precise order is difficult to determine. For many years, scholars held widely different views, based on literary and philosophical features of the dialogues as interpreted according to scholars' varying opinions on Plato's likely development. However, by employing sophisticated stylometric and other techniques, scholars have been able to divide the dialogues into three rough periods, which are accepted by most scholars, though important differences remain. These are referred to as the early, middle, and late works. Order of the dialogues within the groups has been more difficult to determine. There is less agreement about the order of the early dialogues than about the middle, and much less than about the late works. The conclusions of five leading authorities on dating the dialogues—Arnim, Lutoslawski, Raeder, Ritter, and Wilamowitz—strongly agree about the order of the late dialogues and which dialogues constitute a middle group, though they disagree about the order of the early and middle works.[3] Numerous other scholars have performed stylometric studies, and their results generally support this pattern.[4] Most recently, the findings of all these scholars have been confirmed by the stylometric analyses of Leonard Brandwood and G. R. Ledger.[5] Given the strong similarities between the findings of many different scholars, whose methods varied and some of whom were not aware of the work of others, their overall findings should be accepted. Although the tripartite division of the dialogues has been criticized, it is still the dominant hypothesis, and I believe it should

---

[2] See C. C. W. Taylor, 'The Origins of Our Present Paradigms', in *New Perspectives on Plato, Modern and Ancient*, J. Annas and C. Rowe, eds. (Washington, DC, 2002).

[3] Their results are presented by W. D. Ross, *Plato's Theory of Ideas* (Oxford, 1951), ch. 1.

[4] Summarized in L. Brandwood, *The Chronology of Plato's Dialogues* (Cambridge, 1990). Brandwood, 'Stylometry and Chronology', in *The Cambridge Companion to Plato*, R. Kraut, ed. (Cambridge, 1992); and C. Kahn, 'On Platonic Chronology', in *New Perspectives on Plato*, are excellent brief overviews.

[5] Brandwood, *Chronology*; G. R. Ledger, *Re-counting Plato* (Oxford, 1989). I should note, however, that Brandwood's and Ledger's attempts to determine the order of dialogues within the groups is on ground less firm than identifying the groups themselves (as Kahn points out, *Plato and the Socratic Dialogue* [Cambridge, 1996], pp. 44–6).

be regarded as established as firmly as it is possible to establish anything in Plato scholarship.[6]

I reproduce here the groupings of the dialogues presented by F. M. Cornford, an important Classicist of the first half of the twentieth century.[7] These groupings are similar to those of the scholars I have noted and represent a reasonable position, to which, with one exception, I will adhere in this work. In this list, the dialogues are not ordered within the separate groups; the division between groups is relevant here.

Early works: *Apology, Crito, Laches, Lysis, Charmides, Euthyphro, Hippias Minor, Hippias Major, Protagoras, Gorgias, Ion;*
Middle works: *Meno, Phaedo, Republic, Symposium, Phaedrus, Euthydemus, Menexenus, Cratylus;*
Late works: *Parmenides, Theaetetus, Sophist, Statesman, Timaeus, Critias, Philebus, Laws.*[8]

This grouping is based on a combination of stylometric and philosophical and literary considerations.[9] Though not universally accepted, something along these lines is supported by most scholars and undoubtedly has more support than any other view that is significantly different. On strictly stylometric grounds, the division between late and middle dialogues is sharper than that between middle and early. Still, on these grounds alone, it is not always possible to locate a given work in the middle as opposed to the early group, or the late as opposed to the middle. Along with elements of difference there are strong elements of continuity between groups, while once again, it should be borne in mind that relative dates or order of the dialogues within the groups cannot be settled with precision. While the last six members of the late group listed here are firmly placed by stylometric considerations, these alone do

---

[6] See Kahn, 'On Platonic Chronology'; for dissenting views, see H. Thesleff, *Studies in Platonic Chronology* (Helsinki, 1982); J. Howland, 'Re-Reading Plato: The Problem of Platonic Chronology', *Phoenix* 45 (1991); Annas, *Platonic Ethics, Old and New* (Ithaca, NY, 1999); see also, J. Cooper, 'Introduction', in *Plato: Complete Works*, Cooper, ed. (Indianapolis, IN, 1997), pp. xii–xviii.

[7] F. M. Cornford, 'The Athenian Philosophical Schools', in *Cambridge Ancient History*, Vol. VI, J. B. Bury, S. A. Cook, and F. E. Adcock, eds. (Cambridge, 1927), p. 311 ff. These groupings are supported by W. K. C. Guthrie, *A History of Greek Philosophy*, 6 vols. (Cambridge, 1962–81), IV, 50. For another similar, influential view and justification, see G. Vlastos, *Socrates: Ironist and Moral Philosopher* (Ithaca, 1991), ch. 2, sec. 1.

[8] I regard the *Alcibiades* I as genuine; for brief discussion with numerous references, see P. Friedlander, *Plato*, 3 vols., H. Meyerhoff, trans. (Princeton, 1958–69), Vol. II, ch. 17; N. Denyer, ed., *Plato: Alcibiades* (Cambridge, 2001). This is supported on stylometric grounds (see Ledger, *Re-counting Plato*, p. 144), although stylometric evidence makes it difficult to date the work (Denyer, pp. 17–24; cf. Ledger, pp. 218–25).

[9] This is pointed out by Kahn, 'On Platonic Chronology', pp. 96–7; see also Brandwood, *Chronology*, pp. 250–1.

not separate the *Theaetetus* and *Parmenides* from the *Republic* and *Phaedrus*. Similarly, the *Meno*, *Phaedo*, and *Symposium* cannot be separated from the early group on stylistic grounds alone. The main reason for placing these three works in the middle group is philosophical proximity to the *Republic*, in that they present aspects of the theory of Forms (on which, more below). Stylometric considerations support locating the *Phaedo* and *Symposium* as late members of the early group.[10]

Scholars frequently appeal to Plato's first visit to Sicily, in the year 387, to explain the major differences between the early and middle works (see below, pp. 65–8), but although a work such as the *Meno* is generally considered a middle dialogue, there is some disagreement as to whether it was written before or after the visit to Sicily.[11] Still, in a case such as this, the scholars who place it in the early group generally argue that it is a late member of that group, which is in accordance with the stylometric evidence. Obviously, no great weight should be placed on matters of this sort. For the purposes of this study it is necessary to locate one particular dialogue, the *Gorgias*, in the middle group. This is the exception to Cornford's ordering mentioned above—though even in this case, placing the *Gorgias* late in the early group instead would make little difference. But because leading scholars date this work after Plato's first visit to Sicily,[12] the *Gorgias* should be considered a middle dialogue, and will be throughout this work. One final point, because the first Book of the *Republic* is strikingly similar to a number of the early dialogues, certain scholars have argued that it was originally written as an independent Socratic dialogue, the *Thrasymachus*, and only later used as the introduction to the *Republic*.[13] Though this view is not impossible, on balance there is little evidence to support it. However, because *Republic* I is so much like several early dialogues, it is commonly regarded as an early dialogue for purposes of evidence. I follow this practice here, but will not base any important claims on this evidence.

On the whole, these chronological details do not strongly affect the argument of this book. The crucial points for our purposes are separation between the early dialogues and the *Republic* and then between the *Republic* and the *Statesman* and *Laws*. These points are firmly established on stylometric grounds and reinforced by other considerations we note. Around this basic frame, we are reasonably secure in placing other dialogues.

As I have noted, this grouping of the dialogues is supported by philosophical and literary considerations. Some of these are as follows. To begin

---

[10] Brandwood, *Chronology*, p. 252 (but cf. note 5, above).

[11] For references, see Guthrie, *History*, IV, 236.

[12] E. R. Dodds, ed., *Plato: Gorgias* (Oxford, 1959), pp. 26–7; Guthrie, *History*, IV, 284–5.

[13] Friedlander, *Plato*, II, ch. 3.; H. von Arnim, *Platos Jugenddialoge und die Entstehungszeit des Phaidros* (Leipzig, Germany, 1914), pp. 71 ff.

with, the early dialogues are highly dramatic, with their dramatic action frequently revolving around the elenctic mission described by Socrates in the *Apology*. These works frequently feature some particular inquiry initiated by Socrates, which ends in irresolution, or *aporia*. In these works, the views under consideration are generally presented as the interlocutors' own. Socrates insists that the interlocutors actually hold them and is interested in their characters as well as their opinions. It seems clear that one of Plato's main purposes in these dialogues is to preserve something of the character and personality of the Socrates he knew. Thus these works are commonly referred to as Plato's 'Socratic dialogues'. Other associates of Socrates wrote similar compositions. According to Aristotle, the 'Socratic dialogue' (*Sôkratikos logos*) was a recognized literary genre. Aside from Plato's works, various compositions of Xenophon and some fragments of Aeschines survive as examples of this form.[14] It is worth noting that this form probably arose from the efforts of associates of Socrates to preserve something of his unusual oral teaching by writing down actual conversations in which he took part.[15]

The middle dialogues are far less dramatic and preserve relatively little of the tentativeness of the early works. Their philosophical content is generally conveyed in lengthy expositions by Socrates or some other spokesman. In the late dialogues, the role of Socrates diminishes. He is Plato's main spokesman in only the *Theaetetus* and *Philebus*, while he is entirely absent from the *Laws*. These works frequently verge on treatises instead of dialogues—on which, more below. Clearly, as his literary career progressed, dramatically representing the character and teaching of Socrates came to occupy a lower place in Plato's priorities.

In terms of content, the early works largely centre on moral questions, exploring the nature of different virtues and of moral knowledge. Much of this concern with moral themes is carried over into the middle and late works, but Plato's interests also become more abstract and philosophical in a technical sense. Metaphysical and epistemological questions receive increasing emphasis. Perhaps the single most striking difference between the philosophical contents of the early and later groups of works is the theory of Forms—discussed in Chapter 6—which begins to play an important role in the middle works. In conjunction with the theory of Forms, Plato begins to

---

[14] The most important work of Xenophon is the *Memorabilia*; see also the *Symposium* and the *Apology of Socrates*. The fragments of Aeschines are available in English translation in G. C. Field, *Plato and His Contemporaries*, 3rd edn. (London, 1967), pp. 147–52. For discussions of this genre, see R. B. Rutherford, *The Art of Plato* (London, 1995), ch. 2; Kahn, *Plato*, ch. 2.

[15] For evidence of this, see *Theaetetus* 143a–c; Diogenes Laertius, II, 122; Athenaeus, XI, 505b; Aristotle, *Poetics* 1447b9; see Guthrie, *History*, III, 343–4.

pay considerable attention to specific doctrines associated with Orphic and Pythagorean religious and philosophical traditions, especially the immortality and transmigration of the soul (see below, pp. 65–8). The influence this has on his psychological theories is discussed in Part II.

(2) We turn now to problems associated with the dialogue form. Plato is unusual among great philosophers in never expressing himself in his own voice—outside of his epistles, at least two of which I view as genuine.[16] Rather than writing treatises, Plato of course wrote dialogues. It is notable that Aristotle regards the Socratic dialogues as a literary genre, which he likens to the mimes of the Sicilian poet, Sophron. To some extent—perhaps a large extent—Plato's use of the dialogue form can be explained by his place in the development of a written as opposed to an oral culture.[17] When Plato wrote, the treatise was not an established genre. In his *History of the Peloponnesian War*, written perhaps a decade or two before Plato's earliest works, a great deal of Thucydides' meaning is conveyed in speeches put into the mouth of his characters, which raise problems of interpretation related to those we encounter with Plato.[18] The main problem is how far we can identify what Plato's different characters say with his own views. In dramatic compositions, it is generally unwise to do this. Consider the problems in accepting the utterances of Hamlet, Lear, or Macbeth as Shakespeare's own thoughts. Still, I believe this problem is on the whole less worrisome with Plato than with other dramatic authors. The main characters of many of Plato's dialogues appear to speak with authority. As a rule, as we move from the early Socratic dialogues to the middle and late works, the ironic, purportedly ignorant, questioning Socrates of the early works gives way to a figure—still identified and to some extent recognizable as Socrates—who appears to expound a philosophical system. Accordingly, certain scholars argue that, as we move to the middle dialogues, the question and answer method continues to be retained mainly as a holdover from the early works and no longer fulfils a philosophical function.[19] An extreme view is that of Cornford, who edited out the interlocutor's replies in his edition of the *Republic*, because he believed they impede the flow of the argument.[20] Though few scholars would go as far as Cornford

---

[16] See above, ch. 1, n. 1. Comparison between Plato's *Epistles* and the contents of different dialogues, construed according to principles of interpretation discussed in this chapter, supports these principles. For the relationship between the *Republic* and *Epistle 7*, see below, ch. 10, sec. 3; for the relationship between the *Laws* and *Epistle 8*, see below, ch. 13, sec. 4. (The authenticity of *Epistle 8* is briefly discussed in Chapter 11, sec.1.) For discussion, see G. Klosko, 'Politics and Method in Plato's Political Theory', *Polis*, 23 (2006).

[17] See E. Havelock, *Preface to Plato* (Cambridge, MA, 1963).

[18] See P. A. Stadter, ed., *The Speeches in Thucydides* (Chapel Hill, NC, 1973).

[19] R. Robinson, *Plato's Earlier Dialectic*, 2nd edn. (Oxford, 1953), pp. 75–84.

[20] Cornford, ed. and trans., *The Republic of Plato* (Oxford, 1941), p. vii.

and tamper with Plato's text,[21] many scholars believe that, in the middle and late works, the main character—whether Socrates, Timaeus, the Eleatic, or Athenian Stranger—speaks for Plato, and we are more or less able to identify what he says as Plato's own views.

This brief statement—any brief statement on this complex issue—is obviously an oversimplification. Plato was a great literary artist and undoubtedly had important reasons to employ the dialogue form and used it for different purposes. We should note especially that use of this form stimulates the readers to think for themselves as they follow the spokesperson's train of argument.[22] The dialogue form also allows narrative flexibility and so easy digressions. An important example is the myth of the Golden Age, in the *Statesman*, discussed in Chapter 11.

In recent years, scholars have developed interpretations based heavily on literary aspects of even the middle and later dialogues. Especially important to the subject of this book, ironic interpretations of Plato have become common. As I use the term, this designation covers a large number of interpretive strategies. What they have in common is that literary or dramatic details of different dialogues are employed in order to undercut what various characters say.[23] Interpretations along these lines raise many complex issues that cannot be discussed here. But once again, the main point to note is differences between the early and middle and late dialogues. The early works are far more complex dramatically than the others, and I believe Plato does manipulate the dramatic aspects of several of these in order to undercut what Socrates says in important ways (on which, more below). But things are significantly different in the more expository middle and late works.[24] Although these works still retain interesting dramatic elements and flashes of Plato's literary brilliance, I believe

---

[21] Comparably subject to criticism, though in the other direction, is the approach of C. D. C. Reeve, who edited the text into a direct dialogue, as opposed to one narrated by Socrates (*Plato: Republic* [Indianapolis, IN, 2004]); a similar approach was employed by I. A. Richards, ed. and trans., *Plato's Republic* (Cambridge, 1966).

[22] Scholars argue that it also forces the reader to think about the authoritative status of the main spokesperson; see esp. M. Frede, 'Plato's Arguments and the Dialogue Form', *Oxford Studies in Ancient Philosophy*, Supp. Volume (1992).

[23] Most familiar in regard to Plato's political theory are the interpretive claims of Leo Strauss and his followers, especially Allan Bloom; for interpretation of the *Republic*, see Strauss, *The City and Man* (Chicago, IL, 1964), ch. 2; Bloom, 'Interpretive Essay', in *The Republic of Plato* (New York, 1968). For discussion and further references, see Klosko, 'The "Straussian" Interpretation of Plato's *Republic*', *History of Political Thought*, 7 (1986). Also see E. Voegelin, *Plato* (Baton Rouge, 1966). In regard to more mainstream approaches, see Annas and Rowe, eds., *New Perspectives on Plato*; C. Gill and M. McCabe, eds., *Form and Argument in Late Plato* (Oxford, 1996). See also C. Griswold, ed., *Platonic Writings, Platonic Readings* (New York, 1988); G. Press, ed., *Who Speaks for Plato?* (Lanham, MD, 2000).

[24] This is as a rule; there are possible exceptions. Among the middle works, the most notable is *Republic*, Book I, for reasons mentioned above.

it is generally safe to identify the content of the positions Socrates or other main speakers advance as Plato's own views. I should emphasize that I am not saying that one may simply ignore the dramatic aspects of the middle and late dialogues, that utterances abstracted from their dramatic context constitute Plato's philosophy. As a rule, in reading Plato, one must always be aware of dramatic elements. Each conversation Plato depicts is a distinct dialectical encounter between specific characters under specific circumstances.[25] However, in general, throughout the middle and late works, the dramatic circumstances lend themselves to authoritative exposition by the main character. In these circumstances, dramatic context is relatively unimportant, and what the main characters say may well contain straightforward presentation of Plato's philosophy.

There are strong reasons for adopting interpretive principles along these lines. In commenting on Plato's works, Aristotle, who was of course Plato's student, takes what the main character of the *Republic* and *Laws* says to be Plato's views.[26] In general, in Plato's middle and late works, the dialogue form is far less involved than in the early dialogues. It frequently appears to be only a shell, as epitomized by the *Timaeus* and *Laws*, the bulk of which are straight discourse. Also important is the source of the premises of the arguments that are developed in different works. In the early dialogues, Socrates repeatedly insists that the views examined must be the interlocutor's own, and accordingly requests that his interlocutors say only what they believe.[27] Thus, as depicted by Plato in these works, Socrates maintains important distance from views that are examined, which may generally be attributed to his interlocutors. Things change significantly in the middle and late works, in which Socrates frequently answers questions posed by other characters rather than asking them himself. For this and other reasons, the philosophical material discussed in these works should be viewed as from Socrates—or the other main characters.[28] In these works, although the dialogue form is retained, interlocutors are often interchangeable. In several late dialogues,

---

[25] For an excellent overall discussion of Plato's use of dramatic elements, see Rutherford, *Art of Plato*.

[26] T. Irwin, *Plato's Ethics* (Oxford, 1995), pp. 5–7. I should note that Aristotle appears to refer to the *Laws* as a 'Socratic' work (*Pol.* 1265a11), while much of the substance of what he says about the *Republic* especially is questionable; for discussion, see Klosko, *History of Political Theory: An Introduction*, 2 vols. (Fort Worth, 1993, 1995), I, 116–20; cf. R. F. Stalley, 'Aristotle's Criticism of Plato's *Republic*', in *A Companion to Aristotle's Politics*, D. Keyt and F. D. Miller, eds. (Oxford, 1991).

[27] e.g., *Ethp.* 9d; *Cri.* 49c; *Prt.* 331c–d; *Rep.* 349a; *Grg.* 458a–b.

[28] The *Theaetus* and *Philebus* are perhaps to some extent exceptions; see also the literature cited, below in the next note.

they are clearly identified as unimportant.[29] For instance, in the *Parmenides*, the eponymous main spokesman requests an interlocutor who is not overly curious as well as most likely to say what he thinks; 'Moreover, his replies would give me a chance to rest' (*Parm.* 137*b*). In the *Sophist*, among the Eleatic Stranger's requirements for his interlocutor are that he be tractable and give no trouble (217*c–d*). Accordingly, problems of interpretation are less formidable in the middle and late dialogues. The implication for the study of Plato's political theory is that the political theory of the middle and later works can generally be construed directly from what the different main characters say—Socrates in the *Republic*, the Eleatic Stranger in the *Statesman*, and the Athenian Stranger in the *Laws*.[30]

Because of the nature of the early dialogues, they pose severe difficulties for the commentator. Not only are they often characterized by significant philosophical interchange, but many of Socrates' arguments seem hasty and/or unfair, intended to score debating points rather than for the sake of patient, careful examination of points at issue.[31] To complicate matters further, Socrates was famous for his irony, and it is not always clear that what he says can be taken at face value.[32] For instance, is his frequent claim of ignorance—most apparent in the *Apology*—sincerely intended, or meant to induce his interlocutors to reveal their views—as Thrasymachus accuses in *Republic* I (337*a*). If the avowal of ignorance is sincere, how do we reconcile this with strong statements Socrates also makes about knowing certain moral truths?[33] Because of these and other problems, in the early dialogues, one cannot always identify what Socrates says with what Plato believes (or believed at the time he wrote the works in question). Although some scholars believe that, as a rule, the views expressed in the early works do represent Plato's own views when he wrote given dialogues, I believe this position is too rigid and does not sufficiently take into account the dramatic elements of different works. In interpreting the early dialogues especially, one's conclusions often depend on what one makes of the nuances of dramatic action as well as more hard evidence. I do not believe these problems of interpretation can be avoided.

[29] For contrary views, see Gill and McCabe, eds., *Form and Argument in Late Plato* and the other literature cited in note 23 above.

[30] This is not to suggest that dramatic elements play no role in the late works. On the *Statesman*, see M. Lane, *Method and Politics in Plato's Statesman* (Cambridge, 1998); on the *Laws*, see A. Nightingale, 'Writing/Reading a Sacred Text: A Literary Interpretation of Plato's *Laws*', *Classical Philology*, 88 (1993); C. Bobonich, 'Reading the *Laws*', in Gill and McCabe, eds., *Form and Argument in Late Plato*.

[31] See R. K. Sprague, *Plato's Use of Fallacy* (London, 1962); Robinson, 'Plato's Consciousness of Fallacy', *Mind*, 51 (1942); see also the articles cited below in n. 42.

[32] For an excellent discussion of irony in Plato, see Friedlander, *Plato*, Vol. I, ch. 7.

[33] See Vlastos, *Socratic Studies*, M. Burnyeat, ed. (Cambridge, 1994), ch. 2; T. Brickhouse and N. Smith, *Plato's Socrates* (Oxford, 1994), ch. 2.

As a result, any account of these dialogues is necessarily to some extent the author's own interpretation, which is strongly affected by the assumptions he or she brings to the texts. Because the persuasiveness of a given interpretation depends on 'the mutual support of many considerations, of everything fitting together into one coherent view',[34] to borrow John Rawls's language concerning justification in moral philosophy, the proper standard is comparative. No view can be expected to solve all difficulties. We should ask which one best encompasses the significant evidence. Which allows the most coherent overall account of the dialogues in question? Throughout this study, I attempt to work out what I believe is the most coherent overall interpretation of Plato's political theory, which proceeds from the assumptions discussed in this chapter.

(3) The two remaining topics, the 'Socratic problem' and the unity or development of Plato's thought, will be discussed separately, though they are closely related. The Socratic problem centres on disentangling the Socrates who is a character in Plato's dialogues from the historical Socrates. Specifically, the question is: to what extent should the doctrine presented in different dialogues, put into the mouth of Socrates, be attributed to Socrates, and to what extent to Plato? To a large extent the views one defends depend on the positions on the chronology of the dialogues and questions of interpretation discussed so far. Obviously, if one takes the position that at least some dialogues were intended to represent the historical Socrates, then the contents of those works should be attributed to Socrates. The problem then becomes ascertaining at what point Plato ceased presenting historical reconstructions of Socrates' thought and began to present his own. Early in the last century, two influential scholars, Burnet and Taylor, strongly argued that Plato's presentation of Socrates throughout his entire corpus was primarily historical, that Plato's Socrates is always meant to represent the historical Socrates.[35] This position is now all but universally rejected. The decisive consideration in the eyes of most scholars is the evidence of Aristotle, who in the *Metaphysics* clearly distinguishes the metaphysical positions of the historical Socrates and Plato, attributing the theory of Forms to the latter but not to the former.[36] Since in Plato's corpus the theory of Forms first appears—or more accurately, first receives serious consideration—in the middle works, most scholars hold that Plato begins to present his own thought in the middle dialogues. This position is supported by the fact that the Socrates in Xenophon's

---

[34] J. Rawls, *A Theory of Justice* (Cambridge, MA, 1971), p. 21.

[35] For a brief discussion of this position, including references, see Guthrie, *History*, III, 351–2.

[36] 1078b17–32; 987b1–6; on this see esp. Field, *Plato and His Contemporaries*, pp. 202–13. The Socratic problem is discussed at length along the lines taken here by Guthrie, in *History*, Vol. III, with numerous references; see also Ross, 'The Problem of Socrates', *Proceedings of the Classical Association*, 30 (1933).

compositions—mainly the *Memorabilia*—is much closer to the Socrates of Plato's early dialogues than to that of his middle works. Thus scholars hold that historical motives largely lie behind Plato's early dialogues. As Guthrie says, in the early dialogues, 'It may be claimed that Plato is imaginatively recalling in form and substance the conversations of [Socrates], without as yet adding to them any distinctive doctrines of his own.'[37] However, although I believe this is largely true, I think it is overly simple, as we will see momentarily.

Aristotle provides strong evidence for the essentially Socratic nature of the views expressed in the early dialogues. In addition to differences between the metaphysics of the early and middle works, it will be seen below that the moral and psychological views he attributes to Socrates are similar to those presented in the early dialogues and that here too the middle dialogues are quite different. Although this correspondence has received less attention from scholars, the correlations in these areas are as close as those in metaphysical views. Accordingly, in this study, I argue from the generally accepted position, that the views of the historical Socrates can in large measure be reconstructed from Plato's early dialogues, and that this material generally coincides with what Aristotle says about Socrates and Xenophon's portrayal in the *Memorabilia* and some of this other works. This position is not without controversy, as there are conflicts in the evidence. Still, like most scholars, I believe the evidence is largely reliable and basically consistent. One implication of this position is that, as Plato eventually moves away from Socratic views, there is clear development in his thought. To this subject we now turn.

(4) The main positions in the literature concerning the development of Plato's thought are (*a*) that it changes and develops between the different groups of dialogues (we can call this the 'development' view) or (*b*) that it does not (the 'unity' view). Able scholars have argued for both positions and countless variations thereof. Each position has advantages and disadvantages, and it is unlikely that disagreements between scholars will ever be resolved.

In the literature, scholars present different interpretations of the relationship between early and middle dialogues, depending primarily on how they construe the early works. The three main alternatives are that these dialogues (*a*) primarily provide dramatic depictions of the historical Socrates, (*b*) present Plato's own views at the times he wrote the works, or (*c*) contribute to a single coherent body of work that culminates in the *Republic*. Adherents of the unity of Plato's thought focus on the last alternative. The major point in favour of their interpretation is that the early dialogues appear to have been carefully constructed so that the problems they successively raise but

----

[37] Guthrie, *History*, IV, 67.

do not answer are decisively resolved in the *Republic*.[38] These scholars are also interested in hints dropped in various early works that seem to point directly at the *Republic*. They contend that the fact that Plato does not discuss certain aspects of his philosophy in various dialogues does not mean that at the time he wrote those works he did not believe in them or had not yet worked them out. Rather, Plato purposely withheld these doctrines; when he wrote the early dialogues, he had already worked out the main lines of the *Republic*, which these works suggest. Thus, unity scholars discount both development views and views that emphasize the historical dimension of the early works.

As I have noted, for much of the last 200 years, a developmental paradigm has dominated the literature, although this has also been criticized.[39] This book defends a development view, as is clearly indicated by its title. However, it is important to recognize different interpretations of how Plato's thought develops. In particular, I distinguish the view presented in this book from other accounts, which I believe to be overly rigid. On the whole, development between the middle and late dialogues is relatively straightforward and worked out in Part IV. The relationship between the early and middle works requires sorting out, once again in large part because of the heavily dramatic nature of the former. I believe the evidence requires a complex view of Plato's literary and philosophical intentions.

At the present time, the most prominent development view is that advanced by Gregory Vlastos, in his book *Socrates: Ironist and Moral Philosopher*. Vlastos argues for what we may call a 'strong development view', according to which each dialogue reflects more or less exactly what Plato thought at the time he wrote it. In Vlastos' words:

Plato makes him [Socrates] say whatever *he*—Plato—thinks at the *time of writing* would be the most reasonable thing for Socrates to be saying just then in expounding and defending his own philosophy.[40]

Such a strong development view assumes that differences between dialogues always reflect changes in Plato's philosophy, rather than his literary intentions in given works. Thus, according to this view, the main differences between the early and middle dialogues can be attributed to changes in Plato's thinking.[41] In extreme form, a view along these lines contends that, if a given

---

[38] See P. Shorey, *What Plato Said* (Chicago, IL, 1933), 62–73; the classic account of the 'unity' interpretation is Shorey's *The Unity of Plato's Thought* (Chicago, IL, 1903). For a recent statement of a similar position, see Kahn, *Plato*; cf. also Annas, *Platonic Ethics*.

[39] See Annas and Rowe, eds., *New Perspectives*; Kahn, *Plato*; Annas, *Platonic Ethics*.

[40] Vlastos, *Socrates*, p. 50 (his emphasis).

[41] For an extensive list of differences between the early and middle works, see ibid. ch. 2.

dialogue ends in *aporia* (puzzlement), this is not because Plato wished to depict Socrates' practice of the *elenchos*, but because Plato had not completely thought through the given subject. I believe such a position is obviously overstated. Once again, it pays insufficient attention to the literary aspects of Plato's works and his intention to portray the historical Socrates. Still, I believe an interpretation along these lines contains a good deal of truth. As I have noted, I reject the unity view, or at least a strong version of it. However, I believe there is a good deal of truth in the unity view as well. How is this possible?

The details of a solution to this problem cannot receive the attention they deserve, in this context. Full defence would be unduly lengthy; to a large extent, this book as a whole is a defence of what I believe is the proper perspective. Briefly, upon examining the evidence it is difficult to dispute either (*a*) that the early dialogues depict philosophical views that are superseded in the middle dialogues, or (*b*) that the former works raise a number of questions that are carefully and comprehensively addressed in the *Republic*. Thus one reason both the unity and development views have scholarly adherents is that there is strong evidence in support of both. However, the evidence supports only moderate, as opposed to strong, versions of these two interpretations. Strong versions of both the unity and development positions fall short in not adequately recognizing the Socratic nature of the views expressed in the early dialogues. To some extent, a position such as Vlastos' takes this into account in contending that, at the time he wrote these works, Plato was a Socratic. However, what this interpretation neglects is a third point that I find difficult to deny: (*c*) in many early works, Plato is interested in depicting something of the Socrates he knew, and that the Socrates he depicts is generally consistent with our other evidence concerning Socrates. In other words, Plato does more than advance Socratic ideas. He puts them into the mouth of the fully developed character of Socrates, who is obviously closely related to the historical Socrates (as Plato knew him), and is one of the foremost dramatic characters in Western literature.

An interpretation according to which the Socrates of the early dialogues is simply a literary device used for working out Plato's philosophy has difficulty explaining the *ad hominem* nature of the discussions depicted in these works. As I have noted, many of Socrates' arguments appear hasty, while others appear to contain blatant fallacies.[42] Such arguments are difficult to explain as efficacious means used by Plato to develop his own positions. In a

---

[42] For discussion, see the works cited above, in n. 31. See also Klosko, 'Toward a Consistent Interpretation of the *Protagoras*', *Archiv für Geschichte der Philosophie*, 61 (1979); 'Criteria of Fallacy and Sophistry for Use in the Analysis of Platonic Dialogues,' *Classical Quarterly*, NS 33 (1983); 'Plato and the Morality of Fallacy', *American Journal of Philology*, 108 (1987).

larger sense, the same could be said of the *elenchos* as a whole as a mode of philosophical reasoning. (The *elenchos* is discussed in the following chapter.) The point to note here is that it is a method of refutation, used to test the views of Socrates' interlocutors, generally to refute them, in accordance with the mission of moral reform Socrates undertook. As I have noted, in several dialogues all views put forth are refuted, and discussions end in irresolution. If Plato's purpose was to establish the positions he held at the time of writing, depicting discussions of this kind was a peculiar way to go about it.[43] Thus it is not surprising that when presenting and defending his philosophy becomes Plato's primary concern, the *elenchos* fades into the background, and the dialogues focus on Socrates' attempts to *explain* various matters to interested interlocutors. Further clarifications are introduced when the interlocutors are unable to understand various points and ask Socrates for elaboration.

Although the evidence strongly indicates that Plato wrote the early dialogues largely in order to represent the historical Socrates, I believe he also had other ends in mind. When he wrote these works, Plato was aware of some of the major shortcomings of Socratic thought. I believe he also knew where improvements could be made and indicated this in several early works.[44] For these reasons, Plato maintains a certain dramatic distance from the proceedings, including the views Socrates expresses. The upshot of this position is that the early dialogues are not only historical, but are also 'proleptic'. They 'look forward' to the fully developed philosophical theory presented in the middle dialogues. I quote Jaeger on the proleptic nature of Plato's early dialogues:

Since his very earliest works, starting from different points, all lead with mathematical certainty to the same centre, it is evident that a fundamental feature of his thought is this architectonic awareness of the general plan, and that it marks an essential difference between the books of the poetical philosopher Plato and those of every non-philosophical poet. He well knew the end towards which he was moving. When he wrote the first words of his first Socratic dialogues, he knew the whole of which it was to be a part. The entelechy of the *Republic* can be quite clearly traced in the early dialogues. But this way of writing is a new and unique thing. It is one of the greatest revelations of the Greek power of organic creation. Under the guidance of a powerful intelligence which seems in matters of detail to create with all the freedom of untramelled play, and yet works steadily towards a supreme and ever-present end,

---

[43] The most notable attempt to interpret the *elenchos* as a positive method is Vlastos, *Socratic Studies*, ch. 1; see also Irwin, *Plato's Ethics*, pp. 18–21; Brickhouse and Smith, *Plato's Socrates*, ch. 1.

[44] I find it natural to believe that, in the course of depicting Socrates in his first compositions—in accordance with his original intentions—Plato perhaps differed from other practitioners of the Socratic dialogue in coming to understand problems with his teacher's philosophy and so became concerned to work them into his dialogues, while still depicting the Socrates he knew.

Plato's philosophy appears to grow with the liberty and the certainty of a magnificent tree. It would be a serious mistake to believe that, when he wrote these little intellectual dramas, Plato's spiritual range was no broader than their foreground.[45]

In the very process of raising questions that Socrates asked but never answered, Plato also indicates the direction of his own projected solutions. And so, as Jaeger says, many of the early dialogues point directly at the *Republic*. Because Plato's solutions often require rejecting views of the historical Socrates, the early works often feature a deep irony. In addition to the confrontation between Socrates and his interlocutors depicted in a given dialogue, at the very time he is being depicted, the historical Socrates frequently also serves as a kind of interlocutor for Plato, who is aware of the shortcomings of Socrates' positions and points at them in the works. Thus Plato incorporates foreshadowing of the mature views presented in the *Republic* in many works. Only in the light of the *Republic* is it possible to look back on these dialogues and realize the full implications of what Socrates is saying or Plato otherwise depicts. In spite of the apparent complexity of this contention, there is powerful evidence for it in a series of dialogues.[46] I believe that one aspects of this overall strategy bears particularly on Plato's political theory. His concern with the failure of Socrates' mission and eventual death is central to the development of Plato's own views. This theme is discussed in Chapter 4.

It is impossible to demonstrate that this reading of the dialogues is correct—especially in this context. But I should note that this interpretation has the great advantage of recognizing the three considerations I have mentioned: (*a*) that there is a depiction of the character and teaching of Socrates in the early dialogues, much more than in the middle and late groups; (*b*) that there is development in the philosophy presented in different dialogues, as the views expressed in the *Republic* and other middle dialogues differ sharply from those advanced in the early works, which are also closely related to those of the historical Socrates; and (*c*) that the early dialogues are part of an overall artistic construction that culminates in the *Republic*. Throughout this study, then, I assume that Plato presents a historically accurate Socrates in the early works, but also does so in a way that hints at the shortcomings of Socratic thought, thereby revealing the necessity of the quite different philosophical positions assumed in the middle works. By working out the details of this approach, I

---

[45] W. Jaeger, *Paideia*, 3 vols., G. Highet, trans. (Oxford, 1939–45), II, 96. Cf. the different proleptic view recently presented by Kahn, *Plato*; Kahn, 'Proleptic Composition in the *Republic*', *Classical Quarterly*, 43 (1993).

[46] Examples are Socrates' remarks concerning endurance at *Laches* 194a; the depiction of his lust at *Charmides* 155d–e; and the sophistication of Protagoras' view of education in his great speech, *Prt.* 323c–26e; for discussion, see Kahn, *Plato*; M. J. O'Brien, *The Socratic Paradoxes and the Greek Mind* (Chapel Hill, NC, 1967).

attempt to show that it affords the basis for a reasonable—indeed the most reasonable—interpretation of the movement of Plato's thought.

Throughout this study, I trace the development of Plato's political theory from his Socratic early works to his Platonic middle and late ones. For simplicity of reference, I refer to the philosophical contents of the early dialogues as the position of 'Socrates' or as 'Socratic' thought, and attribute the doctrine of the later groups to 'Plato'. I will supplement the contents of the early dialogues with aspects of some later dialogues that appear to be in clear reference to the historical Socrates,[47] and with evidence from Aristotle and Xenophon (occasionally labelled as referring to the 'historical' Socrates).

Since it is probable that Plato was in his youth heavily influenced by the philosophical doctrines of Socrates, it is likely that throughout the early and middle dialogues he has presented something of his own intellectual development. He allows the reader to retrace the steps that led him from Socratism to Platonism.[48] We concentrate most heavily on the rise of the political theory of Plato's middle dialogues—primarily the *Republic*, since Plato's reputation as a pre-eminent political philosopher has always rested on this work. We discuss the *Statesman* and *Laws* in less detail, largely in regard to aspects of the political theory of the *Republic* to which they adhere or from which they depart. In the *Politics*, Aristotle says (freely translated), 'one shall not attain the best insight into things, until one actually sees them growing from the beginning' (1252a24–26). In this study we trace the origin and development of Plato's political thought, from the beginning, as it unfolds, to bear fruit in the *Republic*—as it unfolds, as Jaeger says, like an organic creation.

[47] Cf. the evidence Burnet uses, in his attempt to avoid controversy, in his seminal article, 'The Socratic Doctrine of the Soul', *Proceedings of the British Academy*, 7 (1915–16), pp. 237–8.

[48] In his sense, I believe the strong development view is correct, although, once again, it neglects literary aspects of Plato's presentation of Socrates and questions he may have had about Socrates' views at the time of writing at least some early dialogues.

Part I

The Political Theory of Plato's Socrates

3

Socrates' Mission

Plato's political theory had its origin in the mission of moral reform under-taken by Socrates, which is described in the *Apology* and depicted in a number of the early dialogues. We see that the development of Plato's political thought is complex. Though he remained faithful to certain aspects of the end Socrates sought—though not others—Plato was forced to reject Socrates' means as inadequate to attain that end. Plato eventually came to question some of Socrates' basic assumptions, especially psychological ones, and this led to major changes throughout his political theory. In examining the Socrates of Plato's early dialogues, then, we must pay special attention to three things: (*a*) the end Socrates sought; (*b*) the means he employed; and (*c*) certain basic assumptions he made, especially concerning moral psychology, that enabled him to proceed in his inimitable fashion. We discuss Socratic psychology in detail in the next chapter. This chapter will be devoted to Socrates' end and means.

Problems in reconstructing the political theory of the early dialogues have been touched on in the last chapter. Rather than directly presenting a set of doctrines that is attributed to Socrates, Plato generally depicts Socrates practising his *elenchos*, asking questions without answering them. In order to construct his philosophy we must inquire into what he is depicted as doing as well as what he says. For Socrates, philosophy was not a system of abstract truths but a way of life. And so his philosophy, as presented in the early dialogues, must be looked at in conjunction with his personality and life as a whole. In the case of his political philosophy, we are able to identify a number of propositions concerning political matters and demonstrate that Socrates held them. But Socrates did not 'hold' his political philosophy: he embodied it.

The *Apology* is the one case in which we find something that approaches a general account of Socrates' mission. This work of course presents a series of speeches made by Socrates at his trial. Socrates was charged with impiety and corrupting the young, but rather than confining his attention to these specific charges, he presented a defence of his entire life. It is difficult to ascertain the degree to which Plato's *Apology* is faithful to the actual defence of the historical Socrates. But this need not concern us. The *Apology* is the manifesto

of Plato's Socrates, and in the following discussion we make constant reference
to it.

3.1. SOCRATES' DEFENCE

A number of political ideas are associated with Socrates and are often presented as his contribution to political thought. Two ideas spring to mind
most readily. First, Socrates popularized a cogent criticism of the Athenian
democracy's practice of appointing high government officials by lottery. Since
the Assembly required the advice of recognized experts on certain matters—
ship building or construction, for two examples—Socrates thought it foolish
not to require similar expertise in the far more important matter of governing
the *polis*. The argument that government is a craft like other crafts and therefore requires technical knowledge is a basic Socratic doctrine. In the *Rhetoric*
(1395*b*5–8) Aristotle reports a version of this argument used by (the historical)
Socrates, which runs something like this. If you wanted someone to perform
surgery, you wouldn't choose him by lot; if you wanted someone to run a race,
you wouldn't choose him by lot; if you wanted someone to navigate a ship, you
wouldn't choose him by lot. Therefore, how can you choose people to govern
the *polis* by lot?[1]

Socrates' opinion of democracy is complicated by the fact that he appears
to express a favourable view of the laws of Athens in the *Crito*. However, he
is harshly critical of Athenian politics in the *Apology* (see below, p. 36), and
also refers to Sparta and Crete as well governed in the *Crito* (*eunomeisthai*,
52*e*–53*a*). It is likely that Socrates described these states in this way in order
to contrast them favourably with Athens. The historical Socrates was reputed
to be favourably disposed towards Sparta (Aristophanes, *Birds*, 1281–3). But
although it is inherently important to tease out Socrates' view of democracy,
this is less important than it might otherwise be, because of the distance he
maintained from the Athenian political system.

Also attributed to Socrates is a collection of opinions concerning the so-
called 'social contract' and the almost unconditional duty to obey the laws
that the 'contract' incurs. These ideas are discussed at length in the *Crito*.[2]
However, though I do not doubt that Socrates' criticism of democracy and his
social contract theory are interesting and worthy of study, the true nature of

---

[1] Many arguments used by Plato's Socrates make similar points; see *Prt.* 319*b–e*; *Meno* 92*b–*
94*e*; *Grg.* 455*a* ff.; *Lach.* 184*d* ff. See also Xenophon, *Mem.* I, ii, 9, III, ix, 10–12.

[2] See *Crito* 50*c*–54*c*; for discussion, see G. Santas, *Socrates: Philosophy in Plato's Early Dialogues* (London, 1979), pp. 19–29; R. Kraut, *Socrates and the State* (Princeton, NJ, 1984),
chs. 4–6.

Socrates' political thought must be approached through other means. Guthrie is correct in calling the ideas just mentioned Socrates' political 'views'.[3] It is because they can be removed from Socrates' philosophy as a whole and discussed in isolation from his life and personality that these ideas are no more than political views. One main difference between Plato's Socrates and Xenophon's is that the latter presents us with Socratic doctrine abstracted from Socrates' personality. To do this is to transform the towering figure that Plato has left us into an ordinary street-corner moralist. There is a real Socratic political theory, a political theory of uncompromising aspiration, but it is only to be found at the centre of the intertwined mass of life and thought that is the genuine philosophy of Plato's Socrates. Though perhaps 'political theory' or 'political philosophy' is too strong a term (though I continue to use both), at the heart of Socratic philosophy lies a political ideal, a conception of what man can be. It is according to this ideal that Socrates lived and for it that he died.

The nature of Socrates' political ideal is not found in any direct relationship to the Athenian government. It is a well-attested fact that Socrates largely exempted himself from the Athenian political process that was so much a part of his fellow citizens' lives. Though he fulfilled the duties of his citizenship and performed military service in the Peloponnesian War (*Ap.* 28*d–e*, *Symp.* 220*d*–21*c*, *Lach.* 181*b*), and though on one occasion he secured a place in the Council and fought to defend the laws of Athens against abuse (*Ap.* 32*a–c*), his general attitude to Athenian politics is exemplified by his conduct on another occasion. According to the *Apology*, when the Thirty Tyrants seized control of Athens and 'wished to implicate as many in their crimes as they could', Socrates and four other men were ordered illegally to arrest one Leon of Salamis. Socrates' reaction was typical: 'The other four arrested Leon, but I simply went home' (*Ap.* 32*d*).

In general, Socrates had as little as possible to do with Athenian government. This is one thing for which Plato actually has him apologize: 'Perhaps it may seem strange that I go about and interfere in other people's affairs to give ... advice in private, but do not venture to come before your assembly and advise the state' (*Ap.* 31*c*). His explanation for this is characteristically Socratic: 'As you have heard me say at many times and places ... something divine and spiritual comes to me'. It is Socrates' 'divine sign' and it opposes his engaging in politics (*Ap.* 31*c–d*). In the *Gorgias*, Plato makes much of Socrates' abstention from politics, and Callicles concludes his great speech with an exhortation for Socrates to forsake his philosophizing and to practise

---

[3] Guthrie, *History*, III, 411–16; also N. Gulley, *The Philosophy of Socrates* (London, 1968), pp. 168–79.

'the fairer music of affairs' (*Grg.* 484c–86d). Thus, on the face of it, it seems puzzling to say that Socrates' life was a life of never-ending political activity, but this is the claim that Socrates makes in the *Gorgias*:

I think I am one of few, not to say the only one, in Athens who attempts the true political art (*tê hôs alêthôs politikê technê*), and the only man of the present time who manages affairs of state, because the speeches that I make from time to time are not aimed at gratification, but at what is best instead of what is most pleasant. (521d)

In this passage we see that Socrates' political activity, the politics in which he is engaged, is of a higher order. Whereas he dismisses existing democratic politics and politicians as institutionalized pandering to the mob (esp. *Grg.* 502d–3d, 513a–19a), Socrates calls himself a true politician because he aims at what is best rather than what is most pleasant.

Socrates avoids Athenian politics because he believes they are hopelessly corrupt: 'Do you believe that I could have lived so many years if I had been in public life and had acted as a good man should act, lending my aid to what is just and considering that of the highest importance?' (*Ap.* 32e). And so he must pursue his activity, his mission, in a private capacity. Thus the position we are left with is that Socrates abandoned traditional political activity in favour of political activity of a higher order. Though his opinions concerning ordinary Greek politics—the lower politics—are not uninteresting, his real importance as a political figure, if not exactly a political thinker, lies in the higher activity he pursued.

In the *Apology*, Socrates gives a well-known account of his mission. He says that his activity began in reaction to a puzzling response that his friend, Chaerophon, received from the Delphic oracle. Chaerophon had asked the oracle if anyone was wiser than Socrates. The answer, of course, was 'no' (*Ap.* 20d–21a). Since Socrates knew that in fact he was not wise, his mission began as an attempt to discover the true meaning of the oracle's response. In order to test the oracle, Socrates began to examine those of his fellow citizens who were reputed to be wise. He discovered that, aside from the craftsmen (each of whom knew his craft), they knew no more than he did and, moreover, were not aware of their own ignorance. Thus, supposedly, it was with the intent to validate the oracle that Socrates undertook the herculean labour of invalidating his fellow citizens' claims to wisdom. It is in this role that he is most often pictured, and this activity is given as the cause of the hatred he incurred (*Ap.* 21b–e, 23a–e).

Socrates' investigation of the oracle proved successful. Not only did he find that the puzzling response was indeed correct, but he discovered what he believed to be its true meaning:

[T]he fact is, gentlemen, it is likely that only the god is really wise and by his oracle he means this: 'Human wisdom is of little or no value.' And it appears that he ... merely uses my name and makes me an example, as if he were to say: 'This one of you, O men, is wisest who, like Socrates, recognizes that he is in truth of no account in respect to wisdom.' (*Ap.* 23*a–b*)

Whereas Socrates speaks of the mere investigation of the meaning of the oracle as 'the god's business' (21*e*) and as performed 'at the god's behest' (22*a*), from the very beginning Socrates' mission entailed more than this. From the first he thought it necessary to inform others of his findings. Socrates was not content merely to discover that the first person he examined, one of the politicians, did not possess any real wisdom. He felt obliged to make this known to him (*Ap.* 21*c*). Informing his interlocutors of their ignorance was an integral part of Socrates' mission:

I am still even now going about and searching and investigating at the god's behest anyone, whether citizen or foreigner, who I think is wise; and when he does not seem so to me, I give aid to the god and show that he is not wise. (23*b*)

Socrates' service to the god, then, is not merely proving the oracle correct, and it is not refuting people for its own sake. It is showing people that they are not wise. This is done as part of a larger process of teaching the message of the oracle—that what had up until his time passed as wisdom 'is of little or no value'.

Socrates' peculiar negative teaching is undertaken as a preliminary to his positive teaching. As Socrates continues his defence, the content of his positive teaching, the higher wisdom of the god, becomes clear:

I shall never give up philosophy or stop exhorting you and pointing out the truth to any one of you whom I may meet, saying in my accustomed way: 'Most excellent man, are you who are a citizen of Athens, the greatest of cities and the most famous for wisdom and power, not ashamed to care for the acquisition of wealth and for reputation and honor, when you neither care nor take thought for wisdom and truth and the perfection of your soul?' (29*d–e*)

And again: For I go about doing nothing else than urging you, young and old alike, not to care for your persons or your property more than for the perfection of your souls, or even so much (30*a–b*). Thus we see that Socrates' message to his fellow citizens is that they should 'care for their souls (*psuchai*)'. Later, when he says, 'I tried to persuade each of you to care for himself and his own perfection in goodness and wisdom rather than for any of his belongings' (36*c*), by 'caring for himself' Socrates means 'caring for his *psuchê*'.

At first sight, it might seem to us that Socrates' teaching could not possibly have been anything so commonplace, so banal, as 'care for your souls'.

However, as Burnet first pointed out,[4] before (the historical) Socrates began his mission, not only was it not a moral truism that we should care for our souls, but the very concept 'soul' was not generally believed to encompass those human attributes worth caring for. In fact, as Burnet says, Socrates' exhortation probably sounded as peculiar to the Athenians as the exhortation 'care for your ghost' would sound to us.[5] Though it is not necessary to discuss the details of Socrates' innovations concerning the concept of the soul—as this has been done many times[6]—it seems clear that the philosophy of Plato's Socrates (and, no doubt, the historical Socrates) is rooted in his conception of the soul. If the *Alcibiades* I is to be trusted, Socrates argues that a man's soul is his true self and that it stands in relation to his body as a craftsman to his tools, as user to a thing used (*Alc.* I, 129*b*–31*b*).

The offshoot of this doctrine is an exalted conception of the *psuchê*. *Aretê* (virtue, or excellence), the proper excellence of man, is to care for his *psuchê*, to make sure that it is as good as possible. The ethical implications of this are drawn in full: 'I tell you that virtue does not come from money, but from virtue comes money and all other good things to man, both to the individual and to the state' (*Ap.* 30*b*). Socrates says that a man's *psuchê* is that which is 'most dear to him' (*Prt.* 313*a*) and that 'on which depends the good or ill condition of all [his] affairs, according as it is made better or worse' (*Prt.* 313*a*). It is on the values of the soul that Socrates and Plato erect their new conception of politics. In the *Gorgias*, politics is defined as the art 'which has to do with the soul'. The two aspects of politics, 'justice' and 'legislation', are described as having as their object and function the inculcation and maintenance in the soul of a state of health analogous to that which gymnastic training and medicine are intended to promote in the body. The end of politics is 'to make the citizens' souls as good as possible' (*Grg.* 503*a*). This conception of politics, clearly implied in the *Apology*, proclaimed in the ringing tones of the *Gorgias*, is brought to fruition in the *Republic* and the *Laws*.

3.2. THE SOCRATIC IDEAL

We have seen that Socrates' goal was to induce his countrymen to 'care for their souls'. To a certain extent this injunction is clear. Socrates' message was

---

[4] J. Burnet, 'The Socratic Doctrine of the Soul', *Proceedings of the British Academy*, 7 (1915–16).

[5] Ibid. 256.

[6] See esp. ibid.; also W. K. C. Guthrie, *A History of Greek Philosophy*, 6 vols. (Cambridge 1962–81), III, 467–9; D. J. Furley, 'The Early History of the Concept of the Soul', *Bulletin of the Institute of Classical Studies*, 3 (1956).

that some things are more important than others, while those he believed to be worthy of most consideration were not the things his fellows recognized. To the extent that Socrates' philosophy centred on an attempt to turn the Athenians from their existing values it is not difficult to grasp. But understanding what he wished to put in their place is quite a different matter. One thing that is clear is that Socrates' philosophy was built on the ideal of reason. Whatever else Socrates may have meant by his exhortation 'care for your soul', it is certain that he meant two things: he wanted people to pursue certain values, and he wanted them to do so in a certain way. It would not have been enough for Socrates if a person were able to pursue the values of the soul, unless he did so as the result of a process of rational deliberation and rational choice.

For Socrates, the *psuchê* was identical to the rational faculties. The Socratic concept of *aretê* is linked up with the ideas of function and performance, and denotes the special excellence through which something accomplishes its own particular function or task. Clearly, the most important function of the *psuchê* is guiding or directing the individual's life—as a craftsman guides or directs his tools (*Alc.* I, 129*b*–31*b*; cf. *Rep.* 353*d*). For Socrates, reason is the essence of the soul; 'wisdom and truth and the perfection of one's soul' (*Ap.* 29*e*) are all of a kind. Each man is to live a rationally ordered life, to deliberate and decide and act according to the dictates of his decisions. As Socrates proclaims in the *Crito* (46*b*): 'I am not only now but always a man who follows nothing but the *logos* [reasoning, argument] which on consideration seems to me best'.[7] Socrates expresses his faith in the products of rational deliberation in the so-called 'Socratic paradox', 'virtue is knowledge'.

As far as systematic moral theory is concerned, it seems that Plato's Socrates—as, no doubt, the historical Socrates—does not succeed in working one out. According to the evidence of the dialogues, Socrates holds a number of firm convictions. Probably most important is his insistence that the individual refrain from injustice, from harming other people. Part of what Socrates undoubtedly means by 'caring for the soul' is that injustice harms the soul of the person who inflicts it (*Crito* 47*e*, 49*a*–*d*; *Rep.* 335*b*–*e*). It is also clear that Socrates believes that moral knowledge will itself be sufficient to make people good. As we see below (pp. 50–2), it is basic Socratic doctrine that all wrongdoing is due to a lack of moral knowledge, to ignorance. And so Socrates believes that if people can be induced to care for their souls through the pursuit of knowledge, they will begin to behave morally as well.

---

[7] I depart from Burnet's reading of 46*b*4 (*Plato's Euthyphro, Apology of Socrates and Crito* [Oxford, 1924], ad loc.), in favour of the generally accepted reading, given for example by J. Adam, *Platonis Crito*, 2nd edn. (Cambridge, 1891), text and ad loc.

Aside from the belief that wisdom is of the highest importance, and the injunction to practise justice and avoid injustice, Plato's Socrates does not give a systematic account of how one should care for his soul. The values Socrates holds are held tenaciously; he dies for them without hesitation. But his convictions rest as much on a kind of faith as on reasoned arguments. There is a powerful streak of religious faith running through all Socrates' beliefs, and so there is no real contradiction between his clear 'knowledge' of certain things on the one hand and his repeated avowal of ignorance on the other (on this more below).

Even if Socrates does not present a systematic account of the content of his good, he does seem to have worked out the 'practical' side of his theory. We have seen that he believes that we must order everything according to the knowledge that is virtue. He is also clear about the relationship that the individual must bear to this knowledge. Socrates demands moral autonomy; moral knowledge must be the individual's own. This is the message conveyed by the most famous of all Socratic dicta, 'the unexamined life is not worth living' (*Ap.* 38*a*). As Socrates proclaims in the *Apology*: 'I say that to talk every day about virtue and the other things about which you hear me talking and examining myself and others is the greatest good to man' (*Ap.* 38*a*).

The moral autonomy strand of Socrates' ethics appears to be its strongest. He does not seem concerned about competing claims present in his theory. Socrates says two things: (*a*) there is an objective moral truth, which the individual can discover, according to which he must live, and which will make him happy; and (*b*) the individual must be morally autonomous and live according to his own knowledge. It is probably because Socrates is never able to formulate (*a*), the knowledge that we need, that this conflict never develops into anything of which he must take notice.[8] As things stand, it seems that Socrates emphasizes (*b*) more than (*a*), and it is to this that we now turn.

We are able to abstract from Plato's early dialogues a Socratic theory of what it means to live according to reason. We can almost say that Socrates completed the form of his philosophy without completing its content. This side of Socrates is a startling combination of a belief that human knowledge 'is of little or no value' on the one hand, and an absolute faith in human knowledge on the other. There are two main ideas to be discussed here. We begin with Socrates' lack of faith in human knowledge, his 'provisionality'.[9]

---

[8] Though conflict between (*a*) and (*b*) is not unavoidable, it is possible. In the middle dialogues Plato stresses (*a*) at the expense of (*b*).

[9] Following R. Robinson, *Plato's Earlier Dialectic*, 2nd edn. (Oxford, 1953), pp. 107–9, to whose discussion I am indebted.

By provisionality I mean, basically, an attitude of extreme open-mindedness. As a result of his discovery of the limited value of human wisdom, Socrates became convinced that no human opinion can be taken at face value. All must be subject to constant scrutiny at the bar of reason. Socrates demands the complete overthrow of all intellectual authority. Moral convictions shall remain convictions only so long as they can be supported by the best available arguments.

The first requisite of this Socratic ideal is self-knowledge. From the very outset Socrates has in mind the one respect in which he was wiser than other Athenians, his awareness of his own ignorance (*Ap.* 29*b*; also 21*b*–22*d*). Socrates accepts beliefs only if he is able to defend them. He demands the rigorous examination of all convictions, while convictions based solely on authority are not worthy of consideration as such.

The principle that beliefs must be proved acceptable applies to beliefs that have been proved acceptable in the past. Perhaps the most remarkable feature of Socrates' thought is his insistence that the struggle against ignorance lasts an entire lifetime. Not only is every question an open question, but it remains open for life. As Gomperz says: 'No proposition . . . is so self-evident, so universally true, that we may not be called upon, good ground being shown, to reconsider it on first principles and test its validity anew'.[10] This aspect of provisionality is revealed in many of the dialogues, as time and again Socrates is depicted as willing to go over ground already covered to make sure his arguments are sound. We see this, for example, in the *Euthyphro*: 'Then', Socrates says, 'shall we examine this again, Euthyphro, to see if it is correct, or shall we let it go and accept our own statement, and those of others, agreeing that it is so, if anyone merely says that it is?' (9*e*). Of course it is decided to go over the matter once again.

I have mentioned that Socrates holds a number of beliefs that are grounded in something like religious conviction. Examples are his faith that virtue and happiness coincide, that no harm can come to a good man, and that committing injustice is greatly harmful to oneself (esp. *Ap.* 41*c*–*d*, 30*c*–*d*). But even these convictions must be reassessed at any time, should questions about them arise. This is seen especially in the *Crito*, which presents the clearest example of Socratic provisionality in the entire corpus.

The conversation depicted in the *Crito* professes to be a re-examination of the conclusions of past arguments. The situation given in the work is familiar. Crito has come to Socrates' cell and pleads with him to escape while there is still time. Socrates responds, characteristically, that he will act according to the

---

[10] T. Gomperz, *The Greek Thinkers*, 4 vols., L. Magnus and C. G. Berry, trans. (London, 1901–12), II, 58–9.

moral principles he believes most likely to be true, which are the ones he has always followed. Even though he has abided by these principles throughout his life, he is willing to re-examine them:

And I wish to investigate, Crito, in common with you, and see whether our former argument seems different to me under our present conditions, or the same, and whether we shall give it up or be guided by it. (46*d*; 46*b–d*)

The result of the ensuing inquiry is that it would be unjust for Socrates to flee, and so he elects to stay and bear the consequences. But the matter is not yet settled: 'Be assured that, so far as I now believe, if you argue against these words you will speak in vain. Nevertheless, if you think you can accomplish anything, speak' (54*d*). But Crito has no fresh arguments, and Socrates' previous beliefs stand.

Although Socrates holds his opinions with no great faith in their ultimate certainty, he does not hold them lightly. As remarkable as the open-mindedness he brings to bear in testing his convictions is the single-mindedness with which he acts according to those arguments that best survive examination. Even if certainty is not to be had in this life, we must act, and so our actions must be based on the arguments that seem most likely to be true. Socrates' general procedure has been seen in our look at the *Crito*, while a glimpse at the *Apology* shows how seriously he takes his convictions. As he sees his situation at his trial, Socrates must choose either to desist from his mission, which he believes would be in defiance of the god and therefore unjust, or to die. Though the general run of men fear death and wish to avoid it, Socrates believes that such fear is rooted in ignorance (*Ap.* 29*a*). Since he knows that the other alternative is bad, his decision is not difficult:

I do know that it is evil and disgraceful to do wrong and to disobey my superior, whether he be god or man. So I shall never fear or avoid those things concerning which I do not know whether they are good or bad rather than those which I know are bad. (29*b*)

As we have seen, in the *Crito*, Socrates proves to Crito that it would be unjust to flee, and so the road taken in the *Apology* is followed to its denouement.

Thus we see that Socrates holds his beliefs, even his deepest beliefs, only provisionally. But as long as a given conviction proves worthy, his commitment to it is absolute. As we see in the *Apology*, he willingly dies rather than violate his convictions, and would willingly die 'many times over' (*Ap.* 30*b–c*). Socrates presents the striking position of absolute adherence to convictions he is willing to reconsider at any time.

To sum up, then, it seems that there are a number of linked strands in Socrates' conception of the ideal for human life. According to Socrates, the individual must care for his soul, which means caring for reason and justice. Throughout the dialogues, Socrates insists that injustice damages the soul of the perpetrator. He couples this with the idea that the virtue or excellence of the soul is reason, and so the individual must think about moral questions and decide for himself the principles according to which he wishes to live. Because Socrates has little faith in human wisdom, he in effect prescribes an endless search for moral knowledge. In the final analysis, it is perhaps this search itself that constitutes caring for one's soul, the end of life for man.

3.3. THE SOCRATIC METHOD

Socrates teaches his doctrine of the soul in no ordinary way. In light of what it is to care for one's soul, this is not surprising. We have seen that the examined life is more form than content. While Socrates' message can be analysed and summarized—much as it has been in the preceding pages—and thus learned by rote, it will not be *learned* until the individual examines it and decides on its validity by the light of his own reason. Thus the only effective means of teaching is to get people to think for themselves. This doctrine is personified by Plato in his description of Socrates as a 'midwife', who, through his questions, assists in the birth of knowledge from his subjects' souls (*Tht.* 149a–51d). It is brought to its logical conclusion in the great doctrine of the middle dialogues, that all learning is recollection (*anamnêsis*).

Given this conception of teaching, we can begin to understand Socrates' mission. Socrates believes that, in order for people to pursue the values of the soul, they must not only know certain things, but they must do certain things: they must begin to think. The great discovery of Socrates' inquiry into the oracle was that people are ignorant, and so his mission is designed to overcome this.

Socrates believes that ignorance has serious consequences. Individuals acquire knowledge only through hard thinking, and one never attempts to learn something until he realizes that he does not know it. Since the Athenians believe that they possess moral knowledge—though of course they do not—this false belief prevents them from seeking to attain it. Thus they must be brought to realize the hollowness of their claims to moral wisdom, and it is this awakening function that Socrates assumes.

There can be no better description of Socrates' mission than that of the *Apology* (30e–31a), where he describes himself as a 'gadfly'. He says that he attaches himself to the city as a gadfly to a horse. The horse, 'though large and well bred, is sluggish on account of his size and needs to be aroused by stinging'. He continues: 'I think the god fastened me upon the city in some such capacity, and I go about arousing, and urging and reproaching each one of you, constantly alighting upon you everywhere the whole day long'.

To counteract the ignorance of his subjects, Socrates developed his characteristic method of moral reform, the *elenchos*. The dictionary definition of *elenchos* is 'argument of disproof' or 'refutation'. As Socrates practises it, the *elenchos* generally involves two steps. In the first, Socrates elicits his interlocutor's opinion concerning some moral question, about which he believes himself to possess knowledge. In the second stage, Socrates attempts to disprove this answer. Generally, he asks his subject a series of additional questions and utilizes the responses in order to construct a logical proof, the conclusion of which contradicts the original answer. In Socrates' hands, this logical procedure is practised as a method of moral reform.

In discussing the *elenchos* as a method of moral reform, we must move beyond the relatively uncomplicated theme of how it is supposed to work and attempt to understand why it is supposed to work. We must examine the presuppositions and assumptions on which its use rests, for these are the presuppositions basic to Socrates' mission as a whole. In his role as gadfly to the Athenian people, Socrates uses the *elenchos* in order to produce shock and shame in his subjects, to rouse them from the lethargy of their ignorance. And so the *elenchos* must work in such a way that it can produce these reactions. Thus, in any given encounter, Socrates must do more than merely win an argument and so refute a belief. The belief he refutes must be one that is so important to his subject that having it refuted results in shock and consternation—the sting of the 'torpedo-fish' Meno is made to feel (*Meno* 80a–b). Socrates' belief that the *elenchos* is capable of producing these powerful reactions is based on important psychological assumptions, which will be discussed in detail (esp. in Chapter 4, sec. 1).

As can be gathered from Socrates' doctrine of provisionality and his demand that individuals be morally autonomous and act according to their own beliefs, he believes that people's actions bear an intimate relationship to their general moral principles. These principles are central to their lives; we might almost say that, for Socrates, a life is the application of a set of moral principles. In Socrates' hands, the elenctic examination of a person's moral principles is an examination of his life as well. This is described by Nicias in the *Laches*:

[W]hoever comes into close contact with Socrates and has any talk with him face to face, is bound to be drawn round and round by him in the course of the argument—though it may have started at first on a quite different theme—and cannot stop until he is led into giving an account of himself, of the manner in which he now spends his days, and of the kind of life he has lived hitherto, and when once he has been led into that, Socrates will never let him go until he has thoroughly and properly put all his ways to the test. (187e–88a)

Socrates attempts to refute people's moral principles in order to turn them around, to awaken them to the importance of their souls. The basic idea behind his use of the *elenchos* is that to refute a person's moral principles is to refute his life as well. It is this that causes the necessary shock and shame, and these will be directed back at the subject himself, as he comes to realize that he has spent his life pursuing unworthy ends. Socrates places heavy emphasis on the psychological effects of often complex logical considerations. And so, as Socrates has it, once the subject's basic principles have been found to be inconsistent, his greatest desires will be to redress this situation and to discover true principles. He will dedicate his life to this search and so will begin to care for his soul.

Many dialogues depict the elenctic examination of various subjects. Socrates frequently focuses discussion on the meaning of common moral terms, for example, courage in the *Laches*, temperance in the *Charmides*, piety in the *Euthyphro*, justice in *Republic* I. In all these works the interlocutors are unable to define terms they commonly use, terms, according to Socrates, a clear understanding of which is central to a properly conducted life. According to Socrates' method, the discovery of their ignorance should have transformative moral effects and send them off in search of true values. But as we see below, the *elenchos* only infrequently brings about this result.

Putting aside all other concerns for the moment, let us suppose that the interlocutor can be won over by the *elenchos*. As practised by Socrates, the *elenchos* is meant to produce converts to philosophy, which for Socrates is what the word literally implies: *philos sophia*, love of wisdom. As Friedlander notes, Plato often likens the learning experience to a journey; it is the ideal of Plato's Socrates to induce others to travel with him.[11] Because the truth cannot be communicated directly, Socrates uses his constant discussions to help others discover it for themselves. Presumably he will help them learn those principles that best survive his constant scrutiny. As Socrates says in the *Republic*, 'the measure of listening to such discussions for reasonable men is the whole of life' (450b).

[11] P. Friedlander, *Plato*, 3 vols., H. Meyerhoff, trans. (Princeton, NJ, 1958–69), I, 65–7.

4

Socratic Politics

I said in the last chapter that we should pay special attention to the pre-suppositions about human nature that governed Socrates' mission. In this chapter, we examine these and draw out their political implications. We pay special attention to Socrates' intellectualism, a view widely associated with the historical Socrates and espoused in Plato's early dialogues.

According to the *Magna Moralia*, the historical Socrates' conception of human nature was deficient in the following way:

According ... to Socrates, all the virtues arise in the reasoning part of the soul, from which it follows that, in making the various virtues branches of knowledge, he ignores the irrational parts of the soul, and thus ignores passion and the moral character. (1182*a*18–23)

What the *Magna Moralia* says of the historical Socrates is also true of Plato's Socrates. The Socrates of Plato's early dialogues is a remarkably unperceptive judge of human nature. One particular trap he appears to have fallen into is this. According to Ernst Kapp, 'for many centuries, beginning with Aristotle ... logicians were inclined to substitute logic where psychology was required'.[1] I believe we encounter something similar in the thought of Socrates. As has been noted, he tends to view human conduct as strongly influenced by abstract principles. We have seen that he always follows the *logos* that seems to him best. By some unfortunate feat of empathy, he manages to see other people behaving in the same way. Since adherence to abstract principles does play a role in human behaviour, to a certain extent there is nothing wrong with Socrates' view. But behaviour is influenced by additional factors, and to the extent that Socrates concentrates on abstract principles, he tends to ignore these. We see below that Plato came to see Socrates in this light, as the introduction of the tripartite soul represents the decisive rejection of the Socratic conception of human nature. In Section 4.1 of this chapter we examine the view of human nature showing through Socratic ethics, especially the notorious 'Socratic paradoxes'. The political implications are discussed in sections 2 and 3 below.

[1] E. Kapp, *The Greek Foundations of Traditional Logic* (New York, 1942), p. 16.

4.1. THE SOCRATIC PARADOXES

The Socratic paradoxes can best be understood as the epigrammatic expression of a group of interrelated ethical doctrines, undoubtedly held by the historical Socrates, which are a major concern of Plato's early dialogues. The tangled mass of doctrine represented by the paradoxes is somewhat as follows. All men desire the good, and so all action is undertaken in pursuit of the good. It is through knowledge that we attain our ends, and through lack of knowledge that we fail to attain them. Since justice is essential to happiness, it is only through ignorance of this that we commit injustice. Because virtue is knowledge, it is like other crafts or technical skills. But while the craftsman can reject the end for which his craft is designed, the good man cannot abuse his skill. Though a doctor would make the best poisoner or an accountant the best embezzler, the good man cannot do wrong.

In unravelling this clump of doctrine we see that the paradoxes rest on a conception of human nature in which the irrational components of the soul are not given their due. Socrates is strongly committed to psychological egoism, the view that the behaviour of individuals is motivated by a desire for their own good. This view is expounded repeatedly in the Socratic dialogues, perhaps most forcefully in the *Protagoras*: 'It is not in human nature ... to wish to go after what one thinks to be evil in preference to the good' (358c). According to Socrates, the action of individuals is motivated by calculations of the good—their own good. Thus, if individuals knew where their good actually lay, they would pursue it.

In order for individuals to attain happiness, they must know how it is attained. Socrates believes that a great deal of unhappiness is caused by ignorance of one fundamental truth that happiness and moral goodness coincide. Socrates believes that injustice is harmful to the perpetrator, that it taints his soul, and without a healthy soul, life is not worth living (esp. *Crito* 47c–48a). As we have seen above, Socrates' belief that justice and happiness coincide was deeply held. He died for it without hesitation, though it probably rested more on faith than on reason. This view is given strong statement in the *Apology*:

Bear in mind this one point, which is true, that no evil can come to a good man, either in life or after death, and his fortunes are not neglected by the gods. (41c–d)

As Gerasimos Santas has argued,[2] the Socratic paradoxes flow from a combination of Socrates' belief that all men desire their own good and seek to attain it in their actions, and belief that one's highest good, happiness, is

---

[2] Santas, 'The Socratic Paradoxes', and 'Plato's *Protagoras* and Explanations of Weakness', both rpt. in Santas, *Socrates: Philosophy in Plato's Early Dialogues* (London, 1979).

realized through justice. According to Socrates, unjust individuals inevitably create unhappiness for themselves and others. Of course, if they realized the consequences of their conduct, they would change their ways, and so their wrongdoing is caused by ignorance. Socrates argues that virtue is knowledge, that is, knowledge of what virtue is and that it is necessary for happiness. He holds that knowledge of justice makes people just.

Throughout the dialogues a number of arguments are presented in support of Socrates' moral position. A striking proof that virtue, or justice—in many contexts the words are interchangeable—is knowledge is presented in the *Gorgias*. Socrates employs a simple induction, consisting of three examples. The man who has learnt building is a builder; he who has learnt music is a musician; and he who has learnt medicine is a medical man. Socrates generalizes from these examples: 'He who has learnt a certain art has the qualification acquired by his particular knowledge'. According to this principle, then, 'he who has learnt justice is just' (460*b*). There is good evidence that this was a chain of reasoning employed by the historical Socrates, as similar arguments are attributed to Socrates in both Xenophon's *Memorabilia* (IV, ii, 20) and Aristotle's *Eudemian Ethics* (1216*b*6–9).

A striking feature of this proof as well as many arguments employed in the early dialogues is its use of the analogy between virtue and craft knowledge (*technê*), or more specifically, the kind of knowledge required by craftsmen to achieve their ends. In reading the early dialogues one is repeatedly struck by Socrates' use of this analogy. As Alcibiades says in the *Symposium*, Socrates is always talking about 'smiths, cobblers and tanners' (221*e*).

To a certain extent Socrates' attraction to the craftsmen is readily explained. As we saw above, when Socrates undertook to confirm the oracle by examining his fellow citizens, he discovered that the craftsmen alone possessed knowledge. In matters concerning their crafts, such people could respond to questions and relate their activity to a clearly held end or purpose. Socrates appropriated such technical knowledge as a paradigm for what it is to know some subject matter, especially morals. The individual with moral knowledge must demonstrate the same fluency with his field; he too must be able to connect his actions to a clearly perceived end or purpose.

Socrates was, however, aware of differences between the crafts and moral knowledge. Especially important is the fact that crafts are neutral, capable of being used for bad ends as well as good, which is not true of moral knowledge. This is the implied message of the *Hippias Minor* and a series of arguments used by Socrates against Polemarchus in *Republic* I (333*e*–34*b*). According to these arguments, the skilful doctor is best at committing murder undetected as well as saving patient's lives; the skilful accountant would be best at embezzling as well as balancing books, etcetera. It would follow by analogy that the just man would be best at injustice, but Socrates clearly indicates that this conclusion is unsatisfactory. He believes that moral knowledge is not neutral: he who knows justice is invariably just. This view shows through the argument from the *Gorgias* quoted above and others of Socrates' arguments as well.

In the final analysis, Socrates' belief in the non-neutrality of moral knowledge, along with other major aspects of the paradoxes, rests on his psychological assumptions. In order to examine these, we begin by looking briefly at the evidence of Aristotle. In the case of metaphysical views, Aristotle's testimony is commonly used to distinguish Plato's own doctrines from those he inherited from Socrates (above, p. 23). His evidence can be used similarly in regard to psychological views. The psychological position Aristotle attributes to Socrates coincides with what is found in the early dialogues and conflicts sharply with the middle works. Thus, Aristotle's evidence not only confirms the accuracy of our reading of the moral psychology of Plato's Socrates, but it also indicates the probability that in this regard at least, in depicting Socrates, Plato, and Aristotle were both largely faithful to the historical Socrates.

To put matters simply, the gist of Aristotle's evidence is that Socrates had an extremely one-sided, intellectualistic conception of human nature. We have seen this point of view expressed in the (probably pseudo-Aristotelian) *Magna Moralia*. Throughout the *Nicomachean* and *Eudemian Ethics*, Aristotle repeatedly notes Socrates' belief that virtue is knowledge, especially that courage is knowledge.[3] Aristotle's evidence is especially significant because of striking parallels with Plato's depiction of Socrates.

The most important part of Aristotle's testimony is his account of Socrates' position concerning moral weakness or *akrasia*. Aristotle discusses Socrates' view in Book VII of the *Nicomachean Ethics*, as a preliminary to his own discussion of moral weakness. This passage demands close scrutiny because it contains an unmistakable allusion to Plato's *Protagoras* (*EN* 1145b23–24; *Prt.* 352b8–c2). We see that Socrates' position there is extremely similar. The core of Aristotle's discussion is as follows:

Socrates was entirely opposed to the view in question [that a man may judge rightly but behave incontinently], holding that there is no such thing as *akrasia* [moral weakness]; no one, he said, when he judges, acts against what he judges best—people act so only by reason of ignorance. (*EN* 1145b25–27)

These lines are compressed. In order to understand what Aristotle is saying, we must give a specific content to the words, 'when he judges'; that is, we must say what a man judges that prevents him from doing wrong. In the continuation of

[3] See esp. *EN* 1116b4–5; *EE* 1229a14–16, 1230a7–10; *MM* 1190b27–29. Aristotle's evidence is collected and translated into French, with a judicious commentary, in T. Deman, *Le témoignage d'Aristote sur Socrate* (Paris, 1942).

the passage, we see that Socrates' view is that 'no one acts contrary, to what has seemed to him the better course' (1145*b*33). And so the full sense of the crucial lines is: 'No one, he said, when he judges (that what he does goes against what is best) does what goes against what is best—people act so only by reason of ignorance'. According to Aristotle, then, Socrates' theory is that people never do *x* while believing it is bad for them; they do *x* only if they are ignorant of the fact that it is bad for them.[4]

Thus, Aristotle believes that Socrates' moral view is extreme in its intellectualism. Aristotle goes on to say that Socrates' view contradicts the 'observed facts' of human experience (1145*b*27–28). In addition, because Socrates did not present an adequate account of human motivation, Aristotle believes that he could not adequately respond to the all important question of how people can be made virtuous. Commenting on Socrates' inquiry into the nature of the different virtues, Aristotle writes in the *Eudemian Ethics*:

Socrates... thought that the End is to get to know virtue, and he pursued an inquiry into the nature of justice and courage and each of the divisions of virtue. This was a reasonable procedure, since he thought that all the virtues are forms of knowledge, so that knowing justice and being just must go together, for as soon as we have learnt geometry and architecture, we are architects and geometricians; owing to which he used to inquire what virtue is, but not how and from what sources it is produced. (1216*b*2–10)

Thus, according to Aristotle, because Socrates relied on a conception of virtue that laid exclusive emphasis on its intellectual side, he did indeed, as the *Magna Moralia* states, ignore passion and the moral character. He never considered the role these sides of man's nature play in virtuous conduct and so never addressed himself to the question of how they could be made conformable with virtue.[5]

The position of Plato's Socrates is similar. As we have seen, in Plato's early dialogues Socrates holds that man is strongly motivated by egoistic considerations. This leads him, too, to deny the existence of moral weakness. Though a point by point comparison between Plato's Socrates and Aristotle's could be presented, this is not necessary here. Additional evidence concerning the

---

[4] This construal of the passage is supported by R. A. Gauthier and J. Y. Jolif, eds., Aristotle, *L'Ethique à Nicomaque*, 2nd edn., 3 vols. (Louvain, Belgium, 1970), ad loc.

[5] The evidence of Xenophon gives mixed support to Aristotle's account of Socratic ethics. At *Mem.* III, ix, 4–5, Xenophon's Socrates denies the existence of *akrasia* on similar grounds. But Socrates directly contradicts this view in other passages, e.g. IV, v, 6. The emphasis placed on self-mastery (*enkrateia*) by Xenophon's Socrates (at e.g. I, iv, 4–5 but throughout the entire *Memorabilia*) is sharply at odds with the Socrates of Aristotle and Plato's early dialogues. It should be noted that other evidence of Xenophon conflicts with Plato's account; see esp. *Mem.* II, vi, 35, where Socrates says that virtue consists of helping friends and harming enemies; cf. *Rep.* 335*b–d*.

intellectualism of the early dialogues is presented in the next section, while a certain amount has been seen above, including at least one direct correspondence between the Socrates of Plato and Aristotle (and Xenophon; above, p. 48). For our present purposes it is enough to examine one specific argument, the long and elaborate final argument of the *Protagoras*.[6] This argument is especially useful for two reasons. First, it contains the fullest single statement of Socrates' moral psychology found in the early dialogues. In addition, as we have noted, it is taken seriously by Aristotle, explicitly referred to in Book VII of the *Nicomachean Ethics*. The subject of the argument in the *Protagoras* too is moral weakness, and the view expressed here corresponds to that attributed to Socrates by Aristotle.

The final argument of the *Protagoras* is lengthy and complex. For reasons of space it cannot be analysed here in depth, though certain of its basic features must be looked at. Socrates' intention in the argument is to prove the dominance of knowledge in human behaviour, to demonstrate that 'knowledge is something noble and able to govern man' and that 'whoever learns what is good and what is bad will never be swayed by anything to act otherwise than as knowledge bids' (*Prt.* 352c). Socrates argues against the common view that there are cases of moral weakness, cases in which a person with knowledge 'is not governed by it, but by something else', that in fact knowledge is often dragged about like a slave by such things as passion, pleasure, pain, love, and fear (*Prt.* 352b–c). Socrates attempts to prove the common view wrong. He argues that cases in which a person appears to be overpowered by these opponents of reason and to do wrong knowingly are actually cases of intellectual error, and intellectual error of a rarified type, such as that made by a craftsman in his attempt to measure some object of his skill.

It is clear that Socrates' proof operates through a gradual process of transforming an ostensible situation of moral weakness, in which the subject is overcome by pleasure, into one in which the subject *chooses* what he perceives to be the greater of two pleasures. The series of moves that Socrates makes in order to carry out this proof allows a glimpse at his most basic psychological assumptions. His key assumption is that all human actions are intentional actions, which are based on choices. Even actions committed under the influence of intense desire, passion, pleasure, or pain are based on choices—and, again, the choices he has in mind are paradigmatically rational calculations.[7]

---

[6] The discussion here is supported by G. Klosko, 'On the Analysis of *Protagoras* 351B–360E', *Phoenix*, 34 (1980), which contains numerous additional references.

[7] For additional substantiation of these important points, see ibid. 315 ff.; compare the view of Xenophon's Socrates, who reduces madness (*mania*) to ignorance: 'What is the difference between ignorance and madness?' he asks (*Mem.* I, ii, 50).

On the basis of this psychological view, Socrates declares the ordinary account of being overcome by pleasure to be untenable. What really happens is that the subject is deceived by the nearness of a lesser pleasure and incorrectly takes it to be larger than another though more distant pleasure, which is actually larger. There can be no other reason why the subject would choose the lesser good. Thus, Socrates roots his proof in the *Protagoras* unshakably in the laws of human nature, which are stressed repeatedly (esp. 356*b–c*, 358*b–d*). It is in this context that he presents the strong commitment to psychological egoism quoted above (p. 47). Accordingly, Socrates argues that all that is needed to put an end to all cases of being overcome by pleasure is an art of measurement capable of eliminating the distortion caused by the nearness and remoteness of pleasures (esp. 357*a–e*). In other words, knowledge of this art (or craft) is enough to make people virtuous, granted Socrates' other basic assumption that the virtuous course is always the better course.

The upshot of Socrates' denial of the existence of moral weakness is that he is unable adequately to deal with the phenomenon of psychological conflict. He believes that all men desire the good and pursue it in their actions. In effect, he sees the soul as dominated by a single good-seeking desire, while the problem of action is concerned solely with directing it. This is indeed, as Kapp says (p. 46), to substitute logic for psychology. Socrates interprets the moral agent who is torn between alternatives as rationally choosing which to pursue. This is only partly correct, as the emotions and passions are overlooked. Socrates transforms the situation in which the agent is 'driven and dazed by his pleasures' (*Prt.* 355*a–b*) into a situation in which he is deciding which course of action to take so as to maximize his pleasures. The playwright Euripides is widely believed to be responding to Socrates' view, in the *Medea*.[8] The title character, spurned by her husband, resolves to murder her children, saying: 'I understand the horror of what I am going to do; but anger, the spring of all life's horror, masters my resolve' (1078–80). The shortcomings of Socrates' view are apparent in his inability to account for this kind of behaviour. They are if anything even more evident in his contention that the art of measuring pleasures will put an end to cases of moral weakness. The aspects of moral training that he overlooks will be discussed at length in subsequent chapters.

Throughout the other early dialogues, Socrates demonstrates similar psychological views. Because many of his arguments are directed at specific interlocutors and are brought to a close once the interlocutors have been refuted, it is difficult to work out a detailed interpretation of his moral position. But

---

[8] See E. R. Dodds, *The Greeks and the Irrational* (Berkeley, CA, 1951), pp. 186–7; J. Walsh, *Aristotle's Conception of Moral Weakness* (New York, 1964), p. 20; G. Vlastos, 'Introduction' to *Plato: Protagoras*, M. Ostwald, trans. (Indianapolis, IN, 1956), pp. xliii–xlv.

in works such as the *Laches* and *Charmides* the thrust of his arguments is strongly intellectualistic. Almost no attention is paid to the need to control desire, and the roles that conditioning and habituation play in moral life. To the extent that a coherent theory can be pieced together, it seems to centre on the identification of virtue and knowledge. The all-important knowledge is never explicitly identified in the early dialogues, but Socrates appears to believe that its subject matter is good and evil, and that possession of it will make an individual unfailingly good.

More fully, Socrates seems to see all the virtues as different aspects or parts of the knowledge of good and evil. This view, generally referred to as the 'unity of the virtues', is argued for, though in a somewhat elliptical fashion, in the *Protagoras*, and appears to be the hidden message of the *Laches*.[9] It follows from the unity of the virtues that, as Socrates hints in the *Laches* and *Protagoras*, courage is one aspect of the knowledge of good and evil— knowledge of what is and what is not to be feared (*Lach.* 194*d*–95*a*; *Prt.* 357*b*–60*e*). Similarly, temperance is connected up with the knowledge of good and evil in the *Charmides* (174*a* ff.). For our purposes the crucial point is the psychological status Socrates assigns to knowledge, his unquestioning belief that it prevails over other psychic forces. Here too Socrates appears to have worked out the form of his philosophy without completing the content. Thus, for Socrates virtue is knowledge; he who knows what is right will do it. Equally important, Socrates believes that all wrongdoing is caused by lack of this moral knowledge, or ignorance.

4.2. SOCRATIC POLITICS

Socratic political ideas must be understood in the light of psychological views discussed in the last section. Because Socrates believes that man is rational and misled only by intellectual errors, he is able to leap to the conclusion that people can be reformed through the use of logical persuasion, rational arguments alone. Those factors in human nature which, if adequately recognized, would prevent him from holding this view are overlooked. In this sense, what is not said in the early dialogues is almost as important as what is. In addition, Socrates is convinced that basic rationality is common to all his fellow citizens; it is not the exclusive preserve of the few.

[9] On the unity of the virtues, see esp. T. Penner, 'The Unity of Virtue', *Philosophical Review*, 82 (1973); G. Vlastos, 'The Unity of the Virtues in the *Protagoras*', in *Platonic Studies* (Princeton, NJ, 1973); D. Devereux, 'The Unity of the Virtues in Plato's *Protagoras* and *Laches*', *Philosophical Review*, 101 (1992); 'Socrates' Kantian Conception of Virtue', *Journal of the History of Philosophy*, 33 (1995).

The evidence is strong that Socrates believes all individuals (all Greeks?) to be basically equal. As his very demand that individuals become morally autonomous indicates, Socrates believes that every individual has the capacity to develop his rational faculties and to be governed by them. The soul is identical to the rational faculties, and so every soul can be developed to achieve rationality. Perhaps it is because Socrates has so little regard for human reason that he believes every soul is capable of attaining the heights accessible to others. But however we account for this, there can be no doubt that he addresses his message to everyone: 'I shall never give up philosophy or stop exhorting you and pointing out the truth to any one of you whom I may meet' (*Ap.* 29*d*); 'This I shall do to whomever I meet, young and old, foreigner and citizen' (*Ap.* 30*a*); 'I go about arousing and urging and reproaching each one of you' (*Ap.* 30*e*–31*a*); 'For I tried to persuade each of you' (*Ap.* 36*c*, and see 33*a*–*b*). The necessary presupposition of Socrates' attempt to waken all men is the assumption that all have the potential to be wakened.

Socrates' political practice amounts to a new kind of politics. Every individual has a rational soul, and so every individual can be awakened to become morally autonomous and to rule himself. Socrates devotes his life to a sustained attempt to waken his fellow citizens to his conception of the virtues of the soul, to a life devoted to reason and moral autonomy. In keeping with the traditional Greek view that a chief responsibility of the *polis* is to see to the moral betterment of its citizens, Socrates' goal must be judged 'political'. But Socrates' pursuit of this end is distinctive in that he sought to attain it without recourse to political means. We saw in the last chapter that Socrates remained ineluctably opposed to the political system of his city, and pursued his mission in a private capacity. Accordingly, he sought to bring about the moral reform of his fellows through the use of arguments alone. As he says in the *Apology*, his method is moral persuasion; he takes his fellow citizens aside, 'individually like a father or an elder brother' (*Ap.* 31*b*), urging each to care for virtue.

Though the belief that rational argument alone is a suitable instrument of political reform is a peculiar one, it seems that Socrates' psychological views allowed him to hold it, and he devoted his life to putting it into practice. In the *Crito*, Socrates acknowledged, in regard to his belief in the ultimate evil of injustice, 'I know that there are few who believe or ever will believe this' (49*d*). But in the *Gorgias*, in the course of the most crushing defeat of his method that Plato depicts (see below, pp. 57–8), Socrates says to Callicles 'if we come to examine these same questions more than once and better, you will believe' (513*c*–*d*).[10] As Burnet says, the fact that Aristophanes utilizes Socrates as the arch-Sophist in the *Clouds* is a strong indication that, at the

---

10 The importance of this passage was pointed out to me by Daniel Devereux.

time the *Clouds* was first produced, in 423, (the historical) Socrates was already a familiar figure in Athens, and hence that Socrates' mission most probably started some years before.[11] This is taken for granted in Plato's *Apology*, where Socrates alludes to the *Clouds* (*Ap.* 19c) and says that he has been active on his mission for a long time. And so for some thirty years Socrates pursued his mission of reforming the Athenians through argument. This is the mission through which Plato most probably met Socrates. Plato depicts this mission in many dialogues and presents its philosophical groundwork in the *Apology*. The inescapable reason for attributing to Socrates the theory of moral reform discussed in this chapter is the fact that he spent several decades of his life attempting it.

Various objections could be raised against this account of Socrates' political activity. For instance, it could be argued that Socrates would have had no reason to rely solely on argument; that is, it could be argued that, though Socrates did not use coercive means, he would have had no reason not to approve of their use. But, aside from the fact that there is no evidence that the Socrates of the early dialogues—or the historical Socrates for that matter—ever considered the use of coercion to achieve moral reform, a good case could be made that various doctrines he holds strongly suggest that he is in principle opposed to such means. First, in the *Crito* (51b–c) Socrates argues that it is never right to resist the commands of one's state through violence and that one is limited to attempting to show the state what is really right through persuasion. This creates at least a presumption that, in attempting to show the individual citizens of the state what is really right, one is also limited to persuasive means. Second, the Socratic conception of what it is to care for one's soul and the weight Socrates places on moral autonomy, that each person must examine his own life (esp. *Ap.* 38a), does not rest well with advocating coercive means to achieve this end. In light of the paucity of our information concerning exactly what Socrates means by 'caring for the soul', it is not possible to demonstrate that this is logically incompatible with all coercive means. But because of the lack of evidence to the contrary, this again creates a presumption that Socrates would have opposed the use of coercion to attain his ends.

In order to lend additional support to our interpretation, let us look briefly at our other evidence concerning Socrates. We have seen above (p. 50) that Aristotle criticizes Socrates for not paying sufficient attention to the question where virtue comes from. Because Socrates believes that virtue is knowledge, according to Aristotle he naturally assumes that the question of making people virtuous is a question of inculcating knowledge. In the next section, we see

---

[11] J. Burnet, 'The Socratic Doctrine of the Soul', *Proceedings of the British Academy*, 7 (1915–16), 238–40.

that Aristotle presents a direct criticism of the view we have attributed to Socrates in Book X of the *Nicomachean Ethics*—though without mentioning Socrates by name. Thus, it appears that the evidence of Aristotle concerning the historical Socrates offers some support for the position we have attributed to Plato's Socrates.

Support for this position is also found in Xenophon. Though Xenophon's treatment of Socrates' political views is anything but systematic, his report of Socrates' forecast of what would happen should the definition of justice be found speaks for itself: 'Juries will cease to split their vote; citizens will stop wrangling, going to court, and raising revolts in the cause of justice. States will cease to differ about what is just, and cease to make war' (*Mem.* IV, iv, 8).[12] Thus, Xenophon confirms the view that (the historical) Socrates believed that political problems could be solved by knowledge.

4.3. THE LIMITS OF PERSUASION

Of course readers of the *Republic* and *Laws* recognize the distance that separates the political views of the early dialogues and those woven into the ideal states presented in these two works.[13] In Part II we examine in detail the new moral psychology presented in Plato's middle dialogues, which brought such changes about. We see that, for Plato in the middle dialogues, virtue entails a proper order or harmony among the parts of the soul in addition to a commitment to correct moral principles. As a necessary consequence of this shift, Plato must abandon Socrates' position concerning the means through which people can be made virtuous. From the rejection of Socrates' position grows Platonic political theory.

It is important to note that Plato not only comes to reject Socrates' political position, but his concern with Socrates' shortcomings is a significant theme in a number of works. Our account of this aspect of the dialogues must be kept brief, but it should be realized that the fact that Plato is concerned with criticizing and rejecting the position on moral reform discussed in the last section lends strong additional support to both the view we have presented and the degree of Plato's interest in fundamental moral reform.

Though Plato's criticism of the Socratic view of moral reform is not often recognized, it is an important theme in many dialogues, including the *Republic*. The reason that this aspect of the dialogues has gone unrecognized,

---

[12] Cf. *Euthyphro* 7b–d.

[13] A great virtue of J. Gould, *The Development of Plato's Ethics* (1955; rpt. New York, 1972) is that, in juxtaposing the ethical views of the early dialogues and the *Laws*, he demonstrates the enormous distance between them.

as it seems to me, is because of the way Plato chooses to present it. Instead of discussing this matter directly, Plato *illustrates* it in various works by manipulating their dramatic elements. The situations depicted in many dialogues centre on Socrates' mission of moral reform. By examining how Plato depicts Socrates in the pursuit of his mission, we gain insight into Plato's opinion of that mission and the extent to which he believed it could succeed. The point to note is that Socrates is repeatedly depicted as failing in his attempts to persuade various individuals to care for virtue. In a number of works he is unable to reach his interlocutors for a variety of reasons. Most significantly, in several works the interlocutors are simply unwilling to commit themselves to serious discussion of their views.[14] In the *Philebus*, for example, the title character refuses to participate and stands by mute while Socrates engages in discussion with Protarchus, to whom Philebus has bequeathed his role in the discussion. Similarly, though Alcibiades is won over by Socrates' arguments in the *Alcibiades* I, in the *Symposium*, which depicts his relationship with Socrates some eighteen years later, he has reverted to his original views, while he refuses to engage in further discussion of them with Socrates (esp. *Symp.* 216a–c).[15]

This theme is encountered most sharply in the *Gorgias*. The main dramatic action of this important political work revolves around Socrates' failure to persuade Callicles of the importance of virtue. The central theme of the dramatic action of the *Gorgias* is that the experience of having his views refuted by Socrates does little to shake Callicles' commitment to them. Each time Socrates presents an argument against his position, Callicles brushes its conclusion aside, until he eventually withdraws from the discussion. For much of the dialogue, Socrates is forced to go on alone, answering his own questions. In the person of Callicles, then—and in similar interlocutors depicted in other dialogues—Plato reveals his awareness of the problems of attempting to use rational persuasion alone as a means to induce people to be virtuous.[16]

Besides the tremendous attention Plato lavishes on Socrates' failure at moral persuasion in the *Gorgias*, this work is important because it begins

---

[14] This theme is explored at greater length in Klosko, 'Rational Persuasion in Plato's Political Theory', *History of Political Thought*, 7 (1986); and Klosko, *The Politics of Philosophy: The Origin and Development of Plato's Political Theory* (unpublished Ph.D. dissertation, Columbia University, 1977).

[15] The *Alcibiades* I is situated around the year 433, when Socrates was about 37 and Alcibiades about 15 years of age (P. Friedlander, *Plato*, 3 vols. H. Meyerhoff, trans. [Princeton, NJ, 1958–69], II, 232). The banquet in honour of Agathon's victory—and so the *Symposium*—took place in 416 or 415 (W. K. C. Guthrie, *A History of Greek Philosophy*, 6 vols. [Cambridge, 1962–81]), IV, 365–6), when Socrates was around 55 and Alcibiades around 33 years of age.

[16] This aspect of the *Gorgias* is discussed at length in Klosko, 'The Insufficiency of Reason in Plato's *Gorgias*', *Western Political Quarterly*, 36 (1983).

to signal an explanation for Socrates' difficulties. At one point Socrates tells Callicles why he is so hard to win over: 'Because the love of *Demos* [the people, collectively], Callicles, is there in your soul to resist me' (513*c*). Callicles is a lover of power and glory, and against the orientation of Callicles' entire personality, Socrates' arguments are powerless.

Socrates' failures in the *Gorgias* and these other works have important implications for Plato's political theory. There is strong evidence that, by the time he wrote the *Gorgias*, Plato was aware of the complexity of the *psuchê*, that the psychological views of the *Gorgias* are closer to those of the middle dialogues than to Socratic intellectualism.[17] Granted these new psychological views, Plato must reject the idea that arguments alone can change characters. The reasons for this will be seen throughout the following chapters. Put very briefly, as Plato sees things, the rational faculties of most people are held hostage by their desires, and so there is a definite limit to what arguments can do to help them.

An explicit rejection of moral persuasion as a means of reform is found at the end of Aristotle's *Nicomachean Ethics*, in the transition to the *Politics*.[18] In this context, Aristotle takes up the question of the means through which people can be made virtuous and begins by considering the views of previous thinkers. The first view discussed is the one we have attributed to Socrates that people can be made virtuous through moral persuasion. Aristotle rejects this, because he believes it conflicts with obvious facts:

> Now if arguments were in themselves enough to make men good, they would justly, as Theognis says, have won very great rewards, and such rewards would have been provided; but as things are, while they seem to have power to encourage and stimulate the generous-minded among our youth, and to make a character which is gently born and a true lover of what is noble ready to be possessed by virtue, they are not able to encourage the many to nobility and goodness. (*EN* 1179*b*4–10)

Aristotle believes that the many's lives are governed by passion and the pursuit of pleasure, and accordingly that they are not suited to moral persuasion: 'What arguments would remould such people? It is hard, if not impossible, to remove by argument the traits that have long since been incorporated in the character' (1179*b*16–8). According to Aristotle, people are not made good through arguments or teaching alone, but through a combination of arguments and habituation. Reason works only on those who have been made susceptible through proper upbringing. On those who have not been raised

---

[17] For evidence of Plato's more mature psychology in the *Gorgias*, see T. Irwin, ed. and trans., *Plato: Gorgias* (Oxford, 1979), notes on 491*d*4, 493*a*, 499*e*–500*a*, 505*b*–*c*, 507*a*–*b*.

[18] Whether Socrates is the direct target of Aristotle's remarks is disputed by scholars. For reasons to believe that he is see N. Gulley, *The Philosophy of Socrates* (London, 1968), pp. 135–8.

properly, reason is not effective, and such people must be reformed through other means (1179*b*23 ff.)

Aristotle's own position is that good habits and good character take hold best when they are inculcated from an early age. This, practically speaking, requires that the young be brought up according to good laws in a properly governed *polis* (1179*b*31 ff.). Accordingly, Aristotle argues that the inculcation of virtue is a job best left to the *polis* (1180*a*5 ff.). In a nutshell, if people are to be receptive to moral reasoning, they must be made receptive. This requires habituation, which requires compulsion, which requires laws, and hence the *polis*. If such matters are neglected by the polis, it is up to the individual to do whatever he can (1180*a*24–31), but, given the foregoing, the individual will be most effective if he makes himself skilled in legislation (see 1180*a*32–34). Arguments alone have been shown not to work, and so other means must be utilized.

The evidence strongly indicates that, by the time he wrote the middle dialogues, Plato's own position on the possibilities of moral persuasion had come to be similar to Aristotle's. I believe that it is his realization of the limitations of persuasion that led Plato to manipulate the dramatic action of works such as the *Gorgias* in the fashion I have noted. This same realization bears fruit in the new political theory presented in the *Republic*. The political theory of the *Republic* grows directly out of the rejection of the view of Socrates, and this is an important theme in the work.

Plato's concern with moral persuasion is evident at the very opening of the *Republic*. We come across the following exchange on the first page. As Socrates and Glaucon are heading back to Athens from the Piraeus, they are accosted by Polemarchus and some friends. Polemarchus initiates the discussion:

Socrates, Polemarchus said, it looks to me as though the two of you are setting off back to town.

That's right, I replied. [Socrates is narrating.]

Well, he said, do you see how many of us there are?

Of course.

You'd better choose, then, he said, between overpowering us and staying here.

Well, there is one further possibility, I pointed out. We might convince you to let us leave.

Can you convince people who don't listen? he asked

Impossible, Glaucon replied.

Then I think you should know that we won't be listening to you. (*Rep.* 327*c*)

Socrates agrees to stay, and the entire company moves to the house of Polemarchus, where the rest of the dialogue takes place.

The points made in this little scene are obvious. The connections with the themes we have raised are readily seen, while these intimations bear fruit in Plato's discussion of the means through which the ideal state can be brought into existence in *Republic* V and VI. In the analysis of the parable of the ship of state in Book VI, Plato expounds on the futility of the philosopher's trying to save even the best, most gifted members of a corrupt society. Plato's analysis is based on his belief that the social environment profoundly affects the souls of all inhabitants. In attempting to educate even a single individual against the tide of the many, the private teacher would be competing with the all-embracing public opinion of the *polis*, and the outcome is foreordained. 'You see, it's quite impossible, as the present and the past show, for any educational programme to alter anyone's character, as far as goodness is concerned, contrary to the conditioning he receives in the public arena' (492e).

As the philosopher is unable to convince his individual subject in Book VI, he fares no better in confronting society as a whole. In a well-known passage in Book VII, Plato describes what would happen if the prisoner who had been freed from the cave and seen the light were to return in order to aid his former fellows: 'And wouldn't they—if they could—grab hold of anyone who tried to set them free and take them up there, and kill him?' (517a).

Returning to Book VI, we have Plato's recommendation for those philosophers who survive in corrupt societies. Their role is not to be a public one. They should not take part in the governments of their cities, nor should they pursue the private politics of a Socratic mission. According to Plato, the true philosopher 'lies low and does only what he's meant to do'. Like a man who takes refuge under a wall 'during a storm with the wind whipping up the dust and rain pelting down, lawlessness infects everyone else he sees, so he is content if he can find a way to live his life here on earth without becoming tainted by immoral or unjust deeds, and to depart from life confidently, and without anger and bitterness' (496d–e).

Thus, Plato argues that philosophy alone is powerless to remould souls. Individuals whose personalities are formed cannot be reshaped by the pull of reason. The conclusions Aristotle draws at the end of the *Ethics* are also drawn by Plato. But while Aristotle simply states his findings, Plato communicates his less directly. Philosophy's inability is seen repeatedly in the dramatic action of many dialogues and in the depiction of the fate of the philosopher in the central books of the *Republic*.

Plato's rejection of the Socratic view of moral reform is bound up with the development of his psychological views. At some point in his career, Plato came to see the intellectualistic moral psychology of the early dialogues as simplistic. In the theory of the tripartite soul presented in the middle dialogues, the irrational components of the *psuchê* are given their due and incorporated into a fully developed moral psychology. The moral psychology of the middle dialogues is discussed below. Here it must be seen that Plato's new psychological views bring about the rejection of the intellectualistic account of the different virtues presented in the early dialogues. Whereas the Socratic definition of courage is knowledge of what is and what is not to be feared (*Lach.* 194d–95a; *Prt.* 357b–60e), in the *Republic* courage is defined as a kind of 'preservation' (*sôtêrian*, 429c): '[t]he preservation of the belief which has been inculcated by law... about what things and what kinds of things are to be feared.... keeping it intact and not losing it whether one is under the influence of pain or pleasure or desire or aversion' (429c–d). Whereas, in the *Charmides*, Socrates attempts a number of definitions of temperance, none of which depends on a relationship between reason and desire, in the *Phaedo* temperance consists of 'not being excited by the passions and in being superior to them and acting in a seemly way' (68c). In the *Republic* to be temperate 'is somehow to order and control the pleasures and desires' (430e). As we shall see below (p. 76), in light of this account of temperance Plato finds the analysis of moral weakness in the *Protagoras* severely lacking. As for justice, Plato of course describes it in the *Republic* as that condition in which each part of the soul stays in its proper place and does its own job. In the soul of the just man, reason dictates to the two lower parts, keeping appetite in place with the aid of spirit (442a–b). On the whole the essence of Plato's account of justice is psychological harmony (443c–e). According to Plato's middle works, some semblance of this psychological order is a necessary condition for virtue. Knowledge or correct opinion alone is not enough. Thus, Plato advocates a programme of education in the *Republic* far removed from anything seen in the early dialogues.

These changes in Plato's moral psychology force him to move beyond Socratic politics as well. In order to succeed as a moral reformer, the philosopher must have political power; he must be a king as well as a philosopher. These matters will be discussed in detail below. For now, in the briefest possible terms, the philosopher is forced to ally himself with political power because of the need to bring about in his subjects' souls the psychic order that is a necessary component of virtue. Believing, like Aristotle, that virtue requires the conditioning and habituation of the citizens' souls while they are young and most malleable, Plato believes that the philosopher must control the state and shape it to his educational purposes. In addition, because of the strong effects of the social environment on the souls of the inhabitants, the would-be moral reformer must have complete control over his society. As for the moral reformer without power, he is, as we have seen, unable to succeed. He must not engage in politics; most important from our point of view, he must not embark on a Socratic-type mission of reform.

Part II

The Moral Psychology of the Middle Dialogues

The evolution of Plato's political thought is part and parcel of the evolution of his thought as a whole. Thus it is important to realize that a chasm of change looms between his early and middle works. Though each middle dialogue does not of course differ from the early ones in all respects, placed alongside the Socratic works as a group, the world of the great cycle of middle dialogues—the *Meno, Phaedo, Phaedrus, Symposium*, and *Republic*—is simply a different world. Though the gulf is to some extent bridged in such transitional works as the *Gorgias, Meno*, and *Phaedo* (on which, more below), no amount of apparent continuity can belie the fact that the middle dialogues as a group signify a radical break from Plato's earlier works.

At bottom the break is due to the presence in the middle works of an entire philosophical theory, commonly referred to as 'Platonism', which is absent from the early dialogues. Though language used in various early works can be construed to show inklings of the theory of Forms, it is not until we reach the middle dialogues that such bits and pieces of Platonism are gathered together into a coherent whole. As Cornford says, the 'twin pillars' of Platonism are the theory of Forms and the immortality of the soul,[1] and it is not until the *Meno* and *Phaedo* that these doctrines are brought together as the core of a system. Only then do we have the characteristic Platonic 'two-world view', and it is around this core that Plato weaves his other doctrines: the tripartite soul, the theory of Eros, and the theory of *anamnêsis*, that all knowledge is 'recollection'.

It is beyond the scope of this work to examine all facets of Plato's middle theory, though this would contribute to a full understanding of his political thought, for 'Platonism' with all its ramifications is the lifeblood of the *Republic*. We will see that this new philosophical system has important implications for Plato's political theory, that its new distinctions and variables result in a view vastly more elaborate than Socrates'. Though we cannot discuss the origin of the break between the early and middle works in great detail, some discussion is in order.

It is clear that the middle dialogues are suffused with doctrines of a distinctly Orphic or Pythagorean cast, and many influential scholars attribute the differences between the early and middle works to the influence of this school of philosophy. According to the best ancient evidence, that of Cicero, Plato undertook his initial voyage to Sicily for the purpose of learning Pythagorean philosophy:

[A]fter Socrates' death, Plato went on journeys, first to Egypt for purposes of study and later to Italy and Sicily in order to become acquainted with the discoveries of Pythagoras... And so, as he loved Socrates with singular affection and wished to give

---

[1] F. M. Cornford, ed. and trans., *The Republic of Plato* (Oxford, 1941), p. xxvii; *Plato's Theory of Knowledge* (1934; rpt. Indianapolis, 1957), p. 2.

him credit for everything, he interwove Socrates' charm and subtlety in argument with the obscurity and ponderous learning of Pythagoras in so many branches of knowledge. (*De Republica*, I, 16)

The Pythagorean influence is seen in many aspects of Plato's philosophy. For instance, the theory of Forms is described by Aristotle as basically Pythagorean in origin and influence. Aristotle says that Plato's theory 'accorded with' (*akolouthousa*) the Pythagoreans in most respects (*Metaphysics* 987a29–31). Aristotle's remarks imply more than mere similarity: at least some direct influence is meant.[2] Other elements of Plato's middle dialogues bear a Pythagorean stamp. Some of these, taken from a list compiled by Guthrie, are as follows:

Plato's interpretation of philosophic understanding in terms of religious purification and salvation, his passion for mathematics as a glimpse of eternal truth, his talk of kinship of all nature, of reincarnation and immortality and of the body as the temporary tomb or prison of the soul, his choice of musical terminology to describe the state of the soul... and finally his adoption of the doctrine of the music of the spheres in the myth of Er.[3]

Some additional themes not mentioned by Guthrie bear on Plato's moral and political thought, for example, the doctrine of the 'three lives' (discussed below, p. 78). It is also possible that the ideal of the philosopher-king was influenced by Plato's acquaintance with Pythagorean philosopher-politicians. The most obvious example is Archytas of Tarentum, who was a successful political leader as well as an eminent mathematician. He was elected general of his city seven times and was never defeated in battle (DL VIII, 79, 82). Most important for our purposes, he was also a friend and associate of Plato. Also worth mentioning is Epaminondas, who was the leading figure in Thebes— and probably the Greek world as a whole during the twenty or so years preceding his death in 361. Epaminondas was a pupil of the Pythagorean philosopher Lysis and lived in accordance with Pythagorean precepts. In the *Rhetoric* (1398b18), undoubtedly in reference to Epaminondas, Aristotle writes: 'At Thebes, as soon as those who had the conduct of affairs became philosophers, the city flourished'. But regardless of what one makes of these particular connections, the overall relationship is clear. Guthrie describes Platonism as a 'great synthesis of Socratic and Pythagorean philosophy'.[4]

---

[2] W. D. Ross, *Aristotle's Metaphysics*, 2 vols. (Oxford, 1924), ad loc.; G. C. Field, *Plato and His Contemporaries*, 3rd edn. (London, 1967), p. 204.

[3] W. K. C. Guthrie, *A History of Greek Philosophy*, 6 vols. (Cambridge, 1962–81), IV, 35.

[4] Ibid. IV, 191; according to Cornford, 'Pythagorean influence is everywhere traceable in the dialogues of the middle period' (*Before and After Socrates* [Cambridge, 1932], pp. 62–3). Other scholars agree, e.g. E. R. Dodds, *The Greeks and the Irrational* (Berkeley, 1951), p. 209; T. Gomperz, *The Greek Thinkers*, 4 vols., L. Magnus and C. G. Berry, trans. (London, 1901–12), II, 356–7; R. G. Hackforth, *Plato's Phaedo* (Cambridge, 1955), pp. 5–6. Some different accounts of the development of Plato's thought are presented by R. Robinson, *Plato's Earlier Dialectic*,

Plato's interest in Pythagorean doctrines shows up in a series of dialogues, which occupy a transitional place between the early and middle groups. The ignorant, ironic, elenctic Socrates of the early works gradually gives way to a Socrates who knows. Instead of asking questions, Socrates begins to give answers and to discourse confidently about the deepest truths of human existence. Dialogues in which the transition is most apparent are the *Gorgias*, *Meno*, and *Phaedo*. All these works have close connections with the world of the early dialogues, but all unmistakably introduce something new. Perhaps the *Republic* too could be added, because the Platonic teaching in Books II–X is preceded by the 'Socratic' first book (see above, p. 17).

The *Gorgias* begins as an inquiry into the nature of rhetoric, with Socrates asking the questions and Gorgias answering. But as the discussion progresses, Socrates is led to explain the moral basis of his objections to rhetoric, and in doing so to reveal depths of his philosophy unobserved in the early works. In response to Callicles' praise of the life of unbridled hedonism, Socrates brings up the teaching of Euripides, that perhaps 'to live is to be dead, and to be dead to live':

I once heard one of our sages say that we are now dead and the body is our tomb, and the part of the soul in which we have desires is liable to be over-persuaded and to vacillate to and fro, and so some smart fellow, a Sicilian, I daresay, or Italian, made a fable in which... he named this part... a jar. (492e–93a)

Once Socrates begins expounding his new wisdom, the dialogue becomes virtually a monologue. Callicles—as we have noted—falls silent, as Socrates goes on to unveil political ideas that prefigure the main teachings of the *Republic*. Scholars generally identify the 'sages' in the above quotation, and also the 'smart' Italian or Sicilian, as Pythagoreans.[5] This is one reason for believing that the *Gorgias* was written upon Plato's return from Sicily, where he had been in contact with adherents of that school. Other signs of Orphic-Pythagorean influence are present in the *Gorgias*, notably the account of cosmic order and harmony at 507e–8a, and the myth of the afterlife with which Plato closes the work. Similar myths are found at the ends of the *Phaedo* and *Republic*.

In the *Meno* too Plato brings up unknown sages, as Socrates moves from asking questions to giving answers. In the first portion of this work, Socrates refutes Meno with a series of not uncharacteristic, elenctic arguments. The transition occurs when Meno asks Socrates a question designed to cast doubt upon the possibility of attaining knowledge. Socrates replies by referring to something he has heard from 'wise men and women who told of things divine' (81a):

2nd edn. (Oxford, 1953); T. Irwin, *Plato's Ethics* (Oxford, 1995); J. Gould, *The Development of Plato's Ethics* (1955; rpt. New York, 1972).

⁵ E. R. Dodds, ed., *Plato: Gorgias* (Oxford, 1959), pp. 297–8.

They were certain priests and priestesses who have studied so as to be able to give a reasoned account of their ministry.... They say that the soul of man is immortal, and at one time comes to an end, which is called dying, and at another is born again but never perishes. (81a–b)

In the continuation of the dialogue, Socrates raises for the first time the doctrine of *anamnêsis* (81c ff.). The unnamed wise men and priests mentioned here are also commonly identified as Pythagoreans.[6]

Similar topics are presented in the *Phaedo*, as, in his death cell, Socrates undertakes to explain how philosophy is a 'preparation for death' (61d). This most mystical of the middle dialogues is given a definite place and time, in a firmly grounded historical situation. The work is widely, though probably erroneously,[7] believed to present an historically accurate account of Socrates' death. But its historical dimension is in sharp conflict with its philosophical contents, which are of a piece with the middle dialogues, and Pythagorean influence is apparent throughout.[8]

Thus, I believe that the break between the early and middle dialogues can be attributed to Plato's adaptation of themes from the Orphic-Pythagorean philosophical tradition. We cannot say with certainty how Plato came to be interested in Pythagoreanism. He may have encountered Pythagoreans on his travels, or perhaps as Cicero and various modern scholars say, he went to Sicily expressly to study with them.[9] Plato was undoubtedly shaken by the death of Socrates, and it seems reasonable to believe that he began to search for answers to the problems Socrates had raised and reasons why Socrates' mission had failed. The appeal of Pythagoreanism is apparent in so far as it helps to provide solutions to these questions. Of course, even if we could explain the origin of Plato's philosophy in the middle dialogues, this would not explain his philosophy itself. However, throughout the following chapters we repeatedly see that many of the most baffling—and most characteristic— facets of Plato's philosophy must be understood in the light of the Pythagorean premises from which he begins.

In the following chapters, we confine our attention to the implications that Plato's philosophy have for his political thought. We concentrate especially upon his moral psychology. On the whole, Plato's theory of political reform, like Socrates', must be understood in the light of the end he wished to realize, given the situation with which he was faced and the means he had at his disposal. Here in Part II we discuss the end that Plato wished to achieve in the light of his new moral psychology. Examination of the means he hoped to utilize is reserved for Part III.

---

[6] Guthrie, *History*, IV, 249.

[7] See C. Gill, 'The Death of Socrates', *Classical Quarterly*, 23 (1973).

[8] For a brief discussion, see Guthrie, *History*, IV, 338–40.

[9] J. Morrison, 'The Origins of Plato's Philosopher-Statesman', *Classical Quarterly*, 8 (1958).

5

The Tripartite Soul

In order to unravel the moral psychology of the *Republic*, it is necessary briefly to examine the central argument of the work. At least ostensibly, the *Republic* centres on an attempt to define justice and to prove that it benefits its possessor. By the end of Book I, Socrates has refuted various attempted definitions, when at the beginning of Book II Glaucon and Adeimantus challenge him to define it and to show exactly how it pays. Glaucon presents a classification of goods. Some are (*a*) beneficial in themselves, others (*b*) both in themselves and for their consequences, and others (*c*) beneficial only for their consequences. An example of the first sort is joy, which is immediately beneficial, though it does not have significant consequences. Sight and health are beneficial in both ways. Having them is immediately beneficial and allow one to attain additional important benefits. Finally, medical care is desirable for its consequences, though because it is painful, it is not beneficial in itself. The nub of the argument is Glaucon's and Adeimantus' claim that justice is a good of the third sort. Like medical treatment, it is beneficial because of its consequences though undesirable in itself. Consider going to the dentist. This is often thought to be a particularly uncomfortable experience, but highly beneficial because of its long-term consequences, avoiding various painful conditions and for the long-term health of one's teeth. Glaucon views justice analogously. Though unpleasant in itself—in that it entails forgoing opportunities to profit at others' expense—it too has beneficial consequences, which in this case centre on having a good reputation for justice, which causes other people to treat one well. If one is regarded as unjust, one will be ostracized from society and punished.

Glaucon argues that justice originated in a crude social contract. Knowing they were vulnerable to abuses at the hands of others, people agreed not to take advantage of one another in exchange for not being taken advantage of, while actions that violated this pact would be called unjust and punished. The implication here is that justice is practised only out of lack of power to take advantage of others with impunity. Accordingly:

The point is that any real man with the ability to do wrong would never enter into a contract to avoid both wrongdoing and being wronged; he wouldn't be so crazy (*mainesthai*). (*Rep.* 359a–b)

This message is reinforced by additional arguments. Glaucon claims that anyone with the ability to commit injustice without fear would do so. His example is Gyges, a Lydian shepherd who discovered a ring that made him invisible. Gyges used this to seduce the queen, murder her husband, and become tyrant of Lydia. According to Glaucon, under similar circumstances, anyone else would behave similarly, take whatever he wanted, have sexual relations with anyone he wanted, kill whomever he wanted, and generally, 'act like a god among men' (360*b–c*). Turning Socrates' famous utterance on its head, Glaucon claims that 'no one is just willingly', but only for fear of the consequences of being thought unjust. Glaucon provides an additional argument to prove that it is the reputation for justice that is good, as opposed to justice in itself. His position is fortified by Adeimantus, who argues that, in Greek culture, people are taught to be just, not for the sake of justice itself but for 'the good reputation it brings' (362*e*–63*a*):

Not a single one of you self-styled supporters of morality has ever found fault with injustice or commended justice except in terms of the reputation, status, and rewards which follow from them. What each of them does on its own, however, and what the effect is of its occurrence in someone's mind, where it has been hidden from the eyes of both gods and men, has never been adequately explained either in poetry or in everyday conversation. (366*e*)

Socrates' task is formidable, to explain what justice is and show how it itself benefits its possessor, apart from consequences attached to its reputation. The advantages of injustice are immediate and tangible. Socrates is required to show how forgoing these is preferable to having them, even if one could commit injustice with impunity, unobserved by gods and men.

In order to meet this challenge, Socrates introduces an analogy between city and soul, on which the remainder of the *Republic* turns. Because the justice of a city would be larger and easier to discern than the justice of a single human soul, Socrates proposes to discuss the latter by means of the former. His strategy is to outline a just city and to analyse the virtues present in it, which he can then use as a guide in locating the virtues of the individual (*Rep.* 368*c*–69*a*). To complete this argument Plato examines various types of unjust cities and analogous souls. The benefits of justice, then, are shown by comparing the harmonious, well-ordered, just city, and just soul to the various discordant, unjust cities, and corresponding souls. This analysis is conducted in Books VIII–IX, while in Book IX two additional arguments are developed to prove the superiority of justice to injustice.

We can put off a detailed examination of the just city until Part III. For now we need only note that it is organized around a three-class structure. The rulers are to govern, in the interests of the city as a whole; the auxiliaries, the city's fighting force, are to be the rulers' loyal subordinates and allies; and the lowest class, the farmers, craftsmen, or producers, is to carry on the economic life of the state. Throughout his discussion of the city, Plato is deeply concerned with what we can call the 'principle of specialization', that each individual is supposed to perform only the one task in the community to which he is by nature suited. The virtues of the state, as identified in Book IV, revolve around this principle. The city is wise because it has wise rulers, who exercise their foresight for the good of the whole. It is courageous because it has a brave fighting force. Temperance, unlike these virtues, is not based on the function of only one class, but is a virtue of the entire city; it is a general agreement among all classes as to who should rule and who should be ruled (430*b*–32*a*). Finally, justice is said to be the principle of specialization itself, or some form or image (*eidolon*) of it. This allows the other virtues to appear in the city and to continue to exist, as long as the rulers rule, the auxiliaries perform military functions, and the farmers perform their economic tasks, with all classes willingly acquiescing in this overall scheme of things. Thus, the justice of the city is defined as each class performing its own task (*to ta hautou prattein*) and not meddling with the tasks of others (433*a*–*d*; see below, pp. 142–3).

Given this account of the city's virtue, if the virtues of the soul are analogous, the soul must possess parts analogous to those of the city. And so Socrates argues that the soul, like the city, is composed of three 'parts' or 'elements'.

5.1. THE TRIPARTITE SOUL

As has been anticipated in the preceding chapters, in the middle dialogues Plato moves beyond Socrates' psychological views. Socrates' psychology had been defective in concentrating almost exclusively on rational aspects of human nature, while Plato takes the irrational elements into account and analyses their role in the soul. As it says in the *Magna Moralia*: 'Plato rightly divided the soul into a rational and an irrational part and assigned to each its befitting virtues' (1182*a*24–26). We see that this recognition of the irrational components of the psyche has profound implications for the moral and political theories of the middle dialogues.

The nature of the soul and virtue is discussed in a variety of contexts throughout the *Republic*. The sections most important for our purposes are the extended comparison of the state and soul in Book IV and the additional arguments in Book IX that prove the superiority of justice to injustice. We will also look at portions of Plato's account of various unjust men in Books VIII and IX, and some isolated passages elsewhere. What is of immediate concern is that the points Plato chooses to emphasize vary between contexts. The discussion in Book IV, centring on the analogy between state and soul, describes psychological relationships in political terms, in terms of different elements 'ruling' and being 'ruled'. The discussion here is tentative and must be supplemented by the account of the soul in terms of streams of desire in Book IX. One problem we face in analysing Plato's conception of virtue in the *Republic* is reconciling these different accounts.

In order to present a fully rounded view of human nature, Plato argues that the soul is composed of different elements or parts. These are distinguished in Book IV through a long and tortuous argument based on the 'principle of opposites', that one thing cannot experience opposite states or tendencies towards some other thing in the same respect, at the same time (436*b*). Plato raises as one possible counter-example a man who stands still but moves his hands. It could be said that the man simultaneously experiences opposite states, viz. rest and motion. But this would be wrong; only parts of him move, while other parts are at rest. Plato argues, then, that since it is common for individuals simultaneously to feel opposed urges, for example, to drink and not to drink, there must be distinct elements in the soul as well (437*b*–39*e*).

Though Plato's view is generally discussed in terms of 'parts' of the soul, as in the very term 'tripartite', this is misleading. The word 'part' is far too rigid for what Plato has in mind. Though in the *Timaeus*, a later dialogue, Plato actually describes the parts of the soul as located in different parts of the body (69*d* ff.), the view presented in the *Republic* is more flexible. Plato uses a number of terms interchangeably to refer to the parts, most generally *eidos* ('form', one of the words commonly used to denote Platonic Forms or Ideas) and *genos* (kind), words which do not have precise English correlates. The word for part, *meros*, is not used until Plato is well into the discussion, first appearing at 442*b*11. Probably more common than these terms are various relative pronoun constructions, which are quite common in Greek but awkward and unnatural in English. Accordingly, spirit is often referred to as 'that with which we feel anger', while talk of spirited or reasoning parts of the soul is uncommon.

Plato is vague, perhaps deliberately so, about exactly what constitutes a particular part of the soul, or exactly how or where the line is drawn that differentiates one part from others. At times he suggests that there is more to the soul than what he actually discusses; for example at 443*d* he mentions the three 'kinds' (*genē*) in the soul 'and all the others there may be between them'. Thus Plato does not feel obliged to present a fully developed psychological theory, but discusses only what specific purposes require. In the present context his primary concern is explaining psychological conflict, and so he argues the need for different elements in the soul, without feeling pressed to describe in great detail what they are or how they work.

In accordance with the principle of opposites, the example of thirst is used to distinguish two parts of the soul, appetite and reason. As described initially, appetite is quite primitive. It is desire for gratification, most typically of physiologically rooted urges. Though there is a large class of appetites, its most conspicuous members are said to be thirst and hunger (437d). It is made up of impulses that draw and drag the individual (439d), driving him like a beast to drink (439b). It is especially notable that appetites do not look past their objects; they desire only satisfaction, with no regard for the individual's greater good.

Reason is contrasted with appetite precisely in that it does look towards the individual's greater good. It is initially described as that with which the soul calculates or deliberates (logizetai, 439d5; cf. 353d). More fully rendered, its function is to calculate 'what is better or worse' (441c), meaning for the good of the soul as a whole (442c). In this sense it is analogous to the class of rulers in the city, who apply their wisdom to the betterment of the city as a whole. Thus by implication the conflict between urges to drink and not to drink is between appetite, wishing for gratification, and reason, calculating that for some reason it would not be to the individual's overall advantage to drink. An example would be a situation in which a thirsty man sees some water which he would like to drink, but, believing that the water might be polluted, decides not to. His desire for his greater good, in this case his health, presided over by reason, comes into conflict with his thirst, which is concerned only with its own satisfaction.

Plato's initial account of reason and appetite is complicated by what is said in Book IX. Here reason is described as possessing the attributes of a desire (580d); it is a lover of learning and truth (581b). Similarly, the appetitive part is described a bit differently. The class of appetites is said to be too varied to be given a single name. But as a whole it is the money or gain-loving part, because money is the chief means through which it is able to achieve gratification (580d–81a; also 442a). These aspects of Plato's theory will be discussed below.

The third element, spirit, is initially described in Book IV as that with which we feel anger (439e). As his example Plato relates an anecdote about Leontius, a young man who wished to look at the corpses of some execution victims, but felt an aversion and resisted. Eventually he was overpowered by his desire and rushed up to look, but cursed himself for doing so (439e–40a). This self-directed anger is spirit and is distinct from the other two elements. It sides naturally with reason in its struggles with appetite, and so cannot be appetite. It can be distinguished from reason on two grounds. First, it is found in animals and young children, who are not or not yet reasonable. Second, it must sometimes be rebuked by reason. Apparently, though spirit naturally sides with reason against appetite, it is capable of going against reason and so must be resisted on occasion. Moreover, though spirit is naturally allied with reason, it can be corrupted by improper upbringing, which presumably would sever the alliance. Described a bit more fully, spirit is anger motivated by an individual's conception of what is just. It rages fiercely when he feels he has been wronged, but is docile when he believes himself to be in the wrong (440c–d). In Book IX it is characterized somewhat differently as a lover of honour, victory, and good reputation (581a–b). The link between these different descriptions is, briefly, that spirit covers a range of emotions concerned with someone's image of himself and his desire that others share that image. Thus it gives the individual perseverance. For example, someone who sees himself as a superior athlete will undergo privation and hardship in order to accomplish the goals that will lead others to recognize his prowess. It is perhaps this fortifying role of spirit that allows Plato to assimilate the assertiveness of animals and small children to 'spirited behaviour', though, clearly, they are not motivated by self-image. Aside from these two exceptions, Plato's position is consistent and generally clear.

The range of behaviour Plato associates with spirit is familiar. It is common to see an individual refrain from some action, even if the chances of being discovered are slight, because it would conflict with how he sees himself; for example, it would not be 'honest' to steal from a charity collection box or 'fair' to grade a student especially severely because of her race or religion. Should one do these things anyway, he would be angry with himself. Should he do them and be found out, his reaction would probably be embarrassment or shame, with his anger again directed back at himself. From these examples we can see the nature of the alliance between spirit and reason. Because spirit derives its emotional force from the desire to live up to certain standards, it is naturally allied with reason, which supplies the standards. The judgement whether a given act would be 'decent' must be made by reason, and is made by applying one's general moral principles.

Once these elements have been distinguished, Plato describes the relationships between them that constitute virtue. All the virtues are rooted in a proper order in the soul, analogous to that which constitutes the virtues of the city. The individual is wise because his reasoning element rules, looking out for the interests of the entire soul. He is courageous because his spirited part is allied to reason, preserving even through adversity the opinions handed down by reason about what is to be feared and what is not. His temperance lies in the harmonious interaction between his soul's parts in regard to the question of which is to rule and which are to be ruled. Finally, justice is described as this general psychological harmony. It is the principle by which each part stays in place and does its own job. In Plato's words:

It does not lie in a man's external actions, but in the way he acts within himself, really concerned with himself and his inner parts. He does not allow each part of himself to perform the work of another, or the sections of his soul to meddle with one another. He orders what are in the true sense of the word his own affairs well; he is master of himself, puts things in order, is his own friend, harmonizes the three parts like the limiting notes of a musical scale, the high, the low, and the middle, and any others there may be between. He binds them all together, and himself from a plurality becomes a unity. (443c–e; Grube trans.)

Thus Plato's conception of virtue centres on psychological harmony. In the just soul each element stays in its own place and performs the task to which it is naturally suited. The result is a condition analogous to health in the body. The chief benefit of justice is that it allows this condition of psychological harmony to come into existence and to be maintained in the soul.

Plato believes that psychological harmony can be achieved only if reason rules in the soul. And so we must look into exactly what this entails. In Book IV the rule of reason should be understood in political terms. Throughout Plato's discussion in this context, the recurrent metaphors are political. This is hardly surprising in the light of Plato's basing his account of the parts and virtues of the soul on their analogues writ large in the state. Accordingly, in this context 'rule' should be understood in terms of political struggle between the soul's parts. As in an ordinary political system, conflicts are settled by force or the threat of force. In any given case, we have element X wishing to do something, and element Y wishing not to do it, while the course the soul ultimately chooses is determined by the relative strengths of the two elements. The stronger element rules by enforcing its will on the weaker. Rule in this sense can be referred to as 'direct rule':[1]

Direct Rule: With element X wishing to do A, and element Y wishing to do not-A, if the soul chooses to do A, X rules over Y.

According to the analysis in Book IV, then, reason 'rules' in the soul by being the strongest element. Its rule is exercised in conjunction with its ally spirit, and so Plato holds that virtue is largely bound up with ensuring that spirit can be broken to the will of reason, and that these elements combined are stronger than appetite.

We see in the next section that when Plato incorporates additional material into his analysis, a second conception of rule is called for as well. But before

---

[1] For analysis of rule in the soul, I am indebted to R. Kraut, 'Reason and Justice in Plato's *Republic*', in *Exegesis and Argument*, E. N. Lee et al., eds. (Assen, The Netherland, 1973).

dealing with these complexities, we must discuss how this view has moved beyond Socratic psychology. As seen especially in the *Protagoras*, Socrates is unable satisfactorily to explain psychological conflict and is forced to deny the existence of moral weakness. Plato, as we have seen, not only takes psychological conflict into account but constructs large portions of his theory around it. It is the view of many scholars that the argument in *Republic* IV represents the decisive rejection of Socratic psychology,[2] and I believe this is correct.

In the *Protagoras*, as we have seen, psychological conflict is reduced to intellectual calculation. Consider an agent who is tempted by some pastries but is on a diet and knows she should not eat them. The problem of virtue would involve an additional feature as well, ascertaining the morally correct course, which is far more complex than the question of whether to diet. But we may set these additional complexities aside. According to Socrates, the nearness of the pastries makes the pleasures of eating them seem disproportionately large as compared to the more distant, though in the long run far greater pleasures of thinness, good health, etc., which would be gained by dieting. Thus according to Socrates, an individual conventionally described as morally weak or as 'overcome by pleasure' actually makes a purely intellectual mistake. She commits an error of measurement. Were she to learn the purely technical skill of measuring pleasures, analogous to other purely technical skills, she would be able to avoid such errors in the future.

The view in the *Republic* is significantly different. Here too, let us assume we are faced with the situation of a dieting person under temptation. The key difference is the existence of different parts of her soul, with different desires. Rather than one good-seeking desire dominating her soul as a whole, we have a conflict between different parts and their different desires. As we have seen, such conflicts are resolved politically. If the desire to eat wins out, we have an instance of precisely the kind Socrates denied. This clearly would be a case of moral weakness, in which the individual is overcome by pleasure.

It is in their lack of concern for the individual's overall good that the desires of the appetitive part most clearly break with Socratic moral psychology. The Socrates of the early dialogues could doubtless recognize the appetites discussed in the *Republic*. For example, the physical desires that are responsible for *akrasia* are discussed in the *Protagoras*. Socrates refers to the powerful pleasures associated with food and drink and sexual acts (353*c*). But according to the analysis there, these desires are components of the single overall good-seeking desire that regulates behaviour, which follows calculations of measurements made by the soul. As we saw, *akrasia* is described as incorrectly

---

[2] M. Pohlenz, *Aus Platos Werdezeit* (Berlin, 1913), pp. 156–7; T. Irwin, *Plato's Ethics* (Oxford, 1995), chs. 13–14; J. Walsh, *Aristotle's Conception of Moral Weakness* (New York, 1964), ch. 2.

giving too much weight to specific desires, because of the errors of perspective they cause. And so these can be cured if the individual learns the true art of measurement.

In the *Republic*, the desires of the appetitive part are explicitly said to be independent of any overall process devoted to maximizing one's good. The desire to drink is a desire *only* to drink, without reference to how this desire ties in with the individual's overall good. 'When someone is thirsty, then, the only thing—insofar as he is thirsty—that his mind wants is to drink. This is what it longs for and strives for' (439*a–b*). These desires can be described as 'good-independent' desires.[3] To the extent that a calculative, overall, good-seeking process is retained in this model of the soul, this is solely assigned to *to logistikon*, the reasoning or calculating part. Because the desires of the appetitive part are not components of an overall good-seeking process, they must be trained ('educated' is probably too exalted a term) to be subordinate to the rational faculties, so the latter can exercise political rule. Accordingly, differences in Plato's understanding of the good-independent desires bear fruit in radically different views of how these should be controlled.

In the light of this conceptualization of the good-independent desires, the break with Socratic moral psychology is clear. According to the analysis in the *Republic*, mastery of intellectual techniques is not enough. The respective strengths of the soul's elements is also a crucial variable, and so a programme of habituation and conditioning—designed to strengthen reason, to bend spirit into alliance with it and to weaken appetite—is also necessary. Therefore, Plato sets up a programme of education designed largely to do this as the centrepiece of his ideal state.

5.2. DIRECT AND NORMATIVE RULE

Our account of Plato's psychological views is complicated by a description of the parts of the soul quite different from what we have seen. In our account in the last section, based primarily on *Republic* IV, the soul is understood mainly in political terms. The three parts interact in political relationships such as conflict, alliance, and rule—direct rule. Elsewhere in the *Republic*, primarily in Book IX but in other contexts as well, Plato discusses the parts of the soul according to the metaphor of streams of desire, and also employs a different conception of rule. Though Plato never works these two sets of metaphors into a developed theory, they do not appear to be incompatible. A consistent interpretation can be worked out and I present it in outline here.

[3] Following Irwin, ed. and trans., *Plato: Gorgias* (Oxford, 1979).

The parts of the soul are most clearly described as streams of desire in a brief passage in Book IX (580*d*–81*c*). Plato says that each part of the soul is characterized by a kind of desire (*epithumia*), a kind of pleasure, and also a kind of rule in the soul peculiar to it. The reasoning part is a lover of learning and wisdom; spirit is a lover of honour or victory; appetite is money-loving or a lover of gain. Plato says that one of these elements rules in the soul of any given individual, resulting in three basic kinds of people: philosophers or lovers of wisdom, lovers of victory, and lovers of gain.

The theme of the three kinds of people, or 'three lives', is of Pythagorean origin. According to ancient authorities, when Pythagoras was asked what it meant to be a 'philosopher', he replied by comparing life to the Olympic Games, where some went to compete, some to hawk their wares, and others as spectators (DL VIII, 8). For in life as well, there are lovers of glory, gain, and wisdom. These three types of people make up the three classes in the ideal state. The rulers, whose souls are dominated by reason, are lovers of wisdom; the auxiliaries, ruled by spirit, are lovers of honour, while the producers, ruled by appetite, are lovers of gain.

The account of the parts of the soul as streams of desire can be incorporated into our discussion up to this point, if we introduce a few basic distinctions. Though these are somewhat cumbersome and difficult, they are important and will be seen to provide a relatively precise mechanism for explicating the mental workings of different types of people. The principal distinction is between the two ways in which parts of the soul rule. This distinction is necessary because Plato discusses rule in reference to two rather different types of cases. (*a*) A part is said to rule over other parts when it is able to subordinate their demands to its own. As we have seen, reason rules in this sense when it is able to subordinate the demands of appetite to the overall good of the soul. (*b*) A part is said to rule when the soul as a whole is oriented towards values associated with that part. Thus reason rules in this sense if the soul prefers the values of reason, for example, knowledge and truth, to other values, while spirit rules if the soul prefers the values of honour and reputation, and appetite rules if the soul prefers its values, mainly physical pleasure. Thus the three lives result from the rule (in this sense) of different parts in different individuals. In general, Plato talks of rule in sense (*a*) mainly in Book IV in connection with the political account of the workings of the soul. He talks of rule in sense (*b*) mainly in Book IX in connection with the account of the parts of the soul as streams of desire, and in Books VIII–IX in connection with the four unjust souls, which are ruled (in this sense) by inferior elements. We have referred to rule in sense (*a*) as direct rule. We will refer to rule in the second sense as 'normative' rule, because the ruling part infuses the soul with its values or norms:

Normative Rule: If a soul gives precedence to values associated with element X, rather than those associated with element Y, X rules over Y.

Thus we have direct rule, which is concerned with different parts subordinating others, and normative rule, which is concerned with supplying the soul with the ends it pursues.

This basic distinction between kinds of rule enables us to untangle problem areas in Plato's moral psychology. For instance, as we have seen, the appetitive part rules (normatively) in certain souls, making individuals lovers of pleasure. But it is not immediately apparent how the minds of such individuals work. For instance, if appetite rules in their souls, are such individuals able to reason, and if so, how? Similarly, are such individuals able to suppress any of their appetitive urges, or are they at the mercy of whatever desires erupt, demanding immediate satisfaction? Again, if they are able to suppress other appetites, how does this mechanism work? Unless one works out careful solutions to such problems, the result is liable to be a most peculiar psychological view, according to which appetitive individuals would hardly appear to be human—entirely unable to reason and completely dominated by their desires. Indeed, certain commentators have held that the souls of members of the third class are made up entirely of appetite, as the auxiliaries' souls are entirely spirit, and those of the rulers entirely reason.[4] However, this is not only an extreme view, but, as we see, there is strong textual evidence against it. Plato clearly believes that, though spirited and appetitive individuals are not ruled (in some sense) by reason, they have the ability to think. Moreover, even appetitive individuals are able to subordinate certain of their appetites (again, in some sense). The great advantage of the distinction between the two kinds of rule is that it allows us to clear up these troubling cases and others like them in a clear and economical way.[5]

Put roughly and simply, Plato's overall view can be expressed in terms of the idea of plans of life.[6] Plato holds that individuals form plans of life of various sorts; they wish to maximize certain goods, and organize their psyches around

[4] e.g., M. B. Foster, *The Political Philosophies of Plato and Hegel* (Oxford, 1935), pp. 59, 61, 76–7, etc.; criticized by H. W. B. Joseph, *Essays in Ancient and Modern Philosophy* (Oxford, 1935), pp. 114–21.

[5] Note the problems even in J. M. Cooper's sophisticated account, 'Plato's Theory of Human Motivation', *History of Philosophy Quarterly*, 1 (1984), esp. nn. 7, 13, 18. In several contexts Cooper can be seen to be working towards distinctions made in this section, e.g. on p. 10, where he distinguishes 'motivating' reason from calculation.

[6] Especially valuable discussions are N. R. Murphy, *The Interpretation of Plato's Republic* (Oxford, 1951), pp. 1–97; and Joseph, *Essays*, esp. ch. III. Fuller treatments of certain aspects of the discussion here are found in Klosko, '*Dēmotikē Aretē* in the *Republic*', *History of Political Thought*, 2 (1982); and 'The "Rule" of Reason in Plato's Psychology', *History of Philosophy Quarterly*, 5 (1988).

pursuing them. The role of the normatively ruling part is to determine the desired goods or ends, while relationships of direct rule are concerned with the way parts interact in carrying out the plan. I think Plato would argue that most individuals live according to such plans. Therefore, most human souls reflect the basic structure discussed in Book IV, according to which reason rules (directly), supported by spirit, while these combine to keep the appetites in place.

Though Plato does not explicitly couch his psychological discussion in terms of plans of life, an account along these lines can be extracted from what he does say. There is good evidence that he believes that most individuals possess certain reasoning abilities, that is, that they are rational. Reason is commonly said to be a deliberative faculty. Its functions include determining various kinds of relationships, especially the means necessary to attain different ends. Reason in this sense can be referred to as 'instrumental reason'. It is similar to reason in the well-known account of Hume, who describes it as a 'slave of the passions'.[7]

Plato holds that most people possess reason in this sense. Even if they are not under the normative rule of reason, which expresses itself in the overriding urge for contemplation of and union with the Forms, most people are able to perform (with varying degrees of proficiency) the less exalted functions and operations associated with instrumental reason. Most people are able to learn from experience, to assess the probable effects of courses of action, in short to determine the most appropriate means to attain their ends. People also hold opinions and beliefs about their objects of desire. In Plato's psychology these should be attributed to instrumental reason. This is one respect in which Plato's tendency to personify the parts of the soul is disconcerting.[8] To make matters worse, as we see, he also talks about spirit as having opinions.

In order for individuals to pursue their plans of life, they must be able to suppress desires and other urges that conflict with their overriding goals. This task is performed by instrumental reason. In most souls, instrumental reason rules directly, regardless of the overall values the soul pursues, regardless, in other words, of the part that rules normatively. The great importance of the direct rule of reason is seen clearly by contrasting an individual who has it with one who does not. A person not directly ruled by reason is constantly at the mercy of his appetites. He is continually dragged off to satisfy different urges as they arise, regardless of the effects this has on his overall plan of life.

---

[7] D. Hume, *A Treatise on Human Nature*, II, iii, 1.

[8] Plato's personification is well discussed by J. Annas, *An Introduction to Plato's Republic* (Oxford, 1981), pp. 143–6.

For example, an individual of this type normatively ruled by the desire for wealth is not able to marshal his energies in order to make money. His desire to sleep prevents him from waking up on time; his desire to eat exotic delicacies prevents him from arriving at his appointments on time; his desire to possess various baubles has him constantly thieving and in trouble with the law. In short, he lacks the discipline that makes a coherent, purposeful approach to life possible.

In contrast, someone directly ruled by reason has such discipline. She structures her life towards the optimum satisfaction of her goals (regardless of the quality of the goals). Her appetites of course are still present, demanding satisfaction, but she (or her instrumental reason) decides when and how best to satisfy them in a manner compatible with her overall aims. In short, the job of instrumental reason is to blend the various desires of her soul into a coherent plan of life that will satisfy as many as possible as fully as possible. Again, it should be noted that reason exercises this function in all three kinds of men, and so all three classes in the ideal state.

As we have noted, the main function of the element that rules normatively is to infuse the soul as a whole with its desire. In concrete terms this largely amounts to determining which desires shall be preferred in the individual's plan of life, and so which others must be suppressed. In the case of the normative rule of spirit, for example, this largely comes down to ensuring that the soul prefers the goods of honour. Instrumental reason will believe that the goods of honour are the highest and that happiness is best obtained through possession of these. An individual ruled normatively by spirit will admire qualities such as courage and athletic prowess, while despising cowardice, weakness, and so forth.

Textual evidence for this overall view of Plato's psychology is readily supplied. To begin with, according to the view we have developed, Plato believes that most human souls possess instrumental reason. Thus in *Republic* VIII he speaks of even evil men as possessing intelligence. Men who are 'bad but smart' have keen vision in their souls, though this faculty is forcibly enlisted in the service of evil (518c–19a). Similarly, the degenerate men described in Books VIII–IX possess reason, though directed at unworthy ends. In the soul of the oligarchic man especially, reason is literally the slave of the passions, as appetite and avarice set themselves up as king and subjugate reason, forcing it to look to nothing but making money (553c–d).

There is also evidence that the opinions held by instrumental reason are determined by the normatively ruling part. Thus each of the three types of men believes that his own way of life is the most pleasant (581c–d), while the democratic man fortifies his life of indiscriminate pleasure-seeking with the beliefs that all pleasures are equal (561*b–c*) and that such a life embodies true freedom and happiness (561*d–e*). According to Plato, then, individuals pursue objects of desire in the belief that they are desirable.

Spirit as well as reason is controlled by the normatively ruling appetite. In the case of the oligarchic man, enthroned avarice has spirit as well as reason kneeling at its feet, admiring and honouring nothing but wealth and wealthy individuals (553*d*). The values of the democratic man are similarly affected. Under the sway of his desires, he comes to despise such virtues as moderation and reverence, while holding qualities such as shamelessness and insolence in high regard (560*d*–61*a*).

It seems, then, that when a given desire comes to rule the soul normatively, it is able to rule directly through surrogates. By altering the opinions of instrumental reason and spirit, it organizes the individual as a whole around a plan of life devoted to the maximization of its desired objects. This explains how the direct rule of reason is found in souls ruled normatively by appetite, and solves the apparent paradox that an appetitive man is able to suppress certain appetites. In cases of this sort, the appetitive man's reason and spirit unite to weed out appetites that conflict with his overall plan of life. The oligarchic man is said to subordinate his unnecessary appetites—and some of his better ones as well—regarding them as too expensive, and so liable to interfere with his overriding concern with wealth (554*a–d*). Even the democratic man suppresses some desires, the lawless ones which come to dominate the tyrant's soul (571*b–c*).

This should serve to introduce some of the main elements in the working of the soul. The details of normative and direct rule will receive further elaboration throughout the remainder of Part II.

5.3. THE VIRTUES OF CORRECT OPINION

Though the ideal state is organized around a three-class system, a more significant distinction for Plato's moral psychology is that between the rulers and the two other classes. For only the rulers possess knowledge and so the highest form of virtue. Their virtue can be seen to differ in crucial respects from that of the auxiliaries, and while little can be said with assurance about the virtue of the lowest class, it seems that this would be close to that of the auxiliaries.

The perfect virtue of the philosophers will be discussed in detail in the next chapter. We concentrate here on the virtue of the auxiliaries. The virtue of this class falls short of perfect virtue in two respects. Apparently with reference to these deficiencies, Plato calls it 'civic' or 'popular' virtue (*politikê* or *dêmotikê aretê*), terms which I continue to use. It is deficient in being based on an inferior element ruling normatively in the soul, and in being founded on correct opinion rather than knowledge. These differences can be discussed in turn.

In the souls of the auxiliaries, instrumental reason rules directly in the interest of spirit, planning means through which the goals of spirit can be maximized. Members of this class are, accordingly, lovers of honour. We have seen that Plato holds that each type of individual believes that his own way of life is the most pleasant. And so the auxiliaries not only love honour but believe that the pleasures it affords are of the highest sort. According to Plato, the special virtue of this class is courage, which he defines as the ability to pre-serve correct opinions about what is to be feared and what is not even under adverse conditions (429c–d). In practical terms this conception of courage amounts to the auxiliaries' caring more deeply about (and so being more afraid to lose) their honour than anything else. Having been intensively con-ditioned to attach their conception of what is honourable to the importance of behaving morally, they will adhere to their convictions through the most trying circumstances. This of course makes them brave. But their staunch adherence to moral principles will extend beyond the rigours of the battlefield to all circumstances that could possibly deprive them of their principles.

Because the auxiliaries are motivated by love of honour, some commen-tators have argued that their souls are made up entirely of spirit (above, p. 79). In the last section we saw that this view is incorrect, that Plato believes that in their souls—as in most human souls—we find a structure similar to that discussed in Book IV, with reason ruling (directly), supported by spirit, keeping appetite down. However, even if they are ruled by reason in this sense, the auxiliaries are not philosophers. Because they are ruled normatively by spirit, they are virtuous for the sake of self-esteem. In the final analysis, they would fight bravely, not because they love their city or because they think that is the right thing to do, but because their honour depends on it. Plato believes that virtue motivated by this sort of self-interest is inferior to the selfless virtue of the philosophers (see esp. *Phaedo* 68e–69b).

The auxiliaries also fall short of perfect virtue because they are unable to attain knowledge. Plato develops the distinction between knowledge and correct opinion in the middle dialogues and uses it to distinguish two kinds of virtue, one based on knowledge, while the other, a less exalted kind, rests only on true belief. We must avoid becoming embroiled here in the complex philo-sophical problems concerning Plato's distinction between knowledge and true belief.[9] The main point to note is Plato's view that a semblance of virtue can

---

[9] A good brief account, with numerous references, is Guthrie, *History*, IV, 256–8, 487–93; also see, Ch. 6, sec. 2.

exist without knowledge. Though deficient in other respects, true opinion is a suitable guide for practical actions (see *Meno* 97*a*–*b*). Plato declares that certain people, such as well-known statesmen, have been successful because of true opinion, which they received as a sort of inspiration from the gods (*Meno* 99*b*–*d*).

The virtues of correct opinion are important for the moral psychology of the *Republic,* because only the philosophers possess knowledge. Only they undergo the rigorous education in mathematics and dialectic described in Book VII, which is required to glimpse the Forms. The semblance of perfect virtue maintained by the auxiliaries rests only on correct opinion.

As we have noted, Plato's discussion of virtue in Book IV is avowedly tentative (esp. 435*c*–*d*). Only in Book VI does Socrates advance beyond this position and discuss the higher form of virtue, based on knowledge. Thus the programme of early education described in Books II–III (discussed below in Chapter 8) teaches only correct opinion, in contrast to the programme of studies described in Book VII, which is designed to raise the philosophers to knowledge of the Forms. Thus the virtues described in Book IV are those of the auxiliaries rather than of the philosophers. There is strong evidence for this. There is no reference to the Forms in Books II–IV. Courage in the city is defined as preservation of belief (*doxa*) about what is to be feared and what is not. This belief has been inculcated by the legislator through education (429*c*). At 430*c*3, this is referred to as civic (*politikê*) courage, and many commentators interpret this to imply that it is a lower form of virtue. As Adam says: 'The whole of this section of the dialogue is important because it emphatically reaffirms the principle that courage as well as the other virtues enumerated here rest on *orthê doxa* [correct opinion] and not on *epistêmê* [knowledge]'.[10] Thus, the transition from Books II–IV to the later books represents a movement from discussing the virtues based on right opinion to an account of the knowledge of the philosopher and the virtues attendant on that.

Plato holds that virtues based on opinions are inferior to those based on knowledge in two ways. First, opinions can be incorrect, while knowledge, as we see below, is always true. Correct opinion is also less secure. People with knowledge have stronger characters than people with correct opinion. In the *Meno*, Plato says that true opinions have a tendency not to stay with us, and so must be anchored by causal reasoning and converted into knowledge, which is permanent (97*d*–98*a*). People can be deprived of their correct opinions in various ways (*Rep.* 413*a*–*c*). They can be lost voluntarily, through being cast aside in favour of others the individual comes to believe are more correct; or they can be forgotten over time, or removed through persuasion.

---

[10] J. Adam, ed., *The Republic of Plato,* 2 vols. (Cambridge, 1902), I, 232.

An additional way, more important for our concerns, is that they can be lost to the temptation of some pleasure or to fear. Plato believes that knowledge is able to resist all these forces.

Plato's view that a person with knowledge has greater moral strength than someone with only belief is somewhat at odds with more recent accounts of knowledge and belief. According to recent philosophers, knowledge differs from true belief in possessing greater cognitive certainty. This can be expressed by saying that an individual with knowledge has something that a person with belief lacks, some strong grounds for taking his beliefs to be true. Knowledge is backed up with evidential support and is not merely accepted on faith. Plato frequently distinguishes the two states along these lines (e.g. at *Rep.* 506c; *Meno* 98a; *Tim.* 51e). To take one instance, in the *Meno* (97a–b), Plato says that the individual who knows the way to Larisa has first-hand experience. He has travelled the road himself, while the person with correct opinion has (presumably) merely been told the way.

Plato, however, adds to this cognitive superiority moral superiority. The individual with knowledge is able to withstand temptations that would get the better of true belief. Plato's view is odd because, on reflection, it can be seen that there is no general correlation between the strength of various moral convictions and the security of the grounds for holding them to be true. Certainly, beliefs such as religious convictions have been adhered to most fervently in the face of extreme temptations and pressures—often to the extent of martyrdom—though they are held solely on faith, supported by little in the way of convincing arguments or evidence. Though there may be cases in which an individual who knows something to be true would be more likely to withstand temptation than someone who merely believes it, all cases are not of this sort. There does not seem to be a general correlation of the kind Plato posits between the cognitive status of different convictions and their ability to impart moral strength.

Because he believes correct opinion is inherently weaker than knowledge, Plato seeks to compensate by choosing as his auxiliaries individuals who have strong characters and educating them with extreme care. Through proper education an individual's spirited part can be tempered and moulded into harmony with the reasoning part of his soul, resulting in the creation of an alliance (410b–12a, 441d–42b). The proper relationship between these two parts is courage, one main function of which is to preserve moral beliefs against all their foes (442b–c, 429c–d). The courageous soul is like wool which has been treated to hold its dye. In such souls, beliefs are held fast, immune from pleasure and pain, appetite and fear (429d–30b). Thus, Plato holds that courage can anchor true opinions to the soul through a means quite different from converting them into knowledge.

Only because the auxiliaries have innately strong spirited parts are they able to become truly courageous. However, no matter how thoroughly they are drilled, they must remain inferior to the philosophers, who possess knowledge. Philosophers will be able to resist pressures and temptations at least as well as the most courageous auxiliaries. The reason for this is Plato's view that knowledge is a moral condition as well as a cognitive state, and that the attainment of knowledge is not only a process of confirming the truthfulness of convictions but is also a transformation of the moral character. In order to make sense of these aspects of Plato's view, we turn to his account of the nature of the philosopher.

6

The Ascent to the Philosopher

In the central books of the *Republic*, Plato reveals aspects of his philosophy barely hinted at earlier. The material discussed in Books V–VII touches on the highest reaches of 'Platonism' and yields a conception of the just individual, the philosopher, more exalted than anything seen in Book IV. But these books shed light on more than Plato's moral psychology alone. When we examine the ideal state in the *Republic*, we see that many of its most distinctive features can be traced back to Plato's metaphysical and epistemological views. The state's rigid division between rulers and ruled is justified on the grounds of the former's superior knowledge. This in turn rests on their exceptional natural endowments and on Plato's beliefs that knowledge is fundamentally superior to belief and is unattainable by the vast majority of people. These views and others like them are unusual and difficult, but they are among the most important premises of Plato's political thought.

In this chapter, we concentrate on the philosophical foundations for Plato's belief in the superiority of the philosophers. We discuss two central aspects of his philosophy: (*a*) the theory of Forms, including the famous images of the Sun, the Divided Line, and the Cave, and (*b*) his view of the soul, especially his doctrine of Eros.

6.1. THE THEORY OF FORMS

The theory of Forms or Ideas is probably the most distinctive and notorious aspect of Plato's philosophical system. The arguments of many dialogues, including the *Republic*, rest heavily on it, so it is surprising to realize how nebulous Plato's presentation of the theory is. It is expounded fully in no single dialogue. Although it is discussed in many places in a number of different works, the points discussed vary from dialogue to dialogue, and as is frequently the case with Plato, it is not certain that all aspects of the theory touched upon can be synthesized into one consistent doctrine. The *Republic* is generally cited as a chief source for information about the Forms, but here too Plato's account is haphazard. The theory is presented in this work as already familiar to Socrates' interlocutors (e.g. 476*a*, 505*a*, 507*a–b*; cf. *Phaedo* 100*b*), and so it is not fully explained. Its most crucial and central features are presented cryptically and gnomically in highly compressed passages which are nowhere elaborated upon and in the series of famous and striking images that dominate Books VI and VII—the Sun, the Line, and the Cave. We examine these images later in this chapter, but they present problems, especially in drawing the line between what Plato intends seriously and what figuratively. An added problem is that detailed exegesis of the images frequently yields conflicting results, while Plato himself is unhelpful. The image of the Sun is said to be necessary, because Socrates himself is unable to describe the nature of the Form of the Good (506d–e), which is of course the most important of the Forms. Similarly, in another context Socrates says that if he did expand upon the nature of dialectic, the faculty used to grasp the Forms, his interlocutors would be unable to follow (532e–33a).

The Forms have been discussed by numerous commentators. Because of Plato's cryptic presentation, there is widespread controversy about many important aspects, and no reconciliation seems in sight. But there is some consolation in the fact that much of this has little bearing on Plato's political thought. In general, substituting different versions of even major aspects of the theory would not significantly affect its political implications. For our purpose, it should suffice to sketch some central aspects of the theory, while avoiding detailed interpretation. The reader should, however, be advised that even the basic points made in this section are not unchallenged in the vast scholarly literature.[1]

At heart, the theory of Forms concerns absolute, timeless, immutable essences, completely removed from the sensible world. Because they can be perceived only by the mind, Plato locates them in the 'intelligible' realm. Plato uses various Greek words to refer to these entities, especially *eidos* and *idea*, which are used interchangeably and generally translated as 'Form' and 'Idea' respectively. In regard to the translation, Idea, it is important not to be misled into thinking that the Ideas, like the entities denoted by the English word ideas, have no substantial existence outside of people's minds. Plato's Forms or Ideas most certainly 'exist' (in some sense) in the real world, and Plato would argue that they are in fact more 'real' than anything encountered in the sensible world. Thus Form is preferable.

What lies at the centre of the theory is well expressed in a classic article by Harold Cherniss.[2] According to Cherniss, one reason Plato was led to accept the theory is that it answers important ethical, metaphysical, and

---

[1] For references, see (13) under *Further Reading*.

[2] H. Cherniss, 'The Philosophical Economy of the Theory of Ideas', in *Plato: A Collection of Critical Essays*, G. Vlastos, ed. (Garden City, NY, 1970).

epistemological questions and does so in an economical way. As Cherniss argues, and as we have seen, Plato was deeply disturbed by extreme forms of moral scepticism, and so wished to establish moral standards on a secure basis. He was able to do this by postulating the moral Forms, which are absolute, objective standards of value. Since the Forms also supply the objects required for certain knowledge, they also serve to counter general scepticism of the kind represented by Protagoras' 'Man is the measure of all things', about which Plato was also concerned. Moreover, the same entities that provide moral standards and allow the possibility of certain knowledge also answer important metaphysical questions concerning the nature of true Being and the fundamental constituents of the universe. Thus through one unifying theory, Plato believed he was able to clear up basic questions in ethics, epistemology, and metaphysics.

Forms themselves are most easily explained as entities that are what they are absolutely. They possess their qualities in an unqualified way, in comparison to sensible objects which do not. Plato's position here is supported by a number of versions of what is frequently called the 'argument from opposites'. Two versions are sketched in the *Republic* (478e–79c, 523a–25a). Plato argues that sensible objects (a term I use loosely enough to include actions) bear qualified predicates. For instance a tree is and is not large. It may be large in comparison to a rosebush, but it is small in comparison to a mountain. The reason for this is that 'large' is what can be called an 'incomplete' predicate. It contains a tacit reference; it always compares the object described to some other object, and so, depending on the relative size of this other object, the tree will be large or not large. By substituting a series of objects of different sizes, we are able to show that the tree is large in comparison to some and not large in comparison to others. Thus through the argument from opposites, Plato shows that sensible objects possess both attributes and their opposites.

Plato finds this sort of situation deeply paradoxical. It is not entirely clear why this is so, but in *Republic* VII (523b–24b), he says that certain perceptions do not cause problems, such as that which identifies a given object as a finger. But others, like those concerning the large and not-large tree, have to be reconciled. While we would be inclined to say that the tree is large in comparison to some objects and not large in comparison to others, and think little more about the matter, Plato is apparently led astray by the language of Being. *Einai*, the Greek word for 'to be', is also the word for 'to exist', and it seems that at the time he wrote the *Republic*, Plato was not able entirely to disentangle these senses of *einai*. He does make the necessary distinctions in a later dialogue, the *Sophist*, but does so in such a way that it is clear he believes the problem to be difficult and his solution of the greatest importance.

Put simply and crudely, at the time he wrote the *Republic*, Plato seemed to believe that saying that an object 'is not large' implied that it 'is not', taking 'is' in this second usage to refer to existence. Accordingly, Plato apparently took the observation that the tree 'is and is not large' to imply a deficiency in the tree's 'Being'. He expresses this by saying that it 'embodies' (or 'participates in') Largeness only imperfectly, and in the final analysis, that it 'exists' imperfectly. What is true of the tree holds for all sensible objects. All possess attributes that are also qualified by their opposites, and so all bear their attributes deficiently.

While many of Plato's examples employ comparative predicates, such as 'large' or 'heavy', other incomplete predicates he uses are connected with mathematics. For instance four objects are and are not 'double'. They are double two objects, but are only half of eight objects. Plato treats ethical terms in a similar fashion. A given action is always both just and unjust. For instance, it is seen in *Republic* I that returning what one has borrowed may be just under certain circumstances. But under others it may not be, for example, if one has borrowed a sword, and in the meantime the lender has gone berserk (*Rep.* 331c). To give another example, a beautiful woman cannot be beautiful in all respects, from all angles, in the eyes of all beholders. Even the most beautiful woman ages and loses her beauty. Such a woman, then, is and is not beautiful; she possesses her beauty in a qualified way.

Because of these deficiencies of sensible objects Plato is led to posit Forms, which possess their attributes in an unqualified way. The Form of Large is absolutely large, and the same is true of the other examples. Plato's well-known account of the Form of Beauty in the *Symposium* illustrates this:

First of all, it is ever-existent and neither comes to be nor perishes, neither waxes nor wanes; next, it is not beautiful in part and in part ugly, nor is it such at such a time and other at another, nor in one respect beautiful and in another ugly, nor so affected by position as to seem beautiful to some and ugly to others…but existing ever in singularity of form independent by itself, while all the multitude of beautiful things partake of it in such ways that, though all of them are coming to be and perishing, it grows neither greater nor less, and is affected by nothing. (211a–b)

As is clear in the case of Beauty, Plato views sensible objects as falling short of Forms. In the middle dialogues he generally discusses Forms of qualities that admit of degree. Beauty, for example, can be thought of as representing a standard to which beautiful objects approximate in varying degrees. This is in contrast to a quality such as being a finger, in regard to which some given object either is one or is not. Perhaps some object could be thought of as being like a finger in various respects, for example, in being narrow or straight. But it would seem odd to speak of the object as being and not being a finger, or being a finger to some specified degree. Thus Plato speaks of Forms as representing the highest possible degrees of qualities, to which the attributes of sensible objects only approximate.

Reflecting on the deficiencies of sensible objects, Plato makes the leap we have noted. He argues that sensible objects are not only deficient in how they possess their predicates but in their 'Being' as well. Exactly what Plato means by this is subject to controversy, but the most prevalent view is that he believes the sensible world to occupy a lower plane of existence than the Forms.

There are two ideas here to be sorted out. First, Plato believes that sensible things are somehow dependent on Forms for their attributes. In one context in the *Phaedo* (74a–75a), he describes equal things as 'trying to be like' the Form but falling short. Though nowhere else are Forms described as playing precisely this role, Plato generally maintains that they are responsible for the qualities possessed by sensible things. Taking as our example things that are beautiful, Plato believes that these possess their beauty by virtue of somehow reflecting the Form of Beauty. This relationship of reflection is generally referred to as 'participation'. It is a source of great difficulty for Plato; he was probably never able satisfactorily to explain it (see esp. *Phaedo* 100c–d). In fact, in the *Parmenides*, which was probably written later than the *Republic*, Plato remains undecided about participation and criticizes several ways it could work (*Parm.* 130e–35c; see below, pp. 195–6). But however participation works, it is clear that sensible things possess their qualities by virtue of their relationship to Forms. Each attribute is an imperfect replica of the perfect, unqualified attribute represented by some Form.

Our second point is Plato's view that the dependence of sensible objects on Forms extends beyond their attributes to their Being. The sensible world represents a lower order of Being than the Forms. The full implications of Plato's position is a 'two-world' view. We have the world of the Forms, which truly exists or is truly real, and opposed to this the sensible world, which does not fully exist. The most common account of Plato's view connects his concerns with problems raised by two important philosophical predecessors, Heraclitus and Parmenides.

Plato was deeply troubled by the question of change, probably under the influence of the Heraclitean view that the sensible world is in a constant state of flux. In a well-known passage in the *Metaphysics* (987a32 ff.) Aristotle speaks of this influence. According to two of Heraclitus' famous maxims (both of which are cited by Plato at *Cratylus* 402a), 'everything flows', and 'you cannot step into the same river twice'—because by the time you step again, the waters have changed. Plato takes this mutability of sensible objects to be a sign of inferiority. Because physical objects are subject to decay, they are less real than immutable Forms.

The problem of change connects up with the argument from opposites discussed above. Change qualifies the attributes of things. Nothing sensible is permanent; even the largest tree will eventually die and decay. Thus because of change too the tree is and is not large. Though it is large today (in comparison to certain objects), in the future, when it has decayed, it will be not large (in comparison to comparable objects). Plato frequently expresses the superior status of the Forms by comparing them to what is encountered in waking life, while the stuff of the sensible world is compared to dream images, mere likenesses of what really exists (e.g. *Rep.* 476c–d).

Thus the concerns of Heraclitus led Plato to question the 'reality' of the sensible world. He was probably helped along to this conclusion by the influence of Parmenides as well. Parmenides (of Elea, hence the adjective, 'Eleatic') had argued for an exalted conception of Being. According to him, whatever is is—absolutely. He too appears to have been confused by the different senses of *einai* and was led thereby to conclude that Being must be immutable, timeless, and completely removed from the world of the senses. Plato apparently took over this conception of Being and applied it to the Forms. In an important article, Friedrich Solmsen demonstrates that the description of the Form of Beauty in the *Symposium* shows clear signs of Eleatic influence.[3] Like Parmenides, Plato believed that anything that could be described in qualified terms could not be fully real. As he writes in *Republic* V (479c): 'Can you find a better place to put [such things] than that midway between Being and not-Being?' Only Forms, which bear their predicates in an unqualified way, truly are.

This should suffice to introduce the theory of Forms. Though it is a theory obviously not without difficulties, it should be possible to see how Plato believed that the theory provided answers to crucial questions. He believed it supplied the objective moral standards he sought, and that it explained the ultimate building blocks of the universe. As we see in the next section, he believed that it also answered important epistemological questions.

6.2. SUN, DIVIDED LINE, AND CAVE

In Books VI and VII, Plato illustrates the core of his philosophical system in the three striking images of Sun, Divided Line, and Cave. We begin with the Divided Line, which is central to his epistemological views.

---

[3] F. Solmsen, 'Parmenides and the Description of Perfect Beauty in Plato's *Symposium*', *American Journal of Philology*, 92 (1971).

The major concern of Plato's theory of knowledge, as it bears on his political thought, is to counter scepticism by establishing the possibility of certain knowledge. Plato's problems here are compounded by the fact that his conception of knowledge, like his conception of Being, is exalted. He demands that knowledge be infallible (*Rep.* 477e), and therefore argues that the faculty of knowledge covers only what truly is, that is, the Forms.

The image of the Line is discussed by numerous commentators, and so it is not necessary to recount it in detail here.[4] We can confine our attention to its central features. The Line itself is a vertical line divided into four sections. In each section a different cognitive state is correlated with its own particular objects. The top half represents the intelligible world. Here we have (a) 'understanding' (*noêsis*) or 'knowledge' (*epistêmê*)—Plato uses the terms interchangeably—correlated with the Forms; and (b) 'thinking' (*dianoia*) correlated with mathematical objects. On the bottom half, representing the sensible world, we have (c) 'belief' (*pistis*) correlated with visible things, and (d) 'imagining' (*eikasia*) correlated with images.

The key feature of the Line so far as we are concerned is Plato's view that knowledge and belief have different objects. We concentrate on this, treating its other elements more briefly. Within the sphere of the intelligible world, the inferiority of 'thinking' to knowledge lies in the fact that it makes use of visible images and that it relies on unexamined assumptions. For instance, in geometry, one employs visible representations of such things as triangles and squares, and one also begins with a number of axioms and postulates, which are used in formulating proofs but are never critically examined themselves. Thus thinking is inferior to knowledge, which entails a full consciousness of the assumptions on which it is based.

The inferiority of imagining to belief can also be treated quickly. Briefly, imagining is perceiving appearances, the images or reflections of objects, rather than objects themselves (see *Rep.* 596d–98d). In regard to moral ideas, imagining describes the state of mind of someone who has not thought seriously about such matters and so holds his views simply because he has been told to do so. Such an individual is especially prone to deception and manipulation by masters of persuasion. Thus moving upwardly through the series of stages on the Line leads one gradually from a cognitive condition of completely non-critical acceptance to a condition based on rigorous examination of all one's premises and assumptions.

Plato's correlation of knowledge with Forms and belief with sensible objects requires closer examination. The core of this position, and of Plato's

[4] See esp. R. C. Cross and A. D. Woozley, *Plato's Republic: A Philosophical Commentary* (London, 1964), pp. 203–28; R. Robinson, *Plato's Earlier Dialectic*, 2nd edn. (Oxford, 1953), chs. 10–11; R. L. Nettleship, *Lectures on the Republic of Plato*, 2nd edn. (London, 1901), ch. 11.

epistemology as a whole in the *Republic*, is the doctrine that the things that can be known differ from the things that can be believed. Since only what truly is can be known (*Rep.* 477a), only the Forms are objects of knowledge. The sensible world admits no state higher than belief. Accordingly, Plato depicts the movement from belief to knowledge as an ascent entailing not only a change of cognitive faculty but also a change in objects apprehended. In Plato's only partly figurative language, it is a turning of one's apprehension from the sensible world to the world of the Forms.

There are two striking things about Plato's position. First, it must be emphasized that Plato believes the sensible world cannot be known; it allows no cognitive state higher than belief. The reason for this, as we have seen, is that the sensible world is not fully real. Sensible things are in a constant state of change and possess their attributes imperfectly. Thus they are inferior to what is encountered in the timeless, perfect realm of Forms. As Plato says: 'There's no knowledge involved in these cases' (*Rep.* 529b–c).

The second point is that Plato's view that belief and knowledge have different objects is somewhat odd and flies in the face of most recent opinion. According to most authorities, the development of belief into knowledge involves an alteration of cognitive state, with the object remaining the same. For instance, someone might say that she believes that the three angles of a triangle add up to 180 degrees. By saying she believes this, she implies that she is not certain and could be wrong. Once she has worked through the theorem and is assured her work is correct, she would say she knows this, thereby wishing to rule out any possibility that she is wrong. But throughout this process the object of cognition has remained constant, viz., the theorem that the three angles of a triangle equal 180 degrees.

Plato's view is different, because he holds that the imperfection of the sensible world makes knowledge of it impossible. For example, all triangles encountered in the sensible world are defective. All have lines that are not perfectly straight, angles that are not exact, etc. Thus according to Plato, studying these triangles cannot give one knowledge of triangles. In order to attain knowledge, one must leave the sensible world and turn towards the Form of Triangle. Plato's view finds some support in the fact that geometrical reasoning is readily construed as not being concerned with sensible objects but with the perfect figures that mathematicians posit. However, it is important to bear in mind that for Plato these perfect figures are not intellectual abstractions. The Forms of course exist (in some sense of that word) and are more real than anything encountered in the sensible world. Plato believes that mathematical studies are important because they help to raise the mind from the imperfection of the sensible world to the intelligible realm of the Forms. It is primarily for this reason that mathematics comprises the bulk of the curriculum for the would-be philosophers in *Republic* VII.

Plato's view of knowledge extends beyond the sphere of mathematics to the entire range—whatever it may be (see *Parm.* 135*b–d*), of the Forms. Just as sensible triangles or circles fall short of perfect Forms, so moral actions encountered in the sensible world cannot be perfect. A given action is and is not just, courageous, etc. depending on its relationship to circumstances, on one's point of view, and other factors. Accordingly, the study of human actions can yield only opinion, while the attainment of knowledge involves turning from human actions to the Forms they exemplify. It should be said, however, that what might seem fairly reasonable in the case of mathematics is less easy to defend when its concern is moral knowledge. We return to this in Chapter 9.

One final consideration concerns implications that can be drawn from the points discussed so far. As we have seen, Plato divorces knowledge from sense perception and the sensible world. Knowledge is of the Forms, which can be apprehended only by pure thought. Plato's description of the attainment of knowledge in *Republic* VI is extremely condensed and difficult to interpret. He describes the inquirer as ascending the Line, until, using pure reason aided by the power of dialectic, he reaches the level of the Forms. His journey upwards is described as a process of subjecting his hypotheses to rigorous examination, until he reaches something that is not based on hypotheses. This is 'the first principle of all that exists', which he then uses to confirm the validity of the hypotheses that underlie its other knowledge (511*b*). This unhypothetical first principle should surely be connected up with the Form of the Good. Its apprehension is frequently described in visual terms, often in terms of direct apprehension by the eye of the soul. Such language abounds in the *Republic*. For example, throughout 517*c*–18*d*, Plato speaks of the eye and vision of the soul and seeing the Form of the Good. He brings a number of visual metaphors together at 540*a* in describing the culmination of the philosophers' education: 'You must make them open up the beam of their minds and look at the all-embracing source of light, which is goodness itself'.

As is frequently the case, it is not easy to know how seriously we are to take Plato's language of visual apprehension. This language suggests that Plato views the attainment of ultimate knowledge in somewhat mystical terms, as arising from a kind of revelation. Language of this sort appears throughout the middle dialogues, and in a well-known passage in the *Seventh Epistle*: 'Suddenly like light flashing forth when a fire is kindled, it is born in the soul and straightaway nourishes itself' (341*c–d*). Though there is heated scholarly debate about this point, I believe that the evidence suggests that Plato did view final knowledge as arising from a sudden burst of revelation.[5] It should be noted, however, that the irrationalism this implies is tempered by the fact that the revelation in question is possible to only the gifted few, and only then after many years of intensive study. Evidence that the language of revelation should be taken seriously is discussed below in our account of Plato's doctrine of Eros.

Like the image of the Line, the images of the Sun and the Cave are generally familiar, and need not be discussed in detail.[6] What is most important for our purposes is that both images illustrate how tightly Plato synthesizes his answers to different kinds of questions. As we have noted, Socrates is unable to describe the nature of the Good. Instead, he discusses it by means of an analogy, the sun (507a–8b), which he says is not only like the Good but is actually its 'offspring'. The basis of the analogy is that the Good presides over the intelligible world in the same manner that the sun presides over the visible world. As the sun provides light, which is the intermediary between the eye and its object, so the Good provides the intermediary between the mind and its object, thereby making knowledge possible. As the sun is responsible for generation and growth in the sensible world, the Good is responsible for the very Being of the intelligible world. But as the sun, though responsible for generation is not generation but something higher in dignity and power, so the Good, though responsible for Being is superior to and beyond Being in dignity and power.

Given this exalted account, it is difficult to imagine what the Good could be to merit such a description, a situation made worse by Socrates' refusal to explicate it himself. But Plato's meaning can be surmised as the view, quite simply, that the Good is the goal or end towards which the world is directed. In general Plato's conception of 'good' is closely bound up with the idea of function or purpose. He insists that the universe is not purposeless: it is directed by intelligence, with the Good as its object (see *Phaedo* 97b ff.), although exactly how this works is not clear.[7]

Plato carries this point of view into the ethical sphere, where the Good fulfils its role as a Form. It is by relationship to the Good that other things acquire their value (505a). Good things are good by participation in it, in the same way that other things acquire their attributes by participating in their respective Forms. Plato also says that the Good is the object of all human aspiration.

---

[5] See esp. Robinson, *Plato's Earlier Dialectic*, ch. 10; for a different view, see J. Annas, *An Introduction to Plato's Republic* (Oxford, 1981), ch. 11.

[6] See Cross and Woozley, *Republic*, ch. 9; and Nettleship, *Lectures*, pp. 212–37, 259–63.

[7] A classic account is Nettleship, *Lectures*, ch. 10; cf. Shorey, 'The Idea of Good in Plato's *Republic*', *University of Chicago Studies in Classical Philology*, 1 (1895).

All souls pursue it and perform all their actions for its sake, even though they cannot quite make out what it is (505*d–e*).

The Good is also the supreme object of knowledge. Study of the Good is the greatest study (504*d–e*), but even more, the Good is what makes study possible. It gives the mind the power to know, and objects of study the power to be known. Thus Plato says that it is the cause of knowledge and truth (508*d–e*), and as we have seen, of Being as well. Apparently, the Good is not only the Form by virtue of participation in which things become good, but it also encompasses those attributes by participation in which other Forms acquire their identity as Forms. Since only Forms are objects of knowledge, only the Good makes knowledge possible.

Thus it is clear why the Good occupies such an exalted place in Plato's philosophy. Though Plato's precise views concerning the nature of the Good cannot be determined, it is enough for our purposes to see the kind of role that it plays. We return to the Form of the Good and discuss some political implications of the vagueness of Plato's account, in Chapter 10.

According to the allegory of the Cave, the human condition can be likened to that of prisoners in a cave. The prisoners are bound so that they can see only shadows that pass on a wall in front of them, which are caused by puppet figures paraded before a fire behind them by their unseen captors. The prisoners naturally take the shadows to be real; they value them and contend with one another for preeminence in this shadow world. Plato recounts what happens when one prisoner is freed. Since the ascent out of the cave into the light is painful, he must be dragged along. But gradually he is able to view first the fire, and then the outside world, and finally the sun itself, the cause of all light and of the very existence of the world.

The parable conveys basic metaphysical, epistemological and ethical themes. The prisoners in the cave inhabit a world that is not fully real. Their senses perceive only the shadows cast by objects. Thus to attain knowledge, they must move beyond appearances and penetrate to the genuine objects which the shadows represent, and finally to the sun itself. In terms of ethics too the prisoners are removed from reality. The things they value are worthless apparitions. Should they somehow come to realize this, they would begin to value the reality outside the cave. It is important to note that the prisoners' condition is forced on them. They are of course bound and are manipulated by their unseen captors. They hold false opinions and values because they have been conditioned to do so. The connections with Plato's political theory are readily seen. As the prisoners' upbringing in the cave corrupts them, so being raised and educated in a properly run state can give them true ideas and values, and set them free.

6.3. THE DOCTRINE OF EROS

The theory of the tripartite soul is, as we have seen, introduced in the *Republic* for the purpose of explaining psychological conflict, and it is in this connection that it is most often discussed. However, if we look more closely at Plato's account of the parts as streams of desire, we can see one level at which there is a profound element of unity underlying tripartite diversity. We have seen that each element of the soul possesses a distinctive kind of desire: the three parts are lovers of wisdom, honour, and pleasure or gain, respectively. But they are still parts of one soul. These three desires are viewed by Plato as manifestations of a single psychic force or fund of energy, called Eros, which is directed through different channels towards different objects.

Plato varies his psychological metaphors. As we have seen, in the earlier books of the *Republic* the relationships between different psychical elements are generally described in terms of political conflict, with different elements ruling and being ruled. The interactions here are based on the similar account of relationships between classes in the just state. However, when Plato moves to the virtues based on knowledge in the central books of the *Republic*, he changes his metaphors, and begins to discuss the soul in terms of streams of desire. Though there are some problems in reconciling the different accounts, to a large extent they can be worked into a consistent psychological theory.

The centrepiece of Plato's account of the soul as streams of desire is his doctrine of Eros. 'Eros' is the Greek word for 'love', with a strong connotation of sexual desire. According to Plato, each desire is a manifestation of Eros, while the three kinds of men differ in channelling their love in different ways.

We have seen that, according to Plato's political account of the soul, one part rules over others in political terms. We have called this 'direct rule'. Plato's Eros-teaching is bound up with what we have called 'normative rule', one part's imposing its values on the soul as a whole. This is done by channelling the soul's desires. Plato believes that the fund of psychic energy in a particular soul is stable, and so the normative rule of one part over others is construed as a diversion of the major part of this energy in the direction of the dominant part. No soul is characterized by only one form of desire. Within the soul of each individual are present all three psychic parts and so three divergent streams of energy. Thus a concentration of energy in one direction entails a diminution of the force of other desires. As Plato puts this in *Republic* VI (485*d*): 'And we know that anyone whose predilection tends strongly in a single direction has correspondingly less desire for other things, like a stream whose flow has been diverted into another channel'. In accordance with this principle, the bulk of the philosopher's energy is concentrated on the pleasures of the mind, at the expense of his other desires. Thus 'that person is concerned with the pleasure the mind feels of its own accord, and has nothing to do with the pleasures which reach the mind through the agency of the body, if the person is a genuine philosopher, not a fake one' (485*d–e*).

Plato's Eros-teaching leads to an account of the virtues sharply different from what we have seen. According to the political account of the virtues in Book IV, the better elements in the soul dominate and control the worse, which are depicted as basically distinct from and even hostile to them. The Eros analogy mutes this hostility. The lower parts of the soul are no longer construed as a distinct entity to be opposed and suppressed by a distinct higher part. The emphasis now falls on the fact that they are actually made up of the same stuff as the higher part. Plato argues that the lower parts are composed of energy that is only temporarily diverted to the concerns of the body. It is possible to gather up this energy and focus it on the highest objects of desire, the Forms. Since according to this new account, the energy of the lower parts is capable of being channelled upwards, Plato's emphasis falls on the process of channelling.

The upshot of Plato's Eros-teaching is a doctrine of sublimation, in many respects similar to that of Freud. Plato believes that desire can be withdrawn from the physical appetites and the desires for honour and reputation, and focused upwards. He describes this ascent from different points of view in the *Symposium*, *Phaedo*, and *Republic*. In this section, we examine all three.

According to Plato, one function of education is the upward orientation of desire. In the *Republic* this culminates in the vision of the Form of the Good, as it does in the Form of the Beautiful in the *Symposium*. Since a concentration of desire in the reasoning faculty entails a withdrawal of psychic energy from the lower parts, the soul of the man with knowledge is ordered according to a principle very different from that of the soul with the virtue of correct opinion discussed above. Having this order in his soul, the subject is no longer threatened by those desires that cause unjust behaviour, and so will behave in conformity with the highest standards. The Socratic equation of virtue and knowledge re-emerges here on a higher level. Such an ordering in the soul is a necessary condition for knowledge, and, in a new way, a sufficient condition for virtue.

As Cornford notes,[8] Plato's theory of sublimation differs from Freud's in important respects. Whereas Freud's view concerns the upward orientation of sexual energy, Plato believes that the process works in the opposite direction.

---

[8] Cornford, 'The Doctrine of Eros in Plato's *Symposium*', in *The Unwritten Philosophy and Other Essays* (Cambridge, 1950), pp. 78–9.

Throughout the middle dialogues, Plato argues for the immortality of the soul and a theory of transmigration according to which the soul exists in a pure state only outside of the body. The rational faculty especially is naturally 'akin' (*sungenês*) to the Forms, and only when the soul is incarnated in the body does it develop the lower desires. It follows, then, that when the energy of the soul is withdrawn from these desires, it returns to its original source. In Cornford's words: 'This is indeed a conversion or transformation; but not a sublimation of desire that has hitherto existed only in its lower forms. A force that was in origin spiritual, after an incidental and temporary declension, becomes purely spiritual again'.[9]

According to Plato, full philosophic knowledge requires such a spiritual-ization of desire. Knowledge is possible only if the individual gathers all his psychic energy in the rational part of his soul and focuses it on the Forms, which are both the objects of knowledge and the objects of rational love. Only through such a process can the rational part of the soul return to the condition of natural purity it must have to commune with the Forms.

Plato's most explicit account of his doctrine of Eros is in the great speech Socrates puts into the mouth of Diotima in the *Symposium* (201*d*–12*c*). The emphasis here falls on Eros as a progressively developing kind of love. Diotima defines Eros as a desire for good and beautiful things, a desire to possess them, and to possess them always. Permanent possession can be achieved only through creation. Thus, using the language of birth, she declares that Eros is a 'begetting' of the desired objects. The role of Beauty is facilitation; it makes the delivery easier.

According to Diotima, all men are pregnant in body or soul. When they reach a certain age they desire to beget, a desire that is quickened by the presence of beauty. Immortality is achieved through begetting. Some people, like animals, become immortal through their children. Others live on in their reputations after they have died, while others still, among whom Plato num-bers poets and lawgivers, bring forth works of practical wisdom. And these are only the lesser mysteries of Love.

Diotima's account of the higher mysteries concerns an ascent of the ladder of desire. The initiate begins by loving the beauty of a single beautiful body. From this he comes to realize the beauty of all bodies, and eventually to discover the higher beauty of the soul. From the beauty of souls, he moves on to the forces responsible for this beauty, correct customs and laws. From here he comes to care for the beauty of the different realms of knowledge, and having progressed this far, he completes the journey when the Form of Beauty dawns to him in a sudden vision. The vision of Absolute Beauty works on the

---

[9] Ibid. 79.

initiate to inspire generation. In his case this takes the form of bringing forth true virtue in the souls of others. Presumably he will initiate others on the journey up the ladder of love.

Thus in the *Symposium*, Plato's account of Eros concerns the transformation of desire from love of earthly things to heavenly things, and from the desire to possess beautiful things to the desire to engender true virtue in the souls of others. At each stage of the journey upward, the initiate comes to look down on the objects just transcended. The vision of the Form of Beauty makes him forget gold and fine garments, beautiful boys and other objects of desire. Having reached this stage, he discovers 'that state of life above all others ... in which a man finds it truly worthwhile to live, as he contemplates essential Beauty' (*Symp.* 211*d*).

Eros is not discussed directly in the *Phaedo*, but Plato's theme is closely related—the ascent of the soul from the sensible world to the realm of the Forms. Situating the conversation in Socrates' death cell, Plato depicts death as the liberation of the soul from the prison of the body, and uses this image to symbolize the attainment of philosophical knowledge. Philosophy, he declares, is a preparation for death.

Compared to the psychology of the *Republic*, the doctrine presented in this earlier work is markedly crude and represents the least developed theory found in the middle dialogues. The view here centres on two basic dualisms: body versus soul, and reason versus desire. There is a great divide between reason, which is the faculty of the soul, and desire, which is of the body, with little hint that reason and desire are made up of a single psychological stuff that can be lowered or raised from the one to the other. Thus the view presented here concentrates on the process of purification (*katharsis*), ridding the soul of the taint of corporeality, instead of the transformation of desire, as in the *Symposium*, or channelling the energy of the body into the *psuchê*, as in the *Republic*. Still, the view here is closely related to Plato's fully developed Eros teaching, and probably represents an earlier stage in its development. Thus a brief look at the *katharsis* teaching of the *Phaedo* sheds additional light on the view presented in the *Republic*.

In two early sections of the *Phaedo* (64*c*–69*e*, 78*b*–84*b*), Plato presents a series of arguments to defend his doctrine of *katharsis*. First and most basic, the body poses a distraction to the pursuit of philosophical knowledge. The body not only keeps one busy because of its demands for sustenance, but also fills one with fancies and foolishness, passions and fear (esp. 66*b*–*c*).

Appealing to the distinction between sense perception and knowledge, Plato argues that knowledge is of the Forms, which can be known only by pure reason, disassociated from the body and the senses. He who would glimpse the Forms must employ reason alone, leaving, the senses, indeed the entire body, behind. The body is not only a distraction, but under the influence of bodily desires, individuals come to believe in the reality of the objects of these desires. Drawn to the things of this world, they are unable to raise their sights to the Forms (esp. 83*c–e*).

To these arguments can be added another which centres on the likeness of soul and Forms. Plato argues according to an epistemological principle as old as Greek philosophy itself, that 'like must be known by like'. He establishes a number of factors that the soul and Forms have in common—being invisible, uniform, unchanging (78*b*–80*b*)—and so argues that in order for the soul to know the Forms, it must make itself like them. In order to come as close to knowledge as is possible in this life, the soul must purge itself of the body, though of course full release from the body comes only after death (esp. 67*a–b*).

The kinship between soul and Forms is important, and we encounter it again in the *Republic*. Thus it is worthwhile to quote a passage from the *Phaedo*:

[W]hen the soul inquires alone by itself, it departs into the realm of the pure, the everlasting, the immortal and the changeless, and being akin to these it dwells always with them whenever it is by itself and is not hindered, and it has rest from its wanderings and remains always the same and unchanging with the changeless, since it is in communion therewith. And this is the state of soul called wisdom. (79*d*)

The psychology espoused in the *Republic* is in many ways more moderate and more sophisticated than that of the *Phaedo*. Though the *Republic* is often tinged by the rigid body/soul, reason/desire dichotomies of the earlier view, in this work Plato gives the desires their due and recognizes that they play an important part in human existence. In addition, whereas the *Phaedo* recognizes conflict between reason and desire but depicts this as a conflict between the soul and the body, in the *Republic* Plato locates the desires within the tripartite soul and so is able to give a genuine theory of psychological conflict. What is most important from our point of view is the doctrine, also present in the *Republic*, that a specific ordering of the soul is indissolubly bound up with philosophic knowledge.

As in the *Phaedo*, Plato's argument in the *Republic* is closely associated with the principle that 'like knows like'. The programme of higher education spelled out in Book VII is intended to raise the souls of the Guardians, which are akin to the Forms, to the point at which they can commune with and gain knowledge of them.

The attainment of knowledge requires the education of all parts of the soul. To begin with, the philosopher is a rare individual. He possesses a number of extraordinary qualities, without which the pursuit of philosophy would not be possible (475*b–e*, 485*b–87a*). After undergoing the intensive programme of early education, he is subjected to the programme of studies described in Book VII. This higher education is intended to raise the part of his soul that is akin to the divine until it can grasp the divine itself. The goal is expressed in the following passage:

[A] genuine lover of knowledge innately aspires to reality, and doesn't settle on all the various things which are assumed to be real, but keeps on, with his love remaining keen and steady, until the nature of each thing as it really is in itself has been grasped by the appropriate part of his mind—which is akin to say, the part which is akin to reality. Once he has drawn near this authentic reality and united with it, and thus fathered intellect and truth, then he has knowledge; then he lives a life which is true to himself; then he is nourished; and then, but not before, he find release from his love-pangs. (*Rep.* 490*a–b*)

The goal of education is to raise the soul from the objects of opinion to the realm of true Being and the Forms. We have seen that the ascent is depicted as the elevation of desire in the *Symposium*, while the *Phaedo* emphasizes its negative aspects, purging the soul from the taint of corporeality. In Book VII of the *Republic*, Plato discusses this almost entirely from the intellectual angle. The programme of studies to be followed by the philosophic initiate is spelled out in detail. Through a series of increasingly abstract disciplines— arithmetic, geometry, astronomy, solid geometry, harmonics, and dialectic (521*c–35a*)—the soul of the initiate is prepared to grasp the truth. Plato connects this programme with the similes of the Sun, the Divided Line, and the Cave. As the prisoner in the cave is freed and prepared through stages to look on the sun, the philosopher's studies lead him to see the Form of the Good.

Having seen the Good, the philosopher possesses the external signs of knowledge. He is able to give a verbal account of the Good, indeed to take on all comers in debate and respond to all their questions (534*b–c*, 531*e*). But of course knowledge of the Good is much more. It conveys insight into the teleology of the universe as a whole.

This is the knowledge on which the perfect virtue of the *Republic* is based. Such knowledge must inevitably result in perfect conduct. In the soul of the philosopher, the conflict between reason and desire is obviated, since a particular ordering of the psychic energy that is desire is an essential requisite to achieving knowledge of the Good. The ascent to the Good is not a purely intellectual process; it is identical to the ascent of the ladder of love in the *Symposium*, and so involves the education of desire as well.

Plato does not envision *nous*, the rational faculty of the soul, as we envision 'reason'. As we have said, this is also a desire, fully on a par with other desires, and an overly intellectualistic account of it is misleading. Though the programme of higher education presented in the *Republic* might appear to be an ordinary course of university studies, it should be realized that underlying the psychology of the *Republic* is the Eros-teaching of the *Symposium* and the mysticism of the *Phaedo*. In the *Republic*, as in the *Phaedo*, the regimen of the philosopher is founded on the kinship between his soul and the Forms, and it is intended to bring his soul into contact with them. To do this is to realize in full the natural potential of the *psuchê*. As in the *Phaedo*, Plato argues that the true nature of the soul cannot be seen while it exists in combination with the body. In *Republic* X he writes that, because of the contamination of the flesh, the soul is marred and disfigured. In itself it is a pure passion for wisdom. Should we wish to see its true nature, we should 'consider what it is related to and the affiliations it desires, given that it is of the same order as the divine, immortal, and eternal realm. And we should consider what would happen to the mind if the whole of it allowed this realm to dictate its direction, and if this impulse' raised it from an earthly form (611*e*–12*a*).

Because in this life the soul is invariably found in a carnate state, the energy of its passion for wisdom is diffused throughout the body and its passions and desires. But through withdrawal from the desires of the body, the individual can gather up this dispersed energy and approach the purity of his prenatal existence. The highest manifestation of the soul found in human life is that of the philosopher. Being naturally akin to the divine, he is able to regain a divine order in his soul: 'So because a philosopher's links are with a realm which is divine and orderly, he becomes as divine and orderly as is humanly possible' (*Rep.* 500*c*–*d*).

Within such a soul true justice is found, and the Socratic equivalence of virtue and knowledge achieves its Platonic fruition. Needless to say, Platonic virtue is different from the Socratic kind. Whereas the Socratic theory envisions the knowledge that is virtue as practical knowledge—knowledge that will tell us how to live—the fully evolved Platonic theory centres around the notion that the philosopher's knowledge of and communion with the divine make him like the divine and so begets a perfect virtue. Not only does the philosopher possess a knowledge far more exalted than the Socratic kind, but because his desires are focused on the Forms, he cannot be unjust according to common moral standards.

Thus, the virtue of the philosopher is composite, resting on perfect knowledge and a perfect order in his soul. Knowing the Forms, loving their Beauty and focusing the bulk of his psychic energy on them, he possesses a virtue in comparison to which that accessible to the mass of mankind is indeed a poor imitation.

7

Moulding Souls

In spite of the important differences between the virtues of the auxiliaries and rulers, there are strong similarities. Both are bound up with harmony between the parts of the soul. In both classes this is implanted through intensive early education, while the superior psychological condition of the rulers is superimposed upon this order through the higher studies described in *Republic* VII. Plato also holds that both types of virtue are founded on subordination of the appetites. In the souls of the auxiliaries, this is accomplished through political means. The appetites are forcibly suppressed by an alliance of the spirited and reasoning parts. In the souls of the rulers conflict between the parts is largely overcome by the normative rule of reason, as the energy of their appetites is drawn up and focused on the Forms. Plato's position in the *Republic* is that the virtue and happiness of all three classes require that their appetites be carefully controlled.

It is seen in this chapter that Plato's views concerning the appetites provide the transition between his moral psychology and political theory. Plato's position is based on two main propositions. First, he believes that the appetitive life is empty and horrible. He also believes that this is the life most people pursue, and that to live well they must be turned in other directions. The second proposition is that people are not able to free themselves from the domination of appetite without outside help. Plato's psychology of appetite affords the necessary counterpart to the psychology of virtue discussed in the last two chapters, and so the problem that his political theory is designed to solve. In examining various unjust souls and the obstacles to making them just, we see the necessity for the ideal state and the rationale for its most distinctive features.

Throughout the middle dialogues, Plato's low opinion of the appetites is in keeping with the overall thrust of his psychology. As we have noted, he believes that the soul is immortal, that it exists outside the body after death. The soul exists in its pure state only when it is discarnate, while in this world it appears 'maimed by its association with the body' (esp. *Rep.* 611*b*–12*a*). We have seen that Plato emphasizes different aspects of this doctrine in different dialogues. In the *Phaedo* he stresses the fundamental conflict between body and soul. The view in the *Republic* is more moderate, an outlook that can be attributed largely to the important distinction between necessary and unnecessary desires introduced in *Republic* VIII. The necessary appetites are those 'we're incapable of stopping', those 'whose satisfaction is beneficial to us', while the unnecessary desires are those that 'can be dispensed with (given training from childhood onwards) and whose presence certainly does no good, and may even do harm' (558*d*–59*a*). The distinction boils down to an opposition between the appetites necessary for biological life and those pursued for the sake of pleasure. Needless to say, Plato's attitude towards the unnecessary desires is hostile. Something of the *Phaedo*'s rejection of the body survives in the *Republic* in his opinion of these, and in his antipathy towards the 'lawless' desires, which 'wake up while we're asleep' (571*b*–*d*).

Plato is, however, willing to accept the necessary appetites. At the close of Book IX, he illustrates his main conclusions concerning justice by describing a composite creature, like the legendary Chimera, which is divided into three parts, corresponding to the three parts of the soul: an inner man, who represents the reasoning part; a lion, which stands for spirit; and a beast with a ring of many heads, 'of both wild and tame animals', which stands for appetite and includes the distinction between better and worse, necessary and unnecessary appetites. Throughout the extended simile, Plato regards the appetitive part as a whole with loathing. It is referred to as 'the most vicious part' (589*d*), 'the beastlike parts' (589*d*), 'the most ungodly and disgusting part' (589*e*). It is imperative to bring it under control, and this is the function of justice (590*a*). But even as the appetitive part as a whole is subordinated, the necessary appetites are cared for. Plato says that, through justice, the inner man will 'tend to the many-headed beast as a farmer tends to his crops—by nurturing and cultivating its tame aspects, and stopping the wild ones growing. Then he can ensure that they're all compatible with one another, and with himself, and can look after them all equally, without favoritism' (588*e*–89*b*). Thus, according to this passage, not only are certain desires of the beastlike part to be tolerated, but they are actually to be supported and promoted. Though nowhere else in the *Republic* does Plato duplicate this degree of approval, it is clear that in it he recognizes that under the control of reason the appetites have a legitimate role.

But even if Plato is willing to tolerate certain appetites, the virtue of all classes rests upon appetite's careful control. Plato's position is constructed around three distinctions. First, though he accepts the necessary appetites, he is unwilling to accept the unnecessary ones. Second, Plato distinguishes acceptable and unacceptable pleasures. Appetites are admissible in so far as they are necessary for life, but are to be shunned as sources of pleasure. On the whole, Plato believes that only intellectual pleasures are worthwhile. He opposes physical pleasures, regarding them as harmful to psychic order.

Finally, Plato does not believe that the things people enjoy are necessarily good for them. He distinguishes what people desire (or think they desire) from what they really desire, and is willing to extirpate the former for the sake of the latter.

7.1. THE TYRANNY OF APPETITE

In the *Republic*, Plato presents a series of reasons why the appetites must be suppressed. Put rather simply, they are incapable of giving their pursuers real or lasting satisfaction; they cause conflict between people; and they destroy the harmony of the soul.

Plato illustrates the futility of trying to attain happiness through physical pleasure in the 'myth of the water-carriers' in the *Gorgias* (493a–d). He likens the appetitive part of the soul to a leaky jar. The leakiness expresses the fact that the appetites are impossible to fill. In fact, whoever tries to fill them does so by carrying water in a sieve that also leaks. The leakiness of the sieve pertains to pleasure-seekers' souls, for the pursuit of appetite breeds thoughtlessness as well. The upshot of such a life is endless toil and futility, coupled with the pain of unsatisfied longings.

The points made here are elaborated upon in *Republic* IX, where Plato attempts to demonstrate that the just life is not only better than the unjust, but is also more pleasant. Plato argues that physical pleasures are not 'real', because they are bound up with the satisfaction of appetites (583b–85c). We can call such pleasures 'state-related', since to enjoy them, or to enjoy them intensely, the individual must be in a state of want, with his appetites demanding to be satisfied. Because such states of want are painful, Plato argues that the pleasures associated with satisfying appetites are primarily enjoyable as releases from pain. They only seem pleasant in comparison to the pains that precede them. Plato's example is a sick man who would describe health, the release from pain, as the greatest pleasure. States of pleasure and pain exist on opposite ends of a continuum, with a neutral state of quietude between them. The devotee of physical pleasure mistakes the move from pain to quietude for pleasure, while this is actually relatively not absolutely pleasurable.

Several consequences follow from this conception of physical pleasure. First, according to this account, the pleasures of the body are recurrent, but only as releases from recurrent pains. The gourmand experiences alternating states of hunger (and so pain) and replenishment (and so quietude, which he mistakes for pleasure), with the pattern endlessly repeating itself. The extreme form of such a life is vividly described in the *Gorgias* (494c) as constantly itching and scratching, with the scratching taken to be pleasant because it momentarily relieves the pain. Plato believes, moreover, that the appetitive part of the soul is a beast that grows through ministration. This makes the demands of appetite ever harder to satisfy, the pains more intense, and the pleasures more illusory. And so Plato's view of the life of physical pleasure is well illustrated in the image of the Cave. Lovers of pleasure indeed chase shadows, and do so because they have always done so. Knowing nothing of life outside the cave, they mistake their shadow world for reality.

Plato draws important connections between the physical and intellectual aspects of the appetitive life. The *Phaedo*'s image of the body as a prison expresses something he takes seriously. According to the *Phaedo*, the individual whose life is spent attempting to satisfy bodily urges is fooled into believing that the objects of his desires are real (82*d*–*e*). In other words, the devotee of physical pleasure accepts the release from pain as pleasure because he is constantly beset by pain. His appetites have grown fierce and strong through a lifetime of indulgence. As soon as they are satisfied, they begin again to clamour for attention, and he begins to long for their release. Though the life of physical pleasure is actually unpleasant, the individual is prevented from achieving the detachment from the constant press of appetite required to realize this.

According to Plato, the pleasures of philosophy are different. They are pleasant absolutely in comparison to a state of painful deprivation, but only someone who has freed himself from the press of appetites can know this. In *Republic* IX, Plato says that the person who pursues these pleasures fills the part of himself that is more real with things that are more real (585*d*). This language expresses the fact that the intellectual appetites are capable of lasting satisfaction, as the intellectual faculties are capable of development. The pleasures of philosophy are not state-related. To enjoy them one need not be besieged by appetites, and so they are not accompanied by the intellectual distortions brought on by physical appetites. Because they are not accompanied by recurring pains, they allow the individual an intellectual grace period to turn his mind to other things.

Not only are intellectual appetites capable of lasting satisfaction, but their objects of desire are superior as well. The Forms of course are timeless and indestructible. They offer a permanent source of replenishment, which is not available to seekers of physical pleasure, who consume their objects and constantly require replacements. In order to attain the new objects their appetites require, individuals are forced into conflict with one another (esp. *Phaedo* 66*c*). Since Forms, unlike the objects of physical desire, cannot be appropriated, they cannot cause such conflict. In fact, in so far as they have an effect, it would be cohesive; the joys of intellectual pursuits increase as one engages in them with like-minded others.

A final respect in which the appetites play a destructive role is in their implications for psychic harmony. This is the basis for the *Republic*'s central argument concerning the superiority of justice to injustice. Plato argues that psychic harmony is found only in souls ruled by reason, while psychic harmony is even more necessary than health for happiness. He supports this position by comparing the harmoniously ordered, just soul of *Republic* IV with the four factious, disordered, unjust souls encountered on the cycle of cities and souls in Books VIII and IX. Plato argues that all the unjust souls are alike in (*a*) being dominated by some lower form of desire and in (*b*) being racked by conflict and disorder. The connections between (*a*) and (*b*) lie in the inability of appetites to look beyond their own satisfaction. When one of these comes to rule the soul, it blindly pursues its own object of desire, denying and suppressing conflicting urges. As we move down the ladder of souls and corresponding states—from timarchy, to oligarchy, to democracy, to tyranny—the psychic element in control becomes lower—from spirit, to the necessary appetites, to the unnecessary appetites, to the loathsome appetites, with each level revealing a greater degree of discord than the one preceding. In discordant souls, order is maintained through force. Thus, as the just city and soul are characterized by the consent and cooperation of all parts, the unjust forms are racked by faction and sedition, as suppressed urges struggle for release.

7.2. THE CONTROL OF APPETITE

Having seen various ways in which appetites cause problems, we turn to the question of remedies. The solution to the disharmonious ordering of appetitive souls is found in the just souls discussed in Chapters 5 and 6, especially the soul with the virtues of correct opinion. In order for unjust souls to be made just, clearly their appetites must be controlled.

Plato's position draws upon connections, between the goals different souls pursue and how they are ruled. In order to explicate this, we must introduce some terms. We say that a soul is ruled 'factiously' (or is 'factious') if the normatively ruling element looks only to itself, and 'holistically' (or is 'holistic') if it grants all parts proper satisfaction. As we have noted, Plato holds that the normative rule of the appetites—and generally of spirit too—is factious, in contrast to the normative rule of reason, which is holistic. This contrast is important because Plato holds that holistic rule is necessary for happiness. In factiously ruled souls, the elements that are denied must be forcibly suppressed. They cry out for satisfaction, while the soul as a whole is racked by misery and strife. In the oligarchic soul, for example, all other urges are sacrificed to the obsessive pursuit of wealth. An individual of this type cannot think of anything but money and making money; he has no shame where money is concerned; he finds enjoyment in nothing but money. The longings of his unsatisfied urges keep him constantly in pain.

In the soul of the philosopher, however, harmony reigns, as all desires receive proper satisfaction. The contrast is spelled out at length in Book IX:

> Shall we confidently state that, where avarice and competitiveness are concerned, any desire, which succeeds in attaining its objective will get the truest pleasure available to it when it is guided by truth, which is to say when it follows the leadership of knowledge and reason in its quest for those pleasures to which intelligence directs it? ... It follows that when the whole soul accepts the leadership of the philosophical part, and there's no internal conflict, then each part can do its own job and be moral in everything it does, and in particular can enjoy its own pleasures, and thus reap as much benefit and truth from pleasure as is possible for it. (586d–87a)

Plato's position depends upon granting the normative rule of reason the benefit of the several doubts. Offhand, there seems to be little reason why the philosopher could not be as obsessed with the pursuit of wisdom as the oligarch is by wealth. Indeed, the absent-minded professor, whose mind is always on his work, is a familiar type. But Plato believes that this will not happen. Because reason is not only a desire for knowledge and truth but is also the faculty that judges, an individual normatively ruled by reason will judge more accurately than other individuals and so will understand the importance of psychic harmony. He will make sure that all parts of his soul receive satisfaction.

Since souls under the normative rule of appetite are not governed in this way, an individual in such a condition must somehow change his life before he can be happy. His appetites must be tamed in two related but different ways. First, his ruling passion must be moderated to make room for other concerns. Its demands must become less insistent, allowing other legitimate urges to be recognized, and thereby permitting temperance and harmony to reign. Plato's view here is in keeping with the traditional Greek ideal of *mêden agan*, 'nothing to excess'—the idea that moderation in all things is essential to happiness. Though individuals who are normatively ruled by appetite are not capable of the supremely blessed life of the philosopher, balance and harmony can afford them a condition that is far superior to what they would otherwise have.

Appetites must also be tamed by being subordinated to the direct rule of reason. As we saw in Chapter 5, this means that certain appetites must renounce satisfaction; others must postpone it. The connection between the two ways that appetites must be tamed lies in the fact that the stable political structure found in the just soul cannot emerge unless all parts receive proper satisfaction. A situation in which spirit and the appetites are willing to follow the lead of instrumental reason entails that instrumental reason upholds a moderate, harmonious plan of life. And so according to Plato, the narrow, one-sided existence of appetitive men must be shunted aside in favour of moderation. Through the pursuit of more rounded lives, individuals will introduce balance and harmony—and so health and happiness—into their souls. They will care for all legitimate urges, thereby becoming temperate as well, and so insuring the ability of instrumental reason to chart a successful course.

Thus, Plato believes that most individuals are not able to plan their lives effectively. Because they are dominated by appetite, they come to lose all sense of proportion. They devote their lives to satisfying narrow urges and can think of nothing else. Moral propriety and shame are swept aside. Their ethical views are taken over, and they come to regard behaviour as moral or honourable only in so far as it promotes their desired ends. Moreover, because their souls are torn by faction, their specific appetites are constantly in rebellion, undermining even the pursuit of their unbalanced lives.

Plato describes the way most people live as follows: 'They're no different from cattle; they spend their lives grazing, with their eyes turned down and heads bowed towards the ground and their tables. Food and sex are their only concerns, and their insatiable greed for more and more drives them to kick and butt one another to death with iron horns and hoofs, killing one another because they're seeking satisfaction in unreal things for a part of themselves which is also unreal' (586a–b). The main features of the appetitive life as described throughout this chapter are compressed in this image.

7.3. MOULDING SOULS

In order to rescue individuals from the appetitive life, Plato believes that they must be brought up and educated in the ideal state. Plato's position on the possibility of reform is best seen by contrasting it with two other views. On the one hand, we have the view that the lower class of individuals are devoid of reason. This is of course an extreme view, according to which these people are hardly human. Since this view exaggerates the differences between people, we will call it the 'strong inequality' view. It holds that the souls of the lovers of wisdom are pure reason, those of lovers of honour pure spirit, and those of lovers of pleasure pure appetite (above, p. 79). It should be clear, however, that Plato did not subscribe to this view. It has been seen in

Chapter 5 that Plato believes that all individuals have rational faculties and so both the capacity to reason and the potential to reflect the psychic structure seen in *Republic* IV. Still, this view expresses something Plato takes seriously, to which we will return.

The other view, which stands closer to the liberal political tradition, can be referred to as the 'equality view'. This holds that all individuals are equal in important respects, especially in the ability to attain an important level of competence. Though this need not imply that all people are intellectually equal, it does hold that they are generally the best judges of their own interests and should be as free as possible to conduct their lives as they wish. Plato of course does not believe this to be the case. He does not believe that the majority of people know what is good for them, and so in this respect he stands closer to the strong inequality view.

Plato's position can be located between these views. He believes on the one hand that most people are capable of achieving at least some rationality, but also that individuals fall into the three great groups, lovers of wisdom, honour, and pleasure. Only individuals dominated by the love of wisdom are capable of attaining the perfect virtue of the philosopher; other individuals must be content with the virtues of right opinion. Plato holds, however, that even these lesser virtues are beyond the reach of most individuals unless they are helped. Though one might assume that, since individuals possess instrumental reason, they should be able to manage their own lives, Plato does not believe that this is the case.

Plato holds that individuals normatively ruled by appetite have their intellectual faculties taken over. Such individuals cannot ordinarily make proper moral decisions. As we have seen, they mistakenly believe that their objects of desire are real. Apparently, they are also prone to miscalculation (*Rep.* 602*a*–3*d*), and blunder in their choice of plans of life. Though these individuals would be able to reason effectively if they could somehow escape the press of appetite, this potential remains unfulfilled.

Accordingly, Plato's view is in important ways similar to the strong inequality view. Though all human beings have the potential to be rational and independent, most have souls dominated by appetites, which prevents them from realizing this potential. Therefore, some means must be devised to subdue their appetites. If such individuals are left to themselves, they will develop into the cattle-like beings described above.

Plato's belief in this unmet potential suggests a distinction that is of great importance for his political theory. Believing that most people are not happy though they wish to be so, Plato concludes that the things they desire (or think they desire), things that gratify their inflamed appetites, differ from what they really desire—things that will make them happy. We can call things people think they desire their 'empirical interests', and what they really desire their 'real interests'.

Plato discusses the discrepancy between empirical and real interests in various contexts. For instance, this seems to be the sense of his remarks in *Republic* VI that all souls pursue the Form of the Good and do whatever they do for its sake. Plato says that, unfortunately, people do not clearly perceive the Good, and so are unable to hit the mark, though they know it is there (506*d–e*). In the *Gorgias* we find a similar distinction between a person's deepest wish, *boulêsis*, and inferior desires (467*b*–68*e*). *Boulêsis* is a desire for real happiness, as opposed to the appearances people confuse with it. Only someone who pursues his real interests does what he wishes (*ha boulontai*), while other people do instead what seems best to them (*ha dokei autois beltista*). Such apparent goods as political power are not actually beneficial unless they are used well. Power is only a means to the attainment of various ends. It will be beneficial only if the ends it provides are actually good and do not only seem so. Thus, Plato says that the tyrant does not really have power—taking power as the ability to get what one really wants, things that are genuinely good. Instead, the tyrant does only what seems good to him. In Book IX of the *Republic*, this brief sketch is filled in. Having shown that the tyrant's soul is dominated by a mad, overpowering lust which he is able neither to satisfy nor to control, Plato says that the tyrant is hardly ever free to do 'what he wishes'— again using the language of *boulêsis* (577*d–e*). The tyrant uses his power to gratify inflamed desires, under the mistaken opinion they have induced that this will make him happy.

The political implications of the distinction between real and empirical interests are bound up with the idea that one can benefit another individual by treating him in some fashion that goes against his existing wishes. Plato's position here has ramifications concerning a number of issues central to his political theory, which are discussed throughout Part III. For now, to close out Part II, we must explain how the distinction can be used to justify coercion.

Though the distinction between real and empirical interests can easily justify the use of force, force is not necessarily in order. Granted a situation in which an individual has real interests that diverge from his empirical ones, it is possible to bring him onto the right track without using force, but only if his real interests can readily be seen. Consider a case of this sort. The subject is about to step onto an unsafe bridge, as discussed by J. S. Mill, in *On Liberty*.[1] If a good Samaritan were to stop him and explain the condition of the bridge in a convincing manner, he would realize that his desire to cross the bridge was based on faulty information. He really wishes to travel by some other route. In

---

[1] J. S. Mill, *On Liberty*, E. Rapaport, ed. (Indianapolis, IN, 1978), p. 95.

this case what the subject really wishes boils down to what he wishes when he possesses complete information.

In this instance, the divergence between the subject's real and empirical interests need not lead to constraint, because the divergence is sufficiently clear-cut and the subject is sufficiently receptive and rational to enable him quickly to see where his real interests lie. I believe that Socrates' non-advocacy of coercion rests on the assumption that people's moral disabilities are of this sort. In general, force will be deemed necessary in those cases in which the subject is not readily able to grasp the disparity in his interests, while the form coercion takes depends on the nature of his inability. Thus, if a second individual is in more imminent danger of stepping onto the bridge, the good Samaritan may have to tackle or otherwise forcibly restrain him. Force is justified under these circumstances, because other means are not adequate. In this particular case, the constraint would be of brief duration. On being told about the bridge, the second subject would also realize his true interests.

A more difficult case might concern an individual who is delirious as he starts towards the bridge. Assuming that this subject is incapable of grasping the nature of the bridge's structural defects until he recovers, the good Samaritan would surely be justified in forcibly preventing him from crossing it until he is in a condition to see where his true interests lie. Presumably, when this third subject is able to understand the problems with the bridge, his desire too will change, and he will be grateful to the Samaritan. In this case what the subject really wants is what he wants when he has recovered from his delirium as well as when he has complete information.

The second and third cases involve what we can call 'retroactive consent'. Though circumstances necessitate the use of force, when each individual is able to understand these circumstances, he is grateful and agrees that force was justified. Although the second and third individuals cannot consent to being constrained before the fact, in each case circumstances would have them granting their consent after force had been used.

The kind of case Plato has in mind is more complex. It is close to our third case, but with a crucial difference. We have seen that when the third subject recovers from his delirium he is able (*a*) to understand the nature of the situation, (*b*) to bring his desires into accord with the actual circumstances, and (*c*) retroactively to consent to the force used against him. What sets Plato's view apart is that in his eyes individuals whose empirical interests diverge from their real ones must be subjected to an intensive process of education and conditioning before they can realize this, and so before they can move on to (*b*) and (*c*). As we have seen, Plato believes that individuals whose souls are normatively ruled by appetites are subject to intellectual distortions, and are unable to realize where their true interests lie. Since Plato also believes that the mature moral character is not easily remoulded, the subject's appetites can be tamed only if education begins when he is still young and unformed. Accordingly, the mass of people in existing societies are incorrigible. Ironically, because this is so, the question of coercion does not arise in regard to them. Since it would be pointless to attempt to force them to be free, Plato does not recommend doing so. The mass of the incorrigibles have no place in the ideal state. The only force used against them is that required to drive them from the newly acquired state. As Plato says at the end of *Republic* VII (541*a*), all individuals over the age of 10 will be driven from the city. This will leave the philosopher-rulers free to work on properly educating the young.

The aim of moral education in the ideal state is the inculcation of harmony. Even if the majority of people can never become philosophers, they are capable of living balanced, moderate, well-ordered lives. If they can be educated properly, their appetites can be tamed and their reasoning powers imbued with correct opinions. If they can be brought to understand the importance of moderation and harmony, their reasoning parts can rule their souls holistically instead of factiously. When they are convinced of the importance of psychic harmony, they will strive to keep their appetites in place and to refrain from injuring others. They will know that each crime committed to gratify appetite causes them unhappiness in the long run. And so after extensive education, people will come to understand their real interests. They will approve retroactively of the force used against them, thereby making further force unnecessary.

Accordingly, Plato holds that the main task of rulers who wish to promote the real interests of their subjects is moral education and conditioning. Their job is to purge appetites and to mould souls—harmonizing them by leading instrumental reason to rule securely and to rule holistically. Such shaping is of course the central function of Plato's ideal state, given over to its system of education. These aspects of Plato's political theory are examined in the next chapter. For now we should note that in the *Gorgias* and *Republic*—and in the later dialogues—Plato describes the role of the ideal ruler in these terms. In the *Gorgias*, the end of philosophic politics is 'to make the citizens' souls as good as possible' (*Grg.* 503*a*). Because the virtue of anything is a matter of regular and orderly arrangement (*Grg.* 506*e*, 503*e*–4*a*), the politician must order the souls entrusted to him according to the dictates of truth. He is literally a craftsman of souls, analogous to a painter, a builder, or any other craftsman, and the end he has in view is the harmony that is virtue (*Grg.* 503*d*–4*a*). Above all, the virtue of the soul is temperance, and to achieve this the citizens must be weaned from the life of insatiate licentiousness. So long as any soul is in such a state—'thoughtless, licentious, unjust, and unholy'—the desires responsible for this condition must be combatted; only those desires that make men better should be gratified. Throughout the pursuit of his task, the end the true politician seeks is clear: 'How justice may be engendered in the souls of his fellow citizens, and how injustice may be removed; how temperance may be bred in them and licentiousness cut off; and how virtue as a whole may be produced and vice expelled' (*Grg.* 504*d–e*).

The politician is also a moulder of souls in the *Republic*. Here, as we have seen, Plato's emphasis falls upon shaping the souls of the young, freeing their reasoning faculties from the press of appetites, and eventually enabling them to preside over well-balanced lives. Because the majority of people are incapable of attaining this order without outside help, such help must be given. Plato explicitly states these points in *Republic* IX in an important passage from which we quote. He says that, in order to ensure that the ordinary individual achieves a psychic condition reflecting that of the philosopher, he must be enslaved to the philosopher: '[W]e're not suggesting ... that his status as a subject should do him harm; we're saying that subjection to the principle of divine intelligence is to everyone's advantage. It's best if this principle is part of a person's own nature, but if it isn't, it can be imposed from outside, to foster as much unanimity and compatibility between us as might be possible when we're all governed by the same principle' (590*d*). Through the agency of the philosophers, the subject's appetites will be tamed. The political ordering of Book IV will be constructed in his soul. Once this has been achieved, he will be able to pursue a balanced existence, and so to live happily. The political theory of the *Republic*, then, is largely based on training the young: '[T]his is the function of law: this is why every member of a community has the law to fall back on. And it explains why we keep children under control and don't allow them their freedom until we've formed a government within them, as we would in a community. What we do is use what is best in ourselves to cultivate the equivalent aspect of a child, and then we let him go free once the equivalent part within him has been established as his guardian and ruler' (*Rep.* 590*e*–91*a*).

And so, having given an account of the conception of virtue upon which the *Republic* is founded, we can move on to discuss the means through which Plato believed this ideal could be put into practice. But before we turn to the workings of the just city, we should note important problems in the account of justice on which the *Republic* is based.

7.4. THE BENEFITS OF JUSTICE

As noted at the beginning of Chapter 5, the main inquiry of the *Republic* is initiated by Glaucon and Adeimantus, who request that Socrates explain the nature of justice and how it pays. By the end of Book IV, justice has been defined, and Plato proceeds to demonstrate its superiority to injustice. His main argument employs the analogy between city and soul to demonstrate that the just city is superior to the four unjust cities—timarchy, oligarchy, democracy, and tyranny—and that the analogous just soul is superior to the four corresponding unjust souls. This demonstration is carried out in Books VIII and IX, and is supplemented by the additional considerations concerning the nature of pleasure we have seen (pp. 107–8).[2]

The two problems with Plato's argument are as follows. First, although in the dialogue much is made of problems in defining justice, the participants in the discussion have clear ideas about what justice is. In presenting their case for injustice, Glaucon and Adeimantus provide a definite account of the nature of justice and injustice as commonly understood, which builds on the similar account of Thrasymachus, in Book I. As they present it, justice is most clearly seen in the kinds of behaviour it rules out. As Glaucon's account of the social contract and the ring of Gyges illustrates, justice is abiding by the rules that prohibit one from taking advantage of other people; injustice is violating these rules, and so abusing other people for the sake of one's own gain. Recall Glaucon's claim that anyone else with the power of Gyges would take whatever he wanted from other people, have sexual relations with whomever he wanted, kill whomever he wanted (360a–b). Such actions epitomize injustice, while refraining from them, is justice. The speeches of Adeimantus and Thrasymachus present similar views. There is a strong element of common sense in this conceptualization of justice and injustice, which largely corresponds to beliefs in contemporary society, and, one could surmise, in most societies. For ease of reference, we can refer to justice construed along these lines as 'conventional justice'.[3]

The problem is that the justice Plato discusses in Book IV and claims to be superior to injustice is far removed from this. The conventional understanding locates justice and injustice in how people *behave*. Injustice is taking advantage of other people, justice refraining from doing so. However, in the definition of

---

[2] For the third argument, based on the superior ability of the reasoning soul to judge true pleasures, see *Rep.* 580d–83a.

[3] The position of Thrasymachus is clear on this point in his second main speech (343a–44c), although not as clear in his first; on differences between the two speeches, see esp. J. Maguire, 'Thrasymachus ... or Plato', *Phronesis*, 16 [1971]). The positions of Glaucon and Adeimantus might not appear to be entirely consistent, as they speak of justice as something 'within the soul' (358b, 366e). However, the context makes clear that this and similar locutions are equivalent to what justice itself *does to the soul*, as opposed to the consequences of reputation; see esp. 367c–d, 358a. For full discussion, from a different point of view, see D. Devereux, 'The Relationship Between Justice and Happiness in Plato's *Republic*', *Proceedings of the Boston Area Colloquium in Ancient Philosophy*, 20 (2004).

justice that Socrates develops, the focus shifts from how a person acts to his psychological state: 'Its sphere is a person's inner activity: it is really a matter of oneself and the parts of oneself' (443c–d). For ease of reference, we may refer to this as 'psychic justice'. While Glaucon and Adeimantus challenge Socrates to demonstrate that it pays to refrain from abusing other people, his response is that it pays to have a certain psychic condition. So has he actually answered their question?

This problem has attracted enormous attention. The impetus was an article by David Sachs, 'A Fallacy in Plato's *Republic*', originally published in 1963.[4] But the controversy has largely died down. Scholars now generally believe that, although Plato does not address the question directly, a satisfactory answer can be surmised from his discussion.[5]

In order for Socrates to present a satisfactory response, he must clarify the relationship between just and unjust conduct and their corresponding psychological states. He must explain how the quality of justice is possessed by and only by people whose behaviour is conventionally just, that people who commit unjust acts will not possess this condition, and that people with the necessary psychic qualities will not commit injustice.

Briefly, Plato's position turns on two psychological facts. First, he believes that injustice is caused by uncontrolled appetite. As we have seen, it is because of their appetites that people violate social norms and impinge upon the interests of others. The Greek word *pleonexia*, literally 'having more than', is central to the common conception of injustice as behaviour in violation of social norms (see *Rep.* 359c). He who is unjust in the conventional sense takes more than his share, which he must do by taking from other people. The kinds of behaviour that Glaucon describes as unjust are undertaken to gratify appetites. The second point, again as we have seen, is that one's psychic condition is affected by conduct. In particular, feeding one's appetites makes them larger, stronger, and more difficult to control. Thus, indulging appetites forces greater indulgence in the future, while he who controls his appetites weakens them, thereby strengthening reason and making possible a balanced, holistic way of life (esp. 588e–89a; see above p. 106). In Book IV, Plato describes just actions as 'conduct which preserves and promotes this inner condition' that constitutes justice (443e–44a). Both just and unjust behaviour are self-reinforcing. An account of the benefits of psychic justice implicitly responds to Glaucon and Adeimantus, because a person with the requisite qualities will

---

[4] D. Sachs, 'A Fallacy in Plato's *Republic*', *Philosophical Review*, 72 (1963); rpt. in *Plato II*, Vlastos, ed. (Garden City, NY, 1971).

[5] As Guthrie says, the connections are clear 'in light of the *Rep.* as a whole' (W. K. C. Guthrie, *A History of Greek Philosophy*, 6 vols. [Cambridge, 1962–81], IV, 475 n. 1).

be just in the sense they have in mind, while unjust conduct does not pay, because it undermines psychic justice.

Even if we grant that Plato has a response to this problem, we should recognize that, from the perspective of contemporary ethics, his position is objectionable in not sufficiently recognizing other people. This is the second problem. The central argument of the *Republic*, that justice is beneficial to the individual who practises it, is far removed from contemporary notions of justice, which include duties to be concerned with the interests of other people, without regard to whether this benefits ourselves. To a large extent, Plato's position reflects the overall cultural divide between ancient Greece and modern Western society. This subject is too large to discuss here. Very briefly ancient Greek ethics is generally eudaimonistic. Virtue is viewed as worthy of pursuit primarily because of its contribution to the *eudaimonia*, the happiness, or more exactly, the 'flourishing' of the virtuous person.[6] The modern attitude is epitomized in Immanuel Kant's injunction to treat other people as ends in themselves, and not merely as means. Kant presents this as the duty of a rational agent, as opposed to something one should do because it is beneficial to oneself.[7]

Granted the distance between Plato's and our societies, it would be anachronistic to expect Plato's view of justice, or those of other ancient Greek thinkers, to conform to modern standards. However, in certain respects, aspects of Plato's view approximate the modern conception. This side of Plato's moral theory too is not explicitly worked out, which is an indication of the relatively insignificant role modern conceptions of ethical duty play in his moral thought. But he appears to have in mind something that verges on a modern conception of duty.

The position we can ascribe to Plato is rooted in distinctive aspects of his conception of reason, especially as fully developed in the philosophic soul. As we have noted, in addition to functioning as a calculative faculty (*logistikon*), reason is a desire for knowledge and truth. Dominated by reason, the philosophic nature is in love with 'everlasting reality'. Reason is a passion for 'reality as a whole', and so philosophers 'will not willingly give up even minor or worthless parts of it' (485*b*). To use the words of John Cooper, part of what Plato understands by reason is a desire 'to advance the reign of rational order in the world as a whole'.[8]

---

[6] A. W. H. Adkins, *Merit and Responsibility* (Oxford, 1960), esp. pp. 2–3; a recent attempt to qualify this view is N. White, *Individual and Conflict in Greek Ethics* (Oxford, 2002).

[7] I. Kant, *Groundwork of the Metaphysic of Morals*, H. Paton, ed. and trans. (New York, 1965).

[8] J. M. Cooper, 'The Psychology of Justice in Plato', *American Philosophical Quarterly*, 14 (1977), 155.

In recounting the ascent of the ladder of love in the *Symposium*, Socrates describes how the initiate acquires a desire to create beauty, described more precisely as a desire to give birth in the beautiful (*Symp.* 206c–7a). In people with proper understanding, this manifests itself as desire to promote virtue in others. When one glimpses the Beautiful itself, one desires to give birth not to 'illusions but true examples of virtue, since his contact is not with illusion but with truth' (*Symp.* 212a). We are able to surmise that it is a desire such as this that leads the prisoner freed from the Cave to return, to attempt to free his former fellows. Presumably, it was such a desire that moved Socrates to spend his life attempting to waken his fellow citizens, while (as we see later) the philosopher in the just city is similarly motivated to embrace the task of ruling, although he would prefer not to (pp. 144–5) Plato's account of motivation by reason is not fully developed. Once again, the fact that he devotes little or no direct attention to a disinterested conception of virtue is evidence of his overall lack of concern with a conception along Kantian lines. Moreover, even if we grant these implications of the fully developed reason of the philosopher's soul, this kind of motivation is peculiar to philosophers. The great majority of other people, not driven by reason in this exalted sense, would presumably not recognize such duties to other people. It is possible that we could ascribe to Plato a related but lesser conception of this other-regarding virtue as working in the souls of other people. This would be along the lines of the virtues of correct opinion—as compared to virtue based on knowledge— which ordinary people possess. But this is a topic Plato does not discuss, again indicating his lack of concern with the ethical virtues in this sense.

Part III

Platonic Politics

8

Education and Moral Reform

Having seen the conception of virtue Plato wished to bring into existence, we turn now to the means through which he believed it could be realized. As we have seen, the means Plato advocates in the *Republic* represent the rejection of the very different means relied on by Socrates in the earlier dialogues. Since Socrates' belief that people could be persuaded to become virtuous rested on the inadequate, intellectualistic psychology of the early dialogues, once Plato moved to the psychological views discussed in Part II, he could no longer uphold Socrates' position on moral reform. Of course in the *Republic* we find a sharply different view. The task of moral reform is given to the philosophically run state and is its most important function.

The political theory of the *Republic* centres on the ideal state constructed in the work. As is frequently the case, Plato's discussion appears to be somewhat haphazard, with different aspects of the state receiving vastly different degrees of attention, not always in regard to their apparent importance. Since Plato's treatment of the state is formally subordinate to the inquiry into justice that shapes the work, some peculiarities are readily explained. But the state's presentation is still in many ways remarkably sketchy. It is doubtless a testament to Plato's philosophical and literary brilliance that the state he describes numbers among the most influential such constructions in the history of political thought, though it is presented in such a way that Aristotle, his pupil for seventeen years, was able to misunderstand some of its central features (*Politics*, II, chs. 2–5).

Most discussions of the political theory of the *Republic* focus on its institutional structure. This is not surprising in light of the distinctive features Plato's state contains. Its major institutions are based on the principle of specialization, on the three classes staying in place and doing their own jobs, with the rulers ruling, aided by the auxiliaries, and the producing class excluded from political affairs altogether. Other outstanding features are the community of property and of the family prescribed for the two classes of guardians, and the highly structured system of education, controlled by the philosophers, which shapes the state's intellectual life. These institutions are of course important and will be discussed in the next chapter. This chapter will be given over to the system of education.

The seriousness with which Plato regards education, especially early education in poetry and the other arts, is seen in the sheer amount of attention he
gives it. While community of property is run through in a few paragraphs at
the end of Book III, various matters concerning education in the arts dominate
large portions of Books II, III, and X. As we see, the state as a whole is largely
structured around its educational system, and its other features are tailored
to allow the educational system to work. Plato holds that only if the state
performs the crucial task of education properly can it succeed.

Commentators have long noted the importance of education in the ideal
state. Rousseau characterized the Republic as 'le plus beau traité d'éducation
qu'on ait jamais fait'.[1] It has also been observed that Plato uses education
to perform many tasks often thought to be non-educational. As Friedlander
says, 'in the Republic, almost the whole subject of legislation is replaced by
education'.[2] Jaeger agrees: 'Paideia [education] was for [Plato] the solution
to all insoluble questions'.[3] In the *Republic*, education is the means through
which moral reform is accomplished.

For Plato, like Socrates, the aim of education is to improve the subjects'
souls. But because of the distance that separates Platonic and Socratic psychological theories, the Platonic conception of 'caring for the soul' is far
removed from that of Socrates. Platonic education is primarily a moulding
of souls. As we have seen, Plato holds that the virtue of anything, including
the soul, 'is a matter of regular and orderly arrangement' (*Grg.* 506e). It is
the function of education to produce such order, which is a necessary condition for the virtue based on correct opinion and a necessary precondition
for the virtue based on knowledge. Whereas Socrates, who views the soul
as basically rational, sees education as a wakening of thought, Plato believes
education to be concerned as much or more with the non-rational elements
as with the rational. For Plato, early education, the only stage the majority of the population experiences, concerns the soul before it is capable of
reason.

8.1. EDUCATION IN THE ARTS

In order more securely to grasp Plato's views on education, it should be
helpful to isolate and examine some of his basic assumptions. First, Plato
holds that the human soul, especially the young, undeveloped soul, is highly

[1] J. J. Rousseau, *Emile*, Book I; in C. E. Vaughan, ed., *The Political Writings of Jean Jacques Rousseau*, 2 vols. (New York, 1962), II, 146.

[2] P. Friedlander, *Plato*, 3 vols., H. Meyerhoff, trans. (Princeton, NJ, 1958–69), III, 92.

[3] W. Jaeger, *Paideia*, 3 vols., G. Highet, trans. (Oxford, 1939–45), II, 236.

malleable. Plato of course holds that there is an unbridgeable gulf between the intellectual capabilities of different types of people, and that the orientation of desire is determined at birth and cannot be changed. Within these limits, however, people can be shaped. Such questions as whether an individual lives badly or well, and whether he lives happily or unhappily are decided by his upbringing.

Plato stresses early education so heavily because he believes that the soul is most malleable early in life. As an individual develops, his character becomes set. In Plato's words: 'The most important stage of any enterprise is the beginning, especially when something young and sensitive is involved. You see, that's when most of its formation takes place, and it absorbs every impression that anyone wants to stamp upon it' (*Rep.* 377a–b). In reading the *Republic*, it is well to bear in mind that by the time of the *Laws*, Plato's view in this direction had evolved to the point at which he insisted on beginning the process of education before birth, by requiring that pregnant women undertake specified exercises (*Laws* 789a ff.; see below, p. 222). Thus in the *Laws* as in the *Republic*, great emphasis is placed on conditioning the very young: 'Because of the force of habit, it is in infancy that the whole character is most effectually determined' (*Laws* 792e).

A second assumption is that the young character is shaped in a particular way. Throughout his voluminous discussions of education, Plato says little about direct teaching. He concentrates instead on the importance of making sure that young minds are directed properly. The reason for this is found in a well-known passage in Book VII (518b–d). Plato says that education is not providing the soul with something that was not there already, like putting sight into blind eyes. Rather, the soul possesses the ability to see from birth; the task of the educator is to direct its gaze. Education is the art of 'turning around' the soul from darkness to the light.

We saw in Chapter 4 that Plato believes the environment plays a crucial role in shaping character. His discussion of education explains how this works. Briefly, Plato views the mind as an active, probing force, which responds constantly to its environment and is attracted especially to aesthetic creations. Plato is somewhat unusual among political philosophers in the extent to which he believes artistic products affect the soul. Probably no other important political philosopher had as much respect for art, while the political implications are apparent: if art is so powerful, it must be carefully controlled. It is not surprising to see a large portion of the *Republic*—and a smaller though still significant percentage of the *Laws*—given over to regulating the arts.

A third basic assumption is Plato's belief that early education, the period of training that determines the overall course of development, is primarily education of character. The educator's concern during this process is mainly shaping the desires, rather than developing the reasoning capacities. This view is in keeping with the overall thrust of the moral psychology of the middle dialogues, especially Plato's view that a certain ordering of the soul's non-rational elements is a necessary prerequisite for proper employment of the rational. Accordingly, the main concern of early education is developing the preconditions of reason, rather than reason itself.

Plato introduces his programme of early education in connection with the training of the future Guardians. He says nothing about education of the lowest class, though as we see, we are probably justified in reading some programme for this purpose into the state. In examining the substance of the programme Plato does present, it is well to keep in mind that it is for the guardians, as this influences some of its features. However, since Plato wishes to raise the lower class to some semblance of the virtue of the auxiliaries, it appears that their programme of education would be roughly similar.

The programme outlined by Plato is divided into two components: *mousikê* and *gumnastikê*, commonly translated as music and gymnastics. *Mousikê*, however, covers a wider field than 'music'; it includes all arts presided over by the Muses. Thus Grube's suggestion, 'education in the arts', is preferable.[4] The meaning of *gumnastikê* is probably best expressed through the translation 'physical training'. Though one would assume that this would be pursued for the sake of the body, as education in the arts is for the soul, Plato holds that physical training too has the soul in view (410*b*–*c*). This will be discussed below.

The intended goal of early education as a whole is the virtuous soul described in Book IV. Thus, its main concern is forging the alliance between reason and spirit needed to keep appetite in check, while as we have seen, the four virtues are described as different aspects of this overall psychic structure. Plato's emphasis falls especially heavily on shaping the spirited part to temper its natural harshness and break it to the will of reason. The aim is to harmonize the two parts, 'for those two aspects of our nature to fit harmoniously together by being stretched and relaxed as much as is appropriate' (411*e*–12*a*). In Book IV Plato uses the simile of dyeing. The souls of the guardians are not only inculcated with correct beliefs, but they must be conditioned to retain them, like wool which is treated to retain its dye (429*d*–30*b*). Thus early education is designed primarily to impart correct convictions, and to make sure they stick, through the harmonization of reason and spirit.

In the light of our discussion in the last few pages, it is apparent that Plato's approach to education in the arts does not rely heavily on what we would term aesthetic considerations. There can be little doubt that Plato was

---

[4] G. M. A. Grube, trans., *Plato: The Republic* (Indianapolis, IN, 1974), p. 46, n. 12.

deeply affected by works of art. According to ancient tradition, he at one time aspired to be a poet and to have his plays performed. But then he met Socrates and decided to pursue the higher music of philosophy (DL III, 5). Still, evidence of Plato's poetic gifts abounds in the dialogues, which perhaps testify to an unparalleled combination of philosophical and poetic brilliance. An additional indication of Plato's susceptibility to art is his belief that it is such a potent force. But regardless of any feelings of this kind, Plato discusses art in the *Republic* from an almost entirely political point of view. He sees it as a powerful force with great potential for good or for ill, and is therefore anxious to make sure it is used for good. Throughout the *Republic*, art is discussed almost entirely in the light of its social consequences. Perhaps a flicker of Plato's dissatisfaction with this is seen in Book X (607*b*–8*b*), where he grants poets and other lovers of poetry the opportunity to rebut his charges (below, pp. 179–80). Should they prove that traditional poetry is a constructive force, he would gladly welcome it back. But until poets can prove this, most poetry must be expunged from the state, and the other arts are treated similarly.

The bulk of Plato's account of education in the arts is given over to poetry. This is largely explained by the place poets occupied in Greek society. Their position can be roughly described as unofficial moral teachers, as is attested to by repeated references to poets and their works by characters in Plato's dialogues. For instance, in *Republic* I, Polemarchus takes his proposed definition of justice, 'giving each what is owed to him', from Simonides (331*d*–*e*). Similarly, Cephalus supports his observation that the physical desires wane with age by referring to an anecdote concerning the aged Sophocles(329*b*–*c*). Homer in particular was a potent educational force. His works occupied a position in Greek society somewhat analogous to that of the Bible in modern Western society, and accordingly Plato devotes substantial space to direct criticisms of the *Iliad* and *Odyssey*. He analyses numerous specific passages, all of which are seen to be familiar to Socrates and his interlocutors.

Plato begins by discussing the beliefs poetry conveys. He argues, basically, that the very young are impressionable and so easily misled. Since beliefs formed at this age are not easily altered, great care must be taken to ensure that they are consistent with the beliefs that should be held in later years. Since stories and tales, that is, the works of poets, are important vehicles for imparting early beliefs, their contents must be monitored. They should not lead the young to draw harmful conclusions, for example that the gods are responsible for evil or change their shapes in order to deceive. Similarly, stories should not depict evil prevailing over good or heroes behaving in unseemly ways. Death should not be presented as something to be hated or feared, as such a belief would detract from the courage of future warriors. In short,

Plato believes that beliefs that do not promote the overriding interests of the state should not be allowed to develop. Since the works of traditional poets, including Homer, would induce such beliefs, they must be censored.

Having completed his account of the belief-content of poetry, Plato raises the question of whether the guardians should be 'imitative'. The Greek word *mimêsis*, generally translated as 'imitation', refers to artistic representation in general. In the immediate context it is used in reference to performing arts. Plato carefully distinguishes narrative and imitative poetry. In the former, the poet speaks in his own voice; in imitative, he assumes the voices of his characters. Since Greek poetry was generally recited aloud, in imitative poetry the reciter would throw himself into different characters and deliver their speeches with the appropriate affectations. In Greek society, certain individuals known as 'rhapsodes' presented dramatic recitations as a profession. In the *Ion*, Socrates' interlocutor is such an individual, who describes the extent to which he takes such characterization: 'Whenever I recite a tale of pity, my eyes are filled with tears, and when it is one of horror or dismay, my hair stands up on end with fear and my heart goes leaping' (*Ion* 535c).

Plato's concern in Book III is whether the guardians should take part in recitations of imitative poetry. In Book X he returns to the question of imitation, addressing whether the populace should attend imitative performances as spectators. Plato's arguments in the two contexts are similar and may be treated together.

In Book III Plato argues against allowing the guardians to perform, because of the effects this would have on their characters. Plato defends his position by appealing to the principle of specialization. For a guardian to imitate characters outside the range consonant to his position would be for him to engage in work other than his own (394e–95d). Plato's real concern, however, is the effects this would have on the guardian's personality. In simple terms, Plato believes that imitation has lasting effects; something of what one imitates stays with one. Thus for the guardians to act the part of disreputable characters, or even gods and heroes behaving unworthily, would be to increase the chances that they would behave similarly on some future occasion. As Plato puts this:

They should imitate people who are courageous, self-disciplined, just, and generous, and should play only those kinds of parts; but they should neither do nor be good at imitating anything mean-spirited or otherwise contemptible, in case the harvest they reap from imitation is reality. I mean, haven't you noticed how if repeated imitation continues much past childhood, it becomes habitual and ingrained and has an effect on a person's body, voice, and mind. (395c–d)

Similar considerations weigh against attending recitations at which inferior natures are imitated (esp. 604e–6d). As one watches characters yielding to their emotions, one's own emotions are affected. The audience surrenders to the feelings conjured up onstage and believes those poets are best who most successfully evoke such responses. But again, the effects on the audience are harmful. Surrendering to such feelings strengthens them, making them more difficult to control in real life.

Plato's discussion of imitation is regarded most favourably if it is borne in mind that he refers primarily to its effects on the very young. In the movie *A Double Life* (1948), Ronald Colman plays an actor who, as a result of playing Othello countless times, becomes like Othello, and eventually murders his wife, who plays Desdemona in the same production. While this sort of phenomenon is obviously caused by some deep psychic disturbance, Plato's case is probably more in line with normal psychology. It is because the young are impressionable that imitation has so potent an effect on them. Plato's preoccupation with poetic recitation is rather removed from the concerns of our society. But something of his outlook is shared by many modern psychologists, who decry the effects of television watching on children, especially in connection with watching violent shows. One could easily imagine that the effects would be stronger if children, instead of merely watching, repeatedly acted out violent episodes. Plato's view, then, is that by forbidding such forms of imitation—or attending performances of works that include such imitation—undesirable effects can be avoided, while the repeated exposure to and imitation of virtuous conduct will promote patterns of behaviour of the opposite sort. Thus imitative poetry will be discouraged in the state; permissible poetic works will rely heavily on narrative. Plato's discussion of imitation undoubtedly pertains to tragedy and comedy as well as poetic recitations, and so drama is treated similarly. In general, the guardians will be free to assume the roles of and to watch only good men behaving virtuously. Plato is aware that his policies might make for dull performances (604*e*), but again, aesthetic considerations are heavily outweighed by considerations of social utility.

Similar austerity governs the selection of musical modes. Only particular modes are permitted—only those that imitate the conduct of good men in various circumstances (399*a–c*). In talking of 'imitation' in reference to music, Plato undoubtedly switches to the wider sense of the term, using it to signify artistic representation in general. But it is not easy to see how musical matters, including permissible instruments, imitate good and bad characters. Music is generally considered to be a far more abstract medium than poetry, which is able to describe and to reproduce people's words and deeds. In any event, only simple musical modes are permitted, and only simple musical instruments: the lyre, the cithara, and shepherd's pipes (398*b*–99*e*). To settle the question of poetic rhythms, Plato appeals to the authority of Damon, a current expert on music and meter. Whatever Damon says about these matters will be enacted (400*a*–*c*). In sum, then, the elements of acceptable musical compositions must be 'fine speech, fine music, gracefulness, and fine rhythm'—'all adapted to a simplicity of character' (400*d*–*e*).

The principles that govern the selection of proper poetry and proper music are applied to other forms of art as well: painting and other artistic works, weaving, embroidery, and the making of furniture (401*a*). Plato holds that all these media are able to imitate good and bad characters. Again, exactly how this works is not clear, while Plato runs through these media in only a few sentences without explaining it. Perhaps his point is simply that there is a close relationship between harmony, beauty, and proportion in all artistic creations, which are in turn related to corresponding human qualities. We have seen (above, pp. 74–5) that the virtues of the soul are described in terms of order and harmony, while, significantly, Plato employs the analogy of music in his account of justice.

Despite any difficulties we might have with specific details, Plato's overall position is clear. Since the soul assimilates itself to its environment, the environment must be made as beautiful and harmonious as possible. Plato sums up his concern as follows:

We must look for craftsman who have the innate gift of tracking down goodness and grace, so that the young people of our community can live in a salubrious region, where everything is beneficial and where their eyes and ears meet no influences except those of fine works of art, whose effect is like a breeze which brings health from favorable regions, and which imperceptibly guides them, from childhood onward, until they are assimilated to, familiar with, and in harmony with the beauty of reason. (401*c*–*d*)

Thus early education in the arts harmonizes and orders the soul. It seems clear that such training does not directly produce virtue. Rather, it conditions the soul to facilitate virtue's future development. Since, as we have seen, correct moral opinions can develop only in a correctly ordered soul, education in the arts prepares the soul to receive correct opinions, as in the highest class the virtue of correct opinion prepares the ground for the perfect virtue based on reason. Thus, operating on a pre-rational level, such education lays the groundwork for rationality:

A proper cultural education would enable a person to be very quick at noticing defects and flaws in the construction or nature of things. In other words, he'd find offensive the things he ought to find offensive. Fine things would be appreciated and enjoyed by him, and he'd accept them into his mind as nourishment and would therefore become truly good; even when young, however, and still incapable of rationally understanding why, he would rightly condemn and loathe contemptible things. And then the rational mind would be greeted like an old friend when it did arrive, because anyone with this upbringing would be more closely affiliated with rationality than anyone else. (401e–2a)

Early education plays so important a role in Plato's political theory that we should pause and examine some of its implications. It is clear that the eventual aim of the process is to achieve the virtuous soul recounted in Book IV. As we have seen, the virtuous soul is founded on an alliance of reason and spirit, which combine to keep appetite in check. We are able to unravel the basic process through which this alliance is formed.

We have seen above that the range of phenomena covered by spirit centre on one's sense of self and one's wish that others share one's own view. Education in the arts plays a crucial role in shaping that conception. The young child identifies deeply with the poetic characters he encounters and performs; he is similarly affected by the other art of the state. All these influence the way he comes to see himself. Through constant identification with heroes, the young guardians come to see themselves as heroes. Because they are strongly motivated by the desires of their spirited parts, they care deeply about their self-images and behave in accordance with them. Thus Plato's view is in keeping with the familiar notion that military virtue is closely bound up with conceptions of military honour, which are in turn rooted in deeply held convictions concerning how proper soldiers behave.

The direction in which spirit is shaped is clear. From the first stages in the construction of the state, Plato couches the question of educating the guardians in terms of harmonizing the two sides of their characters, the gentle or wisdom-loving, and the high spirited (374e–76d). Spirit is of course necessary if they are to be courageous warriors—the purpose for which they are originally introduced—and so possession of this is one criterion used in their selection. But if they are too high-spirited, they will be overly harsh and brutal, and a danger to the very charges they are to protect. Thus the problem is to temper spirit and make it obedient to reason. The natural tendency towards anger and violence seen in aggressive natures must be transformed into determination and resolve. The image of the hero with which the young guardians are imbued is that of someone who adheres to his convictions under all circumstances. An appropriate example from American history is Nathan Hale, who regretted that he had only one life to give to his country, rather than Achilles, who cared more for his personal honour than for the success of the expedition against Troy. Before the guardians are able to reason, the exploits of appropriate gods and heroes are related to them; soon they are acting, the parts of such characters in dramatic recitations, while the other arts affect them less directly. By these means the young guardians are indelibly dyed with the appropriate views. Through long and constant exposure, their natural aggressiveness becomes the virtue Plato calls courage.

The contribution of such education to the virtue of right opinion should be noted. As we have seen, artistic media are used to condition the soul, before the subject is capable of reason. Through stories and other media, the child is made accustomed to images of virtue and vice, and led to love the one and despise the other. Thus, during his earliest years, the young guardian has a conception of virtue stamped on his soul. As he grows older this attraction to the desired moral type is cemented over with corresponding moral beliefs, and his virtue comes to be actually rooted in opinions. At this stage a true alliance between reason and spirit holds, as the subject is led to hold convictions that coincide with his image of the desirable moral type.

This particular alliance between reason and spirit represents a sophisticated level of virtue. The guardian's virtue is rooted in more than blindly held convictions. Throughout his life he will be able to relate his conduct to a definite moral ideal, and to determine how he should behave under various circumstances by referring to that ideal. So, rather than possessing a rigid code of right and wrong, he is directed by a vivid conception of a virtuous being, to the high standards of which he shapes his own conduct. His virtue falls short of knowledge mainly in his inability to present a reasoned defence of his moral ideal.

Plato's own writings offer strong evidence of the power exerted by a suitably crafted image of virtue. Through his own imitative powers, brilliantly realized in the dialogue form, Plato has left us in Socrates one of the foremost virtuous characters in the world's literature. It is interesting that in doing so Plato departs somewhat from his own recommendations concerning imitation. For while he says that suitable poetry will not imitate varied types of characters, and will certainly not imitate undesirable types, the dialogues are filled with all sorts of characters, frequently several different types in a single work. Some of Plato's most vivid characters, moreover, are of precisely the kinds forbidden in the ideal state, for example Thrasymachus in the *Republic* or Callicles in the *Gorgias*. Callicles especially is so brilliantly realized that he has left a permanent mark on the history of philosophy, influencing the views of Nietzsche among others.[5] In fact, so vividly is Callicles depicted that several scholars have argued that he must be drawn from a side of Plato's own nature that had been forcibly repressed.[6]

[5] See E. R. Dodds, ed., *Plato: Gorgias* (Oxford, 1959), Appendix: 'Socrates, Callicles and Nietzsche', pp. 387–91.

[6] For example, J. B. Skemp, ed. and trans., *Plato's Statesman* (London, 1952), p. 29; Jaeger *Paideia*, I, 324; cf. W. K. C. Guthrie, *A History of Greek Philosophy*, 6 vols. (Cambridge, 1962–81), III, 106–7.

Though, as we have noted, Plato worries that the imitation of good men might prove somewhat dull, he manages to get around this problem in his depiction of Socrates by again stretching his own strictures. Though stories told in the ideal state must not depict the triumph of evil over good, or good men suffering while bad are rewarded, the central drama of the dialogues is the unjust persecution and death of a good man. Socrates is so arresting a character largely because of what happens to him, and how he conducts himself through trial, imprisonment, and death. Plato's presentation of Socrates is a permanent model of indomitable courage and faith.

Plato could defend his portrayal of Socrates' death on the grounds that it is not a case of good being defeated by evil. According to the deepest tenets of Socratic morality, subscribed to by Plato as well, death is not a great evil, and it is worse to do evil than to suffer it. These views are defended vigorously in the *Apology*, *Crito*, and *Gorgias*. But still, the martyrdom of Socrates and the emotions this evokes are crucial to Plato's dramatic technique. As a natural dramatist, Plato is thoroughly aware of the importance of dramatic tension. A work like the *Gorgias* owes its considerable dramatic power to the fact that Callicles resists Socrates' impassioned appeals, though by allowing Callicles to do so, Plato perhaps makes the *Gorgias* unacceptable in the ideal state. Plato is well aware that contrast, tension, is essential to successful drama. The subject matter of imitations permitted in the ideal state allows a certain amount of this (see 399a–c). But one wonders if this is enough. Plato has the utmost faith in art's power to attract, but one wonders if the state's art will preserve this power, if it is so tightly regulated that it degenerates to the banalities of Socialist Realism. This is an aspect of education in the arts that Plato has not adequately addressed, while in his own works he—perhaps instinctively—stretches the bounds of what is allowed in the state.

8.2. PHYSICAL TRAINING

Having discussed education in the arts at length, we will spend far less time on physical training. Plato devotes comparatively little space to this and does not discuss the details of his programme. He does make it clear that this kind of training is designed to produce soldiers, not athletes; it should train men who will be able to endure the rigours of military campaigns under a wide variety of conditions.

Plato says that physical training should parallel education in the arts in simplicity and moderation. Luxury and excess are to be scrupulously avoided; the guardians are to do without the pleasures of the flesh, be they Syracusan cuisine or Corinthian women (404c–d). This abstinence fulfils the important function of helping to curb their appetites, bringing them firmly under the control of reason and spirit. Plato's general emphasis falls on the fact that physical training is not conducted primarily for the body, but is designed to influence the soul. We have seen that education in the arts is intended to temper spirit, to harness it to the will of reason. Physical training has something of the opposite function; it is to strengthen spirit. If individuals engage too heavily in this, they become harsh and rigid. Their tempers flare up at the slightest provocation (411*b*–*c*), and they come to hate both reason and the arts. They are lost to the ways of persuasion and try to have their way in everything through force (411*d*–*e*). But unless they possess highly spirited natures, they are not suited to their role as guardians.

Though the specific connections in Plato's argument are not developed, the overall point is clear. The guardians must have their spirited parts tempered by education in the arts and subordinated to reason, but they must not be soft. As warriors, they must possess courage and resolve in high measure, and so they must be naturally endowed with the characteristics associated with the martial virtues, which can be carefully tempered by proper education to yield the virtuous soul described in Book IV. The main concern of Plato's discussion of physical training is to stress the importance of having these.

As far as chronology is concerned, Plato sets aside the two or three years before the twentieth birthday for physical training. He says that this is to be a period of physical exertion, with little attention given to intellectual training, since exercise and sleep are the enemies of study (537*b*). Plato's proposals here are similar to Athenian practice, which provided for compulsory military service between the ages of 17 or 18 and 20. Thus early education is to last until the age of 17 or 18, to be followed by physical training. Those who are chosen to be rulers will follow these studies with ten years devoted to mathematics, and then five more of dialectic. Their education is completed by fifteen years of political and administrative work in the city, before, at the age of 50, they are raised up to glimpse the Form of the Good. These matters will be discussed in the following chapters. It should be borne in mind, however, that the philosophers are the exceptions. The formal education of the majority of guardians is complete at the age of 20.

The virtue of the auxiliaries is instilled through the programme of education we have examined. The combination of education in the arts and physical training harmonizes their souls, anchoring correct opinions, secure from opposition. Since for most auxiliaries this is the highest virtue that can be attained, for them moral reform begins and ends with habituation and conditioning.

The situation is probably similar in regard to the lowest class, but because Plato does not discuss them, we cannot be sure exactly what he has in mind. It seems probable that members of this class will be raised to some facsimile of the virtue based on correct opinion. Whatever level of education they experience and, indeed, merely living in the properly ordered ideal state will impose this degree of harmony on their souls. In Book X, Plato describes a man 'who had lived . . . in a well-ordered city, and had been virtuous by habit without philosophy' (619c). It is inconceivable that any inhabitant of the ideal city would be inferior to this kind of man in regard to virtue.

What we can be sure of is that, with the exception of the philosophers, the inhabitants of the ideal state receive the virtue of which they are capable through conditioning. Their souls are cared for through state-controlled education, which has little to do with their rationality. Here we see the full magnitude of Plato's shift from the Socratic view of moral reform. While Socrates envisioned a collectivity of free, autonomous souls, with each individual seeking for himself the knowledge that is virtue, Plato sees a tightly controlled city of people having virtue imposed on them from without. In the ideal state, only the philosophers possess moral autonomy, and even in their case this is possible only because they too are subjected to rigorous conditioning in their youths. Thus an important portion of the Socratic ideal has been left behind.

Plato has not, of course, abandoned all facets of Socrates' ideal. Like Socrates, Plato would accomplish reform through education, and as is also true of Socrates, the result would be to improve the subjects' souls. But in light of the differences between their conceptions of education and their views of the soul, it hardly seems that the two are talking about the same thing when they discuss 'moral reform'. The major reason for this is, of course, the fact that Plato was forced to reject the Socratic conception of the *psuchê* and to replace it with his own far more complex psychological theory. In doing this, Plato was forced to reject some basic presuppositions of Socrates' moral mission.

As we have seen in Part I, Socrates views knowledge as the result of a process of weighing and sifting arguments in order to discover the best possible *logoi*. He has a definite conception of knowledge only in so far as he requires that the holder of knowledge possess certain external signs—that is, that he be able to give an account of the matter, not contradict himself, etc. Because Socrates believes that moral knowledge lies beyond the capacity of the human soul, he has an undeveloped conception of such knowledge and believes basically that all individuals are alike in being unable to attain it. It is largely as a result of this conception of knowledge that Socrates is able to believe that all people are fundamentally equal. Again, because moral knowledge is beyond the reach of everyone, all are equal in terms of what they know.

Plato of course has a far more developed epistemology. The Forms are the only objects of knowledge and can be known only through an application of mental capacities beyond the reach of most people. Only the highly gifted few are able to glimpse the Forms, and only then after years of intensive study. Throughout the dialogues, Plato tends to obfuscate the gulf that separates his conception of knowledge from the Socratic. He stresses the important role of Socratic-type question and answer in the ascent to the Forms—though it is difficult to find a sound basis for this position.[7] Plato also insists that the recipient of knowledge manifest the external signs of Socratic knowledge, that is, that he be able to give a verbal account of the matter without contradicting himself. But these somewhat anomalous sources of continuity cannot hide the fact that Platonic knowledge is sharply different.

Because of the epistemology of the middle dialogues, Plato is led to abandon Socrates' egalitarianism. If knowledge is accessible to the philosophic few, these few must rule in accordance with their exclusive truths. Even more striking than the three-class system into which Plato divides the state, is the division into two groups that also pervades the *Republic*. We have one group able to attain perfect virtue, and a much larger group that is not. To achieve whatever virtue is open to them, people in this second group must be subjected to intensive conditioning and indoctrination. In this sense, the members of the two lower classes are subordinated to the philosophers. They lack the ability to achieve virtue themselves, and so the foundation for the absolute rule of philosopher-kings is laid.

It is important to realize the extent of the gulf that separates these two groups. In the ideal state we have the rulers and the ruled. At one point in the *Republic*, Plato goes so far as to call the latter *douloi*, slaves. They must be enslaved to the philosophers, while the reason for this has been seen: 'Subjection to the principle of divine intelligence is to everyone's advantage. It's best if this principle is part of a person's own nature, but if it isn't, it can be imposed from outside' (590*d*). Accordingly, whereas Socrates prescribes a city of free, autonomous souls, Plato gives us a city composed of two great groups, the educators and their pupils, or, as he himself says, the masters and their slaves.

Thus though the *Republic* presents Plato's solution to the problem of moral reform that Socrates could not solve, given the extent to which he has moved from positions held by Socrates, in many ways the problems Plato addresses are quite different from Socrates'. But it would be wrong to deny continuity altogether. In an overall sense, the aim pursued by Plato is that bequeathed by Socrates. The ideal state outlined in the *Republic* exists for the sake of moral reform. Its overriding purpose is to improve the souls of its subjects, though Plato believes that this must be done through a process of education that

---

[7] R. Robinson, *Plato's Earlier Dialectic*, 2nd edn. (Oxford, 1953), pp. 79–83.

denies the moral autonomy for which Socrates fought and died. Nevertheless, Plato, like Socrates, believes that in order to give men the most exalted life possible they must be educated. Even though this requires Platonic and not Socratic education, the result is still the best that can be hoped for in an imperfect world. Thus Plato, who is often dismissed as a hopeless utopian, actually constructs the ideal state outlined in the *Republic* on the rejection of the far more utopian position of Socrates. The ideal state is intended to achieve what can be salvaged from the wreckage of the Socratic programme.

9

The Ideal State

In the last chapter we saw something of Plato's concern with education and its crucial role in moral reform. What remains to be seen is its role in shaping the institutional structure of the ideal state. Plato argues that education is not only the central institution of the state but also the key to the proper functioning of its other institutions. But difficult requirements must be met before education can work.

9.1. RADICAL REFORM

The significance of education to the smooth functioning of the state is discussed in Book IV (423c–27a). Having outlined many important features of the state, Socrates considers what remains to be done. He declares that further legislation is unnecessary. If the all-important programme of education is adhered to, all will be well; if not, there is little hope. Education is the means through which the public spirit necessary for a successful state is created. Good education and good upbringing, if preserved, will produce citizens who will improve with each generation (424a–b).

Because education is so important, the guardians must above all ensure that it is not corrupted (424b). Because of the potency of the arts, the canons discussed in the last chapter must be rigorously enforced. Following the teachings of Damon, Plato asserts that poetry and music cannot be changed without causing changes in the state's most basic institutions. All aspects of early childhood must be carefully watched. Through proper training of the young, a spirit of lawfulness is created which infuses the city as a whole. Though written or unwritten laws could not bring about such results, they will follow naturally from proper education (425b–c). If education is well conducted, only good ensues; if not, the opposite: 'The final result is a single, dynamic whole, whether or not it's good' (425c).

Given the importance of education, Plato places little store in laws. If education is conducted poorly, the resulting social spirit will be poor, and the state as a whole in virtually hopeless shape. Legislation will be able to do little under such conditions. Plato's analogy is a sick man who tries various remedies while refusing to abandon the bad diet and licentious behaviour that have made him sick. Since no partial remedy can succeed under such circumstances, a true lawgiver should not bother with legislative measures. Plato holds that similar legislation is equally useless and unnecessary in a well-ordered state, because the defects it must ordinarily correct will not arise. Virtuous and well-educated citizens will of their own accord do what they must be compelled to do in other states (see 427a).

The real problem, Plato realizes, is that a proper social spirit is not easily achieved. In order for a philosopher to instil it, he must begin by radically reforming the entire city. Proper education requires not only that subjects be brought up under strict regimentation, but, as we have seen, that the entire environment be carefully controlled. In the thought of Plato, then, many problems we ordinarily think of as 'political' are solved once and for all through education, but in order for education to work properly, it must be preceded by radical reform.

Plato's position in the *Republic* is radical in the extreme. He argues that 'the quickest and simplest way' to bring the ideal state into existence is through a complete break with existing society. Once the philosophers have taken power, they will expel all inhabitants over the age of 10 and begin to raise the next generation properly (540e–41a). In Book VI Plato compares the philosopher-king to an artist. Using divine truths as his model, he will be a 'craftsman of moderation and justice and, in general of what it is to be, in ordinary terms, a good person' (500c–d). Like artists, the philosophers must begin by wiping their canvas clean: 'This isn't a particularly easy thing to do, but you'll appreciate that the main way they differ from everyone else is in refusing to deal with an individual or a community, and not being prepared to sketch out a legal code, until they've either been given a clean slate or have made it so themselves' (501a). After the old generation has been expelled, the children will be brought up according to the educational principles discussed in the last chapter. When they reach adulthood, the state will be fully on its feet.

Plato is often criticized for his radical approach to political reform. In his famous work, *The Open Society and Its Enemies*, Karl Popper especially questions Plato's support of such measures, instead of what Popper calls 'piecemeal social engineering'.[1] Piecemeal social engineering entails a thoroughly rational approach to social problems. Rather than attempting to reconstruct society as a whole after the pattern of a fully worked out blueprint, piecemeal reform advocates attempting to overcome specific social evils within the framework of existing society. Piecemeal reform would alleviate real suffering, while each

---

[1] K. Popper, *The Open Society and Its Enemies*, Vol. I, *The Spell of Plato*, 5th edn., 2 vols. (Princeton, NJ, 1966), ch. 9.

attempted change would also be an experiment. By observing the effects of such actions, reformers would be able to learn about the workings of society, thereby increasing their effectiveness in the future.

As Popper sees things, the modesty of piecemeal reform has several advantages. First, it is based on a body of information built up in the past by similar practices. Second, since such reforms are of modest scope, the damage caused by failed attempts and unforeseen consequences should also be modest and therefore relatively easy to contain. In addition, piecemeal reforms are directed against obvious, known evils, and so constituencies in their favour can be mustered within the open political process of a democratic society. Finally, since the consequences of any specific measure should be tolerable to society, the reformers need not shrink from public disclosure and discussion of their work, again making their policy suitable for democracies.

Wholesale reform strikes Popper as irrational. He believes that there are no precedents for such actions, and so little practical knowledge to guide the reformer. Moreover, any attempt to change society as a whole goes far beyond the elimination of obvious evils. Popper questions the feasibility of the reformers' alternative blueprint. Since it does not arise from actual experience, it must have some other source. He believes that Plato's blueprint is unworldly, based on revelation, and so not easily adapted to inevitable changes in the political environment. Because access to the blueprint depends on privileged knowledge, Popper sees no way that disagreements and conflicts about the blueprint could be settled or future rulers trained to perceive it. Furthermore, if the blueprint is not available to large segments of the population, a constituency in favour of reform is unlikely to arise democratically. The reformers will require concentrated political power in order to achieve their ends.

Popper believes that the scale of such reform raises additional problems. Any attempt to reconstruct society as a whole will come into conflict with members of the existing order who do not wish to be uprooted. Such individuals are likely to resist and so the reformer's power must be sufficient to overcome them, while a high degree of conflict and strife seems inevitable. Mistakes made during wholesale reform will probably be far-reaching; unintended consequences will be similarly grave, while such problems will inevitably stir up further resistance. Thus, the reformers would be tempted to limit knowledge of their actions, and so would resist open disclosure and examination of their work.

Popper cites other difficulties that bear less directly on our concerns. But what we have seen so far reveals clear dangers inherent in radical reform. The combination of difficulty in enlisting popular support, resistance by powerfully entrenched interests, and the need to limit disclosure of what is actually being done will lead the reformers towards dictatorial methods. They will tighten their hold on political power and use it to crush dissent. The political history of the twentieth century, which is the source of Popper's fears, certainly bears out much of his concern.

This brief look at Popper's arguments should be sufficient to show the extent to which his basic assumptions about politics differ from Plato's. But because Plato's views are so different, he is able to respond. It will be seen in the next chapter that Plato is aware of some of the difficulties Popper raises. In fact, we see that reasons similar to those Popper cites lead Plato to believe that the state is unlikely to be realized in practice. We also see that the kind of blueprint upon which Plato bases his state is neither quite as rigid nor as irrational as Popper argues. Here we present Plato's replies to several of Popper's specific criticisms of radical reform.

To begin with, it seems that Plato was in fact able to base his plans upon a substantial body of precedents, if not always of the radical reform of existing cities, then of the founding of new ones. In discussing Plato's political theory in the *Republic*, it must be borne in mind that the society he envisions is small; it is a *polis*, not a modern nation state. The problems of reconstructing such a society are vastly more manageable than those confronted in the radical reform of modern countries, for example, those faced by the leaders of the French and Russian Revolutions. Given the instability of much of Greek political life, cities were constantly beset by revolution and consequently by large-scale political changes. More important, through mechanisms such as colonization, entire cities were founded from scratch. A well-known example is the city of Thurii, established around the year 443. A number of distinguished figures took part in its founding, including Protagoras, who drafted the laws, and the famous town-planner, Hippodamus of Miletus. Along similar lines, the ideal state in the *Laws* is imagined to be a colony, a situation which provides the lawgiver with the advantage of starting off with a relatively clean slate, rather than having to clean it himself (*Laws* 735a–36c). Thus Plato's idea that the philosopher-rulers would be able to reconstruct their city from the ground up is not as outlandish or unprecedented as Popper makes it seem.

Plato differs sharply with Popper concerning the nature of the existing political order. Popper finds much of value in existing society, and so is content to work on solving problems on a piecemeal basis. Plato, on the other hand, is thoroughly disenchanted with the existing order and wants it wiped away. Seeing what exists so differently, Plato and Popper differ sharply in their accounts of the irrational and unpredictable elements encountered in political life. While Popper tends to emphasize the unforeseen consequences of actions not yet taken, Plato is confident of the ideal rulers' ability to manage in the future—through mechanisms we discuss below. The irrational aspects of political actions that concern him are those connected with actions that were performed in the past. He believes that existing societies are chaotic and irrational. They are the domain of appetitive men, built up in the pursuit of worthless aims. Thus, he believes it is a great boon to be able to wipe away with a single stroke the residue of centuries of aimless activity. This also benefits the rulers, in that the levelling of existing society will eliminate all possibility of resistance by conservative elements.

Because he views society so differently from Popper, Plato castigates piecemeal reform. He believes that the ills that beset existing societies lie at their very heart and that these will thwart separate attempts to deal with them. Laws passed to correct specific ills will simply be corrupted and rendered ineffective. Plato likens such measures to cutting off a hydra's heads (*Rep.* 426e–27a): for every one removed, two more grow back in its place. The existing order will be defended by entrenched interests, not only in spite of its abuses but because of them. Those who profit from the way things are will resist meaningful reform. The only politicians corrupt peoples will tolerate are those who cater to them, doing their corrupt bidding (426c). Someone telling them the truth is the 'thing they can abide least of all' (426a). Plato is sceptical about the amount of real reform that could be accomplished with popular consent.

9.2. THE IDEAL STATE

The political institutions sketched in the *Republic* should be understood mainly as providing the environment necessary for proper education. Notable institutions are the system of classes and the two forms of communism—of property and of the family. We begin with the class system.

The system of classes around which the state is organized is rooted in unalterable facts of human nature. There are three general types of men: lovers of wisdom, honour, and gain (581c), or those with gold, silver, and bronze in their souls (*Rep.* 415a–c). Justice in the state requires that the principle of specialization be maintained, that each type of man be located in his proper class and perform his function. Plato puts considerable emphasis upon this, at one point calling it 'of all the god's instructions to the rulers, the first and most important' (*kai prôton kai malista*; 415b). It should be pointed out that this principle pertains much more to classes than, as is widely believed, to individuals. Plato does not believe that each individual is able to perform only one task in the state, which only he can do. Indeed, he says that no great harm comes from a carpenter doing the work of a cobbler or a cobbler that of a carpenter (434a). The danger is if individuals are not assigned to appropriate classes. Plato of course wishes to avoid having higher natures waste away in lower stations, especially the philosophers, whose exceptional qualities are rare and valuable. But his real fear is seeing an inferior nature somehow rise to the ruling elite. Should this happen, Plato prophesies, it would spell the end of the state (415c). Correspondingly, in Book VIII Plato depicts the decline of the ideal state as beginning when inferior natures come to rule (546d–47a). On the whole, Plato does not seem to value justice, the maintenance of the system of classes, greatly for its own sake. Rather, it is necessary if the other virtues are to flourish. Justice assures that the state will be wise through the wisdom of the philosophers, brave through the courage of the auxiliaries, and free from faction. The virtue of temperance will spread throughout the three classes, bringing with it general agreement as to who should rule, while justice itself is valuable mainly because it is 'the principle which makes it possible for all those other qualities to arise in the community, and its continued presence allows them to flourish in safety once they have arisen' (433b–c).

In accordance with a proper distribution of civic functions, only true philosophers are to rule. Plato uses education to solve important problems associated with the rule of philosophers. He does not provide any institutional safeguards—checks and balances—to prevent the philosophers from abusing their power. He relies instead on their education. It is in reference to this problem that the question of educating the guardians is first raised in Book II. Socrates notes that, in order to be a suitable fighting force, the guardians must be brave and high-spirited, but they must not be savage or brutal in their dealings with each other or with the citizens they are to protect. Should the guardians behave in this fashion, they would bring about the ruin of the city (375b–c).

Plato realizes that he faces a universal political problem here. In the myth that closes the *Gorgias*, he remarks that power corrupts; the underworld is filled with the souls of earthly rulers who, having the ability to do wrong with impunity, could not restrain themselves (*Grg.* 525d–26b). Plato notes that it is rare to find a good man among the powerful, and more than once in the *Republic* he displays a full awareness of the consequences of being ruled by lesser men (e.g. *Rep.* 421a, 416a). Accordingly, he argues that every precaution must be taken to ensure that the guardians behave properly towards the citizenry. The best means of accomplishing this is through education: 'Wouldn't a really excellent education have equipped them to take the maximum amount of care?' (416b).

In addition to harmonizing their souls, the education of the rulers ensures that they will not abuse their power. Because of the unlimited power they possess, they must be selected according to the strictest possible criteria. After arduous testing, the rulers are chosen from the wider group of guardians

(412*c*–*e*). They must be tested at all ages, more thoroughly than gold is tested in fire (413*d*–*e*). Only those who weather such a programme will rise to the status of ruler.

The testing of the future rulers does not stop with the virtues of right opinion. It continues as they embark upon their exclusive programme of higher studies. As they were tested in regard to 'toils, fears, and pleasures' during their early years, now they must be examined in regard to intellectual matters. Even when the would-be rulers have completed their course of abstract studies and are spending the requisite fifteen years doing administrative work in the city, they are subjected to additional tests. Only those who pass these as well will be led to look upon the Good (540*a*).

As E. R. Dodds says, the intensive programme of testing prescribed for the guardians indicates Plato's desire 'to exploit the possibilities of an exceptional type of personality'.[2] To use language employed in Chapter 6, Plato wants to make sure that his rulers have a divine nature, that their souls are naturally akin to the Forms. Through the process of erotic sublimation that accompanies their rise to the world of the Forms, the philosophers gain more than knowledge. Because their souls are naturally akin to the Forms, association with them rubs off; 'one's behaviour is bound to resemble anyone or anything whose company one enjoys' (500*c*). The philosopher becomes like the objects of his rational love: 'as divine and as orderly as is humanly possible' (500*c*–*d*). Because all—or nearly all—his Eros is focused on the Forms, the philosopher is free from those desires responsible for most human injustice: 'People who've travelled there don't want to engage in human business; there's nowhere else their minds would ever rather be than in the upper region' (517*c*–*d*). Such beings can be trusted to use their power wisely and well.

Thus, we see the beauty of Plato's solution to the problem of ensuring that rulers do not abuse their power. The key is to make sure that they are the kind of people who would gain nothing by doing so. Plato is aware that most rulers of actual states rule for the sake of gain. They are like shepherds who treat their subjects as sheep to be slaughtered and fleeced (343*b*–*c*). The problem of getting better rulers can be solved only by finding men who view ruling as a burden and so do not wish to rule, and forcing them to do so, either through their fear of being ruled by lesser men (347*a*–*d*), or because they know it is their duty to the city that has raised and educated them (519*d*–20*d*).

Plato presents an inverse proportion: a city in which the prospective rulers desire least to rule should be governed best and experience the least strife, while a city with the opposite kind of rulers should end up governed in the opposite way. Thus only if one finds a way of life that is better than governing

---

[2] E. R. Dodds, *The Greeks and the Irrational* (Berkeley, CA, 1951), pp. 210–11.

can one end up with a well-governed city (520*d*–21*a*). In the ideal city, the rulers know of something better than worldly goods, and of this they take their leave unwillingly. They serve their cities 'as an obligation, not as a privilege' (540*b*). Each goes to rule 'as an inescapable duty' (520*e*). And so in their hands, the city is free from internal strife. In fact, Plato is so successful in setting things up in this way that he has some difficulty explaining why the philosophers are willing to rule at all.

The question why the philosophers are willing to rule has been much debated by scholars.[3] Part of the problem is caused by Plato's saying that philosophers who have escaped from the cave and seen the light must be *forced* to descend once again to aid their fellows (519*c*–*d*). It should be noted that this only pertains to philosophers who have not been formally educated by their societies. Those who have been so educated are obligated to govern out of gratitude. There are, however, at least three reasons why philosophers should be willing to rule.

First, as Plato says in Book I (347*c*–*d*), if they do not rule, other people will, in which case the philosophers pay the severe price of being ruled by lesser men. In other words, they are forced to rule as the lesser of two evils. Second, Plato believes in the transformative effects of philosophic wisdom. As we have discussed, the philosopher, who has ascended the ladder of love, has a desire to reproduce divine order in the souls of his subjects. Once again, in the *Symposium*, Plato notes that such a person desires to give birth in the beautiful, which may assume the form of inculcating virtue in other people. In order to accomplish this effectively, he must rule. And so Plato holds that philosophic wisdom includes a disinterested component—although once again, we should note that this is not a developed theme in his political theory. Finally, the philosopher will feel a great commonality of interest with his fellow citizens. He will perceive what is good for them as good for himself, and wish to benefit them (see below, p. 152). In the light of these three considerations, much of the controversy concerning the philosopher's willingness to rule can be set aside.

9.3. COMMUNITY OF PROPERTY

The major institutions of the ideal city, especially communism and the community of wives and children, are designed to strengthen the framework of

---

[3] See esp. L. Strauss, *The City and Man* (Chicago, IL, 1964), p. 124; A. Bloom, *The Republic of Plato* (New York, 1968), pp. 407–10; the arguments of these scholars are criticized in Klosko, 'Implementing the Ideal State', *Journal of Politics*, 43 (1981), 368–71; see also Kraut, 'Egoism, Love and Political Office in Plato', *Philosophical Review*, 82 (1973).

philosophic rule. The explicit rationale for both forms of communism is the principle that governments decay only when discord breaks out in the ruling class; if the rulers remain cohesive, degeneration is impossible (545*d*, 465*b*). To secure the unity of the governing class, Plato advocates for the guardians communal property and communal family. That these measures are introduced in order to strengthen education is seen in his language. Having outlined the guardians' system of education Plato says: 'In addition [to education], their living quarters and their property in general should be designed not to interfere with their carrying out their work as guardians as well as possible' (416*c*–*d*). The guardians' property arrangements are constructed so as not to impede other features of the state, rather than for considerations of intrinsic merit.

The living arrangements for the guardians are described briefly at the end of Book III (416*d*–17*b*). Plato envisions a kind of permanent barracks existence. They are to live as soldiers in camp, with a common mess. As Adeimantus complains, they appear to live more like mercenaries than like the rulers of the state (419*e*–20*a*). They are to have no private property beyond what is absolutely necessary and are strictly forbidden to own gold and silver. In addition, they are to have no privacy; they are forbidden houses or storerooms which anyone who wishes is not free to enter. All real property in the state, including all the land, is to be owned by members of the lowest class, while the guardians are to be maintained by an annual tax upon this class, which they receive as a salary for protecting them.

Thus, the economic system of the ideal state, frequently referred to as 'communism', is actually based on private property. The guardians alone have communal property, but this is closer to generalized poverty than to the common ownership of the means of production that 'communism' generally implies. The guardians' community of property is actually closer to that practised by the monks in a monastery than to that found in an economic system we would be likely to call 'socialism' or 'communism'—for our present purposes, these terms can be regarded as interchangeable. Plato's system differs from systems commonly referred to as communism or socialism in another sense as well. In general, it seems safe to say that communistic/socialistic economic systems arise largely from concerns of economic justice. There are many varieties of socialism, with wide differences between them, but according to most of these, it is because property and other economic goods are important and valuable that they must be controlled by the community. For instance, one typical argument for socialism, presented by Eduard Bernstein, who is famous as a Marxian 'revisionist', describes socialism as an extension or development of liberalism. In political systems described as 'liberal', the state is generally founded upon and guarantees equal political rights. According to Bernstein, the same principles that justify equality of political rights also require equality of economic rights. Thus democracy without socialism is incomplete; socialism is necessary to make democracy real.[4] Plato of course sees property as intrinsically neither good nor desirable. Thus, his socialism is negative rather than positive; it centres upon renunciation of claims to property rather than ensuring their equal distribution.

In one further sense, however, the ideal state could be described as communistic. 'Communism' or 'socialism' implies more than merely communal ownership. It can also designate a wide variety of economic systems, provided that they are characterized by state control for the public good. If we take socialism in this sense, Plato's state is obviously included, regardless of who owns the means of production. There can be little doubt that the ideal state's system of private ownership is subject to state control in important respects. The guardians are explicitly enjoined to make sure the state avoids extremes of wealth and poverty (421e–22a). The tradition of state regulation of economic affairs was long established in many Greek cities, such as Sparta, in which landowners were forbidden to sell their land (Aristotle, *Politics* 1270a15–34). The law in Sparta also provided for free communal use of many types of private property, for example, slaves, horses, and dogs (*Pol.* 1263a31–37). Even in Athens, which had a relatively free economy, wealthy citizens were commonly faced with the dubious honour of having privately to defray various state expenses, for example, by supporting dramatic performances or outfitting a ship for the navy. We see below that Plato incorporates numerous state restrictions on property-holding in the ideal state in the *Laws*. In the *Republic* as well, it seems safe to assume that the guardians would use such measures, should they seem advisable.

Plato's explicit rationale for introducing communal property is its bearing on stability. He says that if the guardians had more than a minimal amount of property, they would end up as 'estate-managers and farmers instead of guardians; they would become despots and enemies rather than allies of the inhabitants of the community'. The inverse proportion between desire to rule and ability to rule discussed above would be upset, and the guardians would spend their lives hating and being hated, plotting and conspiring in order to retain power, fearing their fellow citizens more than foreign enemies (417a–b). In depicting the decline of the ideal state in Book VIII, Plato has the first degenerate form come about when the rulers seize and distribute the state's land as private property, and turn their fellow citizens into serfs (547b–c).

---

[4] E. Bernstein, *The Preconditions of Socialism*, H. Tudor, ed. and trans. (Cambridge, 1993), ch. 4, sec. (c).

We saw above that throughout his writings Plato shows a deep awareness of the almost constant civil strife that plagued Greek cities. He declares that most cities are actually made up of two cities, the warring classes of the poor and the rich (422e–23a, 551d), and he is of course aware of the inherent instability of such conditions (556e, 422e–23a). His natural desire to avoid this in the ideal city is clearly one main reason for his property regulations. Another important consideration is the fact that having all members of the ruling group own the same things, and so use the words 'mine' and 'thine' in common, will contribute to the cohesiveness of the group (464c–d, 462a–e).

It might seem odd that, if Plato believes communism contributes to the cohesiveness of the ideal city, he confines it to the guardians. This might seem especially odd given his desire that the ideal state be 'one city' instead of two, and so avoid the strife encountered in other cities. With the introduction of communism, the ideal state not only has separate classes, but the classes have drastically different economic existences. It is true that there are some advantages to partial communism, especially that it works to satisfy the economic longings of the lower class and also creates ties of dependence between the classes. The fact that the rulers rely on the lower classes for their food and wages forges bonds between them and those they are to guard. But these advantages would seem to be heavily outweighed by the disadvantages. It could be argued that this system has precisely the effect that Plato fears. Aristotle, for one, contends that this system of community property (and community of the family) breaks the ideal state into 'two states in one, and these antagonistic to one another' (*Pol.* 1264a24–26). Plato of course wishes to avoid this outcome, but because of the inferior natural endowment of the third class, he does not believe that communism—of either type—can be generalized. Thus, community of property is instituted for guardians alone as the best system consistent with human nature.

9.4. EQUALITY OF WOMEN AND COMMUNITY OF THE FAMILY

More radical and far-reaching than communal property are Plato's proposals concerning treatment of women and community of the family. The subject of community of the family is raised in Book IV, where it is treated summarily as an incidental feature of the state (423e–24a). But the importance and radicalism of Plato's proposals are seen in Book V, where he discusses them in depth (449a–66d). Plato's discussion in Book V is given over to three separate matters, three 'great waves of paradox', as he refers to them: (*a*) equality of women; (*b*) community of the family, and (*c*) the realizability of the ideal state. We will discuss (*c*) in the next chapter. (*a*) and (*b*), although formally distinct, are closely related and can be discussed together in this section.

In order to appreciate how radical Plato's proposals concerning women's equality were, it is necessary to consider them against the backdrop of more usual Greek attitudes and practices. There were of course many different Greek cities, each with its own customs and institutions, and accordingly a certain variation in the status accorded to women. But most cities placed women in positions of decided inferiority. It is widely known that the Greeks regarded slaves as naturally inferior. The classic discussion of this subject is in Book I of Aristotle's *Politics*, where Aristotle argues that slaves have defective reasoning capacities and so should be viewed as 'living tools' (*Pol.* I, ch. 4). It is important to realize that Aristotle saw women in a similar light. They too have defective reasoning powers and so should be subordinate to men (*Pol.* 1260*a*12–14).

To the extent that Aristotle reflects traditional Greek ideas here, his views justify how women were treated. The legal status of women varied from city to city. In Athens, for example, they were citizens but were not given the rights to hold property or to plead in court, and had restricted rights to initiate lawsuits. In other cities their position was better, for example in Sparta, where they had the right to own property and could, as heiresses, amass considerable wealth. But in general women existed in a condition of almost oriental subjection. They lived in virtual seclusion, in the women's quarters of their houses, rarely going out, and almost never seeing men other than their husbands or other close relatives. They were given away in arranged marriages in their early teens, generally at the age of 15, while this mainly entailed a move from one women's quarters to another. They were not even the primary objects of romantic love, a role occupied by young boys, as is clearly seen in Plato's dramatic dialogues. Though women's most important role was childbearing—giving their husbands legitimate heirs—the Greeks placed little emphasis on family life. Greek men concentrated their energies on the public sphere. As Aristotle says, man is a political animal (*zôon politikon, Politics* 1253*a*3), not a 'family man', while public life was an almost exclusively male world, a 'men's club', as one commentator puts it.[5] Thus men and women inhabited different worlds: women, the confined domestic space of the home; men, the world outside. When Herodotus encountered, among the Egyptians, a society in which men stayed home and wove while their wives went out to the marketplace, this seemed to him to overturn 'the ordinary practices of mankind' (Herodotus, II, 35).

[5] E. Barker, *Greek Political Theory: Plato and His Predecessors* (London, 1918; rpt. 1947), p. 253.

Viewed in the light of such societies, Plato's proposals in the *Republic* are especially striking, and it is not surprising that he finds it necessary to argue for them at length.

There is a close relationship between Plato's proposals to include women as equals in the guardian classes and to abolish traditional family life. In arguing for each proposal, Plato attempts to prove both that it would be beneficial to the state and that it is possible. But the proposals are beneficial in different ways, while it would not be impossible to institute some form of either one without the other.

Plato believes it is in the state's interest to elevate suitable women to the rank of guardian. The principle of specialization requires that individuals perform functions appropriate to their natures. Though Plato believes that men as a whole are far superior to women, that in fact there are no tasks in the performance of which men in general would not outshine women (455c–d), he believes that there are superior women. These women should assume their rightful place as guardians. Plato believes that women are unquestionably different from men in certain respects, but none of these bears directly on their ability to fulfil the roles of guardians, just as the difference between bald and long-haired individuals does not bear on their ability to be carpenters (454c–e). The only relevant difference is that women are physically weaker than men, and so as guardians must be assigned appropriate duties (451e, 455d–e, 457a).

Thus it is with good reason that Plato is recognized as one of the first thinkers in the Western tradition to look beyond women's biological natures to their overall potential to contribute to society. But Plato's achievements in this regard should not be exaggerated. His belief in emancipating superior women should not be construed as a blanket emancipation of all women. Equality is for women guardians alone. In the lowest class some semblance of the traditional family is doubtless maintained, along with private property, and it seems clear that the women of this class will occupy traditional roles.

Because superior women will be elevated to the ranks of the guardians, with some rising to the class of rulers, the common locution 'philosopher-kings' is not entirely accurate. Plato explicitly mentions female philosophers in Book VII (540c). Women guardians must, of course, receive the same education as men (456c–d). If this entails their exercising naked in public alongside men, so be it. Though at first this might seem amusing, in time people will get used to it. As is generally the case, the fact that Plato believes this system is in the state's best interests outweighs other considerations.

One additional advantage of women guardians, not discussed by Plato, bears mention. This system promises to double the available pool of talent from which to select future rulers. In the light of the great value and rarity of the philosophic nature, this is an important consideration and should be recognized (cf. *Laws* 805a–b).

Community of the family is said to benefit the state for reasons of eugenics and of unity. Plato's eugenic argument is straightforward (459a–61e). In raising hunting dogs, pedigree birds, or other livestock, great care is taken to breed from the best stock, and to use animals in their prime. Plato believes that similar reasoning should apply to human beings, and so means must be devised to ensure that the best men breed with the best women, and that less worthy individuals are restrained from reproducing. This line of argument leads to dismantling the traditional family structure for the guardians and erection of Plato's distinctive institutions.

In the system Plato recommends, sexual activity and reproduction are to be tightly controlled (459c–61e). Temporary marriages for the sake of reproduction will be arranged and consecrated at public marriage festivals. The number of marriages each season will be decided by the rulers, in keeping with the city's population requirements. Through a cleverly rigged lottery system, all guardians will be led to believe that their marriage prospects are determined by chance, while in actuality the rulers will make sure that the best men are mated with the best women. Through this means, those who do not receive partners will blame chance, not the rulers. In addition, Plato recommends that guardians who perform especially meritorious service on the battlefield or elsewhere be given extra mating privileges, both as an inducement to valour and to ensure more offspring from the best stock (460a–b). The resultant offspring will be raised in public nurseries, with steps taken to ensure that parents do not know their children or children their parents. People will be allowed to reproduce only during their prime: women between the ages of 20 and 40, men between 30 and 55. Apparently, individuals will be denied sexual outlets until they reach the prescribed ages, while once individuals have passed the age of having children, they will be allowed to copulate freely, barring only adherence to the incest taboos, and the proviso that no children of such unions will be allowed to live (461c).

Thus, the guardians are to be bred like pedigree beasts. The breeding mechanisms are reinforced with the proviso that children of inferior parents, or children born defective, shall be disposed of (460c), probably through infanticide, though Plato's language is vague, and it is possible that he means simply to demote these children to the class of farmers (cf. *Tim.* 19a). It is clear that Plato takes his eugenic arguments seriously. Proof that he is concerned more with this than with controlling sexual activity for its own sake is the fact that sexual restrictions do not apply once individuals have passed their reproductive years.

In addition to helping to improve the stock of guardians, the system of family relations benefits the state by fostering unity. Members of the guardian classes will regard one another as more than fellow citizens or fellow guardians. They will look upon one another as kin. Ties of blood will be supported by appropriate attitudes and sentiments. And so the ruling classes, deprived of traditional families, will become one large family. The entire cohort of guardians is to be bound together by emotional ties. Plato argues for an extreme form of unity; he compares the guardians to parts of a single organism. When one part of the body hurts, the entire body feels the pain. Similarly, among the guardians, what affects one affects all (462c–d).

Plato places great emphasis upon bringing the rulers to associate their self-interest with the interests of the state. Deprived of private property and private family, the guardian will find his self-interest expressed only in the good of the state. As Plato says, in other cities, one sees an individual drag into his own house whatever he can get hold of away from other people; another drags things into his different house to another wife and other children, and so on. This makes for private pleasures and pains at private events. The inhabitants of the just city, on the other hand, will think of the same thing as their own, aim at the same goal, and, as far as possible, feel pleasure and pain in unison (464b–d). It is not an exaggeration to say that Plato aims at effacing each guardian's private self, and replacing it with a new, public self.[6] Because Plato believes political decline is caused by dissension in the ruling class, he has strong reasons to bind the guardians with ties of family and blood.

In the light of the importance of the unity that community of the family fosters, it may be surprising to see this too reserved for guardians alone. Once again, the explanation lies in what Plato considers possible. He no doubt believes that community of the family and property would place unbearable demands upon the majority of people. Only the guardians with their superior natures are able to withstand such pressures, and even then only after intensive education. Plato takes into account the fact that sexual deprivation will cause hostility even among the guardians. Hence the rigged lottery system. Plato's faith in the possibility of creating almost superhuman rulers is coupled with less confidence in the abilities of most people.

---

[6] Cf. the language of Rousseau: 'He who dares to undertake the making of a people's institutions ought to feel himself capable, so to speak, of changing human nature, of transforming each individual, who is by himself a complete and solitary whole, into part of a greater whole from which he in a manner receives his life and being; of altering man's constitution for the purpose of strengthening it; and of substituting a partial and moral existence for the physical and independent existence nature has conferred on us all' (*The Social Contract*, II, ch. 7; *The Social Contract and Discourses*, G. D. H. Cole, J. H. Brumfitt, and J. Hall, trans. [London, 1973], p. 38).

Although community of the family and property obviously involve severe sacrifice, Plato believes these measures will generate great happiness among the guardian classes. Freed from the multitudinous concerns of property and family that plague the inhabitants of ordinary cities, the guardians will also be freed from the long train of abuses such things bring in their wake: lawsuits, mutual accusations, the need for money, the need to flatter the rich, debt, and many others (464c–65c). As a result of this, though the purpose of the ideal state is to ensure the happiness of the state as a whole not any particular class (420b, 421b–c), the guardians will live lives more blessed than those of Olympic victors:

The guardians' victory is more splendid, and their upkeep by the general populace is more thorough-going. The fruit of their victory is the preservation of the whole community, their prize the maintenance of themselves and their children with food and all of life's essentials. During their lifetimes they are honoured by their community, and when they die they are buried in high style. (465d)

Though Plato does not mention this, freed from the usual ties of family, the rulers also benefit by being able more easily to focus their psychic energy on the Forms.

In spite of Plato's arguments for his position, many scholars refuse to take his proposals concerning women and the family seriously. Most familiar is the criticism of Leo Strauss and Allan Bloom, who view the *Republic* as a kind of ingenious satire, actually intended to demonstrate the *impossibility* of radical political reform.[7] They argue that, in making clear the costs associated with a truly just city, Plato intends to show that such arrangements are beyond the possibilities of human nature. As part of this overall argument, Strauss and Bloom contend that Plato's proposals concerning women and the family are intended to be seen as absurd and against human nature. It is difficult to discuss the arguments of Strauss and Bloom in isolation from their distinctive claims concerning how Plato and other great political theorists should be read. But for reasons of space, this matter cannot be explored here.[8] We confine attention to their account of women and the family.

Strauss and Bloom find abundant evidence for the absurdity of Plato's proposals. For instance, Bloom criticizes equality of women because of the ridiculousness of seeing men and women exercise naked together and because Plato overlooks significant biological differences between the sexes. According to Strauss, Plato's system 'abstracts from the most important bodily difference

within the human race'. The absurdity of Plato's proposal is evident in his comparing differences between men and women to those between bald and long-
haired men.[9] But Plato has a ready response. As indicated above, he anticipates
and addresses such criticisms. Plato contends that the sight of naked women
exercising may be ridiculous 'as things stand now (*en tô parestôti*)' (*Rep.* 452*b*),
but attitudes will evolve along with changing practices. He notes that not long
before his time the sight of men exercising naked was considered ridiculous.
In Plato's eyes, only what is harmful or base is truly ridiculous (452*a–e*).
As for the difference between baldness and long-hairedness, this argument
simply ignores what Plato says in the text. Plato's analogy depends on the
fact that, just as the difference between baldness and long-hairedness has little
bearing on one's ability to function *as a carpenter*, so being female or male
has little bearing on one's ability to function *as a ruler*. Plato writes: 'We're
pursuing the idea that different natures should get different occupations... at
the verbal level, but we haven't spent any time at all inquiring precisely what
type of inherent difference and identity we meant when we assigned different
occupations to different natures and identical occupations to identical natures'
(*Rep.* 454*a–b*). Since there is little reason to doubt Plato's belief that some
women are naturally qualified to fulfil the functions of guardians, it is unlikely
that Bloom and Strauss would be able to establish the absurdity of equal
treatment of women.

Community of the family concerns a more outlandish set of institutions,
and so criticisms here may have more bite. Bloom describes the effect of Plato's
proposals as 'to remove whatever is natural in the family and replace it with an
entirely conventional base'.[10] Plato's attempt to subordinate human sexuality
to law violates human nature: 'Thus the unity of the city depends on that same
forgetting of the body which has been a golden thread running through the
whole discourse'.[11] Once again, according to Bloom, Plato is not serious about
his proposals. He 'forgets the body in order to make clear its importance'.[12]
But the obvious counter to such claims is Plato's belief in the educability of the
just city's inhabitants. Strauss and Bloom may be right when they contend that
human desires for property and the family are ineradicable. Similar arguments
have been advanced by influential philosophers, including Aristotle and Hegel.
But in order to demonstrate that Plato constructed institutions that *he* viewed
as obviously absurd, one would have to discount the great weight he places
on education and its potential. Central to Plato's entire political theory is the
idea that, by harnessing the resources of the state, these and other potentially
harmful desires *can* be largely controlled. To a large extent, his political theory

[9] Strauss, *City and Man*, pp. 116–17; similarly, Bloom, *Republic*, pp. 385–7.
[10] Bloom, *Republic*, p. 385.   [11] Ibid. 386.   [12] Ibid. 387.

centres on how the state can and should go about this. Criticism of community of property and the family should not be undertaken in isolation from Plato's crucial background assumptions—an error, incidentally, of which Aristotle is also guilty, in Book II of the *Politics* (chapters 2–5).

An additional consideration indicates Plato's seriousness about his treatment of women and the family. As we have noted, Plato limits his proposals to the guardians. The lowest class retains some semblance of the traditional family, while the reason for this is, presumably, that their inferior natures could not tolerate the demands of communal families. Plato also recognizes that sexual deprivation will generate hostility even among the guardians, a problem he addresses with the rigged lottery. If Plato had wished to create a system of institutions that could not possibly work, his proposals would have been more obviously outlandish if meant for the entire population of the state.[13]

In addition to the institutions we have noted, Plato outlines further measures necessary for the stability of the state. The guardians are charged with defending the state from foreign enemies. It is for this reason that they are initially introduced into the city (374*b–e*), and this remains one of the auxiliaries' most significant tasks. They are to accomplish this through rigorous training, which will yield great courage on the battlefield. What they lack in numbers they will more than make up for in superior conditioning and stealth (422*a*–23*a*, 466*d*–68*e*).

In addition to defending the state from enemies this class must secure it from enemies within (415*d–e*, 414*b*). Because it possesses a monopoly of military training and equipment, this presents few difficulties. The guardians could doubtless overcome internal opposition through the exercise of force alone. But Plato does not want them to rule the lower classes as the Spartans did their subject peoples (below, p. 162). In the myth of the decline of the state in Book VIII, the introduction of this form of rule is one effect of the degeneration of the ideal state into a timarchy (547*c*), which is a Cretan or Spartan type of state (544*c*, 545*a*). Instead, the guardians are to rule over subjects who are willing to be ruled. The ideal city possesses the virtue of temperance, which, applied to cities, manifests itself as a general consensus among the rulers and the ruled as to who should rule (431*d–e*). The most obvious means of securing the acquiescence of the lower classes is education. The producing

---

[13] Cf. Aristophane's proposals in *Ecclesiazusae*. For discussion of the relationship between these and the *Republic*, see J. Adam, ed., *The Republic of Plato*, 2 vols. (Cambridge, 1902), Appendix I, pp. 345–55; Bloom, Response to D. Hall, 'The *Republic* and the "Limits of Politics"', *Political Theory*, 5 (1977), 324–7; Klosko, 'Straussian Interpretation', 282–7; M. Burnyeat, 'Utopia and Fantasy: The Practicability of Plato's Ideally Just City', in *Psychoanalysis, Mind, and Art*, J. Hopkins and A. Savile, eds. (Oxford, 1992), pp. 180–3.

class will be indoctrinated through such devices as the 'myth of the metals' (see below, p. 166), and thereby made to understand the necessity of their position, and presumably conditioned to like it. They will recognize their rulers for what they are, and instead of chafing under their restraint, will regard them as 'protectors and defenders' (463*b*). Again, though Plato says nothing about educating the lowest class, this is an additional function such education would fulfil. Throughout the ruling classes also, there will be a general agreement as to who should rule. The perfect guardians will reluctantly shoulder their burden; the auxiliaries will support their rule; and the state as a whole will exemplify the virtue of justice.

9.5. A RACIST STATE?

Throughout the mid-twentieth century, Popper and other thinkers called sustained attention to uncomfortable resemblances between Plato's just cities in the *Republic* and *Laws* and fascist and communist societies that had arisen in Germany, the Soviet Union, and elsewhere.[14] Although frequently exaggerated or simply incorrect, these criticisms have permanently influenced the way Plato's political theory is perceived. In order to assess the accuracy of such interpretations, I examine two specific charges in some detail: that the just city is racist, in this section; and that it is a totalitarian society, which denies its inhabitants essential freedoms, in the following section.

There are clearly good reasons to view the just city as racist. The rulers and other guardians, who have superior natural qualities, live apart from the other citizens and enjoy special privileges—although they also bear significant burdens. Since Plato believes that those qualified to be guardians will generally have children with similar qualities and takes considerable care with the process through which they reproduce, at first sight something like racism is apparent. This charge is made most forcefully by Popper, but in some form or other it is widely believed.

What sets Popper's accusation apart those of other scholars is its tone. Popper takes quite literally Plato's repeated comparison of the art of ruling to the shepherd's art. In his terms, the primary task of the philosopher-kings is 'managing and keeping down the human cattle'.[15] Though Popper believes that Plato's racism is subordinated to the political end of ensuring the stability of the just city, he says that Plato's proposals centre upon 'breeding the master

---

[14] In addition to Popper, see R. S. Crossman, *Plato Today* (Oxford, 1939); W. Fite, *The Platonic Legend* (New York, 1934); G. Winspear, *The Genesis of Plato's Thought* (New York, 1940); an essential response is G. Levinson, *In Defense of Plato* (Cambridge, MA, 1953).

[15] Popper, *Open Society*, p. 51.

race'.[16] Plato's philosopher-king 'turns out to be a philosopher breeder',[17] whose task is to realize on earth a platonic idea of the pure race.[18] It is for this reason that the philosophers require exhaustive mathematical training, to understand the secrets of mathematical eugenics, expressed in the notorious 'Platonic Number', presented in the beginning of Book VIII.[19] Popper believes that Plato's crucial teaching is epitomized in the myth of the metals, to which he refers as the 'Myth of Blood and Soil'.[20] Popper's inflated language is obviously meant to evoke the spectre of Nazism. But Plato's Nazism can be dismissed out of hand. There is no textual justification for 'master race', 'human cattle', 'Myth of Blood and Soil', and many other Popperisms. Popper's belief in Plato's Hitlerian obsession with racial purity can also be dismissed out of hand.[21] But in order to see this, we must distinguish different senses of 'racism'.[22]

As the term is generally used, a 'race' is a human group distinguished from other groups by characteristics that are transmitted through heredity. Among qualities commonly noted are physical characteristics such as colour of skin, shape of eyes, and texture of hair. But racism generally connotes more than the fact that groups are different; it generally includes a claim that members of one group are superior to members of others. The essence of racism is a claim that group A is superior to group B because of some hereditary characteristics or others. The implication commonly drawn is that, because of their superiority, members of group A deserve superior treatment, for example, larger shares of important social goods. We may refer to a claim along these lines as 'empirical racism', because it is rooted in the empirical fact of group A's superiority.[23] In contemporary Western societies, beliefs such as these are generally viewed as objectionable, but we should note that this is so only if they are false. If members of group A actually are better at some activity or in some other important respect than members of group B and there are good reasons why people who excel in the relevant respects should receive larger distributive shares, then it may well be right that they be rewarded appropriately. Racism is a pejorative notion, and it is not clear that treating people according to their deserts is wrong. However, empirical racism generally posits exaggerated

---

[16] Ibid. 52.   [17] Ibid. 149.   [18] Ibid.

[19] *Republic* 546a–e; Popper, *Open Society*, pp. 151–3.   [20] Popper, *Open Society*, p. 141.

[21] Levinson, *Defense*, pp. 535–43.

[22] Discussion here draws from Klosko, ' "Racism" in Plato's *Republic*', *History of Political Thought*, 12 (1991), which has more detailed discussion and references.

[23] It may seem strange to identify a claim of hereditary superiority as an 'empirical' claim. However, it should be noted that such a claim assumes some established standard and so would be identified by Ernest Nagel as a 'characterizing' value judgement, as opposed to an overtly normative 'appraising' value judgement (E. Nagel, *The Structure of Science* [New York, 1961], pp. 492–5).

differences between groups, to justify significant distributive inequities. Such claims are generally clearly false, meriting strong condemnation of their proponents, with the degree of condemnation reflecting degree of departure from the truth. Representative claims centre upon the intellectual superiority of group X, or its natural (hereditary) possession of desirable psychological traits, for example, greater willingness to work, or ability to control certain objectionable appetites. In general, views we would characterize as empirical racism turn upon incorrect factual beliefs about different human groups—commonly based on racial or ethnic stereotyping—and are condemned accordingly.

To whatever extent we view beliefs along these lines as objectionable, there can be little doubt that Plato subscribes to them. He claims that people with gold in their souls are superior to those with silver, and those with silver to those with bronze, and that the relevant qualities are generally transmitted through heredity. These points are difficult to dispute. However, his holding these views should be regarded as grounds for criticism only if they are false. We return to this question below. What we should note here is that there is a different sense of racism, what we may call 'normative racism', which is more clearly objectionable and is the form of racism generally pursued in racist public policies. Although these two senses of racism are often run together, they are not only different, but to a large extent incompatible.

A proponent of normative racism argues that hereditary characteristics should take precedence over what would otherwise be recognized as appropriate criteria in questions of distribution. As the appellation indicates, 'appropriate criteria' are those upon the basis of which different goods should be distributed. Thus, if a number of musicians audition for spots in an orchestra, the positions should go to those who most clearly demonstrate musical ability. Or in the case of a football league, the limited number of available positions should go to the individuals who best demonstrate the relevant skills. Though there can be problems in identifying the best musicians or football players, the criteria in these fields and others like them are relatively clear, and for our purposes here, it is not necessary to consider more problematic cases. Once we recognize appropriate criteria in some area, we can see how they may be supplanted in cases of racism. This would occur if musicians of particular racial groups were forbidden to play in various musical organizations, that is, if positions were distributed according to race rather than musical ability. In the football example, the supplanting of appropriate criteria would occur if opportunities went to members of specific racial groups rather than to the best players. The racism of Nazi Germany was seen in countless cases along these lines. During the early years of the Reich, Jews were barred from profession after profession—as a prelude to their later physical liquidation. For example, in Frankfurt, in April 1933, German Jewish teachers were forbidden to teach in universities; German Jewish actors were barred from the stage; German Jewish musicians were forbidden to play in orchestras.[24] In regard to the distribution of more general social goods, such as the rights of citizenship, or protection under the rule of law, non-controversially appropriate criteria are less easily identified. But in most Western societies, it is an established belief that these goods should be distributed to all alike because of their fundamental human equality, or human rights. Thus, we look with horror at the Nazi view that differences in rights and obligations should follow from racial differences.[25]

Though empirical and normative racism are not often distinguished, they are to a large extent incompatible. Though claims of both kinds justify distributive inequalities on the basis of race—the reason, I take it, that they are often lumped together—they justify these inequalities in different ways, on the basis of contradictory factual premises. Empirical racists believe that members of group X deserve more social goods, because they are superior: they possess in higher degree the characteristics that are generally viewed as appropriate for distribution of the goods in question. Normative racism begins where empirical racism leaves off. It advocates distributive inequalities even though members of group X are *not* superior in the appropriate respect. Normative racists do not base their distributive claims upon hereditary superiority, but uphold them even though members of their favoured group are not superior in the relevant respects.

The charge that Plato is a racist is of course based upon the distinctive details of his proposed institutions. There is no doubt that he upholds distribution of places in the social hierarchy according to qualifications which, for the most part, are transmitted through heredity, while this overall system is accompanied by the injunction that members of the lowest class should be 'enslaved' to members of the highest. Once again, in these respects, his view should be identified as empirical racism. But the qualification, 'for the most part' (*to men polu*, 415a8) demonstrates the distance between Plato and normative racism.

Throughout this chapter, we have seen that the distinction between human types is essential to the maintenance of the just city. The main reason justice is stressed is Plato's belief that only individuals with souls of gold are qualified to rule. The importance of ensuring that the right people—and only the right people—rule is the major reason for the rigid class system. As Plato says in Book III: 'the first and most important (*kai prôton kai malista*)' instruction of the god to the rulers is that there is nothing they take more care of than the

---

[24] M. Gilbert, *The Holocaust* (New York, 1985), p. 36.
[25] L. Dawidowicz, *The War Against the Jews* (New York, 1975), p. 67.

mixture of the souls in the next generation (*Rep.* 415*b*). Plato adds that there is an oracle, that 'the community will be destroyed when it has a bronze or iron guardian' (415*c*). Accordingly, as we have seen, one of Plato's arguments for community of the family turns on eugenics. In the just city, steps must be taken to ensure that the best breed with the best, and the less worthy are restrained from reproducing. Once again, institutions along these lines appear to smack of racism. But to what extent is this charge accurate?

Compelling evidence against normative racism is the requirement that citizens of the just city be placed according to their qualifications—their qualifications rather than their birth. This 'first and most important instruction of the god to the rulers' can be referred to as the 'placement rule'. To put this rule into effect, the philosopher-kings would have to set up some competitive system of education for all children, though Plato does not discuss such measures in the *Republic*.[26] While Popper contends that Plato is obsessed with the purity of the master race, the placement rule refutes this contention. Plato is obsessed with having the best qualified person do each job, regardless of the identity of his (or her) parents.

Popper's response to the placement rule is as follows: 'It must be admitted that [Plato] here announces the following rule: "If in one of the lower classes children are born with an admixture of gold and silver, they shall ... be appointed guardians, and ... auxiliaries" '. But this concession is rescinded in a later passage of the *Republic*.[27] Popper conveniently neglects to mention that this 'concession' is explicitly identified as the rulers' 'first and most important' duty. He also neglects to mention that the rule is repeated in Book IV. Plato notes 'the necessity of banishing to the other ranks any inferior child who is born to the guardians, and of having any outstanding child who is born to the other ranks join the guardians' (423*c*–*d*). Popper's position on the placement rule centres upon the claims (*a*) that it is not put forth sincerely, and (*b*) that it means only that 'nobly born but degenerate children may be pushed down, but not that any of the baseborn may be lifted up'.[28] These are indefensible assertions. There is no textual evidence for (*a*), while (*b*) stands in clear defiance of the text.

Assessment of Plato's position in regard to distributive equity is complicated enormously by the fact that he does not believe in perfect hereditary transmission. However, because he believes that considerations of birth should give way to merit, his position should be viewed as empirical racism but not normative racism. One could perhaps maintain that Plato is not an empirical racist, because he does not believe in perfect hereditary transmission and stresses

---

[26] Cf. Aristotle, *Politics* 1262a14–24, 1262b24–29.
[27] Popper, *Open Society*, p. 141; his ellipses.   [28] Ibid.

the importance of dealing with exceptional cases. But he believes in almost perfect transmission, while the exaggerated differences he draws between the classes outweigh the force of any exceptions. On balance it is the fact that Plato draws the hereditary differences between groups so starkly that calls for describing him as an empirical racist. Because of the sheer magnitude of these differences, heredity plays an enormous role in the just city. But still the placement rule proves that when there is a clash between birth and appropriate criteria, Plato comes down squarely on the side of appropriate criteria. To be a normative racist, he would have to argue that, *regardless of* mental and moral characteristics, individuals should be assigned to classes according to birth— if, for example, three of one's grandparents were from a given class, then an individual belongs there as well. Measures such as these would be required to maintain racial purity. Because Plato would reject such measures out of hand, he is not a normative racist, although this realization should not obscure the fact that the bulk of the populations is permanently relegated to the third class.

However, that this status is conferred on them because of their natures rather than the identity of their forebears is an important difference. Because of the rarity of exceptions, one could reasonably hold that this has little practical effect. But I believe this claim is incorrect. As we have repeatedly seen, Plato structures his city around what he takes to be the facts of human nature. It is because people naturally fall into three groups that the class structure is as it is. The implication of Plato's rejection of normative racism is that the division of classes is only because of the qualities people possess. Were the facts of human nature different—or if he believed that they were—he would revise the structure of the just city. This is in accord with the political principles discussed in the next chapter (below, pp. 178–80). If the members of the lower class could be shown to be able to rule themselves, radically different arrangements would be called for. This follows from Plato's guiding principle of adjusting political structures to the qualities that people possess.

9.6. PLATO AND INDIVIDUAL FREEDOM

Criticisms of the just city frequently go beyond Plato's alleged racism and often include the claim that he advocates a 'totalitarian' society. Once again, there is a measure of truth to this charge, but as with his alleged racism, there are complexities that should be sorted out.

To begin with, although the ideal state may have some features in common with Nazi Germany, Stalin's Soviet Union and other societies that have been called totalitarian, it also lacks central features of totalitarian societies. Especially important is its lack of a system of 'terroristic police control' to keep its population in check.[29] The security of the just city is to rest on voluntary harmony, not informers, systematic purges, and concentration camps. Though the guardians have the means to terrorize the population, the explicit purpose behind their education and their renunciation of private property is to make sure that they will not do so. A comparison between inter-class relations in Plato's state and Sparta is instructive here, In Sparta the helots were constantly in revolt or threatening revolt. Accordingly, the Spartans adopted severe tactics, going so far as annually declaring war on them in order to legitimize killing them (Plutarch, *Lycurgus*, 28). Spartan youths were commonly sent out to stalk and murder helots they encountered. On one occasion reported by Thucydides (IV, 80), when the Spartans were especially fearful of revolt during the Peloponnesian War, they rounded up some two thousand of the bravest helots, supposedly to free them. But instead, the helots were massacred, under precise circumstances that have never come to light.

Needless to say, tactics of this sort are not what Plato has in mind. Though at one point (590c–d) he says that the lower kinds of men must be enslaved to the higher, this expresses a moral rather than a legal status. The rulers are to govern—unwillingly—in the interests of their subjects, not in order to exploit them. Plato says that members of all classes should as far as possible be alike and *philoi* (590d). *Philos*, the Greek word usually translated as 'friend', connotes more than 'friendship'. It is also the emotional tie between close family members, in this sense covering emotions we would call 'love'. Of course, Plato's desire that the classes to be tied together emotionally does not itself make this possible, and he does not provide a full explanation of the means that will forge these ties. But at least in so far as Plato's intentions are concerned, there can be no doubt that in this crucial respect his ideal state is not totalitarian.

In regard to how the ideal state treats its individual members, the system must on balance be deemed fair. We have discussed Plato's justification for his treatment of the lowest class. Even granted their essentially subordinate position, Plato goes to great lengths to reconcile their position in society with their deepest desires. The guardians do not use their political power to monopolize life's goods. Compare the timarchic state, which comes about when the guardians begin to rule in their own interest and so reduce the other citizens to serfs. As Plato arranges things, the guardians make the enormous sacrifices of community of property and family in order to be worthy of trust.

[29] For the distinguishing features of totalitarian states, see C. Friedrich, 'The Unique Character of Totalitarian Society', in Friedrich, ed., *Totalitarianism* (New York, 1954), pp. 52–3; also Friedrich and Z. Brzezinski, *Totalitarian Dictatorship and Autocracy*, 2nd edn. (New York, 1966), ch. 2.

Although the lowest class is excluded from politics, it controls all the state's property. Because its members are appetitively oriented, they care more about economic goods than political office and so may well be unwilling to exchange places with their rulers.

As Vlastos has shown, the principle of distribution Plato follows in the *Republic* is granting goods solely with an eye to the welfare of the state.[30] The principle of specialization, according to which each individual is to stick to the one task for which he is naturally suited, is obviously based on maximizing the well-being of the state. If turning over all political power to philosopher-kings is best for the state, it must be done. The same holds for depriving guardians of property and families, if this will make them more suited to their tasks. If sexual inducements might make bold auxiliaries even more bold, that is sufficient justification. Similarly, if depriving the producing classes of property would weaken their incentive to produce, they must be allowed to keep their property. The consistent thread running through all these measures is distribution of various goods in accordance with the interest of the state, while all inhabitants are treated impartially according to this principle. Moreover, as Vlastos shows, it is not part of Plato's political theory that the state is something over and above the individuals who inhabit it, with rights that take precedence over theirs. Rather, the interest of the state is identical to the best interests of its populace.[31]

However, although the just city treats its members fairly, it cannot be said to grant them freedom. To a certain extent Plato's disregard for individual freedom can be explained by his historical background. We have discussed the unique relationship between individual and society that the *polis* was able to foster (above, pp. 6–7), and this need not be repeated here. Let it suffice to say that at the time Plato wrote, 'the individual' as he exists in modern Western society, and as he has existed from roughly the seventeenth century on, did not yet exist. Though the Greek cities of course recognized rights belonging to individuals, in general these did not belong to them by virtue of their humanity, considered apart from any social role. Individuals had rights in connection with their positions in society, for example, their citizenship, but the notion of natural rights was largely absent from Greek political discourse. The view expressed in the *Declaration of Independence*, that all men are created equal and are endowed with inalienable rights to life, liberty, and the pursuit of happiness, would have struck the Greeks as odd. The traditional *polis* did not sharply differentiate between society and the state, or between the individual

---

[30] G. Vlastos, 'The Theory of Social Justice in the Polis in Plato's *Republic*', in H. North, ed., *Interpretations of Plato* (Leiden, The Netherlands 1977), esp. pp. 23–4.

[31] Ibid. 15–18; cf. Popper, *Open Society*, pp. 1, 79–80, 169; G. Grote, *Plato and the Other Companions of Sokrates*, 3 vols. (London, 1865), III, 124, 166.

and the community. As we have seen, Plato wished to restore this kind of traditional *polis*.

The relationship between individual and society in Greece was complex. Certain cities, especially Athens, were known for granting individuals a large measure of freedom. Thus, in his funeral speech, Pericles comments upon the openness of Athens: 'We do not look down on our neighbour if he enjoys himself in his own way.... We are free and tolerant in our private lives' (Thucydides, II, 37). Similarly, Nicias says of Athens that 'all who lived there had liberty to live their own lives in their own way' (Thucydides, VII, 69). Plato reports something similar in the *Republic*, where he excoriates democracy for its extreme openness and permissiveness (esp. 557b–d). Thus it is clear that at least some Greek cities recognized the importance of allowing individuals to live as they please—to pursue their own good in their own way, which Mill calls 'the only freedom which deserves the name'.[32] We must ask, then, why Plato did not follow this example.

As can be gathered from our discussion in Part II, Plato's overall position on the freedom of the individual can be traced back to the two-world view underlying his philosophy as a whole. According to Plato's Orphic psychological views, the soul is in essence simple, uniform, and pure, only temporarily imprisoned in the body. The entire subject matter of moral psychology—and the rationale for political theory—is occasioned by the soul's imprisonment. Though it is difficult to know how seriously to take this theme, at the very least it sets a tone of disdain for people's bodies and their desires that permeates Plato's moral and political philosophy. The image of the Cave is telling here. Since ordinary lives are devoted to the pursuit of illusory goals, Plato shows little hesitancy in wiping them away.

The theory of Forms supports this orientation, by posing a counterpart of perfection to existing imperfection. The Forms supply the only proper answers to all moral questions. People who hold values removed from the Forms are simply wrong. As Plato says, they unsuccessfully strive to hit the mark which they know is there but are unable to perceive (*Rep.* 505d–e).

The political implications of Plato's belief in objectively grounded moral truths—and most people's inability to perceive them—were discussed above, in our account of the distinction between real and empirical interests (above, pp. 112–15). The distinction expresses Plato's belief that man as he is is corrupt, and so removed from the realm of absolute value and truth. Accordingly, the individual can have no moral claim to lodge against being educated by the state. Because the goal of the education process is objectively good, his reasons for resisting can lie only in his corrupting flesh—all the more reason to help

[32] J. S. Mill, *On Liberty*, E. Rapaport, ed. (Indianapolis, IN, 1978), p. 12.

him. Again, Plato does not believe that fully formed adults can be reshaped, and so questions of moral reform do not arise in regard to them.

The extent to which Plato believes that individuals must conform to his prescribed values is seen in one of the *Republic*'s more disturbing passages. Plato argues that the practice of medicine must be restricted in the ideal state. An individual who does not respond to treatment should behave in the following way:

> If he's prescribed a long course of treatment, and told to wrap his head in dressings and so on, then his immediate response is to say that he has no time to be ill, and that this way of life, which involves concentrating on his illness and neglecting the work he's been set, holds no rewards for him. Then he takes his leave of this type of doctor, returns to his usual regimen, regains his health, and lives performing his proper function; alternatively, if his body isn't up to surviving, he gets rid of his troubles by dying. (406d–e)

Two things are striking about this passage. First, Plato has no interest in furthering the lives of people who are unable to do their part in promoting the good of the state. If they cannot do what is expected of them, their existence ceases to be of interest to the state. Second and more striking is Plato's assertion that the lives of such individuals hold no rewards for them. Plato does not consider that these people might still wish to live, that they might find their lives rewarding. What they think of the matter does not appear to be a relevant consideration, let alone what others might think—parents, children, friends, etc. Though the end of the state is to further the good of its members, Plato so tightly connects up the good of each individual with the good of all, that he seems not to imagine that someone unable to contribute to the good of all could achieve any other good. The idea that human beings have inherent value simply because they are human is not found in Plato's thought.[33]

Plato's attitude towards individual liberty is closely related. The kind of liberty that concerns us here is so-called 'negative freedom', the kind of freedom most closely associated with the liberal political tradition. This is, basically, freedom from coercive interference by other individuals. It entails some prescribed area in which an individual can be assured of being so free.[34] It is clear that inhabitants of the ideal state are granted little of this. Those liberties that liberals believe to constitute a minimum level of acceptable treatment of the individual—freedom of thought, speech, worship, freedom to live as

---

[33] This is well described by Julia Annas, *An Introduction to Plato's Republic* (Oxford, 1981), pp. 91–4, to whose discussion I am indebted.

[34] This is well described by Isaiah Berlin, in his classic essay 'Two Concepts of Liberty', in *Four Essays on Liberty* (Oxford, 1969), p. 122.

one pleases—are almost completely denied to the inhabitants of the just city. This is seen perhaps most clearly in regard to what they believe. As we have noted repeatedly, the cohesiveness and stability of the just city rest on its members agreeing as to rulers and ruled. Plato is more than willing to have this assent result from a ruthless process of indoctrination. In Book III he declares that falsehoods can often be useful, as a kind of medicine or drug, which the rulers can employ for the good of the state (389*b–c*, 382*d*). In two contexts he recommends that specific deceptions be employed. First is the rigged lottery used to deceive the inferior guardians. They are to believe that their ability to reproduce is curtailed by chance rather than by the rulers. What is striking here is that such deception is advocated for guardians, not for craftsmen.

Guardians are also to be deceived by the notorious 'myth of the metals' (414*d*–15*c*), which we encountered in the last section, in connection with the question of Plato's racism. The myth is intended to foster unity in the city. It is made up of two parts. First, all citizens, including the rulers and auxiliaries, should be made to believe that they were born from the earth, and so that all are brothers. Second, all must believe that, though they are brothers, they fall naturally into three classes. Some were born with gold in their souls and should rule; others have silver and should be auxiliaries, while the rest have bronze and should be farmers and craftsmen. Clearly, the myth affords further evidence of Plato's willingness to deceive, though it should be pointed out that it expresses something he takes to be largely true, that is, the natural differences between the three main kinds of men. But there is little reason to doubt that even if the myth did not express basic truths, Plato would uphold its use anyway, if he believed it to be for the good of the state.

More important than Plato's willingness to countenance deception is his advocacy of intensive education. Such education should be regarded as interfering with the freedom of the state's inhabitants. Complex philosophical issues are involved in this assessment, occasioned by differences between the deprivation of freedom though the employment of direct physical force and by other less direct means. But basically, though once the inhabitants' beliefs have been formed physical force will not be needed to get them to behave in the prescribed fashion, the fact that the state has so tightly controlled what they have been made to think should be regarded as a deprivation of freedom. By educating them in this way, the state has sharply limited the range of their possible choices, just as surely as if it had blocked them off with armed guards.[35]

---

[35] See Berlin, 'Introduction', *Four Essays on Liberty*, pp. xxxix–xl.

Plato clearly sees little reason not to interfere with the liberty of the inhabitants. Unlike recent liberal political thinkers, he does not view such freedom as an essential component of human dignity. In his classic work, 'Two Concepts of Liberty', Isaiah Berlin defends the opposite position: 'To be free to choose, and not to be chosen for, is an inalienable ingredient in what make human beings human'.[36] Plato does not see things in this light; he does not see freedom as an end in itself. But even more, he does not believe it is an important means to the realization of other values. Put very simply, freedom to choose between different values or styles of life loses much of its importance if one set of ideas is believed to be correct, or one mode of life demonstrably best. In these cases the freedom to think differently would boil down to the freedom to be incorrect, and freedom to live differently to freedom to follow an inferior course. Because Plato believes in objectively grounded moral truths and in the demonstrable superiority of a relatively set way of life based upon them, he sees little reason to grant individuals the ability to think or to live differently. Berlin spells out the connection between freedom and objective values— grounded in his conviction that there is no single set of all-encompassing, absolutely valid moral truths:

The world we encounter in ordinary experience is one in which we are faced with choices between ends equally ultimate and claims equally absolute, the realization of some of which must inevitably involve the sacrifice of others. Indeed, it is because this is their situation that men place such immense value upon the freedom to choose; for if they had assurance that in some perfect state, realizable by men on earth, no ends pursued by them would ever be in conflict, the necessity and agony of choice would disappear, and with it the central importance of freedom to choose.[37]

Because Plato believes that there is a single solution to all human problems, that the universe as a whole is divinely directed towards a single goal, he does not see the need to provide individuals with the opportunity to think or to choose differently.

Interestingly enough, in a crucial passage in Book IX Plato explicitly declares that the citizens of his state will be set free. The passage has been discussed above (p. 116), but I reproduce the important sentences here. Plato states that individuals whose reasoning faculties are not naturally strong enough to rule the beast within must be enslaved to and moulded by the rulers of the state, 'to foster as much unanimity and compatibility between us as might be possible when we're all governed by the same principle'. He continues:

---

[36] Ibid., p. lx.   [37] Berlin, 'Two Concepts of Liberty', p. 16.

[T]his is the function of the law; this is why every member of a community has the law to fall back on. And it explains why we keep children under control and don't allow them their freedom until we've formed a government within them, as we would in a community. What we do is use what is best in ourselves to cultivate the equivalent aspect of a child, and then we let him go free once the equivalent part within him has been established as his guardian and ruler. (590e–91a)

The implication of this passage is that, after undergoing some finite period of tutelage to the guardians, individuals will be removed from their control. Exactly what this means is not indicated. But surely Plato is presenting a contrast between the treatment of children and of adults. This sort of contrast is familiar. Since children, especially younger children, are neither fully rational nor in possession of the elementary knowledge needed to survive on their own, it is generally recognized that they must be placed under the supervision of adults until they reach the age of maturity, however defined. Accordingly, Mill finds it 'hardly necessary' to say that liberty should be granted only to people 'in the maturity of their faculties'.[38] It is also widely recognized that once individuals achieve maturity, this period of subordination comes to an end, and individuals must begin to lead their own lives.

The language in the passage quoted above appears to indicate that Plato's position is similar. Plato seems to contrast a period of rule over children, during which they are slaves to the rulers, with a later period after their souls have been properly ordered, during which they should be free. But it is difficult to say exactly what this 'freedom' consists of and how it differs from the earlier slavery. Plato's overall position disallows the contrast in its usual sense. An instance of the usual contrast would have parents watching over their young children to make sure they did not do themselves bodily harm. In a more difficult case, parents would be concerned with the moral well-being of their children, and so would monitor their experiences, to protect them from harmful influences. However, screening the television their children watched or the books they read would be undertaken in the awareness that at some future point the children would come of age and have to choose their own values, their own ways of life, for themselves.

What distinguishes Plato's case is that, aside from the rulers, the citizens of the ideal state never come of age. Certainly, they will never be free to choose from among a variety of kinds of art or from competing philosophical belief systems. The intellectual life of the state is rigidly controlled, with censorship applied to all artistic or other creations that deviate from the one true path. Similar control over individuals' ways of life are probably called for as well. In these important respects, and no doubt in others also, the state never stops

---

[38] Mill, *On Liberty*, p. 9.

exercising parental control over its citizens. In a word, Plato has too little faith in the ability and character of human beings to allow them freely to lead their own lives. As we saw in Chapter 7, he sees the vast majority of people as somewhat less than human—as the philosopher-rulers are regarded as almost more than human. As one commentator says: 'Plato's estimate of the human race is at once incredibly low and incredibly high.... Between the wisdom of the few and the docility of the rest the human race has never been so exalted or so abased'.[39]

[39] T. A. Sinclair, *A History of Greek Political Thought*, 2nd edn. (Cleveland, 1967), p. 166.

10

Philosophic Rule

The last feature of the state to be examined in detail is arguably its most important and distinctive. When Plato addresses the question of the realizability of the ideal state, in *Republic* V, he says that it can be brought into existence only if political power and philosophical wisdom can somehow be united in the same hands. The means through which this miraculous confluence is to come about is explored in the last section of this chapter. But first we must look more closely at the wisdom with which the philosophers are to rule.

10.1. PHILOSOPHIC WISDOM

We have seen that Plato requires the rule of philosophers for reasons of political stability. Since they know of something higher and finer than the joys of power and the worldly goods that power can provide, they can be trusted not to use their office for personal gain. But the ideal state requires the rulers' unique wisdom as well as their special personalities. Throughout the *Republic* Plato repeatedly notes the importance of having rulers who know the Form of the Good. Because it is through their relationship to the Good that justice and everything else of value become useful and beneficial, Plato holds that knowledge of the Good is indispensable (505*a*–*b*). If we do not know it, no other knowledge can benefit us. Whoever is to act intelligently in public or in private must see it (517*c*). Because knowledge of the Good is so important, obviously, in the ideal state of affairs everyone would possess it. But as we have said many times, according to the most basic tenets of Platonism, this is not possible. The best possible state of affairs is realized in the ideal state. Because 'subjection to the principle of divine intelligence is to everyone's advantage', those who have some facsimile of this must impose their wisdom upon those who do not (590*c*–*d*). By virtue of being ruled by philosophers who know the Good, the state as a whole is rendered wise.

We have already encountered Plato's simile of the philosopher-king and the artist (above, p. 139). In the *Gorgias*, the true politician is compared to painters, builders, shipwrights, and other craftsmen. Since the virtue of the soul, like that of anything else, 'is a matter of regular and orderly arrangement'

(506*e*), it is the job of a true ruler to impose this order upon the souls entrusted to him. The parallel between ruler and craftsman is extended in the *Republic*. As an artist, the philosopher-ruler uses the Forms as his model. After wiping his canvas clean, he works with an eye towards the heavens:

[T]he next stage would involve their [i.e. the philosophers'] constantly looking this way and that as they work—looking on the one hand toward that which is inherently moral, right, self-disciplined, and so on, and on the other hand toward what they're creating in the human realm. By selecting behavior-patterns and blending them, they'll produce a composite human likeness, taking as their reference point that quality which Homer too called 'godly' and 'godlike' in its human manifestation. (*Rep.* 501*b*)

Obviously, if the work of the rulers requires knowledge of the Forms, the instillation of such knowledge must be a significant concern of the state. Plato insists that entrusting the state to rulers without this knowledge would be turning it over to the blind (484*c–d*). And so, though the philosophers would prefer not to, they must be persuaded to rule. The philosophic curriculum described in Book VII is an institutionalized means of creating successors to the existing rulers. Only when successors have been brought up and educated can the existing rulers unshoulder their burden and depart to the realm of philosophy (540*b*).

In the light of this repeated emphasis on the importance of philosophic knowledge, it is somewhat surprising to realize that Plato says little about how the philosophers' knowledge actually enables them to rule. The philosophers must undergo the rigorous program of education discussed in Book VII and then spend fifteen years performing administrative service in the city, before they are raised to glimpse the Form of the Good, which gives them perfect knowledge and completes their education. As we noted in Chapter 6, knowledge of the Form of the Good should probably be construed as knowledge of the intelligence behind all things, of the rational pattern according to which the world as a whole is directed. But it must be asked exactly how this knowledge is necessary for ruling a state.

In Book I of the *Ethics*, Aristotle criticizes the kind of moral knowledge supplied by the Form of the Good. His two major arguments concern what we can call (*a*) the vagueness and (*b*) the apparent uselessness of such knowledge.

Starting with vagueness, it is difficult to say exactly what the Form of the Good is and what knowledge of it would entail. The problem of describing the Good was noted above, including Socrates' unwillingness or inability to explain its true nature in *Republic* VI–VII. According to the theory of Forms, the Form of Good must exemplify some quality or set of qualities common to all things of which 'good' can be predicated. However, things (taken in a loose sense) can be called 'good' in many different ways. We can have a good runner, a good book, a good hammer, a good man, a good job, a good time. It is difficult to isolate one specific sense of 'good' common to all these uses. Apparently 'good' does not maintain a constant sense under different circumstances, as the sense of 'white', for example, is constant in white hair, white paint, a white Christmas, and the White House. Many philosophers say that when 'good' is used its sense is always in reference to a set of criteria specific to its object, while these criteria differ in different kinds of cases. For instance, a good hammer is useful in performing the tasks that a hammer is supposed to perform; a good racehorse succeeds in a competitive endeavour by outrunning other horses; a good book satisfies certain aesthetic criteria, about which there is controversy. We have seen that Plato probably believes that the Form of the Good supplies the intelligible principle according to which all things are ordered. If this is true, different objects participate in the Form and so are good by fulfilling their roles in this overall scheme of things. But it is difficult to explain the precise connections between the various senses in which things are called 'good' and their roles in the rational pattern of all things, without saying, tautologically, that the criteria in reference to which different things are deemed 'good' play this role because of their place in the cosmos as a whole. The Form of the Good exhibits only tenuous connections with the different good things in the sensible world.

Because the connections between the Good and the sensible world are so indefinite, it is difficult to identify the practical value of knowing the Form. One difficulty mentioned by Aristotle is that people engaged in the different fields of practical activity do not see the value in knowing the Good for their work (*EN* 1096*a*6–14). The weaver is not interested in the Good, but in how to make good cloth. The cobbler cares about good shoes, the cook about good food. These craftsmen are interested in the specific criteria of goodness pertinent to their arts, rather than the Good itself. The role the Good plays in their arts is difficult to specify, while even if it can be shown to have a role, this has not been recognized by those same craftsmen whose work Plato frequently cites as examples of informed, purposeful activity. One last possibility concerning the role of the Good is presented by Aristotle:

But possibly someone may think that to know the Ideal Good may be desirable as an aid to achieving those goods which are practicable and attainable; having the Ideal Good as a pattern we shall more easily know what things are good for us, and knowing them, obtain them. (1096*b*39–1097*a*3)

As Aristotle notes, this argument has a certain plausibility, but it too is out of keeping with the actual practice of the different arts. For if knowing the Good is such a potent aid, it seems strange that the practitioners of the different arts are not aware of this. Craftsmen attain proficiency in their fields through years of practice and through study of the objects of their crafts, not through studying metaphysics.

In his account of practical wisdom in the *Ethics*, Aristotle presents further grounds for doubting the usefulness of knowing the Good (esp. *EN* VI, 7–8). The subject matter of Aristotle's account is *phronêsis*, generally translated as 'practical wisdom', though alternative translations are 'prudence' and 'sound judgement'. Aristotle's basic point is that while theoretical knowledge is concerned with the abstract and the unchanging, practical wisdom, being concerned with the needs and interests of particular individuals in particular situations, deals with the concrete and the variable. Even more than knowing the general rules of human conduct, the man of practical wisdom must be able to assess particular situations to decide which rules apply. He must be able to evaluate the given situation, to seize upon the relevant facts, and to understand how they interact. Thucydides describes the political genius of Themistocles in terms such as these:

[H]e had the power to reach the right conclusions in matters that have to be settled on the spur of the moment and do not admit of long discussions, and in estimating what was likely to happen, his forecasts of the future were always more reliable than those of others. ... To sum him up in a few words, it may be said that through force of genius and by rapidity of action this man was supreme at doing precisely the right thing at precisely the right moment. (I, 138)

Obviously, this sort of ability is not to be gained from studying metaphysics. Because knowledge of particulars is attained through experience, Aristotle says that it is not found in the young. Though the young can be mathematical prodigies, they cannot be mature in judgement. Indeed, it is often the case that individuals highly gifted in theoretical knowledge are deficient in practical wisdom. In the familiar story, the philosopher Thales was so intent on contemplating the sky as he walked that he fell into a well. Though Thales might have possessed 'a knowledge that is rare, marvellous, difficult and even superhuman' (*EN* 1141b6–7), this kind of knowledge does not necessarily entail abilities that yield beneficial practical payoffs. In the *Prince*, Machiavelli advises the would-be ruler to study history, not philosophy.

A final indication of the questionable nature of knowledge of the Good is found in the report, given by Aristoxenus, of the reaction of the wider public when Plato lectured on the topic:

Such was the condition, as Aristotle used often to relate, of most of the audience that attended Plato's lectures on the Good. They came, he used to say, every one of them in the conviction that they would get from the lectures some one or other of the things that the world calls goods; riches or health, or strength, in fine, some extraordinary gift of fortune. But when they found that Plato's reasonings were of sciences and numbers, and geometry, and astronomy, and of good and unity as predicates of the finite, I think their disenchantment was complete.[1]

Returning to Plato's account of the philosophers' knowledge in the *Republic*, we find that Plato does not explain exactly how this is beneficial to the state, while the necessary connections are difficult to surmise. This is not surprising given the remoteness of absolute Goodness from the lives and concerns of ordinary human beings. If we rough out a sketch of what the rulers of the state actually do and what they must know to do it, it can be seen that knowledge of the Good is not directly required. The rulers' main task is moulding souls. In order to succeed at this, they require detailed knowledge of human psychology. They must know the proper proportions of mental and physical training to be applied to different types of personalities. They must understand the effects of different types of art, and how to turn dubious and dangerous compositions into helpful ones. This knowledge must cover not only poetry but music and all the visual and plastic arts as well. The rulers must know how to devise the crucial series of tests for aspiring rulers, how to weed out those unfit to rule and how to recognize and elevate superior members of the producing class. They must also devise means—probably educational ones—to ensure the loyalty of the lowest class, and thereby spread contentment throughout the state.

Other kinds of knowledge are also required. The rulers must know eugenics, how to breed the best with the best, and how to rig the mating lotteries towards this end. They must also be able to keep the population stable. Various political skills are required. Plato frequently declares that the guardians must be versed in war. They must also be able to negotiate effectively with other states, including the Machiavellian scheming necessary to subvert potential enemies (see 422*a*–23*a*). Plato mentions other tasks as well, for example, avoiding great disparities of wealth and poverty. This list could be extended, but the main point should be clear. In order to rule the ideal state the guardians require a formidable array of knowledge, skills, and talent. But it is not clear exactly how knowledge of the Good contributes to these.

To his credit, Plato recognizes the importance of the rulers' knowing more than the Good. He insists that they be superior in moral knowledge, but also not deficient in practical experience. And so Plato devises means to provide experience. This is an aspect of the rulers' training that is often overlooked, so it should be emphasized here. The clearest provision is the requirement that the philosophers spend fifteen years performing administrative service in the city, before they are given final knowledge and led up to contemplate

---

[1] Aristoxenus, *Harmonics*, II, 30; H. Macran, ed. and trans. (Oxford, 1902).

the Good (539*e*). This is as much time as they spend on mathematics and dialectic combined. Perhaps the greatest additional emphasis falls upon war. The military applications of the philosophers' training are repeatedly mentioned in Book VII. The study of arithmetic, geometry, and even astronomy are all explicitly recommended in this regard. Knowledge of these subjects is required if the rulers are to be able properly to marshal their troops, construct encampments, and array their forces for battle (525*b*–*c*, 526*c*–*d*, 527*c*–*d*). Plato notes that the military applications of these subjects require far less than the detailed knowledge possessed by the philosophers. But if military proficiency is not a primary objective of mathematical education, it is still an explicit concern. Additional attention is paid to war in Book V, where Plato recommends that the guardians be exposed to battle at an early age, as the children of other craftsmen are exposed to their future professions early in life. For the rulers as well as the auxiliaries, war will be an important professional concern (466*e*–67*d*).

Thus, Plato is aware that knowledge of the Good is not a sufficient condition for being able to rule. But his failure to explain exactly how it is relevant to governing is a significant gap in his political theory. Still, Plato has good reasons for insisting that knowledge of the Good is a necessary condition for effective rule. Its moral effects are indispensable. In bringing the philosophers to despise the things of this world, knowledge of the Good supplies an indispensable qualification for their office. In Book VII Plato states that cities ruled by philosophers, who have seen the Good, are in the hands of men who are awake rather than dreamers. As he goes on to describe the superiority of waking to sleeping, this is seen to be not cognitive, but to lie in the philosophers' superior values (520*c*–21*b*). Similarly, in Book VI, when Plato compares the philosophers, who are sighted, to other men who are blind, the former's superiority lies in a different value orientation (484*c*–*d*).

Though Plato stresses the importance of the philosophers' having absolute knowledge, his view seems easier to defend in regard to the moral rather than the cognitive effects of such knowledge. Although Plato does not clearly argue along these lines, according to the most reasonable construal of his view, philosophers must rule, not because of the practical value of their absolute knowledge, but because absolute knowledge ensures proper values. It is not surprising that Plato shifts between the cognitive and the moral aspects of philosophic knowledge in the light of his view that knowledge is bound up with an orientation of desire as well as a cognitive state. For Plato in the *Republic*, intellectual superiority is moral superiority, and regardless of his failure to explain the importance of the former, the philosophers cannot succeed at their appointed tasks without the latter.

10.2. PHILOSOPHIC RULE

Though we are able to say little about the precise contents of the philosophers' knowledge or exactly how it is applicable to their concerns as rulers, we do know one crucial thing: it supplies the state with an active, probing, critical intelligence. This is an important theme in the political theory of the *Republic* and provides strong reasons why the philosophers must have the most exalted knowledge possible—regardless of the precise contents of that knowledge— and so helps to explain why Plato insists that they know the Good. Moreover, in addition to uncovering a key feature of the political workings of the state, this allows us to see how Plato fulfils one of the deepest aspirations of Socratic thought. It reveals a fundamental continuity between the political thought of the early and middle works, and as we see below, a possible discontinuity with the political theory of the later dialogues.

As he describes his mission in the *Apology* and as he is seen practising it in many of the early dialogues, Socrates' intention is to waken the Athenians to the importance of caring for their souls, or caring for virtue. This theme has been explored at length in Part I. The point to bear in mind here is that, in Socrates' eyes, an individual cares for his soul by embarking upon a quest for true moral principles, according to which he is committed to live. We have seen that Socrates holds his moral principles provisionally, subject to re-examination at any time, but as long as a given principle proves the best possible, Socrates commitment to it is unshakable (pp. 40–3).

With the introduction of the philosophical system of the middle dialogues, Plato moves on to a very different conception of what it is to care for one's soul. As we saw throughout Part II, virtue in the middle dialogues is bound up with balance and harmony, the direct rule of reason and control of appetite. Because an individual can achieve this condition only through intensive con- ditioning, the Socratic ideal of each individual caring for his own soul must be cast aside. The introduction of the theory of Forms also leads Plato to oppose Socrates' belief in the limited power of human knowledge. According to the epistemological views of the middle dialogues, the most exalted truths are accessible to man, but only to the highly privileged few. Since only the philosopher can reach such heights, the many must be enslaved to the few if they are to partake at all of divine intelligence. Accordingly, Plato's epistemo- logical views entail a renunciation of the Socratic faith in moral autonomy. Because the many can never know for themselves, they must live according to principles they are taught to believe. The state as a whole is wise only through the wisdom of its philosophers.

Because of these radically different psychological and epistemological views, Plato must depart from Socrates' commitment to critical rationalism. Because the philosophers in the *Republic* contemplate 'all time and all existence' (*Rep.* 486*a*), it is hard to conceive how they would be able to maintain a detached, critical attitude towards such knowledge. What is more, Plato clearly believes that the philosopher-kings will bring such knowledge to bear in ruling the state. Plato depicts them as doing their job with an eye to the heavens, governing the state according to the dictates of their exalted knowledge. One such passage is quoted above on p. 171.

Not surprisingly, scholars have made much of this sort of depiction of the philosopher-king's activity. Popper, for instance, draws a sharp contrast between Socrates in the *Apology* and Plato in the *Republic*. Whereas he sees the former as a great figure in the history of rationalism and open philosophic inquiry, Popper grants Plato an equally prominent place in the history of irrationality and oppressive social thought. He says that the *Republic* reveals a 'magical attitude' towards social laws and conventions, which must make them rigid and all but impossible to change.[2] Popper is not alone in this conviction; scholars more kindly disposed towards Plato are willing to concede much of the same ground. For instance, R. S. Bluck, writing to defend Plato against some of Popper's more outrageous allegations, describes the ideal state in the *Republic* as a theocracy. Bluck locates the central feature of a theocracy in the fact that 'the ultimate author of all law, whether written or unwritten', must be divine.[3] Thus, he believes that Plato wishes for the state to be founded on divine truths, in keeping with which the guardians are to legislate. In Bluck's words: 'The ideal state should acknowledge a divine force external to itself not only as the sanction of its laws, but also as the ever-present guide to interpretation of them, and its Guardians, having constant reference to it, should put these into effect'.[4]

Thus, according to the view upheld by Popper and Bluck, the ideal state is founded upon some divinely sanctioned blueprint or plan of the state. Only the philosophers have intellectual access to this plan, while clearly, according to this view, their role is to mould political reality according to its dictates. This would appear to be the basic meaning of the simile of the philosopher-king and the artist; the philosophers' main intellectual activity is seeing the Forms, according to the dictates of which they are to shape the state. Because this construal of the philosopher-kings' political activity rests so heavily on divinely grounded truths, we can refer to it as a 'mystical' conception of their activity.

---

[2] K. Popper, *The Open Society and Its Enemies*, Vol. I, *The Spell of Plato*, 5th edn., 2 vols. (Princeton, NJ, 1966), I, 172.

[3] R. S. Bluck, 'Is Plato's *Republic* a Theocracy?' *Philosophical Quarterly*, 5 (1955), 69.

[4] Ibid. 73.

Even though mystical interpretations of the *Republic* are widely held, I believe that such views are actually misguided and should be qualified in important respects. Both Bluck and Popper overlook the extent to which Plato shapes the ideal state around the presence of an active, critical intelligence. In order to see this more clearly, and to see exactly what the mystical view neglects, we must examine an important distinction Plato introduces in the *Statesman*.

The political theory of the *Statesman* is discussed in detail in Chapter 11. In the section of the work that concerns us here (292*a*–303*b*), Plato argues that the true or scientific statesman is someone who knows the art of ruling. Plato appeals to the analogy of the true physician, whose claim to this title rests on his grasp of the art of medicine. Plato contrasts the true constitution, presided over by a genuine statesman, with others based on the rule of law. Laws are deficient because of their rigidity and generality. They are drawn up for average people under average conditions and cannot readily adapt to special or extenuating circumstances. They are equivalent to instructions a doctor would leave if he were to be away from his patients for an extended time. The rule of the true statesman is superior because it can adapt to changed circumstances. The true ruler would not be constrained by past enactments. He would simply apply the scientific understanding he had brought to the original codification of the laws to the new conditions. Just as a doctor would feel no compunction to abide by prescriptions he had previously written but would apply his knowledge directly to his patients' present circumstances, the true ruler would not feel bound to abide by the laws.

Thus, in the *Statesman* Plato contrasts the constitution based on the direct rule of scientific intelligence with the inferior constitution based on the rule of law. Though this exact distinction cannot be applied to the *Republic*, something closely resembling it can be. The contrast to bear in mind in regard to the *Republic* is between the role of the philosopher-ruler as (*a*) an active, self-critical intelligence, or as (*b*) an essentially passive implementer of the divinely grounded blueprint of the ideal state. While the views of Popper and Bluck would have Plato subscribing to (*b*), it can be seen that he actually has in mind something closer to (*a*).

Numerous considerations support this view. To begin with, Plato argues in Book VI that the ideal state requires rulers who not only can apply the laws, but also understand them fully: 'The community would have to contain an element which understands the rationale of the political system and keeps to the same principles' that its original founders had in sketching its laws (497*c*–*d*). (The reference to original founders is to Socrates and his interlocutors in the conversation that makes up the *Republic*.) Because they possess this understanding, the philosophers are not merely to put into practice a fully worked-out blueprint that is formulated without any input from them. Rather, they are to implement a plan over which they have final say. The crucial point is that, should they find reasons to alter the blueprint, they are empowered to do so.

Because they have undergone the programme of studies described in *Republic* VII, Plato feels free to leave much of the task of structuring society in the philosophers' hands. Thus, concerning many aspects of the commercial life of the state, Socrates says that he and his fellow interlocutors need not bother spelling out detailed rules and regulations. 'It isn't right to tell truly good men what to do', Adeimantus says. 'They won't have any difficulty, in the majority of cases, in finding out which matters need legal measures' (425d–e). The same goes for other laws as well: 'If [the rulers] receive a good education which makes them moderate, then they'll easily discover everything we're talking about for themselves' (423e; see also 427a).

Many specific aspects of the state are, accordingly, left incomplete, sketched in broad strokes with the remaining details reserved for the rulers. For instance, they must determine the extent to which the state can safely expand beyond its original borders (423b–c), and the number of marriages needed to keep the male population stable (460a). They must originate the programme of trials and tests through which the perfect guardians are selected from their fellows (see 414a). In reference to his programme of early education, Plato states that he is presenting only broad outlines (*tupoi*), while the specific details are the responsibility of the guardians (379a, 412b).

This principle allows us to read into the state features that Plato does not explicitly discuss, for example, an organized system of education for the lowest class. Throughout the preceding chapters we have repeatedly seen the need for such a programme. Because the rulers will recognize this need, Plato does not have to discuss the programme himself. The rulers are empowered to do more than merely fill in what the original founders have left out. Because they possess exalted knowledge, Plato believes it is possible for them to evaluate and criticize the state. He gives them leave to alter features that do not work, even major features. In Book X, a central feature of the state is explicitly said to be open to further examination at any time. Poetry is offered a chance to reply to the charges levelled against it, that is, the reasons Plato gives for treating it as he does. Though this passage is lengthy, its importance requires that we quote a substantial section of it:

[W]e ought to point out that if the kinds of poetry and representation which are designed merely to give pleasure can come up with a rational argument for their inclusion in a well-governed community, we'd be delighted ... to bring them back from exile; after all, we know from our own experience all about their spell. ... Under these circumstance, then, if our allegations met a poetic rebuttal in lyric verse or whatever, would we be justified in letting poetry return?

Yes.

And I suppose we'd also allow people who champion poetry because they like it, even though they can't compose it, to speak on its behalf in prose, and to try to prove that there's more to poetry than mere pleasure—that it also has a beneficial effect on society and on human life in general. And we won't listen in a hostile frame of mind, because we'll be the winners if poetry turns out to be beneficial as well as enjoyable.

Of course we will, he agreed.

And if it doesn't, Glaucon, then we'll do what a lover does when he thinks that a love affair he's involved in is no good for him; he reluctantly detaches himself. Similarly, since we've been conditioned by our wonderful societies until we have a deep-seated love for this kind of poetry, we'll be delighted if there proves to be nothing better and closer to the truth than it. As long as it is incapable of rebutting our allegations, however, then while we listen to poetry we'll be chanting these allegations of ours to ourselves as a precautionary incantation against being caught once more by that childish and pervasive love. (607c–8a)

If poetry is able to present a suitable defence, it must be treated differently, though this would entail significant changes in the system of early education, and perhaps in the entire state.

This is not the only instance in which the state is subject to revision by the rulers. After completing discussion of early education, Socrates stresses its importance in ensuring that the guardians protect their charges and do not abuse them. To Glaucon's remark that such a programme has been devised, he responds:

That's not something we should stake our lives on ... But we should stand firmly by our present position that *whatever constitutes a proper education* (*hêtis pote estin*), it is the chief factor in the guardians' treating themselves and their wards in a civilized fashion. (416b–c; emphasis added)

It is clear, then, that central elements in the ideal state are maintained subject to revision and review.

And so there is strong evidence that the philosophers are to play the role of an active, critical intelligence in governing the state. To employ the analogies of the *Statesman*, the philosophers have the knowledge of the doctor, who writes prescriptions, not merely of the pharmacist, who carries them out. They are not merely to shape their surroundings according to a blueprint that is given. They must take appropriate measures where the blueprint is found to be incomplete or faulty, and presumably when circumstances change as well.

There are, however, problems with this view. A serious difficulty is that some element of the mystical interpretation of the philosophers' activity is undoubtedly true. As we have seen above, the philosophers' attainment of supreme knowledge is generally described in terms of direct visual apprehension. This conception of knowledge as arising in a sudden burst of light has strong mystical or religious overtones and has commonly been interpreted along these lines. Similarly, as we have seen, the philosopher-rulers are repeatedly described in mystical terms, doing their work with an eye to the Forms, shaping the state according to the dictates of a divinely grounded pattern. It seems difficult to imagine how the philosopher could maintain an open, critical attitude towards knowledge that comes to them in a sudden burst of light. But to this troubling objection there is a reply.

In the light of the extraordinary nature of the philosophers' knowledge, it seems that the main difficulty we face runs something like this: 'If the philosophers have certain knowledge of ultimate moral truths, how can this knowledge be subjected to critical examination and discussion?' Alternatively, adopting Bluck's point of view: 'If the philosophers' role is to enforce divinely sanctioned laws, how could they possibly criticize and change them?' We have seen that Plato describes the philosopher-kings as heavenly artificers. But let us look more closely at this simile.

One commentator describes the comparison of the philosopher and the craftsman at *Republic* 501 as follows:

Plato applies the language of the theory of ideas to the 'social tissue' here exactly as he applies it to the making of a tool in the *Cratylus* 389c. In both cases there is a workman, the ideal pattern and the material in which it is more or less perfectly embodied.[5]

This parallel, however, is not exact. In the *Cratylus* we have a carpenter who looks towards the Form of the Shuttle as he makes a shuttle out of wood. As Plato describes him, the nature of his task is easily grasped. He is to envision the Form of Shuttle and to attempt to impose it on his materials, thereby creating a physical object that is a direct imitation of the Form. The activity of the philosopher-king is more complex. Plato does not portray the philosopher-king as looking to the Form of the ordering he wishes to impose upon his material. Plato never mentions a Form of the Ideal State—or a Form of State for that matter—and such a Form plays no role in his political theory.[6] Rather, it is striking that, when the philosopher-king is portrayed as shaping the state according to the Forms, the Forms he looks to are those of moral qualities, Justice, Beauty, Moderation (501*b*), the Good itself (540*a*)—not the Form of Ideal State. His task is to embody these moral qualities in men's souls,

---

[5] P. Shorey, *The Republic of Plato*, 2 vols. (London, 1930–5), II, 70 n.

[6] Though Plato never writes of a Form (*eidos* or *idea*) of the state, he does describe a model or exemplar (*paradeigma*) of the ideal state, notably at *Rep.* 472*d–e* and 592*b*; on this see N. White, *A Companion to Plato's Republic* (Indianapolis, IN, 1979), pp. 39, 245, 151.

while the means to this end must be fabricated. How the philosophers are to shape the political institutions needed for the desired outcome is a problem to the solution of which they are not given metaphysical guidance.

It seems, then, that Bluck is incorrect in his assertion that the ideal state is a theocracy in which divine forces are responsible for all laws. A more proper view is that the philosopher-king is given an end at which to aim, while his political task lies in devising proper means. Though the end perhaps is rooted in mystically apprehended truths, the question of devising means involves prototypically rational considerations. In so far as the philosophers act in this capacity their role does not appear to be different in kind from that of Bentham's lawgiver, who must devise the optimal means to the greatest good for the greatest number. It seems to me that the fact that ruling is this sort of task is one reason Plato requires that the philosophers have practical knowledge, especially that they spend fifteen years gaining administrative experience.

Thus, it appears that the philosophers bear responsibility for devising the institutional structure of the state. Even if they are given a divinely grounded end to aim at, they are not given divine guidance concerning means. There is no reason why they cannot maintain a critical, open-minded attitude towards the laws and institutions of the ideal state. Indeed, if they discover that the censorship of poetry does not have the desired moral effects, or if they can be convinced by poets that it would not have them, there is little reason why they should not alter this feature of the state.

I do not wish to play down the extent to which the *Republic* is rooted in absolute moral knowledge. Plato is vague about these matters, but there can be no doubt that he puts his objective moral truths before all other considerations, even if knowledge of them resists critical scrutiny. But Plato is undoubtedly less rigid about political institutions. We see strong evidence of this in Part IV. In his late works, when Plato has become sceptical of the possibility of finding the superhuman beings required for philosophic rule, he alters fundamental features of his ideal state.

Additional evidence for this reading is the philosophers' unwillingness to rule. The philosopher-kings of course love contemplation of the eternal Forms far more than anything in this world. Quite simply, because they love truth more than political power, they would not be afflicted by the common dictator's fear of making changes that might weaken his position. They should be willing to criticize and reform the state to improve it.

Thus, the central motif of the political theory of the *Republic* is putting philosophical intelligence in control of the state. Though Plato never explains exactly how the philosophers' supreme wisdom is beneficial to the state, his insistence that they possess this appears to express the ideal that the state be governed by the highest Truths. We have seen above that there is a tension in Socrates' thought between his desires (*a*) that individuals discover their own moral principles, and (*b*) that the principles they discover be compatible with those he himself accepts as true (above, p. 40). A similar tension is seen in the *Republic*. The philosophers possess the highest knowledge. They are able to glimpse the Forms and to see the necessity of shaping the state according to the outline sketched in the *Republic*. Like Socrates, Plato makes the highly optimistic assumption that the truths the philosophers will discover are those he himself holds sacred. The possibility that they might come to see things differently is not explicitly taken into account, and so Plato does not explore what would ensue if the philosophers believed it was necessary to modify the state in fundamental ways. Presumably, from what we have seen in this chapter, Plato would have them go ahead, but we must keep in mind that he does not explicitly say this.

In any event, the political theory of the *Republic* centres upon the rule of the state by supreme intelligence. Philosophers must be kings because only they can discover what must be done. The rulers maintain some measure of moral autonomy. They are not merely to accept the structure and institutions of the state as metaphysically grounded givens. They are to understand the state's rational basis, and to alter and improve things whenever necessary. But if the political ideal of the *Republic* is placing an active philosophical intelligence in control of society, we confront another difficulty, how this situation can be arranged.

10.3. IMPLEMENTING THE IDEAL STATE

We have seen above that Plato was forced to reject the Socratic position in regard to moral reform as unworkable. It remains to be seen what he has to offer in its place.

Though Plato is often thought of as an extremely unworldly, 'utopian' political thinker, it can be seen that he took the question of practical political reform seriously. In Part IV we will discuss his involvement with practical politics, in Syracuse and in the Academy. But he also thought long and hard about the means through which the ideal state in the *Republic* could be brought into existence. From his criticism and rejection of the position concerning political reform upheld by Socrates, a more sophisticated view arose—more sophisticated than Plato is frequently given credit for.

In order to show that the *Republic* is less 'utopian' than is commonly maintained, we must make a few distinctions. The adjective 'utopian' can be used in a number of different senses, three of which should be sorted out. Theory *x* can be utopian in that (*a*) the author never thought seriously about bringing it into existence, or (*b*) he never realistically contemplated the political obstacles to its realization, in addition to (*c*) the fact that it is highly unlikely to be realized in practice. In the case of Plato's *Republic*, I believe that (*c*) is true, as is generally recognized. But I also believe that (*a*) and (*b*) are not true. The ideal state is not like Shangri-La, or the ideal society described in Aldous Huxley's *Island*, an imaginary society, the creator of which gave little or no serious thought to how it could be realized. Many literary utopias are of this kind, but the *Republic* is more than '(an employment) of the imaginary to project the ideal',[7] to use one commentator's phrase. It is a political programme to the realization of which Plato did give serious thought.

Plato repeatedly contrasts his construction with mere wishes or prayers.[8] The Greek work *euchê*, means literally a 'prayer'. In the context of utopian theorizing, it can be translated, as Shorey does, as 'wish-thought'. Waterfield and Grube-Reeve translate it as 'wishful thinking'. Perhaps a suitable contemporary translation is 'pipe dream'. In Book V of the *Republic*, Socrates is emphatic that his construction should not be viewed as 'nothing but a wish-thought (*euchê*)' (450*d*; Shorey trans.). At 456*c*, the same term is used in reference to education of female guardians. This too is not 'impossible or a wish-thought (*ouk... adunaton ge oude euchais*)' (456*c*). The term is also used in reference to the possibility of the state at 499*c* and 540*d*. In the latter passage, which wraps up the overall discussion of the realizability of the state, Socrates says that 'our notion of the state and its constitution is not altogether a wish-thought (*mê pantapasin... euchas*), but that though it is difficult, it is in a way possible' (540*d*; trans. following Shorey). As Myles Burnyeat argues, the ideal state is like a *euchê* in being a product of imagination. However, it is not an idle product, a daydream, but is intended to be subjected to 'the test of practicability'.[9]

This contrast between the just city and mere wishful thinking is supported by the fact that the just city is much *more* practicable than the alternative scheme of reform that Plato examines at length, the view of Socrates. Though Socrates too was interested in the realization of his practical ideal, he did not fully recognize the obstacles he faced. Plato, in contrast, subjected these obstacles to prolonged scrutiny. And so, though the ideal state was never

---

[7] G. Kateb, 'Utopias and Utopianism', *The Encyclopedia of Philosophy*, 8 vols., P. Edwards, ed. (New York, 1967), VIII, 212.

[8] My argument here is indebted to M. Burnyeat, 'Utopia and Fantasy: The Practicability of Plato's Ideally Just City', in *Psychoanalysis, Mind, and Art*, J. Hopkins and A. Savile, eds. (Oxford, 1992), esp. p. 179.

[9] Ibid. 179; see also M. Davis, 'On the Imputed Possibilities of Callipolis and Magnesia', *American Journal of Philology*, 85 (1964). Aristotle describes various ideal states in reference to *euchai* frequently in the *Politics*, e.g. 1260*b*29, 1288*b*23–4, 1295*a*29, 1325*b*35–36, 1330*a*25–26.

likely to be realized—and Plato never thought it was—what interests us are the *reasons* for its unlikelihood. For these concern the same impediments that confront any theory of radical political reform.

It is with trepidation that, in *Republic* V, Plato approaches the question of implementing the just state. The question of realizability, as Plato actually formulates it, is to discover the 'the smallest change [that] would enable a community to achieve this type of constitution' (473*b*). But in the *Republic*, Plato is not interested in compromise; the ideal state can come into existence only through radical reform. Plato, however, realizes that the reformer of an actual state must settle for some approximation of the ideal (473*a–b*). The problem, then, is to discover 'how a community's administration could come very close to our theory' (473*a*). Plato's recognition that the just city cannot be realized completely raises important and difficult questions concerning points at which different approximations cease to be satisfactory. But these we will set aside. The question of realizability is answered by the paradox of the philosopher-king. There is one change, says Socrates, that is 'not a small change, however, or easy to achieve, but it is feasible' (473*c*):

Unless cities have philosophers as kings, ... or the people who are currently called kings and rulers practise philosophy with enough integrity—in other words, unless political power and philosophy coincide, and all the people with their diversity of talents who currently head in different directions towards either government or philosophy have those doors shut firmly in their faces—there can be no end to political troubles, ... or even to human troubles in general. (473*c–d*)

The paradox of the philosopher-king is familiar. It is restated a number of times in the central books of the *Republic*, and found in the *Seventh Epistle* as well (above, p. 12). In it is contained Plato's prescription for political action. In order for the ideal city to be realized in practice, philosophy and political power must coalesce.

This can happen in either of two ways: if kings become philosophers, or if philosophers become kings. Although once the ideal state has been established, it will not matter in which of the two ways it was founded, in so far as the actual realization of the state is concerned, it makes all the difference in the world. Two entirely different sets of political problems are involved. Transforming a king into a philosopher involves convincing one man, who is already in power, to follow the path of justice. Transforming a philosopher into a king involves the political problems a specific individual or group of individuals must overcome to secure power. Although either way one turns the problems are virtually insoluble, Plato realizes that these are political problems. They are not to be overcome in the world of rarified deductions, but in the world of facts. The philosopher must enter this world and emerge with power, and depending on which of the two possible ways he turns, the problems he faces are quite different.

In all probability, Plato arrived at the paradox of the philosopher-king as the result of a process of elimination: he had nowhere else to turn. The major trouble with the paradox is that it too is virtually impossible to achieve. But this is not to say that Plato was not interested in establishing the ideal state. Rather, it is only to realize that because of intractable political obstacles, its realization must wait upon the intervention of more than human forces.

As we have said, Plato is convinced that the philosopher cannot hope to reform society—indeed even to save isolated individuals—without recourse to political means. He sees no good coming from a Socratic-type mission of reform. Though Plato nowhere discusses the remaining alternatives in a systematic fashion, we are able to get a fairly good idea of his thoughts on the subject from *Republic* V and VI and from some of his other works, especially the *Seventh Epistle*. What we find is a far cry from optimism. As the philosopher is barred from a Socratic-type mission, other possible courses are also closed to him. First, as we have noted (above, p. 142), he cannot hope to accomplish anything by working within the political system. In a democracy, especially a corrupt democracy, the successful politician must pander to the mob. Socrates realized this, and in the *Apology* he gives this as his reason for not pursuing a political career (*Ap.* 31c–33b). In a corrupt city, the successful politician can win the favour of the mob only by means of an exceptional talent to gratify its harmful desires. If the philosopher is not willing to indulge in such pursuits, he cannot hope for political success, while to work to oppose such measures would mean certain death. Thus, Socrates was forced to steer a private course, and the ironic fact is that this could not possibly have worked either.

Additional factors work against attempting reform through the political machinery of a society. As we have seen, ordinary legislative measures cannot achieve anything of value in a corrupt society. Such a society is fundamentally defective, and it requires fundamental reform. However, what the mob 'can abide least of all' is someone who tries to tell it the truth (*Rep.* 426a). Thus, the philosopher in politics is no better off than the philosopher outside politics. In the *Seventh Epistle*, we see that Plato arrived at his paradox of the philosopher-king when he realized that ordinary political solutions could not work.

In this *Epistle*, as we saw above (p. 11), Plato explains how he came to be disillusioned with Athenian politics (324b–25c). He was bitterly disappointed in the reign of the Thirty, and in the returning democracy as well. Plato describes an important conclusion he reached:

The more I reflected upon what was happening, upon what kind of men were active in politics, and upon the state of our laws and customs, and the older I grew, the more I realized how difficult it is to manage a city's affairs rightly.... At last I came to the conclusion that all existing states are badly governed and the condition of their laws practically incurable, without some miraculous remedy and the assistance of fortune. (325c–26a)

The miraculous remedy in which Plato came to lodge his hopes was the convergence of political power and philosophy, that is, the philosopher-king (326a–b). In this passage, Plato so much as tells the reader that his reliance on the philosopher-king was forced upon him by the sorry state of ordinary political affairs.

As we have said, the philosopher-king can be brought into existence in either of two ways: either philosophers can become kings, or kings can become philosophers. The problem of how a philosopher attains political power is one that Plato does not consider in the *Republic*. Because he says nothing about the use of violent means to attain it—the means attempted in Syracuse by his friend and pupil, Dion (see below, p. 198)—it seems probable that he would not approve of their use. But it is not possible to state Plato's position on this question with assurance.

There is good evidence that Socrates was opposed to the use of violence to accomplish reform—especially violence directed at one's homeland. In a well-known passage in his 'dialogue' with the 'Laws of Athens' in the *Crito*, Socrates says that, when someone disagrees with an ordinance of his city, he must either convince his city through persuasion that he is right, or, if he is unable, he must submit (51b–c). This position on the question of violence is in keeping with Socrates' attempt to reform his fellow citizens through the use of persuasive means alone. But whether this was the attitude of Plato as well is more difficult to say.

From the evidence of the *Seventh Epistle*, it would seem that Plato remained faithful to the position of his teacher. In this Epistle he asserts that one should attempt to warn his city if he thinks it corrupt 'and there is a prospect that his words will be listened to and not put him in danger of his life' (331c–d). But if persuasion will not work, 'let him not use violence upon his fatherland to bring about a change of constitution. If what he thinks is best can only be accomplished by the exile and slaughter of men, let him keep his peace and pray for the welfare of himself and his city' (331d). It is worth noting that the last lines of this quotation almost echo the prescription Plato offers the true philosopher in the *Republic* (above, p. 60). The problem, however, is that, in the *Statesman*, written some time during the period between the composition of the *Republic* and that of the *Seventh Epistle*, Plato is less squeamish about philosophic violence (see below, pp. 204–5).

The basic argument here is that in questions of government, the betterment of the people is the only factor to be considered and so how this is to be achieved is open. Among the means Plato allows ideal rulers are putting citizens to death or banishing them. An indication that this was Plato's attitude when he wrote the *Republic* is the fact that, in that work, he is willing to resort to drastic measures indeed against the population of the soon-to-be reformed state.

It seems to me that the decisive consideration in determining Plato's position on this question in the *Republic* is the fact that he does not say anything about the philosopher using force to seize power in this work. In this matter, I believe, we should accept the argument from silence. It is, however, interesting that Plato seems to shy away from this alternative. For given his premises, this seems to be the obvious solution. If the philosopher requires political power, why doesn't he attempt to take it? Had Plato followed the implications of this line of argument, he would have found himself on territory very close to that of the more traditional political theorists of radical reform.[10] But, for whatever reasons, Plato rejects this alternative. Perhaps he does so for moral reasons, disapproving (at the time he wrote the *Republic*) of 'the exile and slaughter of men' on principle, or perhaps because in his youth he saw, in the Thirty Tyrants, how political coups tend to end up—while the fate of Dion in Sicily would have more than confirmed his darkest fears, and perhaps explains his further retreat from violence in the *Laws* (see below, p. 244). In any event, deprived of the resort to force, the philosopher is placed in an impossible position. He cannot undertake a Socratic-type mission of reform, nor can he hope to wield influence within the political system. If he cannot attempt a seizure of power, he must indeed 'lie low and do what he's meant to do'; all other options are closed to him.

There is, however, one remaining possibility, and this takes us to the other main alternative. Even if the philosopher cannot hope to rise to power, he can hope to influence those who are in power—even granted the severe difficulties he would encounter, of the kind sketched in *Republic* VI. Plato briefly discusses this alternative as a means to realize the less dramatic political transformations required by the 'second-best city' in the *Laws* (709c–11c) and pursued in himself in his dealings with Dionysius II, tyrant of Syracuse (see below, pp. 197–8). In addition, it is likely that Plato founded the Academy as a training ground for future statesmen, for advisers of rulers (see below, pp. 199–200). But Plato does not pursue this line of approach in the *Republic*, perhaps because he does not think it can yield the thoroughly radical reform he has in mind.

---

[10] For discussion of these and paradoxes associated with attempts to seize power, see G. Klosko, *Jacobins and Utopians: The Political Theory of Fundamental Moral Reform* (Notre Dame, 2003).

Plato lodges whatever hope remains in the possibility of a king becoming a philosopher. Though the chance of this ever coming about are pitifully slim, it is not impossible, and it is the fact that it is not impossible that Plato emphasizes throughout the *Republic*. However, unlike the other alternative— the philosopher becoming king—hoping for a king to be born with a philosophic nature leaves the existing philosopher in the unhappy situation of waiting upon events beyond his control. Direct divine intervention is required, as is seen in language that Plato uses to describe this possibility. But still, it is upon this hope that Plato bases his argument for the realizability of the just state.

Plato presents this argument in Book VI. He argues only for the possibility of a king becoming a philosopher. What is required is a series of lucky accidents, and no one can prove this sequence of events impossible. First, no one can say that there is no chance that the sons of kings can be born with the philosophic nature (502*a*), or that if so born they must all be corrupted. Socrates knows that it would be difficult for a potential philosopher to escape corruption, but still, could opponents of the idea maintain that 'philosophical children of kings and rulers are absolutely bound to be corrupted?' (502*a–b*). If, in the fullness of time, one should be saved, the next step is not impossible either: 'If even one remains uncorrupted, ... in a community which is prepared to obey him, then that is enough; everything which is now open to doubt would become a full-fledged reality' (502*a–b*). But would his city obey him? Again, this is not impossible: 'If he, as a ruler, establishes the laws and practices we've described, ... then it's surely not inconceivable that the citizens of the community will be prepared to carry them out' (502*b*). That the entire citizen body over the age of 10 would willingly go out into the fields never to return does strain one's credulity; but perhaps it is not absolutely impossible.

At this point it is clear that Plato is grasping at straws. Not only does he base his case on one unlikely occurrence after another, but he pyramids them. Each improbable event is dependent on the ones that precede it, and so the odds against Plato's miracle increase not arithmetically but geometrically. But the series is complete. Is it possible that the citizenry would be willing to obey their philosophic ruler? It is not impossible (502*b*). And Socrates concludes: 'If our proposed legislation were actually to happen, it would be impossible to improve on it; and its realization may be difficult but is not impossible' (502*c*).

Thus, Plato has little hope for his ideal state. Instead of arguing that its realization is possible, he demonstrates only that it is not impossible, and he must go to extreme lengths to prove even this. Presumably, the philosopher-ruler would have recourse to means—perhaps violent means—that the philosopher without power does not have. All he would have to do is to purge his city of its corruption, to rusticate all citizens over the age of 10. And although it seems beyond comprehension that he would be able to accomplish this, Plato is probably right. It is not 100 per cent impossible.

This is the position that Plato takes throughout the *Republic*. It is 'feasible, and we aren't talking about unrealizable theories', he writes in Book VI, 'though we're the first to admit that it wouldn't be easy' (499*d*). This is also asserted at the end of Book VII: 'The community may be difficult to realize, but it's feasible' (540*d*). At the end of Book IX, Socrates appears to take a different view on this question, giving up all hope.[11] But closer inspection reveals that the message of this passage is essentially the same. Socrates remarks that the city he and his interlocutors have been describing exists in their discourse, though not on earth. Then Socrates says:

> It may be, . . . that it is retained in heaven as a paradigm for those who desire to see it and, through seeing it, to constitute himself its citizen. In fact, it makes no difference whether it exists now or ever will come into being; it's still the only community in whose government he could play a part. (592*b*; trans. following Shorey)

This passage appears to be more pessimistic than the others we have seen. However, closer examination reveals this is incorrect. In this passage, the immediate question is whether the just man will take part in politics (591*e*). Socrates says, 'He certainly will, in his own community. But I agree that he probably won't in the country of his birth, short of divine intervention' (592*a*). As we have noted, although the just city is 'difficult but not impossible', its realization depends on a series of unlikely events, each of which depends on those that have preceded it. These, collectively, constitute 'divine intervention'. But if these circumstances do not arise, the philosopher will not take part in politics. The passage adds to what we have discussed only the fact that, in the absence of divine intervention, the philosopher will take part in the public affairs of only the replica of the just city constructed in his soul (592*b*).

Though it might seem a poor reflection on Plato as a political theorist that he has no firm means to implement his state, this is certainly the case. But on a larger scale, something more should be said on Plato's behalf. Plato understands the grim necessity that forces the philosopher to resort to political means. He sees the futility in trying to use persuasion as a means of reform. A society indelibly stamps the souls of its inhabitants, and Plato pursues this insight to its logical conclusion. To reform the corrupt inhabitants of a corrupt society, this process must be reversed; the indoctrinating mechanism of society

---

[11] Cf. the discussion of this passage in the first edition of this work, p. 179, which is incorrect in presenting a conventional interpretation.

must be used for virtue instead of vice. Thus, Plato not only has an interest in implementing his ideal state, but he perceives both the means necessary for the desired end and the obstacles that bar the way.

But though the solution to the problem is clear in theory, in practice it must be solved by power. And where this power is to come from Plato cannot say. However, the fact that Plato's theory of radical reform is almost impossible to implement does not destroy its value. In rejecting the Socratic position and formulating the means through which a corrupt city must be reformed, Plato accomplishes an impressive theoretical feat. In formulating the principle that the moral reformer requires political power, Plato states a permanent political truth—for good or for ill.[12]

---

[12] To quote Machiavelli: 'Thus it comes about that all armed prophets have conquered and unarmed ones failed' (*The Prince*, ch. 6; trans. L. Ricci and E. R. P. Vincent, *The Prince and the Discourses* (New York, 1950), 22). For discussion, see Klosko, *Jacobins and Utopians*.

Part IV

Plato's Later Political Theory

11

Plato's Later Political Theory

The mood in Plato's late political works has dimmed. Fiery ideals burn less bright; his view of man's nature has fallen; his faith in radical reform has given way to more modest hopes. Though we cannot be certain exactly what caused this shift, it is natural to place considerable weight on Plato's remarkable political experiences in Sicily. The influence of Sicily will be seen repeatedly in this and the following chapters. An additional factor that must be taken into account is changes in Plato's metaphysical ideas.

In the *Parmenides*, one of the dialogues ushering in the late period, Plato offers a trenchant critique of the theory of Forms. This work depicts an encounter between a relatively young Socrates, probably around 18 years of age, and the venerable Parmenides. Socrates outlines the theory of Forms (*Parm.* 128e–30a), and Parmenides criticizes it. The focus of Parmenides' attack is participation, the relationship between the perfect Forms and their imperfect exemplars in the sensible world. All Socrates' attempts to account for this relationship are dispatched, and Parmenides concludes his attack by advising him to get more practice in the art of making precise logical distinctions before tackling such difficult metaphysical issues (135c–d). Parmenides then presents a lengthy demonstration of the kind of dialectical argumentation Socrates should practise. In a series of subsequent dialogues, especially the *Sophist*, Plato analyses crucial aspects of the theory of Forms with a level of logical sophistication not seen before.

Scholarly opinion is divided over crucial aspects of Parmenides' criticism, including the identity of the theory that is criticized, and what the criticisms amount to. It is certainly in keeping with Plato's sense of fun to put criticisms of his earlier views into the mouth of Parmenides, with a teenage Socrates unable to respond. Many scholars hold that Parmenides' arguments are directed against the theory of Forms as presented in the middle dialogues.[1] Evidence for this is that some language in the *Parmenides* is similar to accounts of the Forms found in the *Phaedo* (compare *Parm.* 130e; *Phaedo* 102b).

---

[1] R. Robinson, *Plato's Earlier Dialectic*, 2nd edn. (Oxford, 1953), pp. 229–30; W. D. Ross, *Plato's Theory of Ideas* (Oxford, 1951), pp. 84–5; F. M. Cornford, *Plato and Parmenides* (1939; rpt. Indianapolis, IN, 1957), pp. 70 ff.; cf. R. E. Allen, 'Participation and Predication in Plato's Middle Dialogues,' rpt. in *Studies in Plato's Metaphysics*, Allen, ed. (London, 1965).

In addition, the *Parmenides* is narrated by Cephalus, with Glaucon and Adeimantus featured in its 'frame-conversation'. This unavoidably calls to mind the *Republic*. We have seen that Plato is undecided about participation in the middle works (above, p. 91), and so it seems that, in the *Parmenides*, he returns to some continuing difficulties with the metaphysical views of these dialogues.

A few basic points about the criticisms can be made. First, though Plato apparently attacks central elements of the theory of Forms, this does not cause him to abandon the theory in his later works. A theory of Forms markedly similar to that of the middle dialogues is presented in the *Timaeus*. This has led certain scholars to attempt to change the traditional dating of the *Timaeus*, in order to locate it in the cycle of middle dialogues, but this attempt has probably not succeeded.[2] Aspects of the theory are examined in great detail in the *Sophist* and the *Seventh Epistle*, which was written during Plato's last years, and probably hinted at in the *Theaetetus* and *Statesman*. Most important from our point of view, the final pages of the *Laws* are filled with allusions to the theory of Forms (see below, p. 253).

It seems safe to say that, though the theory of Forms is not abandoned, it does undergo important changes. The Forms' more exalted, religious overtones largely vanish from discussion in the late dialogues. The main exception is the *Timaeus*, but even in this work a cosmic artificer (*dêmiourgos*) is introduced, whose task is to shape the universe according to the Forms. In general, I believe that we can correlate Plato's reduced emphasis on this side of the Forms with his greater direct attention to the gods and religion in the *Laws*. Thus Plato's thought becomes less metaphysical and more religious, as is clearly seen by comparing the *Republic* and the *Laws* (see below, pp. 249–51).

11.1. PLATO AND SYRACUSE

Questions of intellectual causation and influence are notoriously difficult to answer with assurance. But in all probability the movement to Plato's later political theory is influenced by changes in his metaphysics and his involvement in political affairs in Syracuse. The former is highly abstract and so difficult to trace, but the latter shows up clearly in numerous contexts. Whatever we make of the relationship between the development of Plato's metaphysics and political thought, we repeatedly detect the influence of Syracuse on his later political theory.

[2] See G. E. L. Owen, 'The Place of the *Timaeus* in Plato's Dialogues' and H. Cherniss, 'The Relation of the *Timaeus* to Plato's Later Dialogues', both rpt. in *Studies in Plato's Metaphysics*, Allen, ed.; C. Gill, 'Plato and Politics: The *Critias* and the *Politicus*', *Phronesis*, 24 (1979).

The story of Plato's experiences in Sicily is recounted in his *Seventh Epistle*, while many other epistles, most notably the Eighth, are concerned with Plato's affairs there.[3] The main concern of these epistles is Plato's attempts to reform Dionysius II, tyrant of Syracuse and convert him to philosophy. In order to appreciate the magnitude of Plato's undertaking, it is necessary to realize that Syracuse was then the mightiest city in the Greek world. Its power had been built by Dionysius I, who ruled for thirty-eight years, and an idea of whose character can be gathered from Book IX of the *Republic*, in which he serves as the model for the tyrannic man. But Dionysius was effective in preventing Sicily from being overrun by Carthage—while using the Carthaginian threat to legitimize his autocratic methods. At his death Syracuse was a major commercial centre and naval power, with an empire that encompassed two-thirds of Sicily as well as holdings in Italy.

Plato met Dionysius on his first visit to Sicily, in 387. According to Plutarch, their meeting did not go well, as Plato proceeded to relate his ideas about the moral condition of tyrants (*Dion* 5). In return, so the tale goes, Dionysius had Plato sold into slavery. But something important did come from Plato's first visit to the tyrant's court: he made the acquaintance of Dion, brother-in-law to the tyrant. Dion, then a young man, was captivated by Plato's moral teachings. Plato thought highly of his intellectual and moral capabilities in turn, and a lasting friendship was formed.

Twenty years later, Dionysius died, and left his throne to his son, Dionysius II. Dion wrote to Plato, advising him to come to Syracuse and attempt to win the young tyrant over to philosophy: 'What better opportunity can we expect, than the situation which Providence has presented us with?' (*Ep.* 7 327e). What ensued is recounted in the *Seventh Epistle*. For our purposes it is enough that Plato was not confident about the venture, but he was eventually persuaded to go. An important consideration was his desire not to appear to himself 'a pure theorist, unwilling to touch any practical task' (328c).

During his initial months in Syracuse, it seemed that Plato might succeed. Dionysius II was not cut from his father's cloth. He was interested in philosophy, greatly attracted to Plato, and for a time Dion and Plato were his chief

---

[3] For references concerning the authenticity of *Epistle 7*, see above, ch. 1, n. 1. I regard *Epistle 8* too as genuine. For discussion, see G. Morrow, ed., *Plato's Epistles*, rev. edn. (Indianapolis, IN, 1962), pp. 81–8. Cf. the argument of P. A. Brunt, *Studies in Greek History and Culture* (Oxford: Oxford University Press, 1993), pp. 319, 339–41. The authenticity of *Epistle 8* is supported by G. Ledger's analysis of stylometric evidence (*Re-counting Plato* [Oxford: Oxford University Press], 1989, pp. 151–3). W. K. C. Guthrie counts twenty-two scholars who view this epistle as genuine, as opposed to three who doubt this—not counting the eight scholars who accept all the letters and the twenty-four who deny them all (*A History of Greek Philosophy*, 6 vols. [Cambridge, 1962–81], V, 401). Like most scholars, I doubt the authenticity of many of the other letters, although this subject cannot be explored here.

advisers. But other elements in the Syracusan court perceived a threat and secured the banishment of Dion. With this Plato realized the futility of his venture and returned to Athens.

About six years later, Plato was persuaded to return once more. He was told that Dionysius II had taken a great interest in philosophy. Plato was even less optimistic this time, and he was proved correct. Dionysius' commitment to philosophy proved superficial; Plato says that he had a 'coating of opinions, like men whose bodies are tanned by the sun' (*Ep. 7* 340*d*). Plato bided his time until he was able to leave safely and return to Athens.

Although it is not possible to say with assurance exactly what Plato hoped to accomplish with Dionysius, it seems unlikely that he seriously considered transforming him into a philosopher-king. Something more modest was probably intended. The best bet is that Plato wished to transform Syracuse from a dissolute autocracy into a moderate government under the rule of law. Despite one enigmatic phrase in *Epistle 7* (337*d*), his advice to the friends and followers of Dion was to institute the rule of law, which, he says, is what he had also advised Dion (*Ep. 7* 334*c–d*). It is likely that a close connection exists between Plato's concern with the rule of law in Syracuse and the new emphasis on laws in the *Statesman* and *Laws*. Thus it seems that Plato's aim in Sicily was not to found an ideal state but rather to establish some facsimile of the 'second-best' state based on the rule of law recounted in the *Laws*. It appears that Plato founded the Academy as a training ground for political actors and advisers of rulers (on which more below) and his involvement in Syracuse should be seen in the light of the Academy's tradition of political activity rather than as an attempt to fulfil the exalted hopes of the *Republic*. In any event, Plato was not successful, and the aftermath of his attempt was tragedy.

In the year 357 the still-exiled Dion assembled a small army of supporters and invaded Sicily. Because of obligations he had incurred as Dionysius' guest, Plato was unwilling actively to support the expedition (*Ep. 7* 350*b–d*), though there can be little doubt about his sympathies. Despite the vast disparity between Dion's forces and the tyrant's, Dion managed for a time to gain control of Syracuse. But Dion proved unequal to his task. His attempts to secure political power for himself—perhaps as a necessary prerequisite for reform, but perhaps not—were regarded by the Syracusans as a resumption of tyranny. The situation degenerated into a chaos of faction, murder, and anarchy, and Dion was eventually assassinated in 353—by Callipus, an Athenian, who had been associated with the Academy.

The events in Syracuse do little to enhance Plato's political reputation. The *Seventh Epistle* is not only intended to offer advice to the surviving friends and followers of Dion, but is also a defence of Plato and his school, an attempt to put his Syracusan involvement in the best possible light. This apologetic purpose must be borne in mind in assessing the historical accuracy of Plato's account, but even this apology is not enough to dispel criticism. Some commentators are willing to give Plato the benefit of the doubt. For instance, Burnet says that there 'was nothing chimerical in the project', and remarks that, had Plato succeeded in educating Dionysius, he might have done for Syracuse what the Pythagorean philosopher Lysis had done for Thebes in educating Epaminondas.[4] Most scholars are more critical. A representative view is Guthrie's, that Plato's fear was confirmed; he showed himself to be a born theoretician, rather than a successful man of action. As Guthrie says, 'It should cause no surprise that the author of the *Republic* and even of the *Laws* was something of a political innocent, more at home drawing up laws and constitutions on paper than engaging in the rough and tumble of Greek political life.'[5] Other authorities are less gentle. According to one eminent historian, Plato 'misjudged Dion as a man and miscast him as a statesman', while another says of Plato's proposals in the *Epistles*: 'I doubt if anyone could compose a more useless or empty reply to a request for practical advice.'[6]

It seems only reasonable that Plato's experiences with Sicily would have a substantial influence on his political theorizing, and in examining the *Statesman* and especially the *Laws*, we will note specific instances. The *Statesman* was probably written some time between Plato's renewed involvement in Sicily and Dion's expedition.[7] In this work we detect a falling off from the ideals of the *Republic*, and consequently a greater interest in existing states and how they work. The *Laws* is notably more sombre, and it is natural to attribute this at least in part to the sorry outcome of Sicilian events. Plato's work in the *Laws* is based on a vast accumulation of detailed knowledge of the laws and institutions of numerous Greek cities. This research obviously took years, and it seems reasonable to associate this concerted programme of legal research with Plato's active involvement in Syracusan politics.

It is important to recognize that Syracuse did not represent the full extent of Plato's involvement in the politics of actual states. As we have noted, the Academy was intended at least in part to offer practical training to would-be legislators and advisers of rulers. In a famous passage, Plutarch relates something of the extent of the Academy's political involvement (*Adv. Colot.* 1126*c*). According to Plutarch, Phormio drew up legislation for Elis, Eudoxus

---

[4] J. Burnet, *Greek Philosophy: Part I, Thales to Plato* (London, 1914), pp. 295, 300.
[5] Guthrie, *History*, IV, 29.
[6] N. G. L. Hammond, *A History of Greece*, 2nd edn. (Oxford, 1967), p. 520; M. I. Finley, *Aspects of Antiquity* (Harmondsworth, UK, 1968), p. 79.
[7] J. Skemp, ed. and trans., *Plato's Statesman* (London, 1952), pp. 13–17.

for Cnidus, and Aristotle for the Stagirites. Aristonymus was sent to Arcadia and Menedemus to the Pyrrhaeans, while Alexander the Great is reported to have requested advice concerning kingship from Xenocrates, who was the third head of the Academy. Plato too was reportedly asked to draw up laws. According to (the not always reliable) Diogenes Laertius (II, 23), the Arcadians and Thebans asked him to write laws for the city of Megalopolis which they founded. From other sources we learn that two additional members of the Academy, Erastus and Corsicus, were sent to advise Hermeias, tyrant of Atarneus. The probably spurious *Sixth Epistle* concerns their mission. In addition, Aristotle was of course tutor to Alexander of Macedon, while Dion was a close associate of Plato, and many members or associates of the Academy accompanied Dion on his expedition to Syracuse, including Callipus, his killer.

The evidence for all of these instances is not above reproach, but even if specific details are incorrect, a clear pattern of political involvement emerges in connection with the Academy.[8] The unavoidable implication is that Plato, who is often dismissed as a utopian thinker, whose works are often analysed completely removed from the political events of his society, is actually quite the opposite. One could make the case that Plato had as much experience, direct and indirectly through his students, as virtually any comparable figure in the history of political thought. Even if Plato's plans did not always work out, his involvement was extensive. The depth of his concern shows through the *Statesman* and *Laws*, and contributed to the movement of these works away from positions espoused in the *Republic*.

11.2. THE *STATESMAN*

Like the *Laws*, Plato's other late, political dialogue, the *Statesman* discusses a wide variety of topics in what at first sight appears to be a rambling, at times almost arbitrary manner. This is, however, only appearance, as recent scholars have shed considerable light on the work's underlying structure. Still, little of the literary quality of the early and middle dialogues is in evidence,

[8] For discussion, see Morrow, *Plato's Epistles*, pp. 137–42; P. M. Schuhl, 'Platon et l'activité politique de l'académie,' *Revue des Études Grecques*, 59 (1946). For a more recent, essentially positive assessment, see T. Saunders, ' "The Rand Corporation of Antiquity": Plato's Academy and Greek Politics', in *Studies in Honour of T. B. L. Webster*, Vol. I, J. H. Betts, J. T. Hooker, and J. R. Green, eds. (Bristol: Classic Press, 1986). Cf. the more sceptical assessments of Brunt, *Studies*, ch. 10; and M. Schofield, 'Plato and Practical Politics', in *The Cambridge History of Greek and Roman Political Thought*, C. Rowe and Schofield, eds. (Cambridge: Cambridge University Press, 2000); for additional discussion with further references, see G. Klosko, 'Politics and Method in Plato's Political Theory', *Polis*, 23 (2006).

while the break from these works is apparent in the fact that Socrates is only a peripheral character. The main spokesman, obviously Plato's mouthpiece in the work, is an unnamed Eleatic Stranger, while Socrates stands by mute for almost all the proceedings. The *Statesman* is part of a trilogy, also containing the *Theaetetus* and *Sophist*, the latter of which is also dominated by the Eleatic Stranger. The reason for the Eleatic origin of the Stranger is more apparent in the *Sophist*, as that work tackles important metaphysical questions associated with Parmenides, who was from Elea, and whose tradition in philosophy was known as the 'Eleatic'. This trilogy was originally intended to contain a fourth work as well, the *Philosopher*.[9] But, for whatever reasons, Plato did not complete the project—as other late works, the *Timaeus-Critias-Hermocrates* trilogy, also remain incomplete.

Like the *Sophist*, the *Statesman* is structured around an attempt at definition. The Eleatic Stranger and his interlocutor—young Socrates, namesake of Socrates—attempt to identify the nature of the 'statesman' (*politikos*). The Stranger employs the distinctive method of 'division' (*diairesis*), which is a prominent form of dialectic in Plato's late works. According to this procedure, the term to be defined is part of an inclusive class from which it must be distinguished through a series of bifurcations. Separating the *politikos* from related terms will be seen to yield important insights not only in regard to the function of the statesman but also in distinguishing the political art from closely related competitors—those of the general, the orator, and the judge—and clarifying its relationship to them.

The series of divisions begins with the unquestioned assumption that the statesman possesses a kind of art or science (*epistêmê*). This is identified as a practical science, rather than one that merely provides knowledge. The art is intellectual, rather than based on manual labour, and gives orders to others, as opposed to being the activity of a spectator. Through a lengthy and tedious series of steps along these lines, the statesman emerges as a sort of shepherd, who gives orders to the human herd.

Several of these bifurcations have an immediately odd appearance, and it is not clear how seriously we are to take them. The peculiarity of at least some divisions is clearly for pedagogic purposes, as the Stranger intentionally leads young Socrates to mistaken conclusions for the sake of being able to correct him (262*a*–63*a*, 264*a*–*b*, 268*b*–*e*, 274*e*). Plato is however quite serious about the method. The Stranger says that the discussion has been taken up not for the sake of its particular subject matter but 'for the sake of our becoming better dialecticians (*dialektikôterois*) generally' (285*d*). Central to the method is that

[9] See F. M. Cornford, ed. and trans., *Plato's Theory of Knowledge* (1934; rpt. Indianapolis, IN, 1957), pp. 168–9.

dialectical divisions must correspond to underlying realities. As Socrates says in the *Phaedrus*, one should divide according to the location of the 'natural joints', 'not trying to break any part, after the manner of a bad carver' (*Phdr.* 265d–e). For the underlying divisions, Plato uses a variety of terms, mainly *eidos* and *genos*. The primary dictionary definitions of the latter are 'race' and other terms indicating descent and, more generally, 'kind'. *Eidos* is more ambiguous. As we have seen, it is one of Plato's standard terms for Forms in the middle dialogues. In the divisions, *eidos* and *genos* are used interchangeably and should be translated neutrally as referring to 'classes' or 'species'.[10] Scholars generally believe that the underlying realities correspond to Forms in important respects, but stripped of the transcendental attributes familiar from the middle dialogues.[11] Crudely put, what is at issue in the method of division is the ability to recognize the crucial element amidst the welter of particular factors in given circumstances.

Although the Stranger represents this foray into division as useful primarily as a philosophical exercise, the content of the discussion is obviously of great importance for Plato's political theory. Lest there seems to be a disconnect between methodological exercise and political theory, the unity of the *Statesman* lies in the fact that the method of division demonstrated by the Eleatic Stranger is closely related to the political art (*politikê technê*) that is possessed by the statesman and constitutes his qualification to rule.[12] This is eventually described as ability to recognize the objectively correct course amidst a welter of particular circumstances changing through time (see below, p. 206). The faculty of perception this requires is akin to the ability to sort out the similarly real object of dialectical inquiry from the complexities of the wider class in which it is subsumed.

Described in these terms, the art of the statesman is an art of true measurement. According to the Eleatic Stranger, in contrast to relative measurement, which is concerned only with how, for instance, large and small things stand to one another, there is an art of measurement that is concerned with 'due measure (*to metrion*)', which is objectively rooted. More fully described, this art measures 'in relation to what is in due measure, what is fitting, the right moment (*kairon*), what is as it ought to be' (284e). Thus as Plato presents his account of due measure, this too is correct in regard to constellations of particular circumstances. Objective standards are required for the existence of

    [10] A. Diès, ed. and trans., *Le Politique*, Budé series, Vol. IX, pt. 1 (Paris, 1935), pp. xviii–xix; C. Rowe, ed. and trans., *Plato: Statesman* (Warminster, 1995), pp. 5–7.

    [11] Rowe, *Statesman*, pp. 4–8; Skemp, *Statesman*, pp. 75–9; M. Lane, *Method and Politics in Plato's Statesman* (Cambridge, 1998), pp. 16–18; C. Kahn, 'The Place of the *Statesman* in Plato's Later Work', in *Reading the Statesman*, Rowe, ed. (Sankt Augustin, Germany, 1995), pp. 54–60.

    [12] For these crucial connections, I am indebted to Lane, *Method and Politics*.

all arts, including that of the statesman, which are intended to achieve them (284*a*–*d*).

For our purposes it is not necessary to discuss all matters that Plato covers in the *Statesman*. In section 11.3, we examine Plato's account of the true statesman and his function in the state. We then turn to Plato's account of actual states under the rule of law.

11.3. THE IDEAL RULER

The preliminary definition produced by the Stranger's first series of divisions is that the statesman is a practitioner of the art of 'nurturing' or 'rearing' (*trephein*) human herds, which is analogous to the art of the shepherd. However, despite the extravagant care that was taken in arriving at this definition, the Stranger expresses dissatisfaction. Rather than explaining his objections, he launches into a myth, to mix in 'an element of play' (268*d*).

The Stranger's myth divides history into two ages, the age of Cronus and the age of Zeus. The former is a time long past, a golden age during which god directly controlled the universe. In those times men were born from the earth fully grown and aged backwards. It was a time of plenty; there was no need to labour and no want. There was also no need for property, and neither politics nor war. But the age of Cronus came to an end, ushering in the age of Zeus. God no longer directly controlled the course of things, and so men were left to their own devices. Because they lacked knowledge of the arts and fire, and were at the mercy of wild beasts, their very survival was threatened. But the gods sent fire, with Prometheus, and knowledge of the arts, enabling them to preserve themselves.

The myth has an explicit moral, that the divine statesman mentioned above, the statesman as superior to his human flock as a shepherd is to his sheep, does not exist. The earlier definition is explicitly criticized and revised (274*e*–75*e*). What we are left with is that the statesman's art does not pertain to rearing or nurturing his charges, but to 'tending' or 'taking care' of them (*therapeuein* or *epimeleisthai*). The difference between this and the earlier description is that this does not imply that the practitioner of the statesman's art is qualitatively superior to his charges. He is human as they are. Thus in identifying the art of the statesman, the Eleatic Stranger points away from belief in or hope for ideal political arrangements.

It is difficult not to associate the moral of the myth with the rejection of the ideal state of the *Republic* and its government by more-than-human philosophers. This is especially clear in the light of the similar myth employed in Book IV of the *Laws* (713*a*–14*b*; see below, p. 218).[13] Other attempts to explain Plato's meaning have not been successful.[14] Certain details of the age of Cronus recall the *Republic*, especially the absence of property and families, and the fact that the people of that era were earth-born (271*a*; cf. *Rep.* 414*d*–*e*). But there is a problem with this interpretation, because, as the dialogue progresses, Plato elaborates on the nature of the statesman in such a way that he comes close to the *Republic*'s philosopher-king.

During the remainder of the dialogue, Plato fills in this sketch of 'caring for' the human herd. As he argues in many other works, in the *Statesman* Plato holds that the statesman's exalted title rests on knowledge. He has mastered the art (or science) of ruling (292*b*–93*a*), and this is his sole identifying feature. The statesman merits this title whether or not he holds political office (258*e*, 259*a*). In power, his rule is to be untrammelled by either laws or the desires of the subjects. We saw above why the statesman must not be bound by laws (293*e* ff.; above, p. 178). The Stranger's argument is different from that employed in the *Republic* to justify rule without laws. In the *Republic*, Plato argues that laws are useless: in the good state they are unnecessary, while in the bad state they cannot work (see above, pp. 138–9). The argument here is that laws are vague and general; they are designed for average people under average conditions. Again, they are like prescriptions a physician would leave if he were to be away for a lengthy time. This argument seems more convincing if one bears in mind that Greek laws were much less flexible than those enacted in modern states. It was only because laws would often become immemorial, like customs, that the word *nomos* could be applied indifferently to both. The statesman possesses the kind of wisdom that went into drawing up the original laws. Thus he should be allowed to adjust the laws to changed circumstances. It is notable that Plato's argument here deals with laws only in so far as they embody an expression of social desires and aspirations. They are not considered in connection with the need to restrain rulers and protect subjects.

The statesman is also freed from the need to attain the consent of his subjects. Plato argues from another aspect of the analogy of the physician. A doctor is a doctor whether his patients submit willingly to his ministrations. The sole requirements are that he exercise scientific intelligence, and that this be aimed at the good of his subjects (293*a*–*b*). According to the Stranger:

---

[13] I should note that Lane dissociates the two versions of the myth (*Method and Politics*, pp. 116–17). Diès, in contrast, describes the *Laws* myth as an 'extract' from that in the *Statesman* (*Politique*, p. xxxvii).

[14] See esp. Skemp, *Statesman*, pp. 49–66; cf. G. M. A. Grube, *Plato's Thought* (1935; rpt. Boston, MA, 1958), p. 279.

And whether they purge the city for its benefit by putting some people to death or else by exiling them, or whether again they make it smaller by sending out colonies somewhere like swarms of bees, or build it up by introducing people from somewhere outside and making them citizens—so long as they act to preserve it on the basis of expert knowledge and what is just, making it better than it was so far as they can, this is the constitution which alone we must say is correct, under these conditions and in accordance with criteria of this sort. All the others that we generally say are constitutions we must say are not genuine, and not really constitutions at all, but imitations of this one ... (293*d–e*; also 296*d–e*)

Along similar lines, in describing the statesman's art of 'weaving' the fabric of the state later in the work, Plato recommends harsh measures for dealing with individuals with little potential to become virtuous. They are to be executed, banished, or otherwise severely punished (308*e*–9*a*).

Plato's willingness to countenance violence is one aspect of the *Statesman* that is similar to the *Republic*. In that work, as we have seen, the philosopher-kings are able to use drastic means in order to bring the ideal state into existence. One reason for dating the *Statesman* before Dion's expedition is that it seems it would have been difficult for Plato to hold this attitude towards violence afterwards. Indeed, in the *Seventh Epistle*—and in the *Laws*, both of which were written after events had run their course—Plato's attitude is markedly different. In the *Epistle* he writes that, if the wise man thinks that what is best 'can only be accomplished by the exile and slaughter of men, let him keep his peace and pray for the welfare of himself and his city' (331*d*; see above p. 187). A similar attitude is expressed in the *Laws*, as we see (pp. 243–4).

We encounter an important ambiguity in the *Statesman* concerning Plato's attitude towards the subjects' consent. Though, as we have seen, Plato insists that the presence or absence of consent is not relevant for assessing the statesman's rule, at one point earlier in the work he says that consent distinguishes the king, who practises statesmanship, from the tyrant (276*e*). This appears to be a contradiction in the work between what Plato says in different contexts about the need for consent. This ambiguity too should be borne in mind.

In spite of these difficulties, in Plato's exposition, the statesman's art fulfils an unfulfilled aspiration of the early dialogues and represents an advance over the political theory of the *Republic*. There are close parallels with the *Euthydemus*. In that work, the art of ruling is described as a directive art, with the authority to tell other arts when and how they should be applied. Generals know the art of war, but when they have captured a city, they do not know what to do with it and so turn it over to politicians (*Euthyd.* 290*c–d*). But in the *Euthydemus*, the discussion runs into an impasse (291*b*–302*e*). The nature of the art of properly using what has been acquired is not explained. In the

Statesman, this sketch is filled in. Using the simile of weaving as his guide, the Stranger makes clear how the art of the statesman is distinct from subsidiary arts. While there are other claimants to the status of human herdsman (267c–68c), the statesman controls them. While he does not possess the art of the general, the orator, or the judge, his science of ruling allows him to employ these other arts most efficaciously. In the Stranger's words:

> If then one looks at all the kinds of expert knowledge that have been discussed, it must be observed that none of them has been declared to be statesmanship. For what is really kingship must not itself perform practical tasks, but control those with the capacity to perform them, because it knows when it is the right time (*enkairias*) to begin and set in motion the most important things in cities and when it is the wrong time (*akairias*); and the others must do what has been prescribed for them. (305c–d)

Reference to *enkairia*, 'seasonableness', and its opposite, *akairias*, is important in explicating the nature of the statesman's art. These terms are related to *kairos*, which connotes both the right time or season for action and what is advantageous or practical. In the art of rhetoric, *kairos* connotes the appropriate action at the appropriate time.[15] In the *Statesman*, these terms are used to imply the statesman's mastery of the particular circumstances in which the subsidiary arts are exercised. In other words, the knowledge of the statesman is 'knowledge of timing', 'the situating of objective knowledge in a framework of temporal flux'.[16] We have seen that ability to identify proper time is one component of the art of true measure (above, p. 202). Similarly, the statesman's objective mastery of particular factors and how they change through time is what justifies placing him above the law. While laws are inevitably general and inflexible, because of the statesman's command of changing circumstances, he is able to adapt them to particular contingencies.

In describing the statesman's art as ability to recognize the circumstances under which different arts should be employed, Plato not only goes beyond the incomplete discussion in the *Euthydemus*, but fills in important aspects of the ruler's art in the *Republic*. We have seen that, to the extent that Plato describes the special knowledge that allows the philosopher-king to rule, this is in abstract, metaphysical terms. The philosopher-king knows the Form of the Good, but Plato is unclear on how this translates into abilities relevant to ruling a state, although to some extent, the impracticality of Plato's description is mitigated by the fact that the philosopher must also return to the Cave and work in the city for fifteen years. In the *Statesman*, Plato attempts to relate the statesman's knowledge to practical affairs. In this work, Plato does not discuss the programme of studies the statesman undergoes or provide an elaborate

---

[15] For discussion, see Lane, *Method and Politics*, pp. 139–46.   [16] Ibid. 142, 146.

account of the objects of his knowledge. In keeping with the dialogue's focus on identifying the statesman, which entails distinguishing him from practitioners of related arts, Plato focuses on the relationship between his art and these others and his authority over them. In many ways, Plato's attention to the statesman's knowledge of particulars seems closer to the practical knowledge discussed by Aristotle in the *Nicomachean Ethics* than to the theoretical knowledge of the philosopher-king (see above, p. 173). To some extent—a slight extent—the importance of practical knowledge is anticipated in Book II of the *Republic*. In explaining the need for the principle of specialization, Socrates notes that if someone works at many tasks, he may miss 'the proper time (*kairon*) to do something' in connection with one of them (*Rep.* 370b). But in describing the guardians' function in the state, Plato does not follow up on this point.

It seems reasonable to regard Plato's new account of the ruler's art as bound up with his overall concern with the sensible world and its workings that characterizes the late dialogues. As we see in the following chapters, Plato's discussion in the *Laws* required detailed knowledge of the political systems of many Greek cities. But there is a significant problem with the statesman's art. I have noted the resemblance between the concern with particulars evinced in the *Statesman* and Aristotelian practical wisdom. But Aristotle pursues the implications of this kind of knowledge to a far greater extent. As Aristotle notes, this kind of knowledge differs from the theoretical in terms of how it is acquired. Knowledge of particulars, as knowledge of what is individual and changing, must be gained through experience. For this reason, knowledge of this sort is not found among the young (*EN* 1142a11–18). Along similar lines, Aristotle notes that, because this knowledge is concerned with particular factors changing through time, it is inherently inexact:

We must be content, then, in speaking of such subjects and with such premises to indicate the truth roughly and in outline, and in speaking about things which are only for the most part true and with premises of the same kind to reach conclusions that are no better. (1094b19–22)

One mark of an educated person is to look for only so much precision in different subject areas as they allow. Thus one should no more expect rigorous logical proofs from a rhetorician than 'probable reasoning' from a mathematician (1094b22–7).

The problem with Plato's account is that he appears not to recognize distinctive difficulties associated with knowledge of particulars. The statesman possesses an *infallible* science of ruling, which justifies his unchecked rule over others. His authority is qualified by the requirement that he govern people according to their true good, although with the clear implication that he is a better judge of this than people themselves. But the infallibility of such knowledge does not rest well with the requirement that it include knowledge of particular circumstances. To some extent, Plato could have been misled by the analogy between political rule and medicine. In two passages in which he discusses the statesman's ability to use force on his subjects, Plato compares this to the rule of a doctor, which should be judged solely according to whether it is used for the patient's good (293*a*–*c*, 296*d*–97*b*). As it seems to me, Plato fails to distinguish two sides of the medical art. There are principles of medicine that the student learns in medical school and are a kind of theoretical knowledge. But knowing how to apply them is not similarly theoretical. This depends on experience and is far less exact. Add on to this the vastly complicated constellation of particular factors encountered in the political world, and the idea that the ruler possesses infallible knowledge of these is as improbable as the philosopher-king's infallible political knowledge.

The form in which the statesman exercises control over the subsidiary arts is described in accordance with a simile of weaving. Plato says that there are two basic kinds of personalities, dominated by quiet and active principles respectively, or otherwise stated, possessing moderation or energy (306*b* ff.). Plato says that there is 'dissent in some respect' among the virtues (306*c*). People with energy are able to possess the virtue of courage, but resist temperance or moderation. The opposite is true of quiet personalities. The two kinds of personalities are naturally hostile to one another, which makes conflict between them inevitable (307*c*, 308*b*). This helps to explain political instability. In each state there are active and quiet personalities, interpreting events according to their own psychic natures. This leads to the existence of war and peace parties, and so of faction within cities and the fact that cities regularly pursue disastrous, one-sided courses, erring in the direction of either belligerence or passivity, depending on the party in control (307*d*–8*b*).

The art of the statesman is to intermingle or weave the different personality types. He pursues this task through three means. First, he will ensure that marriages are between different personality types, so that the resulting children partake of both natures (310*a*–*d*). Second and more important, he will employ a tightly controlled system of education to counteract people's natural tendencies. Plato's discussion is not only brief but is also dominated by the metaphor of weaving, so it is not entirely clear how this programme of education is to work. But apparently the statesman will attempt to instil correct moral convictions, which will temper souls, making the vigorous ones gentle and the moderate ones sufficiently strong to fulfil their civic obligations. Because the resulting virtues will be based on correct opinion rather than knowledge, they correspond to the civic virtue of the *Republic*—though the metaphors employed are based on weaving rather than political conflict between the parts of the soul. But Plato's opinion of the moral role of correct opinion has improved since the time of the *Republic*. In the *Statesman*, true opinion is referred to as belonging 'to the class of the more than human' (309c), a 'divine' bond, which is capable of uniting the conflicting elements in the personality (310a).

The statesman's third measure is to intermingle the different personality types throughout the constitutional structure. The result is a new kind of mixed constitution. This again is described briefly (310e–11b), but what seems to be suggested is a crude separation of powers. This is achieved by choosing people with both personality types for individual magistracies and sharing other offices among different personality types: 'By choosing the person who has both qualities to put in charge wherever there turns out to be a need for a single officer, and by mixing together a part of each of these groups where there is a need for more than one' (311a). Through this means the state can avoid the one-sided, disastrous policies that plague other cities.

Though the doctrine of divergent personality types must strike one as somewhat peculiar, Plato appears to take it seriously and it is a central feature of the *Statesman*. He declares that the conflict between energy and moderation is found throughout all spheres of life (307b–c). This personality theory is not entirely original in the *Statesman*. We find traces of it in the *Republic*, especially in Book II, where Plato first discusses the psychological qualities required of the guardians. They must be high-spirited, but gentle as well, while this combination will be difficult to find because the two personality types are by nature opposed (*Rep.* 375c). The educational system of the ideal state is introduced to produce the necessary psychic combination, and so there is at least some continuity between the views of the *Republic* and *Statesman* (see also *Rep.* 410b–11e). However, the degree of emphasis that the doctrine receives in the *Statesman* is clearly new, as is Plato's attempt to explain political instability by appealing to destabilizing factors inherent in human nature. It seems probable that Plato arrived at this new psychic doctrine by observing actual human types. Perhaps he was influenced by the turmoil in surrounding cities and felt the need to account for it. It should be noted, however, that to the extent that Plato explains social conflict on the basis of inherently conflicting personality types, he neglects causal factors that might otherwise seem more important, especially the economic factors he is acutely aware of in other contexts. In any event, regardless of how we explain Plato's sudden adherence to this psychic view, it assumes an important place in his political thought.

One aspect of this psychic view, the inherent opposition between different virtues, may represent an important shift in Plato's moral thought. Plato announces the new view with some fanfare. He calls it 'something astonishing' which goes against what 'people are used to saying', that all the different parts of virtue are in mutual accord (306*b*–*c*). The conflict between courage and moderation obviously represents a departure from the Socratic doctrine of the unity of the virtues, and it is natural to interpret Plato's remarks in this context. Some commentators have gone further. For instance, Skemp writes that the position in the *Statesman* represents a 'frontal assault' on the unity of the virtues as described in Book IV of the *Republic*.[17] This seems to me overstated. In both the *Republic* and *Statesman*, proper education is designed to inculcate all the virtues. The function of the statesman in the *Statesman* is not far removed from that of the philosopher-king in the *Republic*, in so far as it pertains to educating the lower classes in the state. The main difference lies in accounts of the moral condition of people not brought up in properly governed states. In the *Republic*, Plato does not say that such people fall into active and passive types. Rather, to the extent that Plato discusses such individuals, they are classified according to the fourfold typology—timarchic, oligarchic, democratic, and tyrannic—depending on the element that rules in the soul. The two accounts of the virtues of correct opinions, though described somewhat differently, are not far apart.

11.4. ACTUAL STATES

The *Statesman* makes important contributions to Plato's political theory in its attention to actual states and how they work. In this respect the work departs significantly from the *Republic*. As Barker says, in his later years, 'Plato makes his peace with reality, and acknowledges that there is room in political life for consent and law and constitutionalism and all the slow unscientific ways of the actual world of men'.[18] Because we no longer live in the age of Cronus and must make do with human rulers, questions concerning actual states must be addressed. However, in spite of Barker's assessment, Plato's consideration of laws falls far short of contemporary constitutional theory.

As we have seen, Plato argues that the rule of the true statesman is superior to law. Plato also considers the rule of law in actual states and presents a position on the relationship between political knowledge and law that is in fact the polar opposite of the statesman's rule. In contrast to the latter, in actual states laws should be rigidly obeyed; there should be strict adherence to unchanging laws. Polar opposition between scientific rule and this strict

17 Skemp, *Statesman*, p. 223, n. 1.
18 E. Barker, *Greek Political Theory: Plato and His Predecessors* (London, 1918), p. 330.

rule of laws eliminates what appears to be commonsensical middle ground, that even in the absence of the statesman's art, inhabitants of ordinary states should deliberate about their laws and revise them, in order to improve them. Plato's position in the dialogue rules this out.

Plato's discussion of laws in ordinary states is somewhat indirect. We have seen how he employs the analogy between the art of medicine and laws. If a doctor was to be away, he would leave instructions for his patients—laws—which they should follow in his absence, while, on his return, he should be free to disregard his former instructions. It follows from this analogy that states that do *not* have scientific rulers should be governed by laws, as patients should adhere to their physicians' instructions in the latter's absence. However, the analogy between the political and other arts entails that to require any art to be bound by unbreakable rules would be absurd.

The Stranger presents an hypothetical historical scenario according to which laws are made for the arts of medicine and navigation. Ordinary people decide that they are mistreated by practitioners of these arts (in terms that recall how the true statesman is allowed to deal with them, though in this account the rulers are pointedly described as corrupt) (298*a–b*). An assembly is called to legislate for these arts. Opinions are sought from the knowledgeable and non-knowledgeable alike. Whatever the majority decides is inscribed on stone tablets and adopted as laws. Other provisions are adopted as ancestral customs (*agrapha patria*) (298*c–e*). Both are to be followed for all time (*panta ton epeita chronon*) (298*e*). To enforce conformity to these rules, magistrates are established, described in terms that infallibly call to mind the Athenian political system (298*e–99a*). To complete the process, a law is enacted, according to which, if anyone is found investigating the subject of either health or navigation, he will be ridiculed as a stargazer or sophist and be subject to prosecution for corrupting the young and undermining the laws: 'If he is found guilty of persuading anyone, whether young or old, contrary to the laws and the written rules, the most extreme penalties must be imposed on him. For (so the law will say) there must be nothing wiser than the laws' (299*b–c*). Allusions to Socrates' prosecution and death cannot be missed, nor can Plato's continuing bitterness about those events.

The Stranger notes that applying such regulations to these or other arts would utterly ruin them. However, in spite of this derogatory account of the genesis of laws, he contends that having them is superior to circumstances in which people disregard them, 'in order either to profit in some way or to do some personal favor' (300*a*). Although laws are only a second best (297*d*, 297*e*, 300*c*), they *are* second-best and should be rigidly adhered to.

As noted above, the Eleatic Stranger requires conformity to law in two senses. People cannot violate them, and also cannot change them. In other words, the Stranger mandates adherence to *unchanging* laws. In the *Statesman*, he does not say anything as strong as what is found in the *Laws* extolling the laws in Egypt, which remained unchanged for thousands of years (see below, pp. 223, 250). But it appears that Plato's thoughts are along similar lines. For ease of reference, we may refer to laws made with objective intelligence as 'good laws' and those made without such intelligence as 'ordinary laws'. Plato's position requires strict adherence to both good and ordinary laws. And in the absence of the statesman, who possesses the political art, both kinds of laws should be left unchanged.

In order more precisely to describe Plato's view, we may practise an art of division of our own and distinguish four possible positions on the rule of law.

(1) The rule of the statesman, who possesses objective knowledge.
(2) The rule of laws made by objective intelligence (i.e. good laws).
(3) The rule of laws made without objective intelligence (i.e. ordinary laws).
(4) A situation in which laws are disregarded.

Plato's main discussion of the analogy of the physician and statesman is intended to distinguish (1) and (2). Even though a set of laws might be made by a physician who had to be away, on his return he could disregard them. Accordingly, even good laws do not bind the true ruler, although it follows from the analogy that such laws should be adhered to in the physician's absence. The Stranger's main discussion of the importance of adhering to law is in reference to (3). In his derogatory account of how actual laws come to be made, the Stranger argues that even laws made by the many, who are explicitly contrasted with experts in the relevant fields, must be obeyed. The relevant contrast is between (3) and (4). Ordinary laws are preferable to what would ensue should the laws be set aside for unsavoury reasons.

Focusing on these two contrasts, the Stranger does not devote sustained attention to the relationship between (2) and (3). He does not consider the possibility that ordinary laws can develop over time, so they come to approximate good laws. He considers an extreme case—superiority to good laws—in order to explain why the statesman is not bound by laws, and a comparably extreme, negative case—strict adherence to ordinary laws—to argue for obeying laws in the statesman's absence.

What is remarkable here is Plato's requirement that ordinary laws be left unchanged, while expressing little regard for them. To modern readers, it is natural to think of laws as capable of being improved through time. But Plato appears to rule this out. The unchanging status of such laws is implied in the statesman's account of the origin of laws. What is legislated are not only laws but ancestral customs. While the former may be changed through legislative action, this is far more difficult for the latter. Moreover, in this account, the rules are explicitly inscribed on tablets of stone for all time. The unchangeable status of the laws is reinforced by the prohibition against inquiring into their underlying principles. In the absence of such inquiry, they could not possibly be improved through the infusion of knowledge.

The Stranger describes ordinary states that adhere to law as 'imitating' the best state (300e–1a). But this imitation consists of never doing anything 'contrary to what is written or to ancestral customs' (301a). As recent commentators have shown, inferior states are able to imitate the rule of the true statesman in only a formal rather than a substantive sense. They do not imitate by having good laws. All they can do is to refrain from changing the laws they have without scientific intelligence. This resembles the good state, because in that regime as well, laws are changed only in accordance with the requisite intelligence.[19]

Plato's rationale for ruling out improving ordinary laws seems to be his lack of faith in political processes. In addition to the derogatory account of arts-legislation we have seen, the Stranger is similarly critical of what transpires in the politics of ordinary cities:

[T]hose who participate in all these constitutions, except for the one based on knowledge, [are] not statesmen but experts in faction; we must say that, as presiding over insubstantial images, on the largest scale, they are themselves of the same sort, and that as the greatest imitators and magicians, they turn out to be the greatest sophists among sophists. (300c; also 300a)

Plato apparently assumes that, because of the corruption of political processes, ordinary laws cannot be changed for the better. It seems that he does not distinguish between violating laws and attempting to change them. Because the latter like the former is inspired by selfish motives, it should be considered a subclass of the former.

In the text of the *Statesman*, there is some ambiguity about the exact status of ordinary laws. After the Stranger has noted the problems with them that we have seen, without explanation, he suddenly appears to evince a more favourable attitude towards them. He describes them as 'established on the basis of much experience, with some advisers or other having given advice on each subject in an attractive way, and having persuaded the majority to pass them' (300b). The Stranger continues in this vein more strongly:

Now, these regulations will reflect the truth in their various ways since they transcribe as accurately as possible what men of knowledge have said. (300c)[20]

[19] Rowe, *Statesman*, on 300e11–301a3; Lane, *Method and Politics*, pp. 156–9.

[20] This is R. Waterfield's translation, in *Plato: Statesman*, J. Annas and Waterfield, eds. and trans. (Cambridge: Cambridge University Press, 1995), which is similar to those of Diès (*Politique*) and Skemp (*Statesman*). Rowe provides a different interpretation (*Statesman*, ad loc.).

This remark is problematic, because the laws under discussion are explicitly identified as ordinary laws, made in the absence of scientific intelligence. Thus it is unclear how they imitate what is produced by 'men of knowledge'. Given that discussion here—and immediately after this exchange—is explicitly devoted to laws made in the absence of the relevant knowledge, to be consistent, the Stranger should describe them as *not* imitating the products of such men. Plato's apparent wavering here between good and ordinary laws is another ambiguity in the dialogue.

In the *Statesman*, the need to adhere strictly to laws is bound up with and to some extent rests on Plato's belief in the rarity of scientific rulers. Plato repeatedly notes that possessors of the political art will be few and far between. For instance:

A mass of any people whatsoever would never be able to acquire this kind of expert knowledge and so govern a city with intelligence, but we must look for that one constitution, the correct one, in relation to a small element in the population, few in number, or even in a single individual... (297*b*–*c*; also 292*e*–93*a*, 300*e*)

In the absence of the true statesman, both good and ordinary laws must be strictly obeyed and left unchanged. In the *Statesman*, Plato's emphasis on law leads to a new classification of states. In the *Republic*, Socrates places the four inferior forms of constitution in descending order of merit: timarchy, oligarchy, democracy, and tyranny. This classification is psychological; the inferior states are identified and ordered according to the psychic principle that holds sway in each. In the *Statesman*, Plato gives a more elaborate classification, encompassing seven kinds of states. We have the ideal state, ruled by the true statesman, and six lesser forms. These six are distinguished according to number of rulers, one, few or many, with a good and a bad form of each. Thus we have the following six forms: monarchy and tyranny, the good and bad forms of rule by one; aristocracy and oligarchy, the good and bad forms of rule by the few; and good and bad forms of democracy—the same word is used for both (302*d*–*e*).

This sixfold classification of states was traditional in Greece. Some semblance of it can be found at least as far back as Herodotus (III, 80–2), while it exercised enormous influence on later political theorists, including Aristotle, Polybius, Machiavelli, and Montesquieu. The criterion Plato uses to

---

This subject cannot be discussed at length here. I should note, however, that, although Rowe's suggestion helps make logical sense of the passage it also, as he notes, goes against the views of all other known commentators. Reasons for this are apparent. Not only does his reading strain the clear sense of the Greek, but while accounting for the apparently anomalous character of 300*c*5–7, it leaves intact the similarly anomalous 300*b*1–6—his account of which is unconvincing (see ad loc.).

distinguish the good and bad forms of states is regard for law: in the good forms, rulers obey the law, while in bad forms they do not. Earlier in the dialogue, Plato classifies constitutions similarly, with the distinction between good and bad forms established in a more complex fashion, according to three variables: whether rule is by violence or consent; wealth or poverty (presumably of the rulers); and whether laws are adhered to or disobeyed (291e). But these additional factors are not pursued, and we are left with the sole criterion of regard or disregard for law. It is important to note that Plato employs the rule of law as his criterion because of concern for how the subjects fare in each kind of state. In order of merit, the rule of one, if law-abiding, is best, followed by the rule of few and many. Of bad forms, the order is reversed. Just as one law-abiding ruler is able to do the most good, so the tyrant is able to do the most harm. Next worst is oligarchy and then democracy. The perverted form of democracy is least bad because of its inefficiency:

> that of the mass, in its turn, we may suppose to be weak in all respects and capable of nothing of any importance either for good or for bad as judged in relation to the others, because, under it, offices are distributed in small potions among many people. (303a)

This sort of reasoning is alien to Plato's earlier works.

The most obvious departure here from the argument of the *Republic* is the reversal of the order of democracy and oligarchy. In the earlier work oligarchy is better; in the *Statesman* it is worse. Perhaps, as Barker suggests, the relative stability of the Athenian democracy throughout most of Plato's life had softened his attitude towards it.[21] In leading up to his new classification of states, Plato expresses surprise—and apparently admiration—at 'how strong a thing a city is by its nature', which enables particular cities to withstand adversity (302a). It is not difficult to construe this as an allusion to Athens, and perhaps to other states as well.

Of course, the reason democracy is judged more favourably than oligarchy is the criterion employed. In the *Statesman* Plato retreats from the divine. To the extent that he is concerned with the rule of law and its consequences, he assesses imperfect states on their merits. Let us not suppose, however, that Plato has become sentimentally attached to democracy. For the faint praise we have seen follows close upon allusions to the trial and death of Socrates, democracy's most illustrious victim (299b–c).

To conclude this chapter we will note some wider implications of Plato's turn to the rule of law. In regard to the philosophical aspects of his thought, this marks an important stage, a break from the 'two-world' view that

---

[21] Barker, *Greek Political Theory*, p. 337, n. 2.

underlies the political theory of the *Republic*. Plato's new-found regard for the rule of law is also an important theme in the *Seventh* and *Eighth Epistles* and, of course, the *Laws*. Plato's metaphysical views in the middle dialogues devalue human experience in comparison to the absolute truths embodied in the Forms. This view is expressed perhaps most clearly in the analogy of the Cave. Throughout the early and middle works, Plato is like the Sophists in accepting the dichotomy between nature and convention (*phusis* and *nomos*) and in unfavourably comparing existing laws and customs to objectively rooted moral standards. Of course his major difference with the Sophists is that he sees different principles rooted in nature. To the extent that rule of law in the *Statesman* entails respect for customs and institutions because they exist as well as because they are rooted in truth (300*b–c*), it departs from this attitude and undermines the distinction between nature and convention (see below, pp. 229–30) and so also the two-world view of the middle works. Plato's position in this work is complicated by his retention of faith in the objectively good ruler, whose knowledge takes precedence over all else and whose authority is predicated on objective moral values that he is able to perceive.

Thus Plato's outlook in the work is ambivalent. Though the age of Cronus has ended, he devotes much of the work to describing the true ruler who passed with that age. His ambivalence is clearly seen in his classification of constitutions. Alongside the six imperfect forms, ranked according to utilitarian considerations, stands the unchecked rule of the true statesman, although Plato realizes the unlikelihood this will ever come about. The rule of the statesman recalls the *Republic*, while the 'second-best' states ruled by law foreshadows the *Laws*. The *Statesman* stands midway between the worlds of Plato's two major political dialogues.

12

The 'Second-Best' State

The *Laws* of course was Plato's last work, left unfinished at his death. According to ancient tradition, it was edited posthumously by Plato's student Phillip of Opus, who also wrote the *Epinomis* in order to complete various matters Plato left incomplete.[1] The *Laws* is an old man's work. In addition to Plato's increased experience of human affairs, in many ways it shows a mood of tiredness and resignation. The aged Plato has turned his back on the world to face the heavens. Human life seems to him a paltry thing, no more than amusement for the gods (803*c*). His faith in man's power and dignity, in man's ability to know, has waned. The implication for political theory is an ideal state that approaches theocracy.

The world of the *Laws* is immediately different from that of the other dialogues. While Socrates' significance has lessened in many of the late works, the *Laws* is the only dialogue in which he does not appear. His place is taken by an unnamed Athenian Stranger, probably a stand-in for Plato himself. The scene is Crete, as the Athenian and his interlocutors, two other old men, Megillus from Sparta and Cleinias from Crete, pass a long day's walk discussing laws. The choice of interlocutors is, as always, symbolic, as the political principles espoused are based on combining features from the Athenian and Doric (i.e. Spartan and Cretan) polities.

Though the work is formally a dialogue, little of Plato's earlier dialogic spirit survives. Throughout most of the work the Athenian discourses without interruption. Portions of the *Laws* show signs of having been written as a treatise and later—and half-heartedly—converted into a dialogue, a process that was perhaps interrupted by Plato's death. For instance, Book V is an unbroken discourse, while Book VI is close to that. The lack of dialectical interchange indicates something about Plato's temper in the work. Though the *Laws* is based on exhaustive empirical and historical research, and demonstrates a vast knowledge of the laws and institutions of countless peoples, Plato is not much interested in the conclusions others might draw from these data. His ideas are

---

[1] For the evidence concerning Phillip of Opus, see L. Taran, *Academica: Plato, Phillip of Opus, and the Pseudo Platonic Epinomis* (Philadelphia, PA, 1975).

set, and he goes so far as to advocate the death penalty for citizens of his state who fail to be persuaded.

The turn from philosopher-kings to the rule of law is of course indicated by the title of the work. In the *Laws* too Plato refers to the myth of the age of Cronus—in a truncated version—and draws the same moral. The age is past when rulers were superior to their subjects. Mortals have been left to rule mortals, and because no human being can be entrusted with irresponsible power, the rule of law must be instituted (713*c*–14*b*). In two contexts Plato more or less explicitly turns away from the ideal of the *Republic*. Describing property regulations for his new state in Book V, he contrasts present conditions with more exalted ones. In the best state, a system of complete communism would be introduced. There would be community of property, wives and children, feelings and ideas. The allusions to the *Republic* are palpable, though Plato fails to mention that the communism in the *Republic* was confined to the guardians—thus suggesting an error that Aristotle makes in criticizing the *Republic* (see *Pol.* 1263*a*27–30, 1264*a*13–18). But such communism is suitable only 'for gods or sons of gods', so we must make do with what is second best (739*a–e*).[2] In Book IX as well, Plato discusses the impossibility of turning over political power to an irresponsible autocrat. No man is able unfailingly to perceive the public interest and to pursue it in his policies. Even were some individual able to understand what must be done, his 'mortal nature' would impel him towards self-aggrandizement, thereby bringing ruin to the state (875*a–d*). In spite of all this, Plato remains attached to the idea of the philosopher-king. He says that if a person of divine grace should arrive, power must be turned over to him. However, such personages are either nonexistent or exceedingly rare, and so here too we must make do with what is second-best (875*c–d*). The rule of law, however, should not be despised. Only this allows human beings to rise above the level of the most savage beasts (874*e*–75*a*).

Plato's abandonment of hope in rule by philosopher-kings redounds to the benefit of ordinary people. Unlike the *Republic*, the *Laws* has no significant class system, and so no classes of guardians separated from the general population by their mode of life. Although, as we see, the state still lays a heavy hand on both economic and family relations, communism in these areas no longer obtains. All citizens live in essentially the same way and are alike in

---

2 Christopher Bobonich argues against reference to the *Republic* in this passage (*Plato's Utopia Recast* [Oxford, 2002], pp. 11–12); in contrast, Andre Laks, says the reference is 'secure beyond any doubt' ('In What Sense is the City of the Laws a Second Best One?' in *Plato's Laws and Its Historical Significance*, F. Lisi, ed. [Salamanaca, Spain 1998], pp. 108–9); he refers to this as a case of 'quasi-citation' ('Prodige et méditation: esquisse d'une lecture des *Lois*', *Le temps philosophiques*, 1 [1995], 20).

pursuing virtue. Towards that end, all citizens receive the same education, which resembles the early education of the guardians in the *Republic*. The extent to which this represents a break from the *Republic* is impossible to say, in the light of Plato's failure to discuss the education of the third class. If, as I surmise, a programme is envisioned in the *Republic* as well, there will be strong continuity between the *Republic* and *Laws*, as the education of the third class presumably would not differ significantly from the early education of the guardians. However we come down on this question, it is notable that such a programme is mandated in the *Laws*, and so the polity will consist of citizens all of whom are educated in the same way.

In the *Laws*, all classes are also similar in their virtue, although the reign of virtue is not accomplished easily. The necessary system of education is extremely rigorous and, as we will see, generally operates on a low level, conditioning attitudes towards pleasure and pain rather more than developing the intellect. This conception of virtue is obviously far removed from that of the philosopher-kings. It is far closer to the virtue based on correct opinion of the two lower classes in the *Republic*, though mandated, once again, for the entire society.

The *Laws* is such a huge, sprawling work that it is not possible to cover all its contents. We confine our attention to its place in the development of Plato's political thought. The political theory of the *Laws* represents a development and extension of the *Republic*, though not without important exceptions. As we did in previous parts, we discuss the aim Plato hoped to achieve, and the means he believed this to require. As ever with Plato, the desired end is virtue.

12.1. MORAL PSYCHOLOGY IN THE *LAWS*

As in the *Republic*, Plato's analysis in the *Laws* operates on two tracks. The avowed purpose of the work is to consider how a state might best be run and how the individual citizen should pass his life (702*a*–*b*). In this work too Plato introduces the analogy between the individual and the state. Both individual and state possess worse and better parts, in the individual's soul passion and reason, in the state the unruly masses and the discipline represented by law, which is a codification of reason (645*a*–*b*). The aim of course is to ensure that reason controls passion in both. This condition is identified as temperance in the individual and the rule of law in the state.

Plato's lack of hope in regard to philosopher-kings extends throughout his psychological views. The *Laws* presents a despairing conception of human nature. Particularly striking is Plato's repeated pronouncement that human beings are at the mercy of powerful forces; they are not actors, but are acted upon. In one famous passage he compares them to 'puppets of the gods':

[W]e have these emotions in us, which act like cords or strings and tug us about; they work in opposition, and tug against each other to make us perform actions that are opposed correspondingly; back and forth we go across the boundary line where vice and virtue meet. (644e)

This is a recurring motif. Individuals are pulled by their emotions and passions, especially by pleasure and pain. At one point Plato says that pleasure, pain, and desire are the 'cords' from which human beings are suspended, and from which their actions stem (732e–33a). Thus in the *Laws* the rational element in the human personality rides a sea of passion.[3]

An indication of how far Plato has come since the early dialogues is a new definition of ignorance presented in Book III. The 'very lowest depth of ignorance' is now a disharmony between the rational faculties and the feelings of pleasure and pain (689a). In Book IX Plato argues once again for the Socratic paradox that 'all wrongdoing is involuntary'. But once again the intellectualism of the early dialogues is long past. The position here is that the agent who commits wrong does so because of a diseased condition in his soul. Crime must be countered by psychological cure, while the incurable must be put to death (862c–63a). This position finds support in the *Timaeus*, where Plato writes that, when an individual appears to do wrong knowingly, he is actually impelled by a disordered soul:

When a man is carried away by enjoyment or distracted by pain, in his immoderate haste to grasp the one or to escape the other he can neither see nor hear aright; he is in a frenzy and his capacity for reasoning is then at its lowest. (*Tim.* 86b–c)

Thus, in his late works, Plato's position verges on Euripides' in the *Medea* (above, p. 52). The element of paradox has been banished from Socratic ethics.

Not only does Plato believe that the rational element is dominated by the non-rational, but his view of the non-rational has not improved. As in the middle dialogues, Plato's position is that appetitive forces are inherently defective. They are impulses 'bred of old in men from ancient wrongs'; unless expiated, they 'course around wreaking ruin' (*Laws* 854b).

Having observed the impediments to virtue, we can see that the solution suggests itself. If individuals are driven by their passions, the key to virtue is ensuring that they are driven correctly. Education must inculcate order,

---

[3] For an influential, alternative construal of the implications of this passage, see Laks, 'Legislation and Demiurgy: On the Relationship Between Plato's *Republic* and *Laws*', *Classical Antiquity*, 9 (1990), 227; 'The *Laws*', in *The Cambridge History of Greek and Roman Political Thought*, C. Rowe and M. Schofield, eds. (Cambridge: Cambridge University Press, 2000), p. 277.

harmony, and direction in the passions. Thus in the simile of the puppets of the gods, Plato also notes a superior string, the 'leading-string, golden and holy, of rational calculation (*logismos*)', which the individual should follow. Since the pull of reason cannot win out over other forces without help, this must be provided by the law (644*e*–45*b*).

Law is a public calculation of pleasures and pains in the state (644*c*–*d*). It must ensure that individuals derive proper pleasures and pains from the performance of virtuous and non-virtuous actions, thus overcoming the new form of ignorance described above. Accordingly, Plato says that 'when men investigate legislation, they investigate almost exclusively pleasures and pains as they affect society and the character of the individual' (636*d*). Plato retains his old conviction that the just life is the happy life, but he has despaired of easily convincing others. It is the job of the state to make justice pleasurable by manipulating pleasures and pains.

12.2. EDUCATION IN THE *LAWS*

Education is the central business of the ideal state in the *Laws*, and the commissioner of education is the state's most important person (765*d*–*e*). Plato recommends a comprehensive system of education, which he describes in elaborate detail, and which is to embrace all aspects of citizens' lives from before they are born until they die. This system of education is similar to that of the *Republic* though it is more rigorous and described in greater detail. Aside from the general education for all citizens, there is a programme of higher studies for a select few, which resembles that of the philosophers in the *Republic* (below, p. 252). But aside from this, the main business of the state is imposing a single conception of virtue on all citizens. We have seen that education in the *Republic* is designed to condition and harmonize the parts of the soul to promote the direct rule of reason. The system in the *Laws* works similarly, though on a lower level. The lower parts of the soul are conditioned more intensively, and reason has a smaller role.

In the light of Plato's emphasis on pleasure and pain, it is not surprising that education in the second-best state focuses on these. Goodness and badness first come into the soul through pleasure and pain, and so great care must be taken to ensure that they spring up correctly (653*a*–*b*). If the child is trained properly, he will be ready to assent to correct moral principles when the time is right.

Throughout the *Laws*, Plato's emphasizes habituation and conditioning. The child is 'moulded like wax' (789*e*). Great store is placed in the plasticity of the young child: 'Because of the force of habit, it is in infancy that the whole character is most effectually determined' (792*d–e*). The child should be given moderate pleasure, raised according to a rough mean between being spoiled and deprived, to ensure an even disposition in later life (792*c–e*). Above all, the child must be convinced of the association between virtue and happiness, that the good life is also the happy one. This is a primary target of all education (660*e*–63*e*).

In order to work properly, education must begin before birth. Plato prescribes a system of prenatal gymnastics, constant movement for pregnant women. When the baby is born, he should be carried constantly, subjected to continuous motion, as if he were on board ship (790*c–d*). This process should be continued throughout infancy, until the child is 3 years old. Plato believes that this motion has a salutary effect and produces courage, as the external movement will drive away the internal motions that constitute fear (790*e*–91*a*).

The system of education encompasses the traditional Greek division between *mousikê* and *gumnastikê*, education in the arts and physical training. This is of course similar to what we find in the *Republic*, though Plato's position in the *Laws* is the traditional one that the latter course of studies is for the body, rather than, as in the *Republic*, for the soul (795*c*). The system is divided into stages. Briefly, the years up to 3 are, as we have seen, devoted to motion. From 3 to 6 the focus is on games, conducted at the village temples. At 6, the sexes are segregated, though the education of women is to parallel that of men as closely as possible. Training until the age of 10 is in various physical activities, such as riding and wrestling, training in arms and dancing. From 10 to 13 the emphasis is on simple intellectual skills, primarily reading and writing. From 16 to 20 we have military training and as much arithmetic as is required for practical purposes.

Plato cares deeply about non-academic as well as academic aspects of children's schooling. He is fond of a particular play on words. The word for education and culture generally is *paideia*, which Plato believes is serious business. This is similar to *paidia*, which means literally child's play. For Plato *paidia* is serious also, for unless children play the right games, they will not grow up properly. Unless each generation repeats the games of the previous one, it will grow up differently, thereby bringing unwelcome changes to the state. Thus *paidia* is *paideia*; what most people regard as the most frivolous matters are actually among the most important. In addition, the *Laws* as a whole is permeated by a mood of gloom and pessimism concerning human affairs, which leads Plato to declare that nothing pertaining to man is truly significant. Only god should be taken seriously, while man is only a 'plaything of God'. Thus, the most serious things—including *paideia*—are actually of little consequence. They are *paidia* to the gods (803*a–c*).

In the *Laws*, as in the *Republic*, Plato attributes great importance to musical forms, especially in early childhood. The child has a natural tendency towards motion and the exercise of its vocal chords. These natural movements must be channelled into rhythm and harmony, which represent the first suggestion of the beauty and harmony of correct moral standards (653*d*–55*b*). Throughout his discussion of songs and dances, Plato is interested in constancy as well as correct form and content. He is staunchly opposed to change or innovation in music. His ideal is Egypt, where he believes music has not changed for literally thousands of years. In his discussion of the corruption of the Athenian democracy in Book III, Plato's centre of attention is changing canons of music, which he believes contributed to the corruption of the state. To achieve stability he recommends a controlled calendar, replete with religious feast days and celebrations. The calendar will be consecrated and maintained from year to year, while the specific songs and dances associated with each occasion will also be consecrated, immune to change (799*a*–*b*). Plato appeals to another play on words, concerning *nomos*, which means 'tune' or 'song' as well as 'law'. Plato wants the one to be as sacred as the other. Songs as well as laws must be adhered to, with penalties for violations (799*e*–800*a*).

Poets and other artists are of course subjected to careful scrutiny and censorship. A board of citizens over the age of 50 will be empowered to select appropriate songs and compositions from those already existing (802*a*–*b*). Other works of art are banned. An idea of what Plato means by appropriate compositions can be gathered from the fact that, when the Athenian wishes to present an example of a suitable literary piece, he appeals to the discourse in which he is presently engaged, that is, the *Laws* (811*c*–*e*). At this stage in his life Plato wishes to put an end to the age-old battle between philosophy and poetry by declaring his philosophy to be the only permissible poetry.

Throughout their early years, children are watched closely. No aspect of their lives should be left unsupervised; no subject is too insignificant for the state's attention. Education is, thus, all pervasive. Plato believes it was a mistake on the part of other lawgivers to ignore apparently trivial matters, and though everything cannot be covered by legislation, what the laws omit should be addressed by customs. The resulting social fabric will serve as a prop to explicit legislation (793*a*–*e*, 788*a*–*c*). Accordingly, the entire state takes a hand in raising children. The young are supervised by their parents and their nurses, and when they leave these people, by their tutors. The tutors in turn are watched by the state as a whole. All citizens are enjoined to punish both children and tutors if they see them do wrong, while anyone who fails to punish is in turn liable for punishment by state authorities (808*c*–9*a*).

The constant scrutiny to which children are subjected expresses Plato's feelings about moral education. By nature the child is deeply flawed, a raw creature to be beaten into shape:

Of all wild things, the child is the most unmanageable: an unusually powerful spring of reason, whose waters are not yet canalized in the right direction, makes him sharp and sly, the most unruly animal there is. (808d–e).

In another context, Plato says that, without the benefit of laws, men would be no different from the most savage beasts (874e–75a). Thus, human nature must be constrained, 'curbed by a great many bridles' (808d–e).

In addition to being all-pervasive, education in the *Laws* works on a remarkably low level. Plato's great attention to prenatal care, infancy, children's games, etc. is indicative of the fact that the education he prescribes is actually moral training—as in the training of animals. This is illustrated by his repeated references to *epôdai*, chants, spells, or incantations. For example, the songs that are learned and constantly sung throughout the state are really 'chants', designed to 'enchant' the young (664b, 665c, etc.), to 'charm' the souls of those who sing them (812c). Plato's discussion of education throughout the work continuously makes use of *epodê* and related words (e.g. 773d, 837e, 887d, 903b). Thus Morrow describes the art of enchantment as Plato's 'fundamental procedure in the *Laws*'.[4] This is, however, unusual and disconcerting, as in his other works Plato's talk of *epôdai* is generally in connection with magic or sorcery and the verbal techniques of Sophists, who enchant their listeners. Thus in the *Euthydemus* (289e–90a) Plato attributes *epôdai* to sorcerers, who use them to charm 'snakes and tarantulas and scorpions and other beasts and diseases', and to Sophists who use them to sway 'juries and assemblies'. In the *Laws*, then, Plato repeatedly and insistently utilizes techniques that he appears to despise elsewhere in his works.

Insistent moral training does not leave off when children become adults. Throughout their lives, Plato's citizens are to be kept constantly busy. Because they do not engage in economic activities, they participate in 'a life-long round of sacrifices and festivals and chorus performances' (835e). This should not be considered a life of leisure, as Plato believes that the entire day and night do not allow sufficient time to achieve virtue (807d).

In the *Laws*, Plato's view is an interesting combination of optimistic and pessimistic: the former in that all citizens are capable of virtue, but the latter in what it takes to achieve this. The pursuit of virtue is a full-time job, and as such precludes citizens from engaging in economic activities (846d–47a). In presenting this precept, Plato clearly alludes to the principle of

---

[4] G. Morrow, 'Plato's Conception of Persuasion', *Philosophical Review*, 62 (1953), 239.

specialization in the *Republic*.[5] But while there pursuit of economic activities was not thought to impede the development of whatever virtue was possible for members of the third class, in the *Laws*, Plato believes that pursuit of virtue must absorb all their energy. This requires that all aspects of life be regulated: 'Every gentleman must have a timetable prescribing what he is to do every minute of his life, which he should follow at all times from the dawn of one day until the sun comes up at the dawn of the next' (807*d–e*, 780*a*). Even citizens' sleep is not their own. Plato insists that people need little sleep, and so his citizens will be allowed to sleep only as health requires (807*e–8c*).

The end result of Plato's prescriptions is an all-embracing public opinion, intruding into every aspect of people's lives. This is created by the system of education and supported by other institutions. What is more, this public opinion is to be unchanging. The laws of the state, once established, are not to change (see below, pp. 250–1). Resistance to change is an important theme in the *Laws*, and Plato has good reasons for stressing it. The ideal is a system in which each generation closely follows the ways of the one before. No one in the state should remember anything ever having been different, and so along with no one desiring change, no one will imagine that change is possible (esp. 798*a–b*). Plato wishes to take his state outside of history, to locate it before the time when men discovered that other peoples had laws and customs different from their own (above, pp. 2–3). Thus one of Plato's tactics for opposing ethical relativism is to arrange things so that none of his citizens has any means of discovering that ethical relativism exists.

12.3. SOCIETAL ARRANGEMENTS

The ideal state in the *Laws* differs from that in the *Republic* in important respects. We have noted the absence of the *Republic*'s three-class system. In the ideal city described in the *Laws*, all citizens live under similar arrangements. Plato's retreat from the ideals of the *Republic* pervades both the institutions he recommends and the means through which he devises them.

In the *Laws*, Plato discusses an imaginary city, but one that is tied more closely to the real world. It has a specific location, in Crete, and a specific kind of territory. It also has a name, Magnesia, and is discussed under the pretext that it is a colony that the Cretans are founding, for which the Athenian is asked to consider suitable laws. Thus the degree of compromise with the

---

[5] Bobonich, 'Plato and the Birth of Classical Political Philosophy', in *Plato's Laws and its Historical Significance*, pp. 100–1.

material world is far greater than in the *Republic*. Plato allows himself some simplifying assumptions, for instance that the new inhabitants are basically sound, so an initial purge of the populace is not necessary (736*b*–*c*). But he generally takes into account the limitations of the material—both human and geographical—with which he must work.

The historical status of Magnesia is indicative of a different attitude towards history in the work as a whole. In the cycle of inferior constitutions in Books VIII–IX of the *Republic*, representative types of actual states are examined as deviations from the ideal. In Book III of the *Laws*, inferior states are discussed as a prelude to the ideal. Plato presents a brief account of early history, beginning with the Deluge, then the origins of government in primitive society, then the rise and fall of the Dorian monarchies. He considers the causes for the decline of the Persian monarchy and Athenian democracy. Plato's historical survey is surely fanciful and largely fictitious, but what is striking and original about the *Laws* is that he makes use of conclusions that his historical investigation casts up. The experiences of actual states are held to be applicable to the ideal state. We discuss specific examples of this below. We also see that many governmental and social features of the ideal society are derived from actual states. At one point the Athenian Stranger says that he has inquired into the laws of nearly all states (639*d*–*e*). Because of the vast historical research that went into the *Laws*, in many ways the work affords a running commentary on the political and legal institutions of all of Greece.

Plato's description of Magnesia occupies the bulk of the *Laws*, and obviously I cannot summarize all the details here. For our purposes, it is necessary to discuss the social and economic system of the city, something of its system of government, and three of Plato's basic principles, the mixed constitution, the rule of law and the place in the state for philosophical understanding. Then we close with a brief account of how the second-best state can be brought into existence.

The social system of Magnesia is obviously modelled on Cretan and especially Spartan forms. This is not surprising, since in the *Republic* Sparta provides the model for the timarchic state that stands one remove from the ideal (*Rep.* 544*c*, 545*a*). Plato was impressed with Sparta's political success even more than its military accomplishments. According to Thucydides, who here expresses common opinion, Sparta had never been ruled by a tyrant and had preserved the same constitution for four centuries (I, 18). This contrasts sharply with the turmoil encountered throughout the Greek world as a whole. Accordingly, admiration of Sparta was widespread, especially among the upper classes. Plato's cousin Critias wrote a treatise on Spartan laws (Frags. 32–7). Socrates shared this sentiment. In the *Crito* (52*e*–53*a*) he is said to have considered Sparta—and Crete—well governed, while Aristophanes writes in the *Birds*: 'Sparta was all the rage. People grew their hair long, they starved themselves, they stopped having baths (like Socrates)' (1281–3). Spartan stability was attributed to many things: its unique constitutional form; its system of state-run education; its citizens' reverence for its laws (esp. Herodotus, VII, 104). Another important factor is that Sparta clung to old-established ways and resisted change. We see that Plato borrowed heavily from Sparta in all these respects.

Plato is most obviously impressed with the Spartan system of education, which he considers vastly superior to the Athenian practice of treating education as each family's own business. But though Sparta marshalled the resources of the state for education, Plato believes that the kind of virtue it produced was extreme and one-sided. Sparta inculcated courage alone, at the expense of the other virtues (625c ff.). The ideal in the *Laws* is to raise citizens to all the virtues, though with an emphasis on temperance or self-control.

In a number of ways that are attractive to Plato, Sparta represented a throwback to the traditional form of *polis*. Like the ideal-type *polis*, Sparta was an agrarian society. Each family was assigned a plot of land that was in theory inalienable—though in practice the system was flawed and many families managed to lose their land. The land was farmed by helots, the subjugated original inhabitants of the Peloponnese, as Spartan citizens devoted their time to civic and, especially, military affairs. The Spartan economy was almost entirely non-commercial; Sparta avoided commercial relations with other states. Spartan citizens were forbidden to own gold and silver, while for internal purposes a special form of iron currency was introduced.

Sparta was also traditional in the relationships it maintained with its citizens. The state enforced its claim upon the individual through rigorous state-run education. Children were taken from their families at an early age, to be raised communally, under harsh conditions. The state intruded into many other aspects of family life, most strikingly in the fact that Spartan men did not live with their wives until the age of 30, and even after that continued to eat their meals in public dining rooms. The state also laid a heavy hand upon intellectual life. Spartans were forbidden to travel abroad. The cultural life of the state was crude, and lasting intellectual achievements almost non-existent. Foreigners were kept out, in order to maintain moral and cultural isolation.

Life in Magnesia is structured similarly. The 5,040 families are assigned plots of land, each of which is separated into two pieces, one near the city and one farther away. Like the Spartan plots these are inalienable, and Plato arranges things so that the plots will stay undivided and the number of households constant at 5,040. Each household possesses slaves to do manual labour, and it is not clear how much labour citizens are expected to do. Perhaps the poorest citizens, who have the fewest slaves, will engage in heavy physical labour. On the whole it seems safe to say that the bulk of the work will be done by slaves, freeing citizens for the pursuit of virtue, which is their real task.

As was the case in Sparta, everything possible is done to remove the city from the world of commerce. Thus, the Athenian is pleased with its location, eight stadia (about ten miles) from the sea, for this will discourage commerce (704*d*–5*b*). The city is also naturally favoured in regard to the fertility of its land. It is neither too fertile, nor not fertile enough. In the former case, it would have a surplus that it would be encouraged to export; in the latter it would be forced to live by trade (704*d*–5*b*). Citizens are discouraged from engaging in trade. The annual produce is divided into three parts: one for the citizens' consumption at the common tables; one for slaves; and one to be sold to foreign residents (847*e*–48*a*). Citizens are forbidden to own gold and silver (743*d*), while as in Sparta, a special currency is devised for internal purposes (742*a*). The accumulation of wealth is discouraged through means not found in Sparta, especially confiscating excessive property. The state is divided into four economic classes. The lowest owns only their land, and the basic tools and implements needed for working it. The second owns property up to twice the value of the land, the third three times, and the fourth four times (744*c*–*e*). All property is recorded, and anything above four times that of the lowest class will be confiscated by the state. Since citizens are debarred from commercial activity, it is difficult to account for differences in wealth. Perhaps, as Plato indicates in one context (744*b*–*c*), they are simply a residue of the unequal possessions of the original colonists. In any case, wealth and poverty will be tightly controlled, and the state free from many possible causes of faction (744*d*).

Economic activity as well as accumulation is discouraged. Because the duties of citizenship occupy all of citizens' time (846*d*), they are forbidden to practise non-agricultural trades. And so the state requires the services of a class of resident aliens—metics—who will work as craftsmen and at other paid trades, including as schoolteachers. The metics will be enticed into the state by the guarantee of protection and freedom from taxation, but they will ordinarily be allowed to stay for no more than twenty years, presumably in order to prevent them from forming an entrenched interest opposed to the citizenry.

The fact that Plato turns his back on the world of interstate commerce and interstate relations is an important aspect of the political theory of the *Laws*. As we have noted above (pp. 8–9), throughout his life Plato wished to retreat to an earlier, simpler state of affairs. This is seen in the *Laws* as well as the *Republic*. In both works Plato believes that commerce exacerbates tensions within societies, leading to polarization and civil war. Thus other states are not one but two, and racked by sedition and strife. In order for Plato's ideal cities to achieve the important values associated with inner harmony and social stability, a retreat from the commercial world is necessary. This argument is more explicit in the *Laws* than in the *Republic*, but the explicit discussion in the *Laws* casts light on the *Republic* as well. It is only in retrospect that one realizes that the ideal city in the *Republic* does not engage in commerce with other cities and does not possess a fleet—though it has a harbour (*Rep.* 425d). The fact that it is removed from the commercial world helps to locate Plato's ideas within the political currents of his time.

Although specific practices in the *Laws* are clearly of Spartan origin, especially the public dining rooms in which all citizens eat and the great emphasis on state-run education, Plato departs from the Spartan model in emphasizing religious ceremonies and devotions rather more than military exercises. He also departs from Spartan practice in his treatment of women. He criticizes Sparta for closely regulating men while allowing women to run more or less free (806b–c). Thus women are carefully attended to. They are educated as men are, eat at public tables (806e), are trained in arms (804d–6b, 834a), and perhaps expected to use them (785b). Women are also eligible for public office (785b), though it is not clear how far Plato takes this principle in practice.

The end result of Magnesia's social system is the creation of virtuous citizens in a stable society. Plato also believes that the citizens will be happy. They spend their lives pursuing virtue, and so are rescued from the horrors of the appetitive life. They are freed from many of the more burdensome aspects of ordinary life. In the *Republic*, Plato argues that the lives of his guardians will be better than those of Olympic victors, as they are free from ordinary cares and burdens (above p. 153). The citizens of Magnesia are placed in a similar situation and should be similarly happy.

Thus it is clear that, in designing the social system of Magnesia, Plato relies heavily on Sparta, but a Sparta criticized and improved. Where education in Sparta was narrow and militaristic, in Magnesia it will produce all the virtues. Plato takes measures to improve upon the Spartan treatment of women and its system of land tenure. Plato also attempts to avoid the problems Sparta experienced with its helots. Whereas Spartan helots were always on the point of rebellion, with extraordinary measures required to deal with them, Plato seeks to avoid this problem, by preventing the formation of a helot class. He wants to avoid large numbers of slaves with a common origin and customs (777c). It seems likely, then, that slaves will not be attained through reproduction. Rather, they will be purchased abroad, or perhaps captured in war.[6]

---

[6] Morrow, *Plato's Law of Slavery in Relation to Greek Law* (Urbana, IL, 1939), pp. 23–4.

In addition, it seems likely that the children of Magnesian slaves will be sold abroad. We see below that Plato also constructs his political system according to the Spartan principle of mixed constitution—though using basically Athenian institutions.

Thus in all these cases, and others throughout the *Laws* too numerous to recount, Plato's procedure is to take what exists and to work out its flaws. This is strikingly different from his procedure in the *Republic*, where the ideal state is more or less deduced from the requirements of virtue. The philosopher-rulers do their work with an eye to the heavens, rather than to surrounding states. In *Republic* VIII, Plato mentions in passing some changes in oligarchic institutions that would increase stability (555c, 556a–b), but he does not pursue this line of thought. In the *Laws*, however, Plato shapes what is in order to bring it closer to the ideal. In building his social system, as throughout the *Laws*, Plato attempts to improve things largely by combining features of different societies. Thus he includes Athenian institutions in Magnesia's basically Spartan economy. Two examples are the system of social classes—the Athenian system is referred to at 698b—and the practice of encouraging extensive economic activity by foreign residents. Plato's aim is a polity that surpasses any formerly seen, but one that also appears to be possible, because facsimiles of its major features have already existed. To a certain extent, then, Plato's procedure here approaches Popper's 'piecemeal social engineering' (above, pp. 139–40)—though Plato fashions the separate pieces into an elaborate whole.

Plato's reliance on the real rather than the ideal has important theoretical implications which we will examine below. But before moving on, we should note one recurrent problem with his institution building. Plato examines features of numerous states and undoubtedly shows a sharp eye for correcting their defects. But, perhaps because he died before ironing out various difficulties, he is less successful in combining the different features of different states into a coherent system. To cite one example, he takes over Athenian economic classes, but does little to harmonize this with other institutions. Throughout the political system as a whole, we find frequent overlap and duplication of some functions, while others, even important ones, are ignored. Thus, regardless of the wisdom that shows through specific aspects of Magnesia, the whole is frequently chaotic and less than the sum of its parts.

Still, we should realize the nature of the procedure Plato follows in the *Laws*. This approach to political reform adds a new dimension to his more abstract theorizing in the *Republic*, and has not received the recognition it deserves. More attention has been paid in recent years, but much remains to be accomplished in this regard.

12.4. GOVERNMENT

If the social and economic aspects of Magnesia reveal the influence of Sparta, the system of government is heavily influenced by Athens. But as Morrow shows, the Athens that Plato has in mind is not the extreme democracy of his own day, but the more moderate democratic regime that existed before the Persian wars.[7] This is to be expected in the light of Plato's discussion of the decline of Athens in Book III, and his disparaging remarks about democracy throughout his corpus. In general, when Plato is critical of democracy, what he has in mind is the extreme form exhibited by the Athens he experienced. His attitude is considerably more favourable towards the less democratic form from which his own state evolved.

There are numerous gaps and other difficulties in Plato's account of the constitution of the state. To some extent these can be attributed to the fact that Plato probably died before completing the *Laws*. Another factor is that much of Plato's constitution is modelled upon Athens. Since his readers were probably largely Athenian and could have been expected to approach the work with some basic presuppositions, one may often presume that, where Plato is silent, he probably means to take over Athenian institutional forms. He devotes much more discussion to respects in which he departs from Athens than to respects in which he remains faithful.

An additional factor is Plato's rough distinction between constitutional law and other legislation that exists on a lower level. At 751*a* he describes his legislative task as consisting of two parts. First he will describe the state's offices and the means used to fill them, and then he will describe the responsibilities of each. But as Morrow notes,[8] instead of discussing the laws of the state office by office, Plato proceeds to examine them topic by topic, for instance, covering family law, then agricultural law, then criminal law. Because he never presents a systematic account of the duties of each office, it is inevitable that gaps result. In discussing the structure of the state, we will note some of the more important lacunae and attempt to fill a few in.

In order to appreciate the constitutional system of Magnesia, it is necessary to look briefly at the system in fourth-century Athens. As was the case in most Greek cities, the government of Athens combined a popular assembly, a council, a system of courts, and magistrates. However, the precise form these institutions assumed shows that Athens was an extreme democracy. In Athens political power was concentrated in the Assembly, which was the main deliberative body, which all adult males were eligible to attend and for which attendance was eventually paid, and popular courts, which were generally

[7] G. Morrow, *Plato's Cretan City* (Princeton, NJ, 1960), esp. ch. 5.   [8] Ibid. 232–3.

made up of large numbers of citizens, selected by lot and also paid, who fulfilled the roles of both judge and jury. The important function of overseeing the Assembly's agenda was lodged in the Council of five hundred. This body was also staffed through the lottery system. It was divided into ten parts or committees (*prutaneis*), consisting of the fifty members from each of Athens' ten tribes (supplemented by one member of each of the other tribes). Each committee sat for one-tenth of the year, with one member chosen by lot to be in charge, and formally head of state—for a single day. Though there were numerous magistrates, who were generally elected annually, on the whole these exercised little power, with the exception of the ten generals, who combined important military and political functions. All magistrates were under strict popular control, not only through the need to be elected, but through careful scrutiny before election and an examination or audit at the end of their terms in which they were held accountable for their conduct in office, subject to trial before popular courts (Aristotle, *Ath. Pol.* 48, 4–5). Thus, it is clear that in the Athens Plato knew, democracy, literally 'rule by the people', had been realized.

The constitutional structure of Magnesia is at first sight similar. There is an assembly that all citizens who have borne arms are eligible to attend, and a council. Like the Athenian Council of five hundred, this is divided into *prutaneis*, each of which sits separately during a portion of the year. There is also a popular court, actually the Assembly, which has jurisdiction in cases involving crimes against the state. Up to this point, the resemblance to Athens holds.

But in other respects Magnesia is quite different. Magnesia is meant to be a 'mixed' state. We discuss exactly what this means in the next chapter. But clearly an important consideration is Plato's resolve to curb the power of popular institutions in favour of the magistrates, of which Magnesia exhibits a dazzling variety. Much of the state's real power is lodged in their hands.

Whereas in Athens the Assembly possessed extensive powers over such matters as war and peace, foreign policy, legislation, constitutional questions, and sentences of death, the Magnesian Assembly has fewer responsibilities. Only four matters are explicitly placed in its hands. Its major responsibility is electing members of the Council and some other officials. It has jurisdiction in trying cases concerning crimes against the state (768*a*); it must grant approval for changes in the laws (772*d*), which Plato clearly believes will be few and far between (see below, pp. 250–1); and it can extend the stay of resident aliens (850*c*). It is likely that the Assembly is also meant to have additional powers, especially in the field of foreign policy. Plato neglects to assign responsibility for such matters as war and peace and alliances. But since these were prerogatives of the Athenian Assembly, it is reasonable to assume that they were intended for the Assembly in Magnesia. Even with these functions added, however, the Magnesian Assembly is but a shadow of its Athenian counterpart.

The Council too has considerably less power than the Athenian Council. It is explicitly commissioned to oversee the ordinary business of the state, deal with foreign emissaries, and to summon the Assembly (758a–d). But this short list of functions makes the reader pause. We can supplement these responsibilities by assigning the Council the task of controlling the Assembly's agenda. This is another important function that Plato neglects to assign, but since it was a prerogative of the Athenian Council, it seems reasonable to assume the Council was meant to have it in Magnesia. Still, in the light of the fact that the powers of the Assembly are rather limited, controlling its agenda does not greatly enhance the powers of the Council.

Thus it is somewhat disconcerting that Plato introduces an intricate, multi-stage procedure through which Council members are elected, in which the class system figures (756b–e; and see below, p. 240), and is, in fact, the class system's main role in the entire constitution. The attention paid to electing the Council seems out of keeping with its limited power. What is more, upon completing his account of these election procedures, Plato remarks that they give the state a 'mixed' constitution (756e). We discuss the nature of this mixture below, but again, Plato's remarks seem odd, in the light of the Council's limited role in the state.

In his treatment of Magnesia's courts, as in the institutions we have looked at, Plato creates democratic institutions but limits their power. He institutes different kinds of courts to try different kinds of cases. Cases against the state are turned over to a public court, which is the Assembly, in recognition of the fact that crimes against the state concern everyone (767e–68a). There is a three-tier system of courts for private cases. It is important to recognize that in Greek law this classification encompassed much more than what are now generally called civil suits, as most crimes were dealt with through legal action initiated by the aggrieved party, and so fell under private law. The basic court for private cases is a board of arbitrators, made up of friends and neighbours of the contending parties (766e, 956b). Appeals can be made to tribal courts that are chosen by lot (768b). The highest level is a court of select judges, made up of one magistrate from each category. Appeals are, however, to be discouraged through a practice of increasing penalties if the verdict goes against the party initiating the appeal (956c). Finally, capital cases are to be heard by a special court, composed of a combination of the select court and the guardians of the laws (855c). Thus, democratic prerogatives are recognized in the composition of the public court and the lottery system used to select tribal courts. But the majority of the magistrates on the higher courts attain their offices through election, which the Greeks regarded as undemocratic. By instituting higher courts to hear appeals and by limiting the role of the lottery in staffing these, Plato largely removes judicial power from democratic control.

Democracy is curbed far more by the three major bodies of magistrates. These are all composed of older men, over 50, while membership of the three bodies to some extent overlaps. First are the *nomophulakes*. The translation is 'guardians of the laws', though maintaining the Greek title is preferable, in order to avoid confusing them with the guardians of the *Republic*. Though officials similar to these existed in certain Greek cities, this body is largely original with Plato. The *nomophulakes* are explicitly assigned three main functions. First, they have a general responsibility to oversee the enforcement of all laws (754*d*–*e*). Second, they are to keep records of all property in the state. Finally, they are to fill in aspects of the legal system that the lawgiver leaves out and to make necessary changes during the early years of the state, until things are working smoothly (esp. 770*a*–*e*, 772*a*–*c*). They are also assigned numerous relatively minor tasks on a somewhat ad hoc basis, but taken together these amount to a grant of power to inquire into and supervise virtually all aspects of citizens' lives.

Nomophulakes must be at least 50 years old and can serve until they are 70. The thirty-seven members are chosen through a complicated system combining election and the lottery system. Plato assigns great importance to their position and provides means for selecting an initial body of thirty-seven at the founding of the state. The Cretan founders will choose eighteen from Cnossos and nineteen from the colonists (752*e*–53*a*). Plato's discussion is confused, as he runs together the initial selection procedure and the procedure to fill vacancies in the board caused by the death or retirement of individual members. Presumably, further revision would have removed this difficulty.[9]

Upon reading almost all of the *Laws*, one naturally takes the *nomophulakes* to be the most important magistrates in the state. They are constantly mentioned and also serve as a pool of talent used to staff other offices. Thus the official in charge of the educational system is elected from the *nomophulakes*. This commissioner of education, as it seems appropriate to call him, is said to hold the most important office in the state (765*e*) and must therefore be the best of all the citizens (766*a*). In addition, the *nomophulakes* are combined with the court of select judges to compose the special court for trying capital cases, and the ten senior *nomophulakes* serve on the nocturnal council.

---

[9] Ibid. 238–40; cf. T. Saunders, 'The Alleged Double Version in the Sixth Book of Plato's *Laws*', *Classical Quarterly* (20), 1970.

There is an attractive symmetry to the *nomophulakes'* being the main magistrates in the state. For then the second-best state, which exists under the rule of law, would be presided over by guardians of the laws, as the ideal state of the *Republic* is presided over by guardians. However, in Book XII, Plato introduces two additional magistracies that seem to assume many of the *nomophulakes'* functions.

The first body of magistrates introduced in Book XII is the examiners. As their title indicates, the main function of these officials is examining magistrates at the end of their terms to ensure that they have been faithful to the laws. Like the *nomophulakes*, the examiners are required to be at least 50 years old, though they can serve until the age of 75. They are chosen by election, through a complex winnowing out process (945e–46b). At the founding of the state, twelve will be selected, with three additional members added to the board each subsequent year (946c). The function of examination was an important feature of Greek cities, primarily exercised by the Assembly or popular courts in democracies. Thus, in this respect as well, Plato assigns a democratic function to elected magistrates.

Plato takes the position of the examiners very seriously. He declares that they must be of surpassing excellence (945c) and so the best members of the state (946b–c). They are honoured accordingly. For instance, they are crowned with laurel (946b, 947a), and have the front seats at public festivals, while the name of the chief examiner is given to the year (947a).

There are some problems with Plato's account of the examiners. First, it is difficult to reconcile their role with that of the *nomophulakes*. Aside from the fact that they come to receive the great esteem that had been earlier assigned to the commissioner of education, there is an institutional conflict. As we have noted, the *nomophulakes'* primary responsibility is ensuring that the laws of the state are observed. One would assume that the official examination of magistrates at the end of their terms would be an important instrument towards this end, but this function is assigned to the examiners. As Barker says, the examiners seem to usurp the function of the *nomophulakes*.[10] It is not impossible to rescue Plato from contradiction here, as the function of examination can be divided into two components. In this case, the *nomophulakes* would inquire into and prosecute suspected wrongdoing, with the examiners sitting as judges. There can be no doubt that the examiners are given the power to pass sentence on offending magistrates (946d). But under this arrangement, the examiners are transformed into a kind of court, and it is not clear how their role can be reconciled with the other courts, especially the popular court for public cases and the special court for capital cases. In addition, Plato allows the

---

[10] E. Barker, *Greek Political Theory: Plato and His Predecessors* (London, 1918), p. 399, n. 3.

verdicts of the examiners to be appealed to the court of select judges (946d–e). Thus, in spite of the great esteem in which the examiners are held, their power is actually circumscribed at both ends. The *nomophulakes* have the power to inquire into and prosecute wrongdoers, while the verdicts of the examiners can be appealed. Thus their role does not justify the honours heaped upon them.

An additional problem is that the most important magistrates are virtually immune from examination. This is true of the *nomophulakes*, because officials are examined only at the end of their terms and the *nomophulakes* serve for up to twenty years. Of course, if they should die in office—not an unlikely possibility—they would not be audited at all. This seems to be an oversight on Plato's part. Since examiners serve terms of up to twenty-five years, a similar problem arises in their case. Though Plato mentions the examination of examiners (946e, 947e), he realizes that this is not sufficient and provides an additional mechanism, special lawsuits, for the purpose (947e–48a). But no similar mechanism is set up for dealing with misconduct by the *nomophulakes*, and so in this respect as well, Plato has not satisfactorily integrated the examiners and *nomophulakes*.

Finally, there is a problem with the number of examiners. As we have noted, Plato says that after the initial twelve have been chosen, three more will be added each year. It is not possible to assess the size of the resulting board with assurance. But if we assume that the typical examiner serves for half of the possible twenty-five years, the resulting board will be composed of some thirty-six examiners.[11] This seems a large number of individuals of such pre-eminence, especially in the light of the fact that the examiners are assigned seats on the nocturnal council. Since each member of that body also brings a younger associate with him, the composition of the nocturnal council is brought into the range of one hundred members, which seems quite a high figure. Presumably, as in the difficulty with selection of the initial and subsequent *nomophulakes*, there is a problem here, which, had Plato lived to revise the work, he would have cleaned up.

The nocturnal council's sinister sounding name derives from the fact that it meets daily between dusk and daybreak, convenient hours for busy officials. This body is introduced quite in passing in Book X in connection with the examination of imprisoned heretics (908a–9a). But in Book XII its role is expanded. Plato contradicts himself slightly in his two accounts of the synod's composition (951d–e, 961a), but it is likely that it was intended to have the

---

[11] Barker puts the number at forty (*Greek Political Theory*, p. 400, n. 2); the figure of fifteen is given by Ritter (cited by Barker), who is followed by E. B. England (*The Laws of Plato*, 2 vols. [Manchester, 1921], III, 636). Morrow says only that the number is 'much smaller' than the possible seventy-five (*Plato's Cretan City*, p. 223).

following members: the examiners, other citizens who have received awards for merit, the ten senior *nomophulakes*, the commissioner of education and surviving past commissioners, and a number of citizens who have travelled abroad where they observed the laws and customs of other peoples. All these individuals are at least 50 years old. As we have noted, each member will nominate a younger associate, who, with the approval of the entire council, will also serve. These individuals are to be between 30 and 40 years of age. Apparently, service on the synod will provide them with background and experience for future high office. Moreover, as Christopher Bobonich especially argues, because of the relatively large number of Magnesians who serve on the nocturnal council during their thirties and then move back into the general population, their experience should significantly raise the deliberative capacities of the citizenry.[12]

The nocturnal council is envisioned as a kind of ongoing seminar. Its main purpose is to achieve a theoretical understanding of the laws of the state. This requires a series of higher studies, which Plato describes only briefly at the end of the work, but which appear to be similar to those recommended for the guardians in *Republic* VII. It was to offer a more complete account of these studies that Phillip of Opus wrote the *Epinomis*. It is not entirely clear what the nocturnal council is to do with its knowledge, as its constitutional position is not specified. We return to this theme and discuss its implications later.

In general, the members of the nocturnal council too achieve their position through non-democratic means. The senior *nomophulakes* have been elected, as is also true of the commissioner of education and past commissioners, and the examiners. The foreign observers and younger associates are selected by the council. Thus by placing considerable power in the body's hands (on which more later), Plato once again acts to limit popular government.

---

[12] Bobonich, *Plato's Utopia Recast*, p. 408.

13

Political Principles

13.1. THE MIXED CONSTITUTION

Because of the complex system of offices we have examined, the *Laws* is frequently said to be a pioneering work in the theory of the 'mixed constitution'. The constitution can be termed 'mixed' in two different respects. Though Plato does not actually refer to Magnesia as having a 'mixed' (*meikitê* or *memeigmenê*) constitution, he does say that it observes a 'mean' or 'intermediary' position between different constitutional forms, and we examine this. But the work also occupies a significant position in the tradition of what we frequently call the 'mixed' constitution, despite Plato's failure to use the term.

In his discussion of the Dorian states in Book III, the Athenian credits Sparta's unique institutions for the fact that she was the only one of the three original monarchies to survive. Sparta was the only Dorian state to establish institutionalized restraints upon the use of power. This was first seen in the distinctive Spartan dual monarchy, and then further solidified with the establishment of the council of elders, or *gerousia*, and the ephors (691*b*–92*d*). As a result of its complex institutions, Sparta resisted easy identification as either democracy, monarchy, aristocracy, or tyranny. It had elements of all four kinds. In some respects the state was democratic, while the double kingship was tyrannical, the *gerousia* was aristocratic, and the ephorate was considered monarchical (712*d*–*e*). Thus, Sparta possessed a recognizable separation of powers, and something of checks and balances. For these reasons it was a forerunner of the American Constitution and those of the Western European countries. Plato's analysis of the Spartan constitution was taken up by later thinkers, for example, Polybius, and following him, Machiavelli.[1]

Throughout the Magnesian structure, powers are separated, with numerous institutions checking others. The examiners' main function is checking other officials, while Plato also institutes a special check on them. We have seen that the *nomophulakes* play an overall supervisory role in the state, perhaps undertaking a portion of the examining function. Other checking institutions

---

[1] Polybius, *Histories*, VI, 10; Machiavelli, *Discourses*, I, ch.2.

are found in the appellate levels of the judicial system, while even the verdicts of the examiners are subject to appeal. It is not necessary to multiply examples; clearly, separation of powers and checks and balances are respects in which the Magnesian constitution is 'mixed'. As one might expect, the theoretical basis for checks and balances is the existence of flaws in human nature, which make it imperative to give no man irresponsible power (713c, 874e–75c).

The other respect in which the constitution is 'mixed' is its situation between monarchy and democracy. In a few contexts Plato discusses the need to combine monarchical and democratic elements, which were embodied in Persia and Athens respectively. In Book III, Plato shows that these two states fared well as long as they pursued moderate courses. But each declined when it became an extreme representative of its type (701d–e). Accordingly, Plato states that the 'two mother forms of constitutions' are monarchy and democracy, and that it is necessary for a properly ordered state to avoid extremes by combining elements of both.

Though Plato never explicitly describes how the two forms are embodied in Magnesia, his position can be surmised. Democracy errs in the direction of freedom. This was seen in the decline of Athenian music, where the mob tyrannically imposed its standards. The same disregard for authority spread throughout the state, until the Athenians finally sought to cast off the authority of the laws altogether (710a–c). In Persia arbitrary rule of the monarch brought the state to ruin (697c–98a). Thus, Plato attempts to find a mean between the extremes of arbitrary rulers and an unbridled, tyrannical mob. He achieves this by instituting the democratic principle of popular authority in certain aspects of the state, but tempering it in important ways, especially by assigning many of the most important functions to magistrates. Though there is no monarch in Magnesia, the monarchical principle is represented by the state's numerous powerful officials. Unlike magistrates in Athens, these officials are granted lengthy terms of office and so are insulated from popular interference. In addition, the verdicts of the courts, which provided an immediate and powerful check upon Athenian officials, are subject to appeal. But the magistrates are not given arbitrary power. Officials in Magnesia are bound by numerous constitutional restraints, which should prevent the abuse of power that plagued Persia (697d–98a).

In the *Laws* as well as in the *Statesman* (above, pp. 208–9) Plato employs similes connected with weaving (734e–35a). He says that all threads in a cloth cannot be of the same quality. The warp must be better and stronger than the woof. So in Magnesia the magistrates with their superior natures are woven into the social fabric as a whole. Thus, by tempering democratic institutions with the power of superior magistrates, and placing the magistrates beneath the law, Plato finds a position between monarchic and democratic principles.

Plato's account of the 'mixed' constitution is amplified in his discussion of the procedures used to elect members of the Council. These procedures are intricate, and we need not review the details. The election takes place in the Assembly over a number of days, with members of the first two classes, but not the other two, generally required to attend. In addition, a pool of candidates larger than necessary is elected, with the lottery used to select the requisite number. Upon completing this description, the Athenian says: 'A system of selection like that will form a mean (*meson*) between a monarchical and a democratic constitution, and our constitution should always stand midway (*meseuein*) between these' (756e). In the discussion that immediately follows, the Athenian launches into an account of the distinction between arithmetic justice (treating equals equally) and geometric or proportional justice (treating unequals unequally), with obvious reference to the institutions just discussed (757a–d).

One respect in which this selection procedure could be said to combine monarchy and democracy is suggested by Aristotle, according to whom Magnesia represents a mixture of democracy and oligarchy (*Pol.* 1266a5–23). Aristotle bases his interpretation upon the fact that it was a common oligarchic practice to require the wealthy to participate in political affairs in various ways not required of the poor (*Pol.* 1298b3–26). Because allowing all citizens to participate in choosing the Council (even if they are not required to do so) is democratic, the selection procedure could be interpreted as a combination of democratic and oligarchic elements.

It seems that we can find a better interpretation than Aristotle's, which conflicts with what Plato says. Plato says, first, that the selection procedure combines democratic and monarchic elements, not democratic and oligarchic. Second, in his account of the two kinds of justice, Plato says that the procedure embodies an element of proportional justice, which entails granting privileges to those superior in virtue. Thus, Aristotle's interpretation implies that Plato regards superior wealth as tantamount to superior virtue. But this does not rest well with the general bias against wealth apparent in all of Plato's works, including the *Laws*.

A more likely interpretation emphasizes the mode of selecting the Council, rather than the role of classes in that selection. In choosing the Council, as is generally true in the *Laws*, Plato combines election and the lottery system. In discussing the two principles of justice, Plato describes the lottery as the supreme embodiment of arithmetic justice (757b) and contrasts this with proportional equality (757b–d). Thus, the discussion of justice appears to be in reference to the mode of selecting officials, and if Plato takes the lot to represent arithmetic justice, then election must represent proportional justice. This is confirmed by the discussion of Athens in Book III, where

Plato contrasts excessive liberty with a moderate government under elected officials (698*a*–*b*). In addition, in discussing the state's 'woven' composition (734*e*–35*a*), Plato says that the need for a 'warp' of superior quality entails that careful means be devised for choosing high officials. The means eventually applied rely heavily on election, so clearly Plato's position is that elections are capable of selecting the most virtuous members of society. Plato realizes that elections can work efficiently only if the populace is properly educated and aware of the qualifications of the candidates (751*c*–*d*). Apparently, he thinks it will work. For instance, the examiners, the three best men in the state, are chosen entirely by election (946*b*–*c*). In the case of the examiners, it is so important to choose men of surpassing merit that the lot is all but eliminated, used only for breaking deadlocks.

It seems then that the Magnesian constitution combines democratic and monarchical principles in two ways. First, the state combines the democratic principle of freedom from arbitrary authority with the monarchic principle of powerful magistrates who are not susceptible to popular whims. In addition, in devising means to choose these officials—and the Council—Plato combines the democratic principle of selection by chance with the monarchical principle of virtue, as determined by elections. It is notable that the bulk of the state's offices are distributed through a combination of these two mechanisms, and so there is justice to Plato's claim to have combined the principles. In light of Plato's traditional suspicion of the lot, which he inherited from Socrates (see above, p. 34), it is surprising that he employs it at all, instead of relying on undiluted elections for all offices. No doubt Plato would say that the lot is a concession to the populace of the state, instituted to allay discontent (757*d*–*e*). Similarly, Plato remarks that the introduction of property classes is a concession to the wealthy (744*c*). Thus here, as in other cases we have observed, Plato employs a democratic institution but checks its egalitarian tendencies.

13.2. EQUALITY AND FREEDOM IN MAGNESIA

It should be clear from the last chapter that, on questions concerning negative freedom, Plato's position in the *Laws* is generally similar to the *Republic*. The totally educated individual, conditioned from before birth, cannot be said to be free in this sense. There are, however, important respects in which Magnesia's inhabitants are far more equal than those of the just city in the *Republic*.

First and most significant is elimination of the rigid class system of the *Republic*. As we have noted, all citizens explicitly receive an education that resembles the early education of the guardians in the *Republic*. All are alike in pursuing virtue as their main end in life and in devoting virtually all their energy to this. We have seen that there is a four-class system of economic classes in Magnesia. But because of the relatively insignificant role this plays in the state, the citizens of Magnesia experience a kind of equality alien to the *Republic*. In Magnesia, all male citizens, and perhaps women also, take part in political affairs and are eligible for all political offices. Political equality in Magnesia is clear in use of the lot in selecting virtually all officials. The lot would be rejected out of hand by the Plato of the *Republic*. Of course, the introduction of political—and moral—equality in Magnesia is based on Plato's loss of hope for superior human types,[2] In addition, our assessment of Magnesian political equality should be qualified in light of the emphasis on election, which is intended to select the best possible office-holders. Though elections are generally employed in conjunction with the lot, certain officials, notably the examiners, are chosen through election alone. However, even if elections were to work as aristocratically as the Greeks believed they would, all citizens are given the vote and so the power to decide who is chosen.

These forms of political participation bring the second-best state into accord with conventional Greek ideals. As Aristotle says, the excellence of a citizen is achieved by ruling and being ruled in turn (*Pol.* 1277a25–7). In selecting their rulers and being eligible themselves, the Magnesians have far more extensive rights as citizens than members of the third class in the *Republic*.

Elimination of rigid differentiation of classes also makes the principles of distributive justice in the *Laws* more complex than what is seen in the *Republic*. As we have noted, distribution in the latter is according to the principle of what is best for the state (above, p. 163). This takes the form of distributing different goods to the three classes. In the second-best state, more complex principles of distribution are applied to the different social goods. Political offices are assigned through a combination of election and the lot, with both means employed fairly, in that everyone is eligible both to vote and to be elected to all offices. There are disclaimers. Procedures are set up to bring about greater participation in certain elections by the wealthy, while some minor offices are reserved for wealthy individuals. In addition are age requirements, generally of at least 50 years, for virtually all important offices. Age qualifications are a significant component of the constitution.

---

[2] In *Plato's Utopia Recast*, Bobonich argues for a more optimistic view of the virtue of ordinary citizens in the *Laws*, as opposed to the *Republic* (C. Bobonich, *Plato's Utopia Recast* [Oxford, 2002]).

The Magnesian economy provides less equality, in that there are different property classes, with some different privileges attached to them. But economic differences are kept within reasonable bounds. Even the poorest citizens have inalienable land, while excessive wealth is confiscated. The benefits of wealth are largely curbed by strict controls on commerce and by institutions such as the common table, which enforce equality. Though some extra-economic benefits accrue to the wealthy, on the whole these are not of great significance. Especially important is the fact that public esteem attaches to virtue, not wealth. In other respects, citizens are treated equally. As we have noted, all receive the same early education. All are also accorded full rights of citizenship and are viewed as equal in their potential to lead virtuous lives. Because of equality in these fundamental respects, the citizens of Magnesia should be regarded as treated equally for the most part, according to combined principles of arithmetic and proportional justice that reflect the mixed constitution. It should be noted, however, that this equality is for citizens alone. Metics and, especially, slaves are debarred from most benefits of living in the state.

The treatment of distribution in the *Laws* illustrates another sense in which Magnesia is a mixed or combined state. In this respect, as throughout much of the *Laws*, Plato forges an accommodation between his moral ideals and conventional beliefs. The slate is not wiped clean, as in the *Republic*; rather, what already exists is carefully improved. It is not surprising that the more conventionally minded Aristotle finds much to admire in the *Laws* and follows it closely in constructing his own ideal state in Books VII and VIII of the *Politics*.[3]

The case is more complex in regard to the citizens' freedom. At first sight, one could argue that Magnesia's citizens are appreciably more free than members of the third class in the *Republic*. For one, they exercise significantly more political freedom.[4] Plato appears to evince similar interest in their negative freedom. In accordance with his ideal of 'spontaneous and willing acceptance of the rule of law' (690c), Plato contrasts two ways a physician can treat his patients (720c–e). The doctor of slaves simply imposes prescriptions. He makes no attempt to convince the patients of the need for treatment; their assent is irrelevant. The doctor of freemen behaves differently:

---

[3] A good discussion of this is found in E. Barker, *Greek Political Theory: Plato and His Predecessors* (London, 1918), pp. 443–4.

[4] This is the freedom of the ancients, or 'positive freedom', according to one construal of that term; see B. Constant, 'The Liberty of the Ancients and the Liberty of the Moderns', in *Constant: Political Writings*, B. Fontana, ed. (Cambridge, 1988); on negative and positive freedom, see I. Berlin, 'Two Concepts of Liberty', in *Four Essays on Liberty* (Oxford, 1969); G. MacCallum, 'Negative and Positive Freedom', *Philosophical Review*, 76 (1967).

[H]is method is to construct an empirical case-history by consulting the invalid and his friends; in this way he himself learns something from the sick and at the same time he gives the individual patient all the instruction he can. He gives no prescription until he has somehow gained the invalid's consent; then, coaxing him into continued cooperation, he tries to complete his restoration to health. (720*d*)

Because the rule of law, like the doctor of freemen's treatment, requires subjects' assent, the lawgiver must use persuasion as well as force.

In order to meet this need, Plato attaches preambles to his laws. This is one of his major theoretical innovations in the *Laws*. Each specific edict is composed of two parts, a straightforward description of the prohibition in question along with a statement of the penalty for violations and a lengthy, philosophical explanation of the reasons for the prohibition and punishment (718*a*–22*c*). Plato takes credit for originating this form of legislation (722*b*–*c*), and many important philosophical discussions in the *Laws* are preambles to different laws. For instance, the theological arguments in Book X constitute the preamble to the laws concerning crimes against the gods, while the striking passage in Book IX concerning the overall need for laws is the preamble to laws concerning the infliction of wounds (874*e*–75*d*). Plato says that laws should be like parents who give loving instruction, rather than despots who order and threaten (859*a*). He notes that someone witnessing a physician of the kind he has in mind might protest that the physician does not treat (*iatreueis*) his patients but educates (*paideueis*) them (857*d*). But, of course, in Plato's eyes, the *polis* is an educative institution, and the laws play a crucial role in this process.

The need for consent to laws sets the *Laws* apart from Plato's other political works. The difference between the positions here and in the *Statesman* is evident (see above, pp. 204–5). In that work Plato says that consent is of no concern, as long as the physician works to promote his patient's good—though, as we noted, there is some ambiguity on this point (above, p. 205). Since Plato employs the analogy of the physician in both works, it seems likely that he is explicitly rejecting the position of the earlier work in the later. In the *Laws*, in the absence of the perfect statesman, Plato not only insists on the rule of law, but on the subjects' consent to law.

Though one might easily fall into discussing Plato's views on consent in terms of the 'right to consent'—as in the last paragraph—this is misleading. First of all, it is not clear that instruction by written preambles amounts to much. In a number of works Plato says disparaging things about the written word. Written compositions are poor teachers because one cannot ask them questions. If one attempts to do so, they merely go on repeating the same thing endlessly (*Phdr.* 275*d*; cf. *Prt.* 329*a*–*b*). Much the same could be said about the preambles. They might represent the fruit of philosophic wisdom, but they are no substitute for philosophers. It is not clear how far they would actually be able to educate the subjects.

It is also unclear whether the subject's assent could be said to be given freely. From before birth, he is intensively conditioned to hold specific moral views. In light of his having been 'moulded like wax' for many years, it does not seem that he would be able not to consent. The preambles represent a codification of what the subject has always been taught to believe. If one of Plato's suggestions were implemented, the actual preambles contained in the *Laws*, along with similar compositions by other hands, would be the only literature he had ever known. Moreover, if some subject were able to withhold assent, it seems unlikely that he would be allowed to do so. One of the less attractive features of Plato's state is its treatment of people who disagree with the theological grounding of the laws. Dissidents receive a five-year term in solitary confinement, visited only by members of the nocturnal council who discuss the disagreements in question. If after this period of thinking it over the dissident still dissents, the penalty is death (908e–9a). Thus, the right of consent is narrowly circumscribed.

Finally, there are important differences between Plato's system and what political theorists generally regard as theories of popular consent.[5] The main point is that theorists upholding consent generally insist that government is not legitimate unless it rests on consent by the populace. Thus, the *Declaration of Independence* says that 'governments [derive] their just powers from the consent of the governed'. The implication here and in theories of consent in general is that if citizens choose to withhold consent or to withdraw it after it has been given, the government ceases to be legitimate. Since Plato would undoubtedly shrink from such implications, his view should not be regarded as a theory of popular consent.

On the whole, it seems more reasonable to interpret the role of consent in the *Laws* as similar to, though more explicit than, the role of temperance in the state in the *Republic*. In that work, as we recall, temperance boils down to the willing acquiescence of all elements of society to the overall scheme of things, and is secured primarily by education. In the *Laws*, temperance in the state entails that all citizens respect the rule of law, and this too is achieved by education. It seems that the primary function of consent is contributing

---

[5] For J. Locke's classic account, see *The Second Treatise on Government*, ch. 6. There is no hint of tacit concent in the *Laws*, though such a doctrine is found in the *Crito* (51c–54c); see above, Ch. 2, n. 2. For a sophisticated analysis of the requirements for consent, and political obligations based on consent, see A. J. Simmons, *Moral Principles and Political Obligations* (Princeton, NJ, 1979), ch. 3–4. It could perhaps be argued that the sense in which 'consent' is maintained in the *Laws* corresponds to what Simmons calls 'attitudinal consent'; see *Moral Principles*, pp. 93, 97.

to respect for the laws, and so consent should be looked at primarily as a mechanism for inculcating temperance. It is towards this end that Plato discusses it and writes preambles to the laws, not because he recognizes an inherent right of consent.

Having said this, we should add that consent is of course not without value. One of Plato's chief goals in the *Laws*—as throughout his political theory— is to design institutions that will promote stability and harmony within both the state and its individual members. The difference between the physician's treatment of slaves and freemen is real; Plato does not want his rulers to hold sway through force alone—as the Spartans ruled their helots—or along the lines of the rulers in the degenerate states in Books VIII and IX of the *Republic*. All parts of Magnesia are to be linked by acceptance of the order of things, and ideally by friendship as well. Though this acceptance is achieved somewhat ruthlessly, it is an important component of the state. Once more, however, it should be mentioned that assent is limited to full members of the state. Plato recommends that slaves be treated leniently in many ways (777d–78a), and recommends other measures to avoid the danger of revolt (above, p. 229) but in general they are ruled by force. Metics are not full members either, but because their presence is not constrained, they should not be dissatisfied during their twenty years of residence.

13.3. THE RULE OF LAW

Because the direct rule of philosophical intelligence is impossible, Magnesia must exist under the rule of law. This is a major difference between the political theories of the *Laws* and *Republic*, while as we have noted, the *Statesman* lies directly between the two works. Plato's main argument for the rule of law is conventional. Human beings cannot be entrusted with unaccountable power, and so must be placed under laws (esp. 713c, 874e–75d). In Plato's words:

Where the law is subject to some other authority and has none of its own, the collapse of the state, in my view, is not far off; but if law is the master of the government and the government is its slave, then the situation is full of promise and men enjoy all the blessings that the gods shower on a state. (715d)

Laws must satisfy certain conditions to be legitimate. Plato is aware of various sociological accounts of the origin of laws. In the *Laws* he repeats the argument made familiar by Thrasymachus in the *Republic* that the laws of existing states were instituted by the stronger members to promote their own interests. Having arranged things in this way, the rulers declared obedience to the law just and disobedience unjust. According to this account, then, law is 'the interest of the stronger' (714*b–e*; *Rep.* 338*d–39a*). However, Plato denies that such edicts are truly laws, as he refuses the title 'polity' (*politeia*) to states ruled in this manner. Instead, they are 'faction-states' (*stasiôteias*) (715*a–b*). The Greek here is difficult to translate, but something of Plato's sense is perhaps conveyed by the difference between 'commonwealth' and 'party-wealth'. In genuine polities, government is for the benefit of all, though in most states a single faction holds power and rules in its own interest. Of course, for Plato the end of government is the benefit of all. He says that the goal of the laws should be to make the state free, temperate, and wise (693*b*, 701*d*).

Thus, for Plato the rule of law requires that the laws aim for the public good. It affords protection from self-interested rulers and can be compared to 'reason free from passion', in Aristotle's *Politics* (1287*a*32). As an instrument to attain the common good, law is indeed a public calculation of pleasures and pains, as Plato calls it in Book I (644*c–d*).

The relationship between reason and law involves some additional factors. As the state is analogous to the soul, the law, or reason in the state, is analogous to reason in the soul. At one point Plato speaks of reason as 'embodied in the law as far as it can be' (835*e*). As we see directly, he holds that reason in the state—and in the soul—is a reflection of the eternal reason that directs all things. In so far as the individual is concerned, the law represents the means through which he becomes rational. It is through education according to law that individuals achieve the virtue of temperance, through which their passions are subordinated to their reason. Without law there would be nothing to distinguish men from beasts (874*e*–75*b*). In addition, since virtue is necessary for happiness, it is by participating in law that individuals become happy. Accordingly, as the individual is suspended like a puppet on strings of pleasure and pain, he should strive to lay hold of the 'golden string' of the law (644*d*–45*a*).

The relationship between temperance in the individual and the rule of law in the state is more than an analogy; it involves reciprocal interaction. Through education under the law, individuals become temperate and rational as far as possible. In its turn, temperance is the lifeblood of the laws. Only if individuals are able to control their passions can they obey the laws. Thus, law as the reason of the state promotes the rule of reason in the individual, while the rational individual enables reason to prevail in the state.

An additional respect in which the laws of the state participate in reason is by reflecting the rational principles of the universe as a whole. The relationship between the state and the cosmos is not spelled out clearly in the *Laws*, just as the connections between the philosopher's knowledge of the Good and his role in the ideal state are not presented clearly in the *Republic*. In the *Laws*, Plato obviously believes that the values promoted by the state, that is, reason and harmony, mirror cosmic principles. But he also insists on a general, though largely unspecified, close relationship between the laws of the state and the rational grounding of the cosmos.

Plato argues in support of this relationship in Book X, where he attempts to prove the existence of the gods and the fact that they control all things. His arguments are directed especially against various materialistic thinkers, who explain all things as the result of the combination of elements through chance. Plato believes that their theories give rise to three specific heresies: that the gods do not exist; that even if they do exist, they do not involve themselves in human affairs; and even if they do become involved, they can be bought off through lavish sacrifices and other bribes. Though Plato attributes the heresies largely to the influence of the cosmologists (890*a*), they were widespread. We see all three heresies in the speech of Adeimantus in Book II of the *Republic*, who says that they represent most people's opinions (*Rep.* 363*e*–66*d*). But because of the cosmologists' role in propagating these beliefs, Plato combats them with cosmological arguments of his own.

It is not necessary to look at Plato's arguments in detail (886*e*–99*d*, 899*d*–905*d*, 905*d*–7*b*). The proof of the existence of God (or the gods—Plato is indifferent to this distinction) is based on the necessity of a prime mover, which in Plato's case is demonstrated to be soul. From the existence of soul, Plato proves the existence of God. Having shown that the gods exist, he then 'proves' that they take concern for human affairs through the analogy of the craftsman. As the good craftsman does not neglect any aspect of his subject matter, so God, who is not inferior to any craftsman, could not neglect human affairs, which fall within his domain. The third argument depends on another analogy. Basically, if God is superior to other watchmen, and it is inconsistent with being an effective watchman to accept bribes, then God cannot accept bribes. It should be noted that Plato's arguments throughout this section are weak and beg various questions at issue.

Though Plato believes in the gods and believes that they enforce the laws of justice, to a certain extent the arguments here can be attributed to good politics. Plato believes that people act out of self-interested motives. Thus, they will behave virtuously only if they believe that it pays to do so. Like his cousin Critias before him (above, p. 3), Plato sees the utility in inventing gods to scare men into virtue. If people believed there were no gods, they would be uncontrollable (907*c*). Thus, the belief that the gods enforce the rules of justice is a 'useful fiction', which the wise lawgiver should do everything in his power to foster (663*b*–*d*). Accordingly, even if the arguments in Book X do not hold, Plato believes it is necessary that people believe that they do. The conclusions of the arguments are so necessary for promoting virtuous behaviour that individuals who cannot be convinced that they are true should be put to death (908*e*–9*a*). It should be noted that the individuals to be dealt with in this way are expressly said to be otherwise unobjectionable; their outer behaviour is in conformity with the law (908*b*–*c*). One is justified in asking if it is because they do not suffer from deranged souls that Plato believes they are so dangerous and must be dealt with so severely.

Upon reflection, it seems that one reason Plato believes it is necessary to establish close connections between the laws of his state and the laws of God is precisely because the connections are not apparent. We have seen that the distinction between nature and convention was frequently employed to undermine faith in existing institutions, and that one of Plato's main goals throughout his works was to establish objective moral standards rooted in nature. In Book X Plato refers to the distinction between nature and convention and explicitly argues for the natural grounding of the laws of the state (889*e*–90*d*). However, as we have seen, to a large extent Plato bases Magnesia upon existing Greek cities. Instead of deducing Magnesia's institutions from the moral demands of the Forms, Plato relies on what men have made. Thus, the rule of law in the *Laws*, as in the *Statesman*, is bound up with a narrowing of the gap between nature and convention, and a movement away from the two-world view of the middle dialogues. Much of the moral teaching of the *Laws* is conventional as well, as is seen in the removal of the paradoxical element from Socratic morality (see above, p. 220).

Thus, in his final work, Plato's overall position resembles the belief system of the traditional *polis* according to which the gods enforce the laws of justice. Because traditional views had come under attack, they could not be asserted uncritically and required defence. In the *Laws*, Plato attempts to defend his own—largely traditional—moral views by arguing for the existence of the gods. But his arguments rely heavily on faith and repeatedly assume what they set out to prove.

I think it is fair to say that the philosophical element in the *Laws* is largely muted. One reason the connections between the laws of the state and of the universe are unclear is that the connections do not rest on reasoned arguments as much as on faith. Plato believes that virtue and happiness coincide, and in so far as the state works to propagate that belief it does God's work. Though Plato's arguments rest, in the final analysis, more on faith than reason, he is not deterred. The *Laws* is in many ways a religious work. We have seen several indications of this, that is, in Plato's talk of man as a puppet of the gods and as a plaything of the gods. If in the early dialogues Plato defends the Socratic position that one's well-being depends entirely on the state of his soul, in the *Laws* he believes that how one fares rests on his relationship with the gods. Throughout the state, religion is taken very seriously. We have noted that religious festivals are a pervasive element. Similarly, the criminal code deals especially harshly with crimes against religion. The citizen who robs a temple commits 'a great and unspeakable offence', should be deemed incurably iniquitous and put to death (854*d*–*e*). The first word of the dialogue is 'God', and God is a fundamental principle throughout. An indication of Plato's sentiments is his revision of the Protagorean dictum, 'man is the measure of all things' to 'God is the measure of all things' (716*c*). Similarly, he says that a proof of the existence of the gods would be the best possible preamble to all the laws (887*b*–*c*).

It is therefore not surprising that in many respects the institutions and practices of Magnesia take on the rigidity of theocracy (see above, p. 225). The subjects are for all intents and purposes required to accept the laws of the state on faith. Though Plato does not explicitly say that laws can never be changed, though in one ambiguous passage (772*c*) he may well do so, this is implied by what he does say. He expresses great admiration for the practice of Egypt, in which all matters pertaining to music and other arts were prescribed in detail and left unchanged for ten thousand years, 'literally ten thousand' (656*d*–57*a*). In describing proper education in Book VII, Plato returns to this theme (797*a*–*d*). Nothing is more dangerous than innovation in children's games. This eventually leads to the desire to change the laws, which is the greatest of all ills to the state. Stable laws are a great good. If people live under unchanging laws, with no recollection of their ever having been different, the laws are reverently upheld. Thus, the lawgiver must devise some means to make this true in his state (798*a*–*b*). Again, the ideal is Egypt, where numerous matters were consecrated for all time (799*a*–*b*).

It would seem, then, that the laws are to be all but unalterable. In only one context does Plato address procedures for changing them. In Book VI he says that the original lawgiver cannot provide for every eventuality, and so the *nomophulakes* must revise and change the original laws as they think necessary (769*b*–71*a*). Precise procedures are not spelled out here, as the Athenian moves on to discuss such things as marriage assemblies and thanksgiving festivals (771*e*–72*a*). But he abruptly returns to the question of improving laws. The details of such festivals must be filled in by the officers of the choirs together with the *nomophulakes* (771*a*). During a trial period that is to last ten years, improvements are to be made, 'until every detail is thought to have received its final polish' (772*a*–*c*). The text continues: 'After that, they must assume that the rules are immutable and observe them along with the rest of the code which the legislator laid down and imposed on them originally' (772*c*). The 'rest of the code (*tôn allôn nomôn*)' here is ambiguous. It could mean all the laws of the state, or merely those concerning festivals presently under discussion. The narrower construal is generally preferred, because of the context.[6] As Guthrie says, this would be 'an oddly casual way' for Plato to introduce so important a feature of the state as the rigidity of all laws.[7] It should be noted, however, that the passage in question appears directly after the discussion of amending laws in general, and so the wider construal is possible.

In the continuation of the passage, the Athenian discusses procedures for change. If after the initial period changes are deemed necessary, proposals must be brought before all the people, all the officials and all the divine oracles. Unanimity is necessary; those objecting to changes must always prevail (772c–d). These all but insurmountable obstacles are a further indication of the degree to which all laws are resistant to change.

Thus, despite the probability that the language at 772c does not prove the immutability of all laws, there is abundant evidence that Plato has this in mind. Forever unchanging laws have desirable effects, while change is a blight. The ideal is Egyptian stability for thousands of years. Thus in the *Laws*, the ideal of rule by reason seen in the early dialogues and only partly repudiated in the *Republic* gives way to rule by faith. Government in Magnesia is according to a blueprint that is accepted whole and is beyond criticism (cf. above, pp. 177–8). This is rule by a detailed prescription the physician has left, rather than by the physician himself. Of course, institutions of this kind leave the *Laws* far removed from Socrates' ideal of the examined life. Everything possible is done to prevent the subjects from examining their moral standards. In this sense moral autonomy is eliminated from Magnesia. The ideal state is static, even in its system of education, which is to be entirely dictated by the laws, designed to instil the moral ideals they enshrine. In fact, the commissioner of education—the most important person in the state—is to do no more than carry out the legislation that has been codified (809a–b). His discretionary authority is minimal, which is as it should be. He is elevated to his position through election. Victory in an election does not guarantee wisdom, and Plato does well not to give an elected official the power to tamper with the system of education.

The unhappy implication, however, is that the moral status of the state and everyone in it appears to depend solely on the wisdom of the laws, while no one in the state is able to assess this. Plato undoubtedly wants the Magnesians to take it on faith that their laws meet the requisite standards, but this has to be accepted on faith, in the absence of any means to confirm it.

---

[6] See e.g. G. Morrow, *Plato's Cretan City* (Princeton, NJ, 1960), p. 571, n. 54; R. F. Stalley, *An Introduction to Plato's Laws* (Indianapolis, IN, 1983), p. 82; Barker, *Greek Political Theory*, p. 363, n. 1; K. Schöpsdau, ed. and trans., *Platon: Nomoi*, 2 vols. (Gottingen, Germany, 1994, 2003), ad loc.

[7] W. K. C. Guthrie, *A History of Greek Philosophy*, 6 vols. (Cambridge, 1962–81), V, 368.

13.4. THE NOCTURNAL COUNCIL

At some point in working on the *Laws* Plato became dissatisfied with the rigidity of the state and took measures to remedy it. In Book XII the nocturnal council is assigned a legislative function, though Plato's account of this is fragmentary, and one cannot be sure exactly what he had in mind or how well his presentation here fits in with the other eleven books. Because of conflicting strands in the evidence, our discussion must be somewhat tentative.

Plato first mentions the nocturnal council in connection with the treatment of heretics in Book X. In Book XII as well, it is introduced in passing, but Plato returns to the subject and treats it with the greatest seriousness. It is first discussed in Book XII in connection with foreign observers. Plato says that it is desirable that qualified individuals be sent abroad to observe the laws and institutions of other states. When they return from their travels, they are to report to the nocturnal council (951*d*). The reason for the observers' journeys is to learn from other states, and so to make it possible to improve the laws of Magnesia (951*c*). Upon their return, the observers are apparently made members of the council, though Plato's two accounts of the composition of the body conflict on this point (961*a*; but cf. 951*d–e*).

The function of the synod is indicated by the observers' commission. Plato says that the laws cannot be 'safeguarded' unless some members of the state grasp them intellectually (*gnômê*) as well as by habit (*ethesin*) (951*b*). To perform their tasks properly, the doctor, the pilot, and the general require a clear understanding of their goals. Thus, the state must provide some members who understand its aim and the best means of attaining it (963*a–b*, 962*b*). Plato places great store in this knowledge. He repeatedly says that it is necessary for the 'salvation' (*sôtêria*) of the laws and of the state (960*b–e*). The presence of this knowledge gives the laws an irreversible quality (960*e*).

Since the aim of the state is the inculcation of virtue, the council must inquire into the nature of virtue, and the relationships between its four components—wisdom, courage, temperance, and justice (963*a–c*). A programme of higher studies is required. The council members must study the relationship between the many and the one (965*b*). They must know of the gods and so grasp the theological arguments presented in Book X (966*c–d*). They also study the nature of soul, musical theory, and the movements of the heavens, which inspire religious faith (966*d–67a*). The study of astronomy probably receives greatest emphasis, but on the whole the curriculum is not described in detail. At one point Plato says that it cannot be spelled out in advance (968*e*).

In several respects the nocturnal council recalls the guardians of the *Republic*. Its members are repeatedly referred to as the 'guardians' of the state (964*d–e*), at one point as the 'real guardians of the laws' (*tous ontôs phulakas... tôn nomôn*) (966*b*). Clearly, the *nomophulakes* take a back seat to the council, though at one point Plato apparently mixes them up with it (964*b*). The council's programme of studies also recalls the *Republic*. There is clear overlap in regard to the study of astronomy and musical theory, and preliminary studies (967*d–e*)—which undoubtedly include mathematics (cf. 817*e*–18*a*). Accordingly, certain scholars argue that Plato does not bother to describe their curriculum in detail, because it is obviously meant to replicate that of the *Republic*.[8]

The nocturnal council recalls the guardians in its objects of investigation. One of its primary subjects is virtue, especially the relationship between the one substance of virtue and its diverse components. The problem of the one and the many is a central concern of the middle dialogues, closely linked with the theory of Forms. At one point in the *Laws* the subject matter to be studied is described as the Forms (*eidê*) of virtue (963*c*). Though this does not necessarily mean 'Forms' in the *Republic*'s sense—this is a question about which scholarly opinion is divided—the allusion to the theory of Forms is probable.[9] Other language associated with the Forms is used. The council will study the essence (*ti pot' estin*) of virtue (965*c–d*). The contrast between dream and reality is mentioned (969*b*). It is significant that in presenting the synod, Plato departs from the arid declamation of the preceding books. The discussion again becomes question and answer; unbroken exposition gives way to dialectic.

In the light of these similarities, it seems possible that the nocturnal council is meant to play a role in the state similar to that of the guardians in the *Republic*. Some of Plato's language suggests this. For instance, the council is called the 'anchor' for the whole state (961*c*); it supervises (*epopteuontôn*) the laws (951*d*). At the conclusion of his account of the body, Plato says that, if this 'divine council' should come into existence, 'then the state must be entrusted to it' (969*b*). Thus, it is not surprising that the council has been interpreted as revamped philosopher-kings.[10] This interpretation is supported by the testimony of Aristotle, who says that, though Plato wishes to make the state

---

[8] e.g. P. Shorey, *What Plato Said* (Chicago, IL, 1933), p. 405; Guthrie, *History*, V, 373–4; L. Taran, *Academica: Plato, Phillip of Opus, and the Pseudo Platonic Epinomis* (Philadelphia, PA, 1975), pp. 27–8.

[9] See esp. V. Brochard, *Etudes de philosophie ancienne et de philosophie moderne* (Paris, 1966), ch. 9; Guthrie follows Brochard (*History*, V, 378–81); cf. Stalley, *Introduction*, pp.135–6. I find the brief remarks of Cherniss convincing (review of G. Muller, *Studien zu den platonischen Nomoi* [Munich, 1951], *Gnomon*, 25 [1953], 377).

[10] Barker, *Greek Political Theory*, pp. 406–10; G. Sabine, *A History of Political Theory*, revised edn. (New York, 1950), p. 85; J. Luccioni, *La pensée politique de Platon* (Paris, 1958), pp. 288–9; G. Klosko, 'The Nocturnal Council in Plato's *Laws*', *Political Studies*, 36 (1988).

in the *Laws* 'more suitable for adoption by actual states, he brings it round by degrees back to the other form, that of the *Republic*' (*Pol.* 1265a3–4). Aristotle's remarks seem to be in reference to the nocturnal council's assuming philosophical control.

In spite of the evidence for this interpretation, it confronts an enormous problem. The introduction of philosopher-king-like figures in Book XII of the *Laws* conflicts with Plato's discussion throughout the earlier books. If Plato intends the council to take over the state, he is remarkably sketchy on how this will work. In a dialogue that goes into endless detail on minor matters, numerous significant concerns relevant to this hypothesis are unaddressed. Plato provides no explicit discussion of the council's constitutional position or the relationship it bears to other institutions. While selection procedures for relatively minor offices are described at length, he devotes only a couple of paragraphs to the composition of the council. This discussion is found in different contexts and is inconsistent. Assigning the nocturnal council legislative authority is badly out of keeping with the bulk of the *Laws*. We have seen in the *Republic* that if rulers can be provided with the same knowledge as the hypothetical founders of the state, the founders need not describe things in detail, as the rulers will be able to provide what is needed. Thus, the incredible detail that Plato goes into throughout the *Laws* sharply differentiates its rulers from those of the *Republic*, while the strong emphasis in the *Laws* on the need to avoid change suggests that little in the way of a legislative function is recognized. Moreover, it is doubtful if Plato believes that anyone has the ability to change the laws. We have seen that he repeatedly casts doubt on whether anyone possesses divine ability—the attributes of the *Republic*'s philosophers. In addition to possessing the highest natural aptitude, the philosopher-kings in the *Republic* are subjected to a rigorous process of education and selection. Their course of higher studies lasts fifteen years, not including further training in dialectic. Members of the nocturnal council do not receive this. They are elevated to this body by virtue of holding other offices in the state, to which they are generally elected. This problem is to some extent alleviated by the fact that the younger members of the council receive some philosophical training during their period of membership. Given their presumably superior attributes, which cause them to be picked for the council, it is not unlikely that they will later be elected to the high offices that staff it. But Plato does not devise means to guarantee this. Aside from this possibility, no means are provided to make sure that council members have philosophical ability. The rigorous programme of studies they undertake begins after they are on the council and is not a prerequisite for membership. In addition, one wonders how much intellectual progress can be made by aged officials, who also have a full slate of public duties to attend to.

Even granted all of these problems, it is not impossible that the nocturnal council is intended to exercise king-like powers. As we have seen, conflict between the unencumbered rule of philosophical intelligence and strict adherence to unchanging laws pervades the *Statesman*. It is possible that Plato wishes to leave a similar pattern in the *Laws*, the rule of philosophic wisdom alongside the rule of law, with these two ideas not reconciled. However, for obvious reasons, an interpretation of the nocturnal council that is able to make it consistent with the rest of the *Laws* is preferred by most scholars. Such an interpretation has been advanced by Morrow in *Plato's Cretan City* and is supported by most scholars.[11]

According to Morrow, the nocturnal council is intended to contribute to improving Magnesia's laws. His interpretation can be referred to as the 'informal view'. It consists of three main claims. First, Morrow argues that the nocturnal council is not suddenly introduced in Book XII. Looking back on the earlier Books of the *Laws* from Book XII, one can retrospectively detect a number of allusions to it.[12] Second and more significant, according to the informal view, although the nocturnal council has a legislative role, this is pursued informally. The council's only formal responsibilities are those noted above, examining imprisoned atheists (908*a*, 909*a*), and interrogating observers returned from abroad. Morrow contends that the council does not need formal responsibilities. Because of the importance of the officials it contains—the ten senior *nomophulakes*, the auditors and the present and past commissioners of education—it would be able to act behind the scenes to influence such matters as formal revision of laws and everyday administration and interpretation of laws.[13] The informal view's final claim is that this account of the nocturnal council is eminently reasonable. The knowledge attained by the council is necessary for the state. If the laws are not to be 'rigidly and unthinkingly adhered to',[14] there must be some body in the state capable of understanding the reasoning behind them. Such knowledge is necessary to preserve a measure of moral autonomy in the state and merits Plato's repeated description of the council as the 'saviour' of the state.

In addition, according to the informal view, the council fulfils another important function, by seeing that top offices in the state are staffed with worthy individuals. Its younger members are selected according to merit

---

[11] C. Kahn, Review of Morrow, *Plato's Cretan City, Journal of the History of Ideas*, 22 (1961), 421; Guthrie, *History*, V, 374; Bobonich, *Plato's Utopia Recast*, ch. 5; Stalley, *Introduction*, p. 112; T. Saunders, ed. and trans., *Plato: The Laws* (Harmondsworth, UK, 1970), p. 516; M. Piérart, *Platon et la cité grecque* (Brussels, 1973), p. 232; R. Hall, *Plato* (London, 1981), p. 134.

[12] Morrow, *Plato's Cretan City*, pp. 501–2.   [13] Ibid. 510–11.   [14] Ibid. 501.

(951*e*–52*a*, 961*a*–*b*), as opposed to the various combinations of election and the lot used to staff other offices. Service in the council publicly identifies certain young men as worthy candidates for future office, and as noted above, is a means through which such people receive philosophical training. Moreover, because of the relatively large number of Magnesians who serve on the nocturnal council during their thirties and then move back into the general population, their experience significantly raises the deliberative capacities of the citizenry.[15]

However, in spite of the persuasiveness of Morrow's analysis, there is strong textual evidence that Plato did not consistently view the nocturnal council in this light.[16] The main problem is that what Plato says about changing the laws in the text of the *Laws* is inconsistent with Morrow's claims. In a series of contexts, Plato explicitly says that laws are to remain unchanged (*akinêta*), and so he apparently rules out the task that Morrow assigns to the council. As noted above (pp. 225, 250), there is strong evidence that, throughout the *Laws*, Plato intends the laws in Magnesia to have the rigidity of theocracy. In only one context does he discuss procedures for changing the laws. As we have seen, the Athenian says that the original lawgiver cannot provide for all contingencies, and so the *nomophulakes* must be prepared to make needed changes (769*b*–71*a*). They are assigned the task of ascertaining what is to be done, but this will be only during a ten-year trial period, after which the laws will be declared to be fixed (*akinêta*) (772*c*4). After that, should it be necessary to change the laws, extremely demanding procedures will be required, rendering them all but impossible to change. Even if we accept the narrower interpretation of this passage as bearing only on religious festivals and the like rather than all laws (above, pp. 250–1), the evidence indicates that the rest of the laws are covered by similar injunctions.

The key consideration is that, although this is the most detailed discussion of procedures for changing the laws, similar procedures are invoked in regard to other areas of the law. Thus in Book VIII, discussing legal procedures for agricultural cases, the Athenian Stranger says that many details remain to be filled in. This task is assigned to the *nomophulakes*; after they finish their work, these laws too will be 'permanently fixed' (*akinêta*) (846*b*6–*c*8). Similarly, in Book XII, in regard to legal procedures more generally, the *nomophulakes* are assigned the task of filling in missing details, while their work in this area too is sealed as unchanging: the *nomophulakes* 'shall put them into practice all their life long' (957*a*1–*b*5).

---

[15] Bobonich, *Plato's Utopia Recast*, p. 408.

[16] For detailed discussion, see Klosko, 'Knowledge and Law in Plato's *Laws*', *Political Studies* (forthcoming).

In at least four other contexts, the Athenian provides for the *nomophulakes* to fill in the details of different aspects of the law, although in these passages, he does not say that, once drawn up, these laws are to remain unchanged. These are regulations concerning festivals (828*b*3–7), rhapsodes and choral competitions (835*a*2–*b*4), sexual matters (840*c*11–*e*7), and certain penalties (855*d*1–4).

If we combine the matters explicitly said to be unchanging in these passages and those discussed above, we have unchanging status of laws explicitly stated in five areas: musical education (656*c*–57*b*); sacrifices and dances (772*c*); children's games, dances, and music (798*a*–*b*); rules for dealing with agricultural cases (846*c*); and general legal procedures (957*a*–*b*). Although it is not mentioned in the text, it is likely that the same is true of the four additional areas just mentioned in which the *nomophulakes* are enjoined to legislate: festivals, rhapsodes and choral competitions, sexual relations, and certain penalties. Although it is not explicitly stated that laws in the last four areas are to be *akinêta*, the procedural similarities between these passages and the others in which the *nomophulakes* are to legislate makes it likely that Plato had this in mind. But, even on a more conservative interpretation in which the last four areas are not included, we have five areas in which it is explicitly said that laws are unchanging. To these considerations, we should add the fact that, with one exception, Plato nowhere describes procedures for changing laws. The exception is of course the 772 passage, and as we have seen, the procedures described make it almost impossible to change them. In all these contexts, Plato does not say that the laws are to be unchanging, subject to review by the nocturnal council. They are unchanging *simpliciter*.

A second consideration concerns the procedures for changing and revising laws that Plato discusses. The problem here is that, in all these discussions, no role is assigned to the nocturnal council. According to the informal view, the council is brought into existence to provide for just these eventualities, and so the fact that Plato leaves it out is difficult to explain. To make matters worse, Plato explicitly assigns these legislative tasks to the *nomophulakes*. In other words, he proposes an alternative procedure. He discusses the *nomophulakes'* role in detail at 769*a*–71*a*, at one point addressing them as 'saviours of the laws (*sôtêres nomôn*)' (770*b*). As we have seen, in many other passages, legislative tasks are explicitly assigned to them. So there can be little doubt that when Plato wrote these sections of the *Laws*, the job of amending and improving laws was intended for the *nomophulakes*. At one point the Athenian says that we must make 'the very same men lawgivers as well as guardians of the laws (*toutous autous nomothetas te kai nomophulakas*)' (770*a*). It should be emphasized that, as the example of revising laws concerning festivals shows, the *nomophulakes* are to make recommendations concerning changes, which must then be acted upon by the appropriate legal authorities. In other words, the role assigned to them here—and presumably in the other contexts where they are discussed—is precisely that which the informal view associates with the nocturnal council.

Morrow's response to this problem is that the nocturnal council is 'obviously' intended to play a role in these proceedings, which he later compares to that of a learned legislative commission in modern countries.[17] On the contrary, the fact that in at least six separate contexts, Plato describes procedures for revising laws, always assigning this responsibility to the *nomophulakes* and never mentioning the nocturnal council, is powerful evidence that, when Plato wrote these passages, he did not intend that the nocturnal council would play such a role. A reasonable assessment of the evidence is presented by Guthrie. He notes the problems in reconciling the informal view with the process for changing laws, and attributes the conflict to 'an organizational change' which Plato did not fully work out.[18] Guthrie appears to posit a break in the *Laws*—a minor one—the implications of which he does not explore.

Thus, Plato's treatment of the nocturnal council gives evidence of incompleteness. Alongside indications that the council is to play a role in the state analogous to that of the philosophers in the *Republic*, there are good reasons to believe it is to fulfil a more mundane—but still essential—function as a source of legal advice within the constitutional system. Given the state of the text, it is difficult to determine exactly how Plato would have reconciled these conflicting strands—as with other problem areas in the *Laws*— assuming that he wished to do so. Once again, it is possible that he preferred to leave apparently conflicting elements intact, as he appears to have done in the *Statesman*. Still, on any interpretation, the introduction of the nocturnal council indicates Plato's unwillingness completely to renounce Socratic moral autonomy. On any interpretation of the nocturnal council, whether as revamped philosopher-kings or as learned legal advisers, its members study the rational grounding of the laws. Accordingly, in spite of the dim view of human nature and capacities that shows through the *Laws*, in the final analysis Plato was unwilling to accept a state in which there was not at least a body of people capable of understanding and revising legislative enactments. To use Friedlander's words, at the end of the *Laws* 'the Socrates in Plato still wins out over the Solon in him'.[19]

---

[17] Morrow, *Plato's Cretan City*, pp. 200, 571.   [18] *History*, V, 369, n. 2.
[19] P. Friedlander, *Plato*, 3 vols., H. Meyerhoff, trans. (Princeton, NJ, 1958–69), III, 444.

13.5. IMPLEMENTING THE 'SECOND-BEST' STATE

In order to bring a state like Magnesia into existence, Plato still confronts the problem of uniting philosophical wisdom and political power. He addresses the question in Book IV of the *Laws*. Plato no longer bases his hopes on combining wisdom and power in a single person—the philosopher-king is no longer in the cards. Rather, it is necessary that a monarch, preferably young, but one with a temperate character and intellectual gifts, come into contact with a wise lawgiver, and the two join forces. This would be 'the quickest and easiest way' for the constitution to come into existence (709e–10d). It is also possible for the lawgiver to win over the ruling clique in an oligarchy or democracy, but the task is easier if power is concentrated in fewer hands (710c–11a). Plato does not describe in detail the means that the enlightened monarch must pursue. He says that the end requires a combination of persuasion and force, while the process will be helped along by the monarch's ability to influence public opinion through the force of example (711b–d).

The alliance between a young tyrant and a lawgiver mentioned here unavoidably calls to mind Plato's experiment with Dionysius in Sicily. This is surprising in the light of the turn that events in Sicily took. It is also surprising to see Plato address the question of how an existing state can be reformed, rather than, as one would expect, how a new state can be founded. Plato runs these two questions together inexplicably. The question of how to bring an ideal state into existence has been pre-empted by the Cnossians' intention of founding a colony and Cleinias' new status (on which, more below). But however we account for this, there is clearly a close relationship between Plato's plans for Syracuse and the political proposals presented in the *Laws*.

More than this, the detailed study of the laws and political systems of many Greek states that shows through the *Laws* is evidence of Plato's deep concern with political reality. Important scholars connect this with the political activity of the Academy. According to this view, the detailed prescriptions of the *Laws*, adapted to realistic conditions, were intended to serve as a practical model to be followed by members of the Academy in their legislation and other political activities throughout the Greek world.[20]

The close connections between the *Laws* and Plato's plans for Syracuse are apparent in the *Epistles*. As noted above (p. 198), Plato's overall hope

---

[20] Schöpsdau, *Nomoi*, I, 132–3; T. Saunders,'"The Rand Corporation of Antiquity": Plato's Academy and Greek Politics', in *Studies in Honour of T. B. L. Webster*, Vol. I, J. H. Betts, J. T. Hooker, and J. R. Green, eds. (Bristol, 1986); A. E. Taylor, *Plato: The Man and His Work*, 6th edn. (1952; rpt. Cleveland, 1956), p. 464; Guthrie, *History*, V, 323, 335; Stalley, *Introduction*, p. 96.

was to transform the Syracusan tyranny into a government under law, while according to Plato, Dion too had hoped to accomplish this (*Ep. 7* 336a). More concretely, Plato's suggestion in *Epistle 7* is for the friends and followers of Dion to invite in lawgivers to draw up a constitution and laws (337b–d). These should be eminent old men, of good families; Plato suggests inviting fifty. When the laws are drawn up, everything depends upon obedience to them, though of course this government of laws is only the 'second-best' form of polity (*Ep. 7* 337d).

Aside from this overall parallel, there is a close correspondence in specific details. In *Epistle 3*, which may or may not have been written by Plato, the author says that, on his second visit to Syracuse, Plato worked with Dionysius at writing preambles to laws (*Ep. 3* 316a). We will not enter into the controversy surrounding the attribution of this epistle. It is worth noting that in Book IV of the *Laws* the Athenian says that the entire discussion up to that point is really a preamble to the legal code he now draws up (722c–d). Scholars have noted that the discussion in Books I–III of the *Laws* is particularly well suited to conditions in Syracuse.[21] Several points discussed in these Books are also mentioned in the epistles. Thus, to impress upon his audience the fragility of absolute monarchy, Plato refers to the fact that of the three original Dorian monarchies only Sparta survived, because she moderated her institutions (*Ep. 8* 354a–b). This closely parallels a discussion in Book III of the *Laws* (esp. 691e; see above, p. 238). In *Epistle 7* Plato mentions the success of Darius, Great King of Persia, in establishing an empire that lasted (332a), while in *Epistle 8*, he briefly discusses the ruinous effects unbridled liberty can have upon democracies (354d). Similar points are made through similar examples in the *Laws* (695c ff., 698a ff.). The conclusion drawn in *Epistle 8* is the necessity of a moderate government, representing a mean between excessive servitude and excessive liberty (354e). This of course is one of the central teachings of the *Laws* (esp. 710e; see above, p. 239). In the epistles as in the *Laws*, Plato presents the idea that for governments to survive, laws must be the lords of men (*Ep. 8* 354c; *Laws* 715d), and that the ruler of the wise man is law, and of the foolish, pleasure (*Ep. 8* 354e; cf. *Laws* 636d–e, 644d–45b).

Plato's specific proposals for the government of Syracuse are strikingly similar to what is presented in the *Laws*. We have already mentioned that Plato and Dionysius may well have drawn up preambles to the laws of Syracuse. In his advice to the friends and followers of Dion, Plato proposes a triple monarchy, unmistakably modelled on the Spartan dual monarchy (*Ep. 8* 355e–56b). This apparently is to have authority in religious matters but is otherwise

---

[21] L. A. Post, 'The Preludes to Plato's *Laws*', *Transactions of the American Philological Association*, 60 (1929), 5–24; Morrow, *Plato's Epistles*, revised edn. (Indianapolis, IN, 1962), p. 92, n. 4.

largely ceremonial (356*d*). Actual political power is to be in the hands of thirty-five guardians of the laws or *nomophulakes*, an assembly and council, and a series of courts. One of these courts, empowered to try capital cases, is to be composed of the thirty-five *nomophulakes* and selected office-holders of the previous year, one from each office (356*d–e*). The parallels with Magnesia are unmistakable.

The reason for the close relationship between Plato's proposals for Syracuse and his second-best state are not clear, aside from the fact that Plato was probably working on the *Laws* during the period in which he composed the two epistles. However, this offers further evidence that Plato's turn away from the ideal state of the *Republic* to the second-best state of the *Laws* went hand in hand with his involvement and interest in political reform in Syracuse. As we have said, the *Laws* shows the fruit of years of intensive research. Plato probably undertook these studies in conjunction with his interest in Syracuse, and his concerns along these lines dominate the political writings—both dialogues and epistles—of his last years.

Plato's greater interest in practical reform is also seen in his ideas concerning bringing his second-best state to life. We have seen that this depends upon an alliance between a willing ruler and a wise lawgiver. No longer must kings be philosophers: they must only listen to philosophers. This too parallels Plato's political activity during his later years. We have noted above that the Academy was a training ground for would-be advisers of rulers and that its members travelled to the corners of the Greek world in pursuit of this task (above, pp. 199–200). Here too we have a parallel between Plato's proposals in the *Laws* and his political activity in Syracuse—and in this case with one major function of the philosophical school he established as well.

Although the political activity of the Academy was extensive, it is difficult to estimate its effectiveness. But Plato has written a success of sorts into the dramatic action of the *Laws*. At the end of Book III, Cleinias springs a surprise on his two companions. He says that it is fortunate that they have been discussing the subject of laws, for he has been named one of ten lawgivers for the city of Cnossos that is about to be founded by Crete (702*b–d*). The coincidence is of course incredible, and through it, the three characters in the dialogue are miraculously transformed from mere old men talking about laws into the founders of a state. Cleinias has the power to put their suggestions into effect.

This power finds its way into the hands of the Athenian as well. At the end of the work, after the Athenian has expounded at length upon the legislation needed to erect a state, Plato has the Athenian's arguments conquer Cleinias. Cleinias requests the Athenian's help in setting up the state and will use every possible means to secure his cooperation (969*c–d*).

And so the long-sought union of political power and philosophical wisdom is achieved, if only in the world of the dialogue. Plato knows, however, that this is a mere dream of his old age. This awareness spills over into the mind of the Athenian too. As he prepares to draw up laws for the new state, he asks his two companions—one of whom is empowered—to pretend along with him that the possibility of its founding is real (712*b*–*c*): 'Like children, we old men love a bit of make-believe'.

Afterword

At the beginning of this study, I mentioned two main themes indicated in the *Seventh Epistle* that can be traced throughout Plato's works. In closing, I return to these. First, Plato was interested in political reform and, second, because of his assessment of surrounding conditions, he believed it could not be accomplished within existing political systems. Plato's lifelong orientation was no doubt influenced by his early experience in Athens, where successive democratic and oligarchic regimes were failures in his eyes, while the disastrous experience of the Thirty Tyrants taught bitter lessons about rule by force. Thus, as Plato says in the epistle, he was led to place his hopes for political improvement in philosophy.

The relationship Plato posited between philosophy and political power changed from early to middle and middle to late dialogues. The Socratic philosopher, removed from the political world, gives way to the philosopher-king, firmly rooted in both worlds. In the *Laws* the king must only listen to philosophers. The changes here reflect the unmistakable movement from the politics of philosophy towards increasing emphasis on political institutions evident in Plato's political thought as a whole.

The reasons Plato's political thought developed in this direction cannot be identified with assurance. Questions of intellectual influence and causation are notoriously difficult, especially in the case of an author so far removed in time. And so I have not insisted on specific reasons why Plato's thought evolved. But connections between changes in his political views and other aspects of his philosophy are obviously important.

In the development of Plato's political thought, metaphysics, epistemology, and moral psychology played the role of base to political theory's superstructure. Psychological views impinged most directly. For a political thinker like Plato, whose primary concern was the inculcation of virtue, moral psychology, which determines the nature of virtue, was obviously crucial. Plato's moral psychology moved in the direction of increasing pessimism. He attributed an ever-increasing role to appetitive and irrational forces, and came to rely on rigorous psychological conditioning to counter them. By the end of his life, in the *Laws*, his disillusionment was all but complete. Human beings are yanked about like puppets on strings, and all of their lives, beginning before birth, must be dedicated to training them to resist.

It has been seen throughout this study that questions of political reform were ever at the forefront of Plato's political thought. This concern was central to his life—from his early temptation to join the Thirty, to his voyages to Sicily, to the foundation of the Academy, which was a school for statesmen—and is reflected in his dialogues. Though as a political reformer Plato is often dismissed as utopian, with the establishment of the ideal state in the *Republic* relegated to the heavens, for much of his life he was interested in realizing it. He wrestled with the problem of unifying theory and practice, but coming up against the political obstacles all reformers face, he bided his time. He did not withdraw from politics out of lack of interest, but out of lack of hope. As we saw in Chapter 10, the founding of the ideal state rests on the unity of philosophic wisdom and political power, although Plato could never say how this unity was to be achieved. In his later years he moved in the direction of more modest reform and compromise states. The rule of philosophy gave way to the rule of law—though always grudgingly, as is seen in the ambiguities of the *Statesman* and the role of the nocturnal council in the Laws. But in the final analysis government by perfect laws must also wait upon the intervention of more-than-human forces. Though the Academy attained political influence, it was not able to realize the ideal—or even the 'second-best' state. No doubt Plato never gave up hoping for the miraculous turn of events that would make the ideal real. The ideal remains 'difficult but somehow possible' (*Rep.* 540*d*). It is impossible 'humanly speaking', but as Plato writes in a related context (*Rep.* 492*e*) 'for the divine, as the proverb says, all rules fail'.

Bibliography

Included are works cited in the text and under Further Reading. Articles under Further Reading that appear in anthologies are not listed separately.

Ackrill, J. L., ed. *Aristotle's Ethics* (London, 1973).

Adam, J., ed. *Platonis Crito*, 2nd edn. (Cambridge, 1891).

—— ed. *Platonis Apologia Socratis* (Cambridge, 1886; rpt. 1916).

—— ed. *The Republic of Plato*, 2 vols. (Cambridge, 1902).

Adam, J. and A. M. Adam, eds. *Platonis Protagoras* (Cambridge, 1893; rpt. 1971).

Adkins, A. W. H. *Merit and Responsibility* (Oxford, 1960).

Allan, D. J., ed. *Plato, The Republic Book 1* (1940; rpt. London, 1953).

Allen, R. E., ed. *Studies in Plato's Metaphysics* (London, 1965).

—— 'Participation and Predication in Plato's Middle Dialogues', in *Plato I*, G. Vlastos, ed. (Garden City, NY, 1971; also rpt. in *Studies in Plato's Metaphysics*, Allen, ed.).

—— *Socrates and Legal Obligation* (Minneapolis, MN, 1980).

Annas, J., *An Introduction to Plato's Republic* (Oxford, 1981).

—— *Platonic Ethics, Old and New* (Ithaca, NY, 1999).

Annas, J. and C. Rowe, eds. *New Perspectives on Plato, Modern and Ancient* (Washington, DC, 2002).

Annas, J. and R. Waterfield, eds. and trans. *Plato: Statesman* (Cambridge, 1995).

Aristoxenus. *The Harmonics*, H. Macran, ed. and trans. (Oxford, 1902).

Armstrong, A. H. *An Introduction to Ancient Philosophy* (London, 1947).

Arnim, H. von. *Platos Jugenddialoge and die Entstehungszeit des Phaidros* (Leipzig, Germany, 1914).

Bambrough, R. E., ed. *Plato, Popper and Politics* (Cambridge, 1967).

Barker, E. 'Greek Political Thought and Theory in the Fourth Century', in *Cambridge Ancient History*, Vol. VI, J. B. Bury, S. A. Cook, and F. E. Adcock, eds. (Cambridge, 1927).

—— *Greek Political Theory: Plato and His Predecessors* (London, 1918; rpt. 1947).

—— ed. and trans. *The Politics of Aristotle* (Oxford, 1946).

Benjamin, A., trans. *Recollections of Socrates and Socrates' Defense Before the Jury of Xenophon* (Indianapolis, IN, 1965).

Berlin, I. *Four Essays on Liberty* (Oxford, 1969).

Bernstein, E. *The Preconditions of Socialism*, H. Tudor, ed. and trans. (Cambridge, 1993).

Bloom, A., ed. and trans. *The Republic of Plato* (New York, 1968).

—— Response to D. Hall, 'The *Republic* and the "Limits of Politics"', *Political Theory*, 5 (1977).

Bluck, R. S. 'Is Plato's *Republic* a Theocracy?', *Philosophical Quarterly*, 5 (1955) [1955a].

—— ed. and trans. *Plato's Phaedo* (London, 1955 [1955b]).

Bobonich, C. 'Reading the *Laws*', in *Form and Argument in Late Plato*, C. Gill and M. McCabe, eds. (Oxford, 1996).

—— 'Plato and the Birth of Classical Political Philosophy', in *Plato's Laws and Its Historical Significance*, F. Lisi, ed. (Salamanca, 1998).

—— *Plato's Utopia Recast* (Oxford, 2002).

Brandwood, L. *The Chronology of Plato's Dialogues* (Cambridge, 1990).

—— 'Stylometry and Chronology', in *The Cambridge Companion to Plato*, R. Kraut, ed. (Cambridge, 1992).

Brickhouse, T. and N. Smith. *Socrates on Trial* (Princeton, NJ, 1989).

—— *Plato's Socrates* (Oxford, 1994).

Brochard, V. *Etudes de philosophie ancienne et de philosophie moderne* (Paris, 1966).

Brunt, P. A. *Studies in Greek History and Culture* (Oxford, 1993).

Burnet, J., ed. *Platonis Opera*, 5 vols. (Oxford, 1900–7).

—— ed. *Plato's Phaedo* (Oxford, 1911).

—— *Greek Philosophy: Part I, Thales to Plato* (London, 1914).

—— 'The Socratic Doctrine of the Soul', *Proceedings of the British Academy*, 7 (1915–16).

—— ed. *Plato's Euthyphro, Apology of Socrates, and Crito* (Oxford, 1924).

Burnyeat, M., ed. *The Theaetetus of Plato* (Indianapolis, IN, 1990).

—— 'Utopia and Fantasy: The Practicability of Plato's Ideally Just City', in *Psychoanalysis, Mind, and Art*, J. Hopkins and A. Savile, eds. (Oxford, 1992; also rpt. in *Plato 2*, G. Fine, ed.).

Bury, J. B. and R. Meiggs. *A History of Greece* (London, 1979).

Bury, R. G., ed. *The Symposium of Plato*, 2nd edn. (Cambridge, 1932).

—— 'The Theory of Education in Plato's *Laws*', *Revue des Etudes Grecques*, 50 (1937).

Campbell, L., ed. *Sophistes and Politicus of Plato* (Oxford, 1867).

Cherniss, H., 'Review of G. Muller', *Studien zu den platonischen Nomoi*, *Gnomon*, 25 (1953).

—— 'The Relation of the *Timaeus* to Plato's Later Dialogues', in *Studies in Plato's Metaphysics*, R. E. Allen, ed. (London, 1965).

—— 'The Philosophical Economy of the Theory of Ideas', in *Plato I*, G. Vlastos, ed. (Garden City, NY, 1971; also rpt. in *Studies in Plato's Metaphysics*, R. E. Allen, ed.).

Constant, B. 'The Liberty of the Ancients and the Liberty of the Moderns', in *Constant: Political Writings*, B. Fontana, ed. (Cambridge, 1988).

Cooper, J. M. 'The Psychology of Justice in Plato', *American Philosophical Quarterly*, 14 (1977).

—— 'Plato's Theory of Human Motivation', *History of Philosophy Quarterly*, 1 (1984).

—— ed. *Plato: Complete Works* (Indianapolis, IN, 1997).

Cornford, F. M. 'The Athenian Philosophical Schools', in *Cambridge Ancient History*, Vol. VI, J. B. Bury, S. A. Cook, and F. E. Adcock, eds. (Cambridge, 1927).

—— *Before and After Socrates* (Cambridge, 1932).

—— ed. and trans. *The Republic of Plato* (Oxford, 1941).

—— *The Unwritten Philosophy and Other Essays* (Cambridge, 1950).

—— ed. and trans. *Plato and Parmenides* (1939; rpt. Indianapolis, IN, 1957 [1957*a*]).

——ed. and trans. *Plato's Cosmology* (1937; rpt. Indianapolis, IN, 1957 [1957*b*]).

——ed. and trans. *Plato's Theory of Knowledge* (1934; rpt. Indianapolis, IN, 1957 [1957*c*]).

Crombie, I. M. *An Examination of Plato's Doctrines*, 2 vols. (London, 1962–3).

Cross, R. C. and A. D. Woozley *Plato's Republic: A Philosophical Commentary* (London, 1964).

Crossman, R. S. *Plato Today* (Oxford, 1939).

Davis, M. 'On the Imputed Possibilities of Callipolis and Magnesia', *American Journal of Philology*, 85 (1964).

Dawidowicz, L. *The War Against the Jews* (New York, 1975).

Deman, T. *Le témoignage d'Aristote sur Socrate* (Paris, 1942).

Denyer, N., ed. *Plato: Alcibiades* (Cambridge, 2001).

Des Places, E. and A. Diès, eds. and trans. *Les Lois*. Budé Series, Vols. XI–XII (Paris, 1951–6).

Devereux, D. 'The Unity of the Virtues in Plato's *Protagoras* and *Laches*', *Philosophical Review*, 101 (1992).

——'Socrates' Kantian Conception of Virtue', *Journal of the History of Philosophy*, 33 (1995).

——'The Relationship Between Justice and Happiness in Plato's *Republic*', *Proceedings of the Boston Area Colloquium in Ancient Philosophy*, 20 (2004).

Diels, H. and W. Kranz, eds. *Die Fragmente der Vorsokratiker*, 6th edn., 3 vols. (Berlin, 1951–2).

Diès, A., ed. and trans. *Le Politique*, Budé Series, Vol. IX, Pt. 1 (Paris, 1935).

Dodds, E. R. *The Greeks and the Irrational* (Berkeley, CA, 1951).

——ed. *Plato: Gorgias* (Oxford, 1959).

Duke, E. A., W. F. Hicken, W. S. M. Nicoll, D. B. Robinson, and J. C. G. Strachan, eds. *Platonis Opera*, Vol. I (Oxford, 1995).

Edelstein, L. *Plato's Seventh Letter* (Leiden, Germany, 1966).

Dover, K. J. *Greek Popular Morality in the Time of Plato and Aristotle* (Oxford, 1974).

Ehrenberg, V. *The Greek State* (Oxford, 1960).

——*From Solon to Socrates*, 2nd edn. (London, 1973).

England, E. B., ed. *The Laws of Plato*, 2 vols. (Manchester, 1921).

Euben, P. *The Tragedy of Political Theory* (Princeton, NJ, 1990).

Field, G. C. *Plato and His Contemporaries*, 3rd edn. (London, 1967).

——*The Philosophy of Plato*, 2nd edn. (Oxford, 1969).

Fine, G., ed. *Plato 1: Metaphysics and Epistemology* (Oxford, 2000 [2000*a*]).

——ed. *Plato 2: Ethics, Politics, Religion and the Soul* (Oxford, 2000 [2000*b*]).

Finley, J. *Thucydides* (Cambridge, MA, 1942).

Finley, M. I. *Aspects of Antiquity* (Harmondsworth, UK, 1968).

——*The Ancient Economy* (Berkeley, CA, 1973 [1973*a*]).

——*Democracy Ancient and Modern* (New Brunswick, 1973 [1973*b*]).

——*Politics in the Ancient World* (Cambridge, 1983).

Fite, W. *The Platonic Legend* (New York, 1934).

Forrest, W. G. *A History of Sparta, 950–192 B.C.* (New York, 1969).

Foster, M. B. *The Political Philosophies of Plato and Hegel* (Oxford, 1935).

Frede, M. 'Plato's Arguments and the Dialogue Form', *Oxford Studies in Ancient Philosophy*, Supp. Volume (1992).

Freeman, K., trans. *Ancilla to the Pre-Socratic Philosophers* (Oxford, 1956).

Friedlander, P. *Plato*, 3 vols., H. Meyerhoff, trans. (Princeton, NJ, 1958–69).

Friedrich, C. 'The Unique Character of Totalitarian Society', in *Totalitarianism*, Friedrich, ed. (New York, 1954).

Friedrich, C. and Z. Brzezinski. *Totalitarian Dictatorship and Autocracy*, 2nd edn. (New York, 1966).

Fritz, K. von and E. Kapp, eds. and trans. *Aristotle's Constitution of Athens and Related Texts* (New York, 1950).

Furley, D. J. 'The Early History of the Concept of Soul', *Bulletin of the Institute of Classical Studies*, 3 (1956).

Gallop, D., ed. and trans. *Plato: Phaedo* (Oxford, 1975).

Gauthier, R. A. and J. Y. Jolif, eds. *Aristote: L'Ethique à Nicomaque*, 2nd edn. 3 vols. (Louvain, Belgium, 1970).

Gernet, L. 'Introduction, Deuxième Partie: *Les Lois* et le droit positif', in *Les Lois*, E. Des Places and A. Diès, eds., Budé Series, Vols. XI–XII (Paris, 1951–6).

Gilbert, M. *The Holocaust* (New York, 1985).

Gill, C. 'The Death of Socrates', *Classical Quarterly*, 23 (1973).

——— 'Plato and Politics: The *Critias* and the *Politicus*', *Phronesis*, 24 (1979).

Gill, C. and M. McCabe, eds. *Form and Argument in Late Plato* (Oxford, 1996).

Gomme, A. W., A. Andrewes, and K. J. Dover. *A Historical Commentary on Thucydides*, 5 vols. (Oxford, 1945–81).

Gomperz, T. *The Greek Thinkers*, 4 vols., L. Magnus and C. G. Berry, trans. (London, 1901–12).

Gosling, J. C. *Plato* (London, 1973).

——— ed. and trans. *Plato: Philebus* (Oxford, 1975).

Gould, J. *The Development of Plato's Ethics* (1955; rpt. New York, 1972).

Griswold, C., ed. *Platonic Writings, Platonic Readings* (New York, 1988).

Grote, G. *Plato and the Other Companions of Sokrates*, 3 vols. (London, 1865).

Grube, G. M. A. *Plato's Thought* (1935; rpt. Boston, MA, 1958).

Grube, G. M. A., ed. and trans. *Plato: Republic*, 2nd. edn., rev. C. D. C. Reeve (Indianapolis, IN, 1992).

Gulley, N. *The Philosophy of Socrates* (London, 1968).

Guthrie, W. K. C. *A History of Greek Philosophy*, 6 vols. (Cambridge, 1962–81).

——— 'Plato's Views on the Nature of the Soul', in *Plato II*, G. Vlastos, ed. (Garden City, NY, 1971).

Hackforth, R., ed. and trans. *Plato's Phaedo* (Cambridge, 1955; rpt. 1972 [1972*a*]).

——— ed. and trans. *Plato's Phaedrus* (Cambridge, 1952; rpt. 1972 [1972*b*]).

——— ed. and trans. *Plato's Examination of Pleasure* (1945; rpt. Indianapolis, IN, n.d.).

Hall, R. W. *Plato* (London, 1981).

Hamilton, E. and H. Cairns, eds. *The Collected Dialogues of Plato, Including the Letters* (Princeton, NJ, 1961).

Hammond, N. G. L. *A History of Greece*, 2nd edn. (Oxford, 1967).

Hansen, M. *Athenian Democracy in the Age of Demosthenes*, J. A. Crook, trans. (1991; rpt. Norman, OK, 1999).

Howland, J. 'Re-Reading Plato: The Problem of Platonic Chronology', *Phoenix*, 45 (1991).

Hume, D. *A Treatise of Human Nature* (Harmondsworth, UK, 1969).

Irwin, T. *Plato's Moral Theory* (Oxford, 1977).

—— ed. and trans. *Plato: Gorgias* (Oxford, 1979).

—— *Plato's Ethics* (Oxford, 1995).

Jaeger, W. *Paideia*, G. Highet, trans., 3 vols. (Oxford, 1939–45).

Jones, A. H. M. *Athenian Democracy* (Oxford, 1957).

Joseph, H. W. B. *Essays in Ancient and Modern Philosophy* (Oxford, 1935).

Jowett, B., trans. *The Dialogues of Plato*, 4 vols. (New York, 1895).

Kahn, C. 'Review of G. Morrow's *Plato's Cretan City*', *Journal of the History of Ideas*, 22 (1961).

—— 'Drama and Dialectic in Plato's *Gorgias*', *Oxford Studies in Ancient Philosophy*, 1 (1983).

—— 'Proleptic Composition in the *Republic*', *Classical Quarterly*, 43 (1993).

—— 'The Place of the *Statesman* in Plato's Later Work', in *Reading the Statesman*, C. Rowe, ed. (Sankt Augustin, Germany, 1995).

—— *Plato and the Socratic Dialogue* (Cambridge, 1996).

—— 'On Platonic Chronology', in *New Perspectives on Plato, Modern and Ancient*, J. Annas and C. Rowe, eds. (Washington, DC, 2002).

Kant, I. *Groundwork of the Metaphysic of Morals*, H. Paton, ed. and trans. (New York, 1965).

Kapp, E. *The Greek Foundations of Traditional Logic* (New York, 1942).

Kateb, G. 'Utopias and Utopianism', *Encyclopedia of Philosophy*, P. Edwards, ed., 8 vols. (New York, 1967).

Kerferd, G. B. *The Sophistic Movement* (Cambridge, 1981).

Keyt, D. *Aristotle: Politics, Books V and VI* (Oxford, 1999).

Klosko, G. *The Politics of Philosophy: The Origin and Development of Plato's Political Theory*, unpublished Ph.D. dissertation (Columbia University, 1977).

—— 'Toward a Consistent Interpretation of the *Protagoras*', *Archiv für Geschichte der Philosophie*, 61 (1979).

—— 'On the Analysis of Protagoras 351B–360E', *Phoenix*, 34 (1980).

—— 'Implementing the Ideal State', *Journal of Politics*, 43 (1981) [1981*a*].

—— 'The Technical Conception of Virtue', *Journal of the History of Philosophy*, 19 (1981) [1981*b*].

—— '*Dêmotikê Aretê* in the *Republic*', *History of Political Thought*, 3 (1982).

—— 'The Insufficiency of Reason in Plato's *Gorgias*', *Western Political Quarterly*, 36 (1983) [1983*a*].

Klosko, G. 'Plato's Utopianism: The Political Content of the Early Dialogues', *Review of Politics*, 45 (1983) [1983*b*].

—— 'Criteria of Fallacy and Sophistry for Use in the Analysis of Platonic Dialogues', *Classical Quarterly*, NS 33 (1983) [1983*c*].

—— 'Provisionality in Plato's Ideal State', *History of Political Thought*, 5 (1984).

—— 'Rational Persuasion in Plato's Political Theory', *History of Political Thought*, 7 (1986) [1986*a*].

—— 'The "Straussian" Interpretation of Plato's *Republic*', *History of Political Thought*, 7 (1986) [1986*b*].

—— 'Plato and the Morality of Fallacy', *American Journal of Philology*, 108 (1987).

—— 'The Nocturnal Council in Plato's *Laws*', *Political Studies*, 36 (1988) [1988*a*].

—— 'The "Rule" of Reason in Plato's Psychology', *History of Philosophy Quarterly*, 9 (1988) [1988*b*].

—— ' "Racism" in Plato's *Republic*', *History of Political Thought*, 12 (1991).

—— *History of Political Theory: An Introduction*, 2 vols. (Fort Worth, TX, 1993, 1995).

—— 'Popper's Plato: An Assessment', *Philosophy of Social Science*, 26 (1996).

—— *Jacobins and Utopians: The Political Theory of Fundamental Moral Reform* (Notre Dame, IN, 2003).

—— 'Politics and Method in Plato's Political Theory', *Polis*, 23 (2006).

—— 'Knowledge and Law in Plato's *Laws*', *Political Studies* (forthcoming).

Kosman, L. 'Platonic Love', in *Facets of Plato's Philosophy*, W. H. Werkemister, ed. (Assen, The Netherlands, 1976).

Kraut, R. 'Egoism, Love and Political Office in Plato', *Philosophical Review*, 82 (1973) [1973*a*].

—— 'Reason and Justice in Plato's Republic', in *Exegesis and Argument*, E. N. Lee et al., eds. (Assen, The Netherlands, 1973 [1973*b*]).

—— 'Comments on Gregory Vlastos, "The Socratic Elenchus"', *Oxford Studies in Ancient Philosophy*, 1 (1983).

—— *Socrates and the State* (Princeton, NJ, 1984).

—— ed. *The Cambridge Companion to Plato* (Cambridge, 1992).

—— ed. *Aristotle: Politics, Books VII and VIII* (Oxford, 1997 [1997*a*]).

—— ed. *Plato's Republic: Critical Essays* (Lanham, MD, 1997 [1997*b*]).

Laks, A. 'Legislation and Demiurgy: On the Relationship Between Plato's *Republic* and *Laws*', *Classical Antiquity*, 9 (1990).

—— 'Prodige et méditation: esquisse d'une lecture des *Lois*', *Le temps philosophiques*, 1 (1995).

—— 'In What Sense is the City of the *Laws* a Second Best One?', in *Plato's Laws and Its Historical Significance*, F. Lisi, ed. (Salamanaca, Spain, 1998).

—— 'The *Laws*', in *The Cambridge History of Greek and Roman Political Thought*, C. Rowe and M. Schofield, eds. (Cambridge, 2000).

Lane, M. *Method and Politics in Plato's Statesman* (Cambridge, 1998).

Ledger, G. R. *Re-counting Plato* (Oxford, 1989).

Levinson, R. B. *In Defense of Plato* (Cambridge, MA, 1953).

Lisi, F., ed. *Plato's Laws and Its Historical Significance* (Salamanaca, Spain, 1998).

Locke, J. *Two Treatises of Government*, P. Laslett, ed., student edn. (Cambridge: Cambridge University Press, 1988).

Luccioni, J. *La pensée politique de Platon* (Paris, 1958).

MacCallum, G. 'Negative and Positive Freedom', *Philosophical Review*, 76 (1967).

Machiavelli, N. *The Prince and The Discourses*, L. Ricci and E. R. P. Vincent, trans. (New York, 1950).

Maguire, J. 'Thrasymachus... or Plato', *Phronesis*, 16 (1971).

Michell, H. *Sparta* (Cambridge, 1952).

Mill, J. S. *On Liberty*, E. Rapaport, ed. (Indianapolis, IN, 1978).

Moline, J. 'Plato on the Complexity of the Psyche', *Archiv für Geschichte der philosophie*, 60 (1978).

Moore, J. M., ed. and trans. *Aristotle and Xenophon on Democracy and Oligarchy* (Berkeley, CA, 1975).

Morrison, J. 'The Origins of Plato's Philosopher-Statesman', *Classical Quarterly*, 8 (1958).

Morrow, G. *Plato's Law of Slavery in Relation to Greek Law* (Urbana, IL, 1939).

—— 'Plato's Concept of Persuasion', *Philosophical Review*, 62 (1953).

—— *Plato's Cretan City* (Princeton, NJ, 1960).

—— ed. and trans. *Plato's Epistles*, revised edn. (Indianapolis, IN, 1962).

Mossé, C. *Athens in Decline, 404–86 B.C.*, J. Stewart, trans. (London, 1973).

Murphy, N. R. *The Interpretation of Plato's Republic* (Oxford, 1951).

Nagel, E. *The Structure of Science* (New York, 1961).

Nails, D. *The People of Plato* (Indianapolis, IN, 2002).

Nettleship, R. L. *Lectures on the Republic of Plato*, 2nd edn. (London, 1901).

—— *The Theory of Education in Plato's Republic* (1880; rpt. Oxford, 1935).

Neu, J. 'Plato's Analogy of the State and Individual: The *Republic* and the Organic Theory of the State', *Philosophy*, 46 (1971).

Newman, W. L., ed. *The Politics of Aristotle*, 4 vols. (Oxford, 1887–1902).

Nightingale, A. 'Writing/Reading a Sacred Text: A Literary Interpretation of Plato's *Laws*', *Classical Philology*, 88 (1993).

Nussbaum, M. *The Fragility of Goodness* (Cambridge, 1986).

Ober, J. *Mass and Elite in Democratic Athens* (Princeton, NJ, 1989).

—— *Political Dissent in Democratic Athens* (Princeton, NJ, 1998).

Okin, S. M. *Women in Western Political Thought* (Princeton, NJ, 1979).

Owen, G. E. L. 'The Place of the *Timaeus* in Plato's Dialogues', in *Studies in Plato's Metaphysics*, R. E. Allen, ed. (London, 1965).

Pangle, T., trans. *The Laws of Plato* (New York, 1980).

Penner, T. 'The Unity of Virtue', *Philosophical Review*, 82 (1973).

Pohlenz, M. *Aus Platos Werdezeit* (Berlin, 1913).

Popper, K. *'The Open Society and Its Enemies', Vol. I: The Spell of Plato*, 5th edn. (Princeton, NJ, 1966).

Post, L. A. 'The Preludes to Plato's *Laws*', *Transactions of the American Philological Association*, 60 (1929).

Pradeau, J.-F. *Plato and the City*, J. Lloyd, trans. (Exeter, UK, 2002).

Press, G., ed. *Who Speaks for Plato?* (Lanham, MD, 2000).

Raeder, H. *Platons philosophische Entwickelung* (Leipzig, Germany, 1905).

Raven, J. E. *Plato's Thought in the Making* (Cambridge, 1965).

Rawls, J. *A Theory of Justice* (Cambridge, MA, 1971).

Reeve, C. D. C. *Philosopher-Kings: The Argument of Plato's Republic* (Princeton, NJ, 1988).

—— *Socrates in the Apology* (Indianapolis, IN, 1989).

—— ed. and trans. *Plato: Republic* (Indianapolis, IN, 2004).

Rhodes, P. J. *A Commentary on the Aristotelian Athenaion Politeia* (Oxford, 1993).

Robinson, R. 'Plato's Consciousness of Fallacy', *Mind*, 51 (1942).

—— *Plato's Earlier Dialectic*, 2nd edn. (Oxford, 1953).

—— ed. *Aristotle: Politics, Books III and IV* (Oxford, 1996).

Ross, W. D., ed. *Aristotle's Metaphysics*, 2 vols. (Oxford, 1924).

—— 'The Problem of Socrates', *Proceedings of the Classical Association*, 30 (1933).

—— *Plato's Theory of Ideas* (Oxford, 1951).

Rousseau, J. J. *The Social Contract and Discourses*, G. D. H. Cole, trans., rev. J. H. Brumfitt and J. Hall, Everyman edn. (London, 1973).

—— *The Political Writings of Jean Jacques Rousseau*, 2 vols., C. E. Vaughan, ed. (1915; rpt. New York, 1962).

Rowe, C., ed. and trans. *Plato: Statesman* (Warminster, 1995 [1995a]).

—— ed. *Reading the Statesman* (Sankt Augustin, Germany, 1995 [1995b]).

—— ed. and trans. *Plato: Symposium* (Warminster, 1998).

Rowe, C. and M. Schofield, eds. *The Cambridge History of Greek and Roman Political Thought* (Cambridge, 2000).

Rutherford, R. B. *The Art of Plato* (London, 1995).

Sabine, G. *A History of Political Theory*, revised edn. (New York, 1950).

Sachs, D. 'A Fallacy in Plato's *Republic*', in *Plato II*, G. Vlastos, ed. (Garden City, NY, 1971).

Samaras, T. *Plato on Democracy* (New York, 2002).

Santas, G. *Socrates: Philosophy in Plato's Early Dialogues* (London, 1979).

Saunders, T. 'The Socratic Paradoxes in Plato's *Laws*', *Hermes*, 96 (1968).

—— 'The Alleged Double Version in the Sixth Book of Plato's *Laws*', *Classical Quarterly* (20), 1970 [1970a].

—— ed. and trans. *Plato: The Laws* (Harmondsworth, UK, 1970 [1970b]).

—— *Bibliography on Plato's Laws* (New York, 1976).

—— ed. *Aristotle: The Politics*, T. A. Sinclair, trans., revised edn. (Harmondsworth, UK, 1981).

—— ' "The Rand Corporation of Antiquity": Plato's Academy and Greek Politics', in *Studies in Honour of T. B. L. Webster*, Vol. I, J. H. Betts, J. T. Hooker, and J. R. Green, eds. (Bristol, 1986).

—— ed. *Aristotle: Politics, Books I and II* (Oxford, 1995).

Schofield, M. 'Plato and Practical Politics', in *The Cambridge History of Greek and Roman Political Thought*, Schofield and C. Rowe, eds. (Cambridge, 2000).

Schöpsdau, K., ed. and trans. *Platon: Nomoi*, 2 vols. (Gottingen, Germany, 1994, 2003).

Schuhl. P. M. 'Platon et l'activité politique de l'académie', *Revue des Etudes Grecques*, 59 (1946).

Shorey, P. 'The Idea of Good in Plato's *Republic*', *University of Chicago Studies in Classical Philology*, 1 (1895).

—— *The Unity of Plato's Thought* (Chicago, IL, 1903).

—— *What Plato Said* (Chicago, IL, 1933).

—— ed. and trans. *The Republic of Plato*, Loeb Classical Library edn., 2 vols. (London, 1930, 1935).

Simmons, A. J. *Moral Principles and Political Obligations* (Princeton, NJ, 1979).

Sinclair, T. A. *A History of Greek Political Thought*, 2nd edn. (Cleveland, OH, 1967).

Skemp, J., ed. and trans. *Plato's Statesman* (London, 1952).

Slings, S., ed. *Platonis Res Publica* (Oxford, 2003).

Solmsen, F. 'Parmenides and the Description of Perfect Beauty in Plato's *Symposium*', *American Journal of Philology*, 92 (1971).

Sprague, R. K. *Plato's Use of Fallacy* (London, 1962).

—— ed. *The Older Sophists* (Columbia, SC, 1972).

Stadter, P. A., ed. *The Speeches in Thucydides* (Chapel Hill, NC, 1973).

Stalley, R. F. *An Introduction to Plato's Laws* (Indianapolis, IN, 1983).

—— 'Aristotle's Criticism of Plato's *Republic* ', in *A Companion to Aristotle's Politics*, D. Keyt and F. D. Miller, eds. (Oxford, 1991).

Stockton, D. *The Classical Athenian Democracy* (Oxford, 1990).

Strauss, L. *The City and Man* (Chicago, IL, 1964).

—— *The Argument and Action of Plato's Laws* (Chicago, IL, 1975).

Susemihl, F. and R. D. Hicks, eds. *The Politics of Aristotle, Books 1–V* (London, 1894).

Taran, L. *Academica: Plato, Phillip of Opus, and the Pseudo Platonic Epinomis* (Philadelphia, PA, 1975).

Taylor, A. E. *Socrates* (1935; rpt. Garden City, NY, 1953).

—— *Plato: The Man and His Work*, 6th edn. (1952; rpt. Cleveland, OH, 1956).

Taylor, C. C. W., ed. and trans. *Plato: Protagoras* (Oxford, 1976).

—— 'Plato's Totalitarianism', *Polis*, 5 (1986) (also rpt. in *Plato 2*, G. Fine, ed.).

—— 'The Origins of Our Present Paradigms', in *New Perspectives on Plato, Modern and Ancient*, J. Annas and C. Rowe, eds. (Washington, DC, 2002).

Thesleff, H. *Studies in Platonic Chronology* (Helsinki, 1982).

Untersteiner, M. *The Sophists*, K. Freeman, trans. (London, 1957).

Vidal-Naquet, P. *Politics Ancient and Modern*, J. Lloyd, trans. (Cambridge, MA, 1995).

Vlastos, G. 'Introduction' to *Plato: Protagoras*, M. Ostwald. trans. (Indianapolis, IN, 1956).

—— ed. *The Philosophy of Socrates* (Garden City, NY, 1971 [1971a]).

—— ed. *Plato: A Collection of Critical Essays, I* (Garden City, NY, 1971 [1971b]).

—— ed. *Plato: A Collection of Critical Essays, II* (Garden City, NY, 1971 [1971c]).

—— *Platonic Studies* (Princeton, NJ, 1973).

—— 'Socrates on Political Obedience and Disobedience', *Yale Review*, 63 (1974).

Vlastos, G. 'The Theory of Social Justice in the *Polis* in Plato's *Republic*', in *Interpretations of Plato*, H. North, ed. (Leiden, Germany, 1977).

—— 'The Virtuous and the Happy', *Times Literary Supplement* (24 February, 1978).

—— 'The Historical Socrates and Athenian Democracy', *Political Theory*, 11 (1983) (also rpt. in Vlastos, *Socratic Studies*) [1983*a*].

—— 'The Socratic Elenchus', *Oxford Studies in Ancient Philosophy* (1983) (also rpt. in Vlastos, *Socratic Studies*; and in *Plato 1*, G. Fine, ed.) [1983*b*].

—— *Socrates: Ironist and Moral Philosopher* (Ithaca, NY, 1991).

—— *Socratic Studies*, M. Burnyeat, ed. (Cambridge, 1994).

Voegelin, E. *Plato* (1957; rpt. Baton Rouge, 1966).

Wallach, J. *The Platonic Political Art* (University Park, PA, 2001).

Walsh, J. *Aristotle's Conception of Moral Weakness* (New York, 1964).

Waterfield, R., trans. *Plato: Republic* (Oxford, 1998).

White, N. *A Companion to Plato's Republic* (Indianapolis, IN, 1979).

—— *Individual and Conflict in Greek Ethics* (Oxford, 2002).

Winspear, G. *The Genesis of Plato's Thought* (New York, 1940).

Woodhead, W. D., trans. *Gorgias*, in *The Collected Dialogues of Plato, Including the Letters*, E. Hamilton and H. Cairns, eds. (Princeton, NJ, 1961).

Woozley, A. D. *Law and Obedience: The Arguments of Plato's Crito* (London, 1979).

Zagorin, P. *Thucydides: An Introduction for the Common Reader* (Princeton, NJ, 2005).

Zimmern, A. *The Greek Commonwealth*, 4th edn. (Oxford, 1924).

Further Reading

Complete references are available in the *Bibliography*.

(1) *Bibliographies*. Comprehensive bibliographies are published periodically in the journal *Lustrum*, and by year in the individual volumes of *L'Année Philologique* and the *Philosopher's Index*. For Plato in general, useful bibliography is found in Kraut (1992) and Guthrie (1962–81), Vols. IV and V. For the *Republic*, in Annas (1981); for the *Statesman*, in Rowe (1995*b*); for the *Laws*, in Stalley (1983) and Lisi (1998). Saunders (1976) is a complete bibliography for the *Laws* up to that date.

(2) *Plato's texts*. The standard edition of the Greek text is Burnet (1900–7). Vol. I has been revised (Duke et al. 1995), as has the *Republic* (Slings 2003). All the dialogues and Epistles are translated in the fine edition of Cooper (1997), which is far superior to Hamilton and Cairns (1961), and with facing Greek texts in Loeb Classics Library editions. Many dialogues are cheaply and easily available in Penguin, Hackett, Library of Liberal Arts, and other editions.

(3) *General works on Plato*. Dialogue by dialogue accounts, including summaries and discussion, are found in Friedlander (1958–69), A. E. Taylor (1956), Shorey (1933), Grote (1865), Guthrie (1962–81), Vols. IV and V, and Gomperz (1901–12), Vols. II and III. Vol. I of Friedlander is a stimulating introduction to Plato as a whole. Kraut's *Cambridge Companion* (1992) is a valuable general source. Important collections of articles are Vlastos (1971*b*) and (1971*c*), and Fine (2000*a*) and (2000*b*). Good brief introductions are found in Field (1969), Armstrong (1947), and Cornford (1932 and 1927). Plato's thought is discussed topic by topic in Grube (1958) and more abstractly and philosophically in Crombie (1962–3), and Gosling (1973). The development of Plato's thought is traced by Raeder (1905). Accounts of the development of Plato's ethics are Gould (1955) and Irwin (1995). The classic account of the 'unity of Plato's thought' is Shorey (1903). A proleptic unity view is advanced by Kahn (1996). A useful reference book on all people mentioned in Plato is Nails (2002).

(4) *Interpretation*. On the Socratic genre, see Rutherford (1995) and Kahn (1996). For stylometry, see Brandwood (1990) and Ledger (1989); good brief overviews are Brandwood (1992) and Kahn (2002). For critiques of traditional dating, see Thesleff (1982), Howland (1991), and Annas (1998). Critiques of straightforward readings are found in Annas and Rowe (2002), Gill and McCabe (1996), Griswold (1988), and Press (2000). Influential alternative interpretations of Plato include Strauss (1964), Bloom (1968), and Voegelin (1966). Works that provide strongly literary readings of Plato include Euben (1990) and Nussbaum (1986).

(5) *Historical background: ancient texts*. Essential background is supplied by Thucydides and Aristotle's *Politics*. Thucydides is conveniently available in a

Penguin edition, with useful notes by M. I. Finley; J. Finley (1942) is an excellent introduction, as is Zagorin (2005); an historical commentary is Gomme, Andrewes, and Dover (1945–81). The works of Herodotus, Aristophanes, and Euripides are also available in Penguin and Loeb editions. Editions of Aristotle's *Politics* with commentaries include Newman (1887–1902), Susemihl and Hicks (1894), Saunders (1981), Barker (1946), and, most recently, the four-volume commentary of Saunders (1995), Robinson (1996), Keyt (1999), and Kraut (1997a). In Book II of the *Politics*, Aristotle presents his well-known criticisms of the *Republic* and *Laws*; for detailed discussion see Newman (1887–1902), Susemihl and Hicks (1894), and Stalley (1991). Aristotle's *Constitution of Athens* is available with commentary in von Fritz and Kapp (1950) and Rhodes (1993), and with other texts, including the 'Old Oligarch', in Moore (1975). Many of Plutarch's *Lives* are of great interest. For Sparta, the life of Lycurgus is especially valuable; for Athens, see esp. *Pericles, Themistocles,* and *Alcibiades*; for Plato's adventures in Sicily, see the life of Dion. Plutarch is readily available, perhaps most conveniently in Penguin and Modern Library editions.

(6) *Historical background, secondary works.* Hammond (1967) and Bury and Meiggs (1979) are excellent general histories. M. I. Finley has written a number of stimulating works (including 1973a, 1973b, and 1983). On Athenian history, politics, and culture, see Jones (1957), Ehrenberg (1973), Mossé (1973), Hansen (1999), Stockton (1990), Ober (1989) and (1998), Vidal-Naquet (1995), and Zimmern (1924); for Sparta, see Michell (1952) and Forrest (1969). Plato is situated in his historical context in Field (1967).

(7) *Socrates, historical evidence.* For the evidence of Xenophon, see especially the *Memorabilia, Symposium,* and *Apology of Socrates*, available in Loeb, Penguin, and Library of Liberal Arts translations. The evidence of Aristotle is collected and translated into French, with good analysis, in Deman (1942). The fragments of Aeschines can be found in English translation in Field (1967). For the evidence of Aristophanes, see especially *The Clouds* and Dover's essay in Vlastos (1971a). Good discussions of the 'Socratic Problem' are Guthrie (1962–81), Vol. III, and Ross (1933). Good brief, general accounts of Socrates are found in Cornford (1932), A. E. Taylor (1953), and Burnet's classic essay (1915–16).

(8) *The Sophists.* The relevant fragments from Diels–Kranz (1951–2) are found in translation in Freeman (1956) and Sprague (1972). Good general discussions are Guthrie (1962–81), Vol. III, Untersteiner (1957), and Kerferd (1981). The moral landscape is filled in by Adkins (1960) and Dover (1974).

(9) *Early dialogues. Apology*: Greek text with commentary is available in Burnet (1924) and Adam (1916). Valuable discussions of the *Apology* are Brickhouse and Smith (1989) and Reeve (1989). Text and commentary of the *Crito* are found in Burnet (1924) and Adam (1891); on the Crito, see Kraut (1984), Woozley (1979), and Allen (1980). Text and commentary of the *Protagoras* are found in Adam (1971); excellent discussions of the *Protagoras* are Vlastos (1956) and C. C. W. Taylor's commentary (1976). On Socratic moral thought, see Santas (1979), chs. 6–7; Penner (1973), Irwin

(1995), Devereux (1992) and (1995), Gould (1955) (criticized in Vlastos [1973], ch. 9), and Irwin (1977), criticized in Vlastos (1978), and subsequent correspondence, and Klosko (1981*b*). Important analyses of the Platonic Socrates, from strongly analytic perspectives are Vlastos (1991 and 1994), Santas (1979), and Brickhouse and Smith (1994). For Socrates on democracy, see Vlastos (1983*a*). The classic discussion of the Socratic *elenchos* is Robinson (1953); for *elenchos* as a positive method, see Vlastos (1983*b*), criticized by Kraut (1983). A stimulating analysis of the *elenchos* in the *Gorgias* is Kahn (1983).

(10) *Middle dialogues. Gorgias*: text and commentary, Dodds (1959); translation and valuable commentary, Irwin (1979). *Phaedo*: text and commentary, Burnet (1911); translations with commentary, Bluck (1955*b*), Hackforth (1972*a*), Gallop (1975). *Symposium*: text and commentary, Bury (1932), and Rowe (1998).

(11) The *Republic*. Text and commentary, Adam (1902); Book I, text and commentary, Allan (1953); valuable translations are Cornford (1941), with some commentary, Grube and Reeve (1992), and Waterfield (1998). Kraut (1997*b*) is a valuable collection of essays. To my mind the best overall treatment is still Murphy (1951), and the best introduction is still Nettleship (1901); also useful are Cross and Woozley (1964), Annas (1981), White (1979), and, more idiosyncratic, Reeve (1988).

(12) *Moral psychology of the middle dialogues*. Good accounts are Irwin (1995); Murphy (1951), pp. 1–97; Joseph (1935), esp. ch. 3; Gosling (1973), esp. chs. 2–6; Moline (1978); and Penner (in Vlastos [1971*c*]); see also Kraut (1973*b*), Klosko (1982) (1988*b*), Cooper (1984), and articles in Vlastos (1971*c*) and Fine (2000*b*).

(13) *Metaphysics and epistemology*. Good general discussions are Cherniss (1965), the chapters from Cross and Woozley (1964) and Robinson (1953) reprinted in Vlastos (1971*b*), Ross (1951), and Crombie (1962–3). Many important articles are collected in Allen (1965) and Fine (2000*a*). A useful summary of Plato's presentation of the theory of Forms throughout his corpus is found in Grube (1958). The Sun, Line, and Cave are well discussed in Cross and Woozley (1964), Nettleship (1902), and Raven (1965).

(14) *Political thought.* General accounts are Barker (1947), Hall (1980), Luccioni (1958), Sinclair (1967), Wallach (2001), Pradeau (2002), and Samaras (2002). Barker (1927) is an excellent brief introduction. Schofield and Rowe (2000) is a valuable general source. Popper's (1966) violent attack has generated tremendous controversy; Levinson (1953) is a lengthy response; additional discussion is collected in Bambrough (1967); see also Klosko (1996) and Taylor (1986). Barker (1947) contains an excellent discussion of communism in the *Republic*. For Plato's views on education, see Jaeger (1939–45), esp. Vol. II; Nettleship (1935) is still well worth reading. On issues concerning the possibility of the just city: Burnyeat (1992), Davis (1964), and Laks (1990). The status of women is well discussed by Okin (1979), chs. 1–3. For the 'organic theory of the state', see Neu (1971). For social justice in the ideal state, see Vlastos (1977). Influential works from alternative perspectives are Annas (1998), Strauss (1964 and 1975), Bloom (1968), and Voegelin (1957).

(15) *Late dialogues.* The best introductions to the philosophy of Plato's later works are translated texts with commentaries. For the *Phaedrus*, see Hackforth (1972*b*); and Cornford's commentaries on the *Parmenides* (1957*a*), the *Theaetetus* and *Sophist* (1957*c*), and the *Timaeus* (1957*b*). On the *Theaetetus*, see also Burnyeat (1990) for the *Philebus*, see Hackforth (1945), and Gosling (1975). Guthrie (1962–81), Vol. V, examines many important issues, with extensive references; see also Crombie (1962–3), Vol. II. For controversy surrounding changes in Plato's metaphysics, see esp. Vlastos (1954) and the numerous responses it generated. An important, though controversial study of changes in moral psychology in the late dialogues is Bobonich (2002).

(16) *Political activity of Plato and the Academy.* For the *Epistles* in translation with exhaustive historical discussion, see Morrow (1962). The political activity of the Academy is discussed by Schuhl (1946) and Saunders (1986), and more sceptically by Brunt (1993) and Schofield (2000).

(17) *The Statesman.* Text with commentary available in Campbell (1867); important editions are Diès (1935), Skemp (1952), Annas and Waterfield (1995), and Rowe (1995*a*). A good general account is found in Barker (1947). Rowe (1995*b*) is a valuable collection of essays. Bobonich (2002) discusses the work's moral thought. To my mind, the most important recent study is Lane (1998).

(18) *The Laws.* Text and commentary, of mainly philological interest, is England (1921). Saunders (1970*b*) is a highly readable translation with some commentary; Pangle (1980) is a translation with notes and interpretive essay. A valuable edition, comprised of text and French translation, with notes and introductions is Des Places and Diès (1951–6). A German translation and commentary (still in progress) is Schöpsdau (1994, 2003). Lisi (1998) is an important collection of essays. Morrow (1960), to my mind the single most important work on the *Laws*, is a massive, indispensable historical analysis. Morrow's discussion of such topics as the state's constitutional structure, its economy, the nocturnal council, and the nature of the mixed constitution have provided the starting points for subsequent discussion. Kahn (1961) is a good review of Morrow which criticizes certain lapses. Klosko (1988*a* and forthcoming) present alternative views of the nocturnal council. Barker (1947) contains a good general account of the work's political theory and Gould (1955) of its moral thought. Guthrie (1962–81) Vol. V contains a useful discussion of the entire work. The outstanding recent work is Bobonich (2002), which presents an iconoclastic account of the development of Plato's later political theory. Laks (1990, 1995, 1998, 2000) and Pradeau (2002) present alternative views of the work's political theory. Stalley (1983) is an excellent philosophical introduction. Plato's view of education in the work is discussed in Bury (1937) and Jaeger (1939–45), Vol. III; for Plato's treatment of the Socratic paradox in the work, see Saunders (1968) and Stalley (1983), ch. 14. Plato's theory of law is discussed in Morrow (Vlastos 1971*c*) and Cairns' essay (Friedlander 1958–69, Vol. III). Plato's treatment of slavery in the work is well discussed in Morrow (1939), and the status of Forms in the work in Brochard (1966), ch. 9. For dramatic elements of the work, see Nightingale (1993) and Bobonich (1996).

Glossary of Greek Words

akrasia weakness of will, moral weakness

anamnêsis recollection

aporia perplexity, puzzlement

aretê virtue, excellence

boulêsis wish

genos kind

dêmiourgos craftsman

dêmos the people (collectively)

dianoia intellect, reasoning

dikaiosunê justice, righteousness

doxa belief, opinion (also reputation)

eidos Form, kind

eikasia imagination

einai to be, to exist (infinitive form)

elenchos refutation, test

epistêmê knowledge, science

epôdê chant, spell, incantation

eros love (especially sexual love)

gerousia Spartan council of elders

gumnastikê physical training

hexis habit, disposition

idea Form, kind

katharsis purification

logos speech, reasoning, argument, word

mimêsis imitation

mousikê music, art in general

noêsis understanding, knowledge

nomophulakes guardians of the laws

nomos law, custom, convention

nous knowledge, intuition

paideia education, culture

paidia play, children's games

paradeigma model, pattern, exemplar

philia friendship, love, affection

phronêsis prudence, practical wisdom

phusis nature, what is natural

pistis belief

polis city, state, city-state

politeia constitution, polity

psuchê soul

sophia knowledge

sôphrosunê temperance, self-awareness

stasiôteia party rule

stasis faction, political instability

technê art, craft, skill

telos end, final state

thumos spirit, anger

Index